Mandarin Phrasebook

true run media 编

中国人口出版社
China Population Publishing House

图书在版编目（CIP）数据

中文短语手册 / 楚人鼎立编．—北京：中国人口出版社，2006.11

ISBN 7-80202-286-X

I．中… II．楚… III．汉语－口语－对外汉语教学－自学参考资料－汉、英 IV．H195.4

中国版本图书馆 CIP 数据核字（2006）第 013436 号

中文短语手册

true run media 编

出版发行	中国人口出版社
印　　刷	北京盛通印刷股份有限公司
开　　本	889×1194　1/48
印　　张	7.375
字　　数	300 千字
版　　次	2006 年 11 月第 1 版
印　　次	2007 年 11 月第 3 次印刷
书　　号	ISBN 7-80202-286-X/C · 290
定　　价	50.00 元
社　　长	陶庆军
电子信箱	chinapphouse@163.net
地　　址	北京市宣武区广安门南街 80 号中加大厦
邮政编码	100054

Mandarin Phrasebook

General Enquiries:
5820 7100
editor@immersionguides.com
www.immersionguides.com
www.thatsbj.com

Managing Editor Adam Pillsbury

Assistant Editors Reid Barrett, Gabriel Monroe, Jackie Yu

Production Manager Susu Luo

Design Yuki Jia, Li Yang, Liu Ying

Illustrators Li Xing, Ray Heng, Joey Guo

Copy Editor Tom Spearman

Cover Design Li Xing

General Enquiries:
5820 7700
Distribution: 5820 7101
sales@immersionguides.com
distribution@immersionguides.com
marketing@immersionguides.com
www.immersionguides.com
www.thatsbj.com

General Manager Michael Wester

Sales Manager Claire Tang

Sales Lynn Cui, Elena Damjanoska, Ada Dong, Kelly Han, David Wan, Cindy Zhang, Julie Zhu, Emma Zhuang

Distribution Manager Zoe Wang

Marketing Manager Alex Chen

Finance & Accounting James Li, Tracy Ye, Angela Zheng

Office Manager Eileen Huang

Reception Cherry Wu

Table of Contents

Introduction

Sidebars

Hotels & Housing

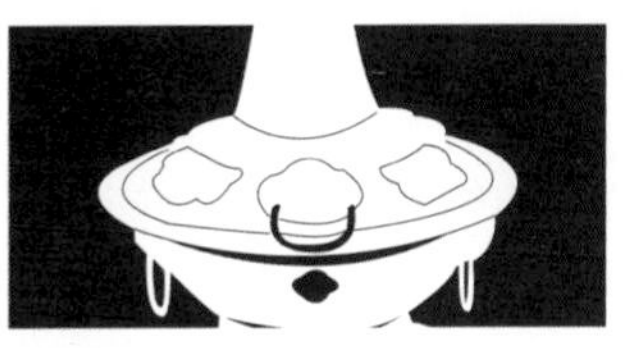

Food

Kids & Family Life

Sidebars

Art & Culture

Sidebars

Sightseeing

Nightlife

Sidebars

Shopping

Sports & Fitness

Health & Beauty

Sidebars

Transportation

Excursions

Sidebars

Business & Work

Sidebars

Adult Education

Sidebars

Useful Info

Glossary

INTRODUCTION ►

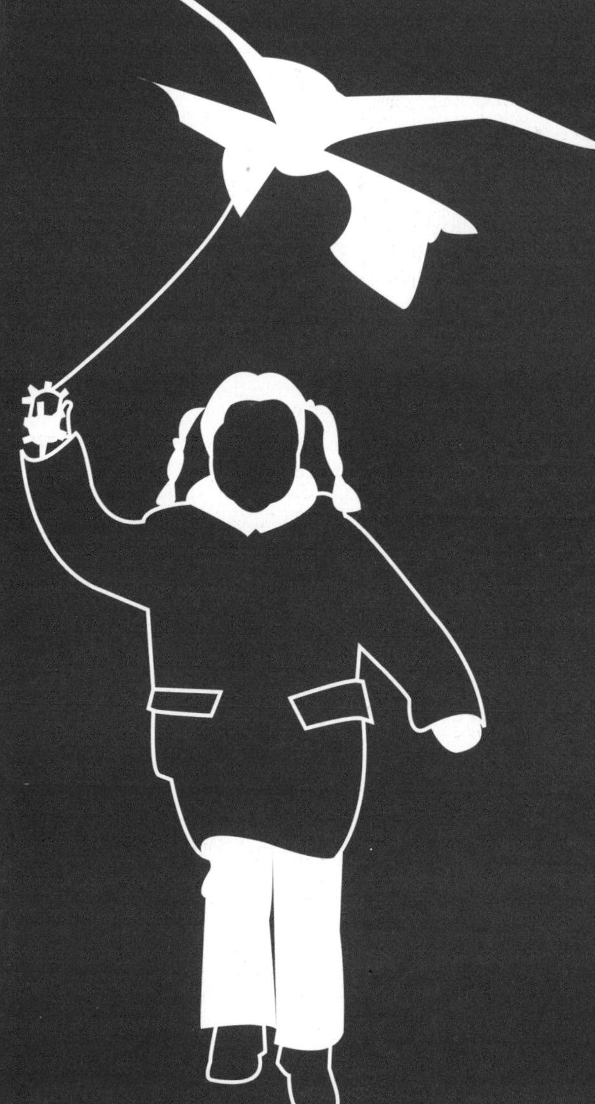

The *Mandarin Phrasebook* is designed to help foreigners get more out of life in Beijing. It introduces essential phrases, vocabulary and slang that enable readers to communicate effectively in the daily situations they encounter in Beijing – from renting an apartment and interviewing an ayi to chatting with a cabdriver and bargaining in the markets.

This book is not a dry textbook, however. To be sure, it is informative and accurate, yet like all true Beijing *ren*, it is also leavened with irreverent humor and favors local idioms over standard Mandarin. Best of all, it promises the benefit of a heightened Beijing experience without the drawback of a final exam.

Organization

Like its companion volume – the *Insider's Guide to Beijing* guidebook – this phrasebook is divided into 15 chapters, each of which tackles a major aspect of life in Beijing (Kids, Housing, Nightlife and so on). This Introduction chapter begins with a primer on the pronunciation and grammar of Mandarin as well as a collection of basic nouns, verbs and adjectives.

All the words and phrases contained in the book are written in English, Chinese characters and Pinyin with tone marks. Each chapter provides examples of how to use relevant vocabulary and phrases, as well as responses typically offered by Beijingers. This material is augmented by illustrations and sidebars that delve into topics both practical and obscure. For convenient reference, an English-Mandarin/Mandarin-English glossary is included in the back.

Thanks to such content, the book should appeal to readers with differing levels of Mandarin proficiency. It promises to teach the proficient speaker things s/he would never, ever learn in a class.

Pronunciation

Adopted by China in the late 1950s, Pinyin is a system of Romanizing the sounds of Mandarin Chinese to make them recognizable to learners. This phrasebook uses Pinyin, in which each sound is the combination of initials (a consonant) and finals (one or more vowels, sometimes with **n** or **ng**). Many letters and sounds in Pinyin can be read normally for English speakers, while some are quite different. Familiarizing yourself with the system pays off, because street signs and proper names are all written in pinyin.

Initials

• The consonants/initials: b, ch, d, f, g, h, k, l, m ,n , p, s, sh, t ,w, y can all be read as in English

- The letters below follow these special pronunciation rules:

c is like **ts** in ha**ts**
j is like the **j** in **j**eans
q is like **ch** in **ch**eek, with a puff of air
x is best described as a hissing cross between s and sh, with a puff of air. (There is no similar sound in English)
z is like **ds** in li**ds**
zh is like a burly j sound, sort of like the **g** sound in **G**erman (similar in tongue position to the 'ch' and 'sh')
r is like the **ur** in plea**sure** (in American English)

Finals

The vowel sounds in Chinese are actually more consistent when written in pinyin than when they are written in English.

a like the **a** in f**a**r
e on its own is a bit like *uh* or the French **oe** in **oe**uf, but when used as a final it is like the **e** in y**e**s
i like **ee** in fr**ee**, but after ch, c, zh, z, sh and s is like the **i** in r**i**p
o like the **o** in m**o**re
u like the **u** in fl**u**te, but like ü when after q, j x
ü like the French *tu*

Combined Letters

an	like *ahn*
ang	like *ahng*
en	like the **un** in **un**der
eng	like **ung** in r**ung**
er	like **er** in murd**er**
ian	like *yen*
iang	like *yahng*
in	like **ean** in m**ean**
ing	like the **ing** in bl**ing**-bling
iong	like *yohng*
ong	like *ohng*
uan	like *oowahn* (or *oowen* after x, j, and q)
uang	like *wahng*
un	*oohn*
üan	like *you ahn*

- Many of these combined vowel sounds (aka diphthongs) are unlike their English pronunciations and must be memorized.

ai	like *eye*
ao	like **ow** in c**ow**
ei	like the **ay** in h**ay**

ia	like **ya** in **ya**rd
ie	like **ye** in **ye**sterday
iao	like **iao** in m**iao**w
iu	like the **ew** in p**ew**
ou	like *oh*
ua	like the **wa** in **wa**ddle
uai	like *why*
ue	like the **you a** in **you a**pe!
ui	like the **ay** in sp**ay**
uo	like the **oi** in c**oi**ffed
üe	like the **ew e** in n**ew e**gg

Tones

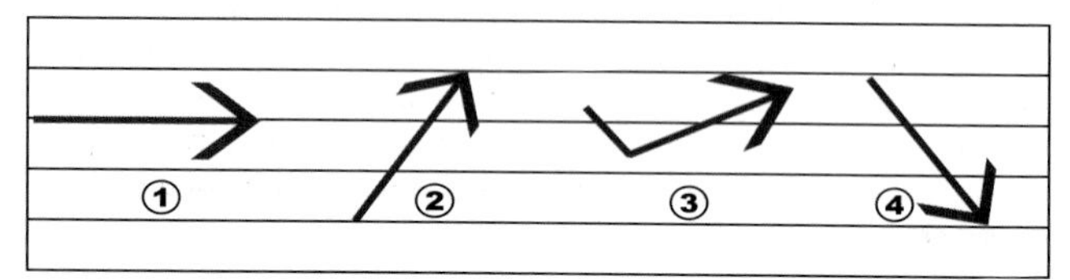

• Tone is variation in pitch by which a syllable can be pronounced. All Chinese pinyin are marked with one of four tones. The four tones are as follows:

1st tone – singing tone; high, flat, continuous
2nd tone – rising; similar to the intonation used to ask a question in English, like "oh?"
3rd tone – dip tone; falls and then rises
4th tone – falling tone, sharp like when you holler "boo!"

• These tones are incredibly important. If you get them wrong, people will not understand what you are saying. Many syllables in pinyin have dramatically different meanings depending on the tone. Take for instance the Pinyin construction *bao*:

bāo 包 wrap   báo 薄 thin   bǎo 保 guarantee   bào 抱 hug

So as you can see, if you're not careful you will accidentally tell someone that you want to hug them, when in fact, you just want to give them a guarantee.

Tone changes and the neutral tone

Two things to keep in mind:

1) Tones sometimes change depending on context. For example, whenever you have two third tone syllables in sequence, the first

character shifts to second tone. With the phrase hěn shuǎng (很爽feels so good), the third - third tone combination changes, and should be pronounced second tone - third tone (hén shuǎng). The change should naturally occur in normal speech. Additionally, certain characters change their tones depending on their usage.

2) The neutral tone. The second character of many phrases have a neutral tone, especially phrases in which a syllable is repeated. This means that you pronounce it without singing, rising, dipping or falling, and let it ride the sound of the character preceding it. For example:

kànkan (看看 take a look) is pronounced 4th - neutral, not 4th - 4th similiarly

bàba (爸爸 father) is also pronounced 4th - neutral, not 4th - 4th while

guānxi (关系 relationship) and

māma (妈妈 mother) are not pronounced 1st - 1st but 1st - neutral

The possessive pronoun de (的) has a neutral tone. If you notice pinyin without a tone mark, it is a neutral tone, not a mistake.

For these reasons, be aware! Even if you have already learned a word, you should still pay attention to the tone marks of the pinyin throughout the book.

The Beijinghua "er"

Mandarin Chinese was the local Beijing dialect before it was chosen to become the official standard dialect of China. Chosen because it was the simplest of all the major dialects in contention (with "only" 4 tones), the Beijing dialect still has a few of its own foibles. Certainly Mandarin Chinese is a living language and is more virile and fluid in Beijing than anywhere else. Of particular note is the piratical phenomenon of "er" slurring. Many words in standard Mandarin have adopted the slurred er (儿) sound over the years, and these common pronunciations can be represented in characters (such as shìr（事儿） and nǎr（哪儿）).

While in Beijing you may encounter widespread indiscriminate "er" slurring. However, be careful of context! Foreigners have been known to enthusiastically mistake the Beijing "er" for the key to Chinese fluency, blending it into every word and massacring the language. Imagine a Chinese person approaching you and speaking in broken English with an exaggerated Creole twang. It would be fun, but it wouldn't fly at a board meeting. Speaking with heavy "er" sounds are best reserved for informal occasions in the company of Beijing people.

Grammar

Chinese grammar is quite a bit simpler than English grammar. There are no articles (a/ the), tenses, gender forms, plurals or verb conjugations. Once you learn a few basic patterns you will find that there is a lot that you will be able to communicate. After that it's just a matter of vocabulary. No sweat, right?

Word Order

Like English, at a basic level Chinese word order is subject-verb-object. For example, the sentences "I want money" or "I eat meat" follow the same grammatical pattern in English and Chinese.

- Wǒ yào qián 我要钱 I want money
- Wǒ chī ròu 我吃肉 I eat meat

Nouns

Nouns are made up of one or two words (syllabic characters), and do not change if they are plural.

- chē 车 car
- chē 车 cars
- yǎnjing 眼睛 eye
- yǎnjing 眼睛 eyes

Adjectives

(For a list of common adjectives, see p23)

Adjectives in Chinese are placed before the nouns they modify, just like in English.

- kuài chē 快车 fast car
- dà lóu 大楼 big building

Pronouns

Subject (e.g. I) and object (e.g. me) forms are the same. Adding the syllable "men" (们) to the end of the pronoun makes it plural.

- wǒ 我 I / me
- nǐ 你 you
- tā 他 he / him
- tā 她 she / her
- wǒmen 我们 we / us
- nǐmen 你们 you all
- tāmen 他们 they / them

Possession

To express possession, just add a "de" (的) between the subject and the object. For example:

- wǒ de shìr 我的事儿 my business
- tā de mìmi 他的秘密 his secret

This possessive de can also be used for descriptive modification:

- hěn guì de yǔsǎn 很贵的雨伞 expensive umbrella

Measure Words

In Chinese, all objects must be modified by measure words, which take the place of pronouns. Many objects have their own specific measure words in Chinese, which are rare in English. For example, in English we have a pinch of salt and a gaggle of geese. In order to speak correct Chinese, you always have to be asking yourself, "What kind of gaggle is that?" For examples, refer to this gaggletastic chart:

five baseball bats 五根棒球棒 wŭ gēn bàngqiú bàng
three cups of alcohol 三杯酒 sān bēi jiŭ
four photographs 四张照片 sì zhāng zhàopiān
one fish 一条鱼 yì tiáo yú
a pair of gloves 一双手套 yì shuāng shŏutào
six horses 六匹马 liù pĭ mă

However, the general measure word gè (个) usually saves the day. As soon as you learn it you'll realize "when in doubt, use ge." Chinese people use ge very frequently, and you'll start to use it too much yourself. Also, the general numerical meaure word is xiē (些), like "a few" in English.

- zhè 这 this
- nà 那 that
- zhège 这个 this (one)
- nàge 那个 that (one)
- zhèxiē 这些 these
- nàxiē 那些 those

Tip

Beijing people almost always pronounce zhège (这个 this) and nàge (那个 that) as "zhèige" and "nèige." This is *Beijinghua*, the local Beijing dialect, not standard Mandarin Chinese. Therefore, in this handbook we have decided to use the zhe and na pinyin spelling predominantly. However, since these are abbreviations of the colloquial forms "zhè yí ge" (这一个) and "nà yí ge" (那一个), we do use the zhèige and nèige spellings in certain places where the context is appropriately informal.

Verbs and tenses

(For a list of common verbs, see p22)

In Mandarin, verbs do not change form, regardless of pronoun or tense.

- wŏ dài 我带 I bring
- tāmen dài 他们带 they bring
- Nĭ míngtiān dài 你明天带 You'll bring it tomorrow

Temporal modifiers

Le (了) is a very important temporal modifier. Le expresses the completion of an action. For example:

- Wŏ dài le 我带了 I brought it
- Wŏ chī le 我吃了 I ate it

However, le is also frequently used for emphasis, which sometimes makes you realize the similarity between completion and emphasis. Completed actions are much more certain than evolving ones, aren't they? For example:

- Wǒ bú qù 我不去 I'm not going

  becomes

- Wǒ bú qù le! 我不去了! I'm not going!

  while

- Wǒ gěi le 我给了 is either "I gave it" or "I gave it!"

Another very common temporal modifier is guò (过), which is used to express or deny previous experience, for example:

- Wǒ hē guò tāng 我喝过汤 I've drank soup (before)
- Wǒ méiyǒu hē guò chá 我没有喝过茶 I've never drank tea

Using le refers to a specific instance, while guò is used in regard to all which has come before. The following examples show difference between guò and le:

- Wǒ qù le 我去了 I went
- Wǒ qù guò 我去过 I have been (there before)

Change of state

When le (了) is used after adjectives rather than verbs, it expresses a change of state. For example:

- Wǒ lèi le 我累了 I'm tired
- Wǒ è le 我饿了 I'm hungry
- Wǒ de liǎn hóng le 我的脸红了 My face is red (I'm blushing)

These sentences implicitly convey that I've *become* hungry and tired, and my face has *become* red.

To Be

In Chinese, the basic verb "to be" (是 shì) is used exclusively with nouns. In other words, when describing *how* something is instead of *what* something is, shì (是) is unnecessary.

In other words, "to be" is implicit when using adjectives. Descriptive adjectives are sometimes used exclusively, but are usually modified (often by the word hěn 很 very).

For example, the following examples use shì (是):

- Wǒ shì huàiren 我是坏人 I am a bad person
- Nǐ shì wǒde péngyou 你是我的朋友 You are my friend

In contrast, using descriptive adjectives often looks like this:

- Wǒ hěn huài 我很坏 I am bad
- Nǐ hěn yǒuhǎo 你很友好 You are friendly

Passive voice (*ba* 把 particle)

One extremely common and important grammar form in Chinese is the passive voice using the bǎ (把) particle. Due to its utility and ubiquity, this is an important structure to be aware of. More importantly, certain constructions in Chinese are impossible to communicate correctly without using bǎ (把).

Most sentences can be communicated using either the bǎ (把)+object+verb+subject pattern or the subject+verb+object structure. However, using the bǎ (把) form is the *only* correct way to communicate the transfer of objects.

For example, although the following two setences are both correct:

- Tā dǎkāi le mén 她打开了门 She opened the door
- Tā bǎ mén dǎkāi le 她把门打开了 She opened the door

The following sentence is grammatically incorrect in Chinese, although it seems to make sense in English:

- Ná gěi wǒ nà gēn gùnzi 拿给我那根棍子 Grab (to) me that stick

Instead, it must be expressed like this:

- Bǎ nà gēn gùnzi ná gěi wǒ 把那根棍子拿给我 Take that stick and grab it to me

Although this grammar structure seems quite funny in English, it elegantly shifts the emphasis of the sentence to the object. In Chinese, the transfer of objects using verbs like bring, send and take can only be conveyed correctly in this way.

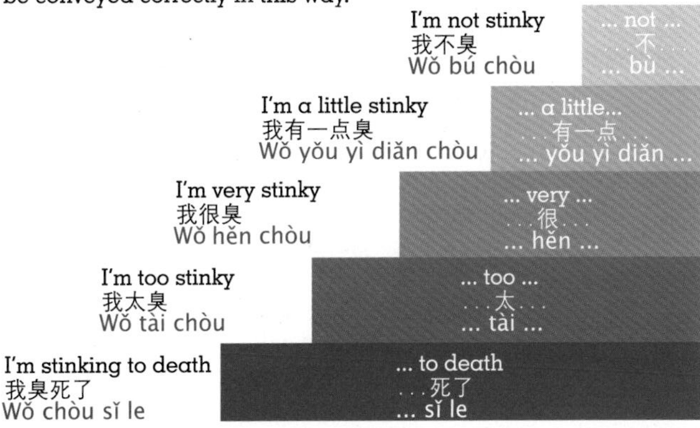

Modifiers

This chart shows the range of emphasis that can be expressed with several common modifiers:

Negatives

There are two basic negative words in Mandarin, bù (不) and méi (没). However, while bù (不) can be used to negate almost any verb, méi (没) is used exclusively with the verb to have (有 yǒu). Bù cannot be used to negate "to have." Even when méiyǒu (没有) is shortened to méi by itself, it still negates by implying absence.

For example:
- Bù zhīdào 不知道 I don't know
- Méi ménr 没门儿 There is no way (lit: no have door)

Two other forms are important for negative advice and warnings:
- búyào 不要 don't (no want) • Búyào kū! 不要哭 Don't cry!
- bié 别 don't • Bié zǒu! 别走 Don't go!

These two forms are interchangeable.

Commands

In Chinese, like in English, commands are indicated by adding verbal stress to a statement. Say it with authority!

Comparison

Comparisons are very simple to make. Just say the word bǐ (比) between the two things you want to compare, followed by the term of comparison (e.g. good, big, smart, beautiful, long).
- Wǒ de xiǎomǔzhǐ bǐ nǐde dàmǔzhǐ hái cū 我的小拇指比你的大拇指还粗 My pinkie is thicker than your thumb
- Tā bǐ nǐ gāo 她比你高 She's taller than you
- Nǐ bǐ wǒ piàoliang 你比我漂亮 You're prettier than me

Conjunctions

- hé/gēn 和/跟 and
  Wǒ hé nǐ shì yí duì 我和你是一对 You and I are a couple
- huòzhě/háishì 或者/还是 or
  Tā fù qián huòzhě wǒ fù qián 她付钱或者我付钱 She pays or I pay

Note: Háishì 还是 sentences are implicty inquisitive. For example:
Tā fù qián háishì wǒ fù qián? 她付钱还是我付钱? She pays or I pay?

- yàoshì/rúguǒ 要是/如果 if
  Yàoshì nǐ bù zhīdào, méiyǒu guānxi 要是你不知道，没有关系
  If you don't know, no problem
- yīnwéi 因为 because
  Wǒ bù dǒng, yīnwéi wǒ hěn bèn 我不懂，因为我很笨
  I don't understand, because I'm very stupid
- suǒyǐ 所以 therefore
  … suǒyǐ nǐ lái le 所以你来了 ... therefore, you came

Tip:

Be prepared to be asked personal questions. For many foreigners, income, age and marital status might be considered private matters. In China these subjects are fair game even during the most brief and casual encounters with strangers. On the other hand, Chinese people are unlikely to discuss sex in public.

Questions - how to ask a question

In Chinese, asking questions is usually indicated by certain question words. One very simple and common inquisitive sentence structure is to add the particle ma (吗 neutral tone) to the end of a sentence. This particle automatically changes the previous statement into a question.
For example:

- Nǐ shì Běijīng rén 你是北京人 You are from Beijing
  becomes
- Nǐ shì Běijīng rén ma? 你是北京人吗？ Are you from Beijing?

The particle ba (吧 neutral tone) is the same as ma, but it is suggestive. Questions that use ba are often leading, rhetorical or interrogative. The answer is assumed, but since it is a question there is still some doubt.
So the sentence:

- Nǐ liǎojiě rényāo 你了解人妖 You understand transsexuals
  becomes
- Nǐ liǎojiě rényāo ba? 你了解人妖吧？
  You understand transsexuals, eh?

A third important particle, ne (呢), also pulls heavy duty. Ending a sentence with ne after an object poses the question; "What about (object)?" This particle is very useful for fostering free flow in a dialogue.
For example the statement:

- Wǒ rènwéi Shànghǎi hěn xiàndàihuà 我认为上海很现代化
  I think Shanghai is very modern
  is very simply followed up with the question:
- Běijīng ne? 北京呢? What about Beijing?

Another common inquiry structure is the positive/negative? construction. By juxtaposing a verb with its negative form, you can ask all sorts of questions.
For example:

- Shì búshì? 是不是？ Isn't it? (Is not is?)
  Tā hěn piàoliàng, shì búshì? 她很漂亮，是不是？
  She's very pretty, isn't she?
- Duì búduì? 对不对？Correct? (lit: correct incorrect?)
  Nǐ yào chī diǎnr chuànr, duì búduì? 你要吃点儿串儿，对不对？
  You want to eat some meat sticks (kebabs), don't you?
- Hǎo bùhǎo? 好不好？Alright? (good not good?)
  Wǒmen chànggē, hǎo bùhǎo? 我们唱歌，好不好？ Let's sing. ok?
- Yǒu méiyǒu? 有没有？Is there any ...? (Have not have?)
  Yǒu méiyǒu dòuzi? 有没有豆子？ Do you have any beans?
  and so on ...

Finally, Chinese has a few question words similar to those in English (who, what, where, why, etc). These words are:
- shéi 谁 who
- shénme 什么 what
- wèishénme 为什么 why
- shénme shíhòu 什么时候 when (lit: what time?)
- zěnme 怎么? how
- duōshǎo 多少 how many/how much

Replies - how to reply

Affirmative replies require only repeating the verb. Negative replies require adding a negative particle to the verb. The positive/negative questions are easy to reply to, because both potential answers are included in the question.
For example:
- Nǐ yǒu méiyǒu píngguǒ? 你有没有苹果 Do you have apples?

Is answered either:
- yǒu 有 yes (lit: have)

  or
- méiyǒu 没有 no (no have)

When people are asking about or confirming something that you want or are asking for, they often use the duibudui pattern. However, the duìbúduì pattern is also important to keep in mind even when answering other questions. Many shìbúshì or ma questions can be answered yes or no using this correct/incorrect dichotomy as a model.
For example:
- Nǐ yào qù huǒchēzhàn ma? 你要去火车站吗?
  Do you want to go to the train station?
- Duì 对 Yes

  or
- Nǐ yào mántou shì búshì? 你要馒头，是不是?
  Do you want steamed buns?
- Búduì, wǒ yào yì wǎn dòujiāng 不对，我要一碗豆浆
  No, I want a bowl of soy milk

1 Basics 基础词汇 Jīchǔ cíhuì

Sentences

- Yes 是 Shì
- No 不 Bù

- Perhaps 也许 Yěxǔ
- Please,... 请. . . Qǐng,...
- Thank you 谢谢 Xièxie
- You're welcome 不客气 Bú kèqi
- Not a problem / No worries 没问题 Méi wèntí
- Don't worry about it / Forget it (passive aggressive) 没事儿 Méi shìr
- Excuse me (to get past) 请让一让 Qǐng ràng yí ràng
- I have to get by 让我过一下 Ràng wǒ guò yí xià
- Excuse me / Sorry to trouble you (to get attention) 对不起，麻烦你 Duìbùqǐ, máfán nǐ
- Can I ask you ... 请问一下. . . Qǐng wèn yí xià ...
- Sorry 对不起 Duìbùqǐ
- Pardon me 不好意思 Bùhǎo yìsi
- I didn't do it on purpose 我不是故意的 Wǒ búshì gùyì de
- I'm really, really sorry 实在抱歉 Shízài bàoqiàn
- Maybe 可能 Kěnéng
- OK 行 Xíng
- That's enough 够了 Gòu le

2 Greetings 打招呼 Dǎ zhāohu

Sentences

- Hello 你好 Nǐ hǎo
- Long time no see 好久不见 Hǎojiǔ bújiàn

Stick to the Script ...

... or read this and toss it out

by Gabriel Monroe

Tired of offering the same replies to the stock questions you are asked daily? Then try one of these snappy rejoinders:

Q: Where are you from? 你是哪国人？/你是什么国家的人？ Nǐ shì nǎ guó rén?/nǐ shì shénme guójiā de rén?

- Evasive answer: Guess ... where do I look like I'm from?
  你猜吧...我像什么国家的人
  Nǐ cāi ba ... wǒ xiàng shénme guójiā de rén?
- Nonsensical: I am moon person! 我是月球人！ Wǒ shì yuèqiú rén
- Exotic: Well, I have an Icelandic passport, but I was born in Israel and grew up in Thailand
  我是冰岛护照，不过我在以色列出生，然后在泰国长大
  Wǒ shì Bīngdǎo hùzhào, búguò wǒ zài Yǐsèliè chūshēng, ránhòu zài Tàiguó zhǎngdà

Q: Can you speak Chinese? 你会说中文吗？ Nǐ huì shuō zhōngwén ma?

- Cheeky: I cannot speak any Chinese whatsoever
  我一点儿中文都不会说 Wǒ yìdiǎnr zhōngwén dōu bú huì shuō
- Modest/moronic answer: I fluently speak horrible Chinese!
  我会流利地说很差的中文！
  Wǒ huì liúlì de shuō hěn chà de zhōngwén!

Q: Your Chinese is excellent
你的中文很标准 Nǐ de zhōngwén hěn biāozhǔn

- Textbook: Where, where – this classic response shows modesty but is subtly boastful 哪里哪里 Nǎlǐ, nǎlǐ
- Clever: "Its only fluff" – i.e. I haven't even scratched the surface of learning Chinese皮毛而已 Pímáo éryǐ
- Cheeky: Now if only I could only get an audition on Super Voice Girls / Guys 还在等着看我能不能上超级女生/男生 Hái zài děngzhe kàn wǒ néng bùnéng shàng chāojí nǚshēng/ nánshēng

Q: Did you come to China to study Chinese/to work? 你来中国学习/工作吗？ Nǐ lái Zhōngguó xuéxí/gōngzuò ma?

- Slacker: Neither, I'm just here to bum around for a few years 不是，我是个流浪汉 Búshì, wǒ shì gè liúlànghàn
- Patriotic/cute: No, I came to take part in the revolution 不是，我来参加革命 Búshì, wǒ lái cānjiā gémìng
- Mysterious, spiritual: Nope, it's just fate 不是，这就是命 Búshì, zhèi jiùshì mìng

Q: What kind of work do you do? 你做什么工作？ Nǐzuò shénme gōngzuò?

- Wannabe: I'm a secret agent! (Follow with shushing motion) 我是特工！ Wǒ shì tègōng!
- Lei Feng: Serve the people 为人民服务 Wèi rénmín fúwù
- Liar: I am a helicopter pilot 我开直升飞机 Wǒ kāi zhíshēng fēijī

Q: What's your salary? 你的薪水多少？ Nǐ de xīnshuǐ duōshǎo?

- Evasive: It's enough ... 还行 … Hái xíng ...
- Make them practice their math: Ten million cents per year (about RMB 8,000 per month) 一年一千万分 Yì nián yìqiānwàn fēn
- Throwback: 20 taels a month 一个月二十两银子 Yí gè yuè èrshí liǎng yínzi
- Currency exchange sadist: 200 Guatemalan Quetzal per fortnight 半个月二百块危地马拉格查尔 Bàngè yuè liǎngbǎi kuài Wēidìmǎlā géchá'ěr

Q: How's the weather in your country? 你们那儿天气怎么样？ Nǐmén nàr tiānqì zěnmeyàng?

- Tough: Where I come from, everyday it rains bullets 我们那边儿每天下子弹 Wǒmén nèibiānr měi tiān xià zǐdàn

Q: Are you accustomed to Beijing? 来北京习惯了吗？ Lái Běijīng xiguan le ma?

- Philosopher: When in Rome ... 入乡随俗... Rùxiāngsuísú ...
- Mama's baby: I only miss my mother's bosom 我只怀念我妈妈的怀抱 Wǒ zhǐ huáiniàn wǒ māma de huáibào

Q: Are you married? 你结婚了吗？ Nǐ jiéhūn le ma?

- Desperate for love: Not yet. Introduce me to someone! 还没.你来介绍吧！ Hái méi. Nǐ lái jièshào ba!
- Devout: I took a vow of celibacy 我发誓独身 Wǒ fāshì dúshēn
- Modest single: I'm too ugly to find anyone 我长得太难看了，找不着对象 Wǒ zhǎng de tài nánkàn le, zhǎo bù zháo duìxiàng
- We are the world: There's no need, isn't all of humanity one family? 不用，世界人民是一家，对不对？ Bùyòng, shìjiè rénmín shì yì jiā, duì búduì?

- Good morning 早上好 Zǎoshàng hǎo
- Good afternoon 下午好 Xiàwǔ hǎo
- Good evening 晚上好 Wǎnshàng hǎo
- How are you? 怎么样啊？ Zěnmeyàng a?

Listen for this

- Háihǎo, nǐ ne? 还好，你呢？ I'm ok, how about you?
- hěn hǎo 很好 pretty good
- bú cuò 不错 not bad
- yì bānbān / mǎmǎ hūhū 一般般/马马虎虎 just so so
- bù zěnmèyàng 不怎么样 not good
- Shénme zěnmeyàng? 什么怎么样？ How am I *what*?

3 Introductions 介绍 Jièshào

Sentences

- My name is ... 我叫... Wǒ jiào ...
- I am ... 我是... Wǒ shì ...
- I'd like to introduce you to (my) ... 我想把你介绍给我的... Wǒ xiǎng bǎ nǐ jièshào gěi wǒ de ...

(1) wife 老婆 lǎopo
(2) husband 老公 lǎogōng
(3) life partner 爱人 àirén
(4) boyfriend 男朋友 nánpéngyou
(5) girlfriend 女朋友 nǚpéngyou
(6) colleague 同事 tóngshì
(7) son 儿子 érzi
(8) daughter 女儿 nǚ'ér
(9) mother 妈妈 māma
(10) father 爸爸 bàba

• What's your name? (formal) 请问您怎么称呼? Qǐngwèn nín zěnme chēnghu?

• What's your name? (informal) 你叫什么? Nǐ jiào shénme?

• Pleased to meet you 很高兴认识你 Hěn gāoxìng rènshi nǐ

• Titles 称呼 Chēnghū

(1) Mister 先生 xiānsheng
(2) Madam 女士 nǚshì
(3) Miss 小姐 / 姑娘 xiǎojiě / Gūniang
(4) grandpa / grandma 爷爷/奶奶 yéye / nǎinai
(5) little boy 小男孩儿 xiǎo nánháir
(6) little girl (young gal) 小女孩儿 xiǎo nǚháir
(7) big bro 大哥 dàgē
(8) dude 伙计/哥们儿 huǒji / gēmenr
(9) auntie 阿姨 āyí

• Hello Miss Tang 唐小姐你好 Táng xiǎojiě nǐhǎo

• What's up dude? 哥们儿怎么样? Gēmenr zěnmeyàng?

• Please teach me more Mr. Wang 王先生请多指教 Wáng xiānsheng qǐng duō zhǐjiào

Listen for this

• Rènshi nǐ hěn gāoxìng 认识你很高兴 It's very nice to meet you

• Jiǔyǎng dàmíng 久仰大名 I've heard a lot about you

4 I beg your pardon (language difficulties) 对不起（语言问题）

Duìbùqǐ (yǔyán wèntí)

Sentences

• I don't speak any Chinese 我一点儿中文都不会说 Wǒ yìdiǎnr zhōngwén dōu bú huì shuō

• I speak a little Chinese 我只会说一点儿中文 Wǒ zhǐ huì shuō yì diǎnr zhōngwén

• Do you speak English? 你会说英语吗？Nǐ huì shuō yīngyǔ ma?

• Is there anyone who speaks English? 有人会说英语吗？Yǒu rén huì shuō yīngyǔ ma?

• I beg your pardon / Could you repeat that? 能重复一遍吗？Néng chóngfù yí biàn ma? / 请你再说一遍 Qǐng nǐ zài shuō yí biàn

• Could you point to the phrase in this book? 你能在这本书里指出这个词吗？Nǐ néng zài zhèi běn shū lǐ zhǐchū zhè gè cí ma?

• Just a minute, I'll look it up 等一下，我找一找 Děng yí xià, wǒ zhǎo yì zhǎo

• I can't find the word/phrase 我找不着这个字/词 Wǒ zhǎo bù zháo zhè gè zì / cí

5 Useful Lists
实用列表 Shíyòng lièbiǎo

Numbers	数字	shùzì
0	零	líng
1	一	yī
2	二	èr
3	三	sān
4	四	sì
5	五	wǔ
6	六	liù
7	七	qī
8	八	bā
9	九	jiǔ
10	十	shí
11	十一	shíyī
12	十二	shí'èr
13	十三	shísān
20	二十	èrshí
21	二十一	èrshíyī
22	二十二	èrshí'èr

30	三十	sānshí
100	一百	yìbǎi
101	一百零一	yìbǎi líng yī
110	一百一十	yìbǎi yīshí
111	一百一十一	yìbǎi yīshíyī
1000	一千	yìqiān
10.000	一万	yíwàn
100.000	十万	shíwàn
1.000.000	一百万	yìbǎiwàn
10.000.000	一千万	yìqiānwàn
100.000.000	一亿	yíyì
1.000.000.000	十亿	shíyì
1.300.000.000	十三亿	shísānyì-China's population

first	第一	dì-yī
second	第二	dì-èr
third	第三	dì-sān

once	一次	yí cì
twice	两次	liǎng cì
etc	等等	děngděng

Orientation & direction
方位和方向 Fāngwèi hé fāngxiàng

Note: Beijing people are more likely to give directions based on cardinal directions than lefts and rights. Also, as a general rule, people are hesitant to commit themselves to an answer if you ask how far away something is. Only if you ask, "about how far is ..." the place that you're looking for, will you be able to get an approximate answer, in time or in distance (km or Chinese *li*). Remember: be patient, and be persistent.

above 上面 shàngmiàn	⟷	below 下面 xiàmiàn
left 左zuǒ	⟷	right 右 yòu
ahead 前面 qiánmiàn	⟷	behind 后面 hòumiàn
front 前面 qiánmiàn	⟷	back 后面 hòumiàn
straight 直走 zhí zǒu	⟷	turn 转弯 zhuǎnwān
inside 里面 lǐmiàn	⟷	outside 外面 wàimiàn
beside两边 liǎngbiān	⟷	between 中间 zhōngjiān
near 近 jìn	⟷	far 远 yuǎn
nearest 最近的 zuì jìn de	⟷	furthest 最远的 zuì yuǎn de
fast 快 kuài	⟷	slow 慢 màn
fastest 最快的 zuì kuài de	⟷	slowest 最慢的 zuì màn de
north 北 běi	⟷	south 南 nán
east 东 dōng	⟷	west 西 xī

Time 时间 Shíjiān

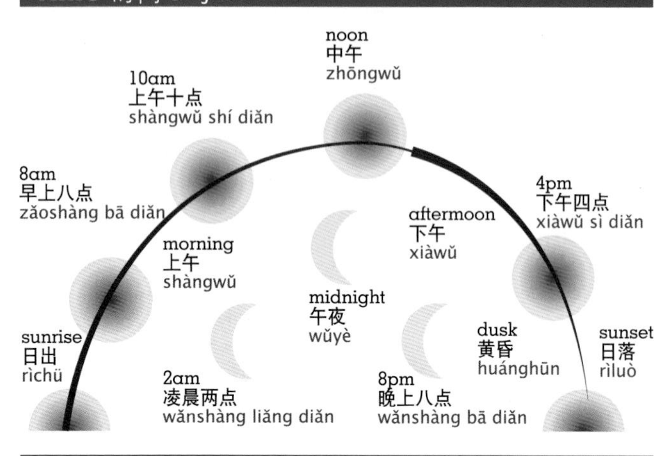

Days of the week 星期 Xīngqī

Note: Days of the week and months are indicated numerically in Chinese, and usually don't have names like they do in English. The word for week (xīngqī 星期) could be literally translated as "star time period," and the days of the week are numbered from one to seven (although Sunday is the exception, usually called xīngqī tiān 星期天; literally "week heaven" or "week day").

Monday 星期一 xīngqī yī	Friday 星期五 xīngqī wǔ
Tuesday 星期二 xīngqī èr	Saturday 星期六 xīngqī liù
Wednesday 星期三 xīngqī sān	Sunday 星期天 xīngqī tiān
Thursday 星期四 xīngqī sì	Weekend 周末 zhōumò

Dates 日期 Rìqī

Note: The twelve months of the year are numbered without exception ("one month," "two month," etc.).

January 一月 yī yuè	March 三月 sān yuè
February 二月 èr yuè	December 十二月 shí'èr yuè
next month 下个月 xiàgè yuè	last month 上个月 shànggè yuè
this month 这个 zhègè yuè	everyday 每天 měitiān

1/9/1953 一九五三年九月一日 yījiǔwǔsān nián jiǔ yuè yī rì

3 years ago
三年前
sānniánqián

this year
今年
jīnnián

6 years from now
六年后
liùniánhòu

past
过去
guòqù

last year
去年
qùnián

next year
明年
míngnián

future
未来
wèilái

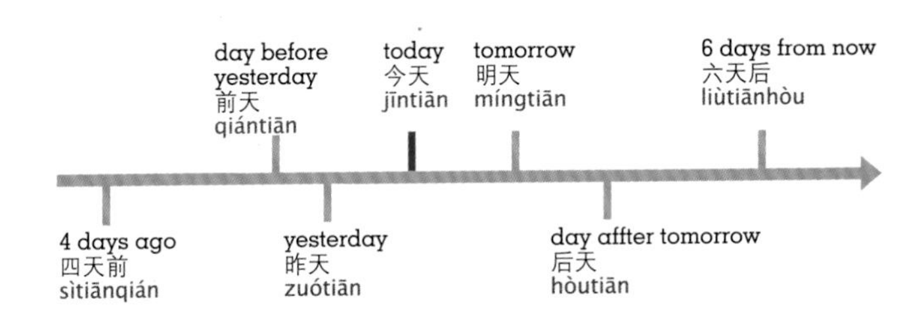

Seasons 季节 Jìjié

winter 冬天 dōngtiān
summer 夏天 xiàtiān
spring 春天 chūntiān
fall 秋天 qiūtiān

Weather 天气 Tiānqì

hot 热 rè
cold 冷 lěng
rain 雨 yǔ
fog 雾 wù
cloud 乌云 wūyún
thunder 雷 léi
dry 干燥 gānzào
dust storm 沙尘暴 shāchénbào
temperature 气温 qìwēn
warm 暖和 nuǎnhe
wind 风 fēng
snow 雪 xuě
sun 阳光 yángguāng
humid / moist 潮湿的 cháoshī de
lightening闪电 shǎndiàn
polluted 污染的 wūrǎn de
clear day 晴天 qíngtiān
Celsius 摄氏度 shèshìdù

Shapes 形状 Xíngzhuàng

round 圆的 yuán de
circular 圆形的 yuánxíng de
square 正方形 zhèngfāngxíng
triangle 三角形 sānjiǎoxíng
rectangular 长方形的 chángfāngxíng de
cube 立方体 lìfāngtǐ
sphere 球体 qiútǐ
line 线条 xiàntiáo
cylinder 圆柱体 yuánzhùtǐ
pyramid 金字塔形 jīnzìtǎ xíng

Colors 颜色 Yánsè

red 红色 hóngsè
brown 棕色 zōngsè
yellow (blond) 黄色 huángsè
green 绿色 lǜsè
silver 银色 yínsè
gray 灰色 huīsè
pink 粉色 fěnsè
light green 浅绿色 qiǎnlǜsè
black 黑色 hēisè
blue 蓝色 lánsè
white 白色 báisè
gold 金色 jīnsè
orange 橙色 chéngsè
purple 紫色 zǐsè
dark blue 深蓝色 shēnlánsè
clear 透明 tòumíng

People 人物 Rénwù

teacher 老师 lǎoshī
secretary 秘书 mìshu
policeman 警察 jǐngchá
adult 成年人 chéngniánrén
friend 朋友 péngyǒu
driver 司机 sījī
tailor 裁缝 cáifeng
neighbor 邻居 línjū
child 孩子 háizi
guest 客人 kèrén

Places 地点 Dìdiǎn

hospital 医院 yīyuàn
bank 银行 yínháng
airport 机场 jīchǎng
post office 邮局 yóujú
embassy 大使馆 dàshǐguǎn
school 学校 xuéxiào
supermarket 超市 chāoshì
office 办公室 bàngōngshì
clubhouse 俱乐部／会所 jūlèbù/huìsuǒ

VERBS 动词 Dòngcí

to arrive 到 dào
to attend 参加 cānjiā
to be 是 shì
to be able 能 néng
to be in / at / on 在 zài
to book / reserve 预定 yùdìng
to bring 带 dài
to buy 买 mǎi
to come 来 lái
to cough 咳嗽 késou
to cry 哭 kū
to do / make 做 zuò
to draw 画 huà
to drink 喝 hē
to eat 吃 chī
to feel 感觉 gǎnjué
to fetch 取来 qǔ lái
to find 找到 zhǎodào
to follow 跟着 gēnzhe
to get 得到 dédào
to give 给 gěi
to go 去 qù
to grow 成长 chéngzhǎng
to look for 寻找 xúnzhǎo
to love 爱 ài
to make a phone call 打电话 dǎ diànhuà
to pick up 捡起 jiǎn qǐ
to post mail 寄信 jì xìn
to pull 拉 lā
to recognize 认识 rènshi
to return 返回 fǎnhuí
to ride (bike, horse) 骑 qí
to sell 卖 mài
to send 发送 fāsòng
to sit 坐 zuò
to sleep 睡觉 shuìjiào
to smile 微笑 wēixiào
to speak / say 说 shuō
to spend 花／用 huā/yòng
to stand 站 zhàn
to study 学习 xuéxí
to taste 品尝 pǐncháng
to tell 告诉 gàosù
to understand (at all) 理解 lǐjiě
to understand (clearly)

to have 有 yǒu
to have to 得 děi
to help 帮助 bāngzhù
to invite 邀请 yāoqǐng
to know 知道 zhīdào
to leave 离开 líkāi
to like 喜欢 xǐhuān
to live 生活 shēnghuó
明白 míngbái
to visit (person) 拜访 bàifǎng
to visit (place) 参观 cānguān
to wait 等 děng
to want / will 要 yào
to want to / miss / think 想 xiǎng
to wash 洗 xǐ
to write 写 xiě

ADJECTIVES 形容词 Xíngróngcí

big 大 dà	⟷	small 小 xiǎo
wide 宽 kuān	⟷	narrow 窄 zhǎi
up 上 shàng	⟷	down 下 xià
open/on 开了 kāi le	⟷	closed/turned off 关了 guān le
tall 高 gāo	⟷	short 矮 ǎi
high 高 gāo	⟷	low 低 dī
expensive 贵 guì	⟷	cheap 便宜 piányi
old (person) 老 lǎo	⟷	young 年轻 niánqīng
old (thing) 旧 jiù	⟷	new 新 xīn
dirty 脏 zāng	⟷	clean 干净 gānjìng
long 长 cháng	⟷	short 短 duǎn
fat 胖 pàng	⟷	skinny 瘦 shòu
thick 厚 hòu	⟷	thin 薄 báo
fast 快 kuài	⟷	slow 慢 màn
full 满 mǎn	⟷	empty 空 kōng
happy 高兴 gāoxìng	⟷	sad 难过 nánguò
tidy 整洁 zhěngjié	⟷	messy 杂乱 záluàn
strong 强 qiáng	⟷	weak 弱 ruò
rich (person) 富 fù	⟷	poor 穷 qióng
dry 干 gān	⟷	wet 湿 shī
difficult 困难 kùnnàn	⟷	easy 简单 jiǎndān
dangerous 危险 wēixiǎn	⟷	safe 安全 ānquán
correct 正确 zhèngquè	⟷	incorrect 错误 cuòwù
noisy 吵闹 chǎonào	⟷	quiet 安静 ānjìng
hard 硬 yìng	⟷	soft 软 ruǎn
late 晚 wǎn	⟷	early 早 zǎo
beautiful 漂亮piàoliàng	⟷	ugly 丑陋 chǒulòu
smelly 臭 chòu	⟷	fragrant 香 xiāng

6 Congratulations and condolences 贺词和悼词 Hècí hé dàocí

Sentences

- Happy birthday! 生日快乐！ Shēngrì kuàilè!
- Wishing you many happy returns (long life) 祝您长命百岁 Zhù nín chángmìng bǎisuì
- Congratulations! 恭喜！ Gōngxǐ!
- Thanks so much for everything 非常感谢您做的一切 Fēicháng gǎnxiè nín zuò de yíqiè.
- It was a lot of fun 真得很高兴 Zhēnde hěn gāoxìng
- Give my best to ... 请替我向...问好 Qǐng tì wǒ xiàng...wènhǎo
- All the best! 祝一切都好 Zhù yíqiè dōu hǎo
- Good luck 祝你好运 Zhù nǐ hǎoyùn
- Please accept my condolences 请节哀 Qǐng jié'āi
- My deepest sympathy 我深表同情 Wǒ shēnbiǎo tóngqíng

Listen for this

- Xièxie nín de guānxīn 谢谢您的关心 Thank you for your concern

Not Exactly ...

Designed to put you at ease, the following expressions should instead put you on your guard

by Jon Campbell

• Yīnggāi méi wèntí 应该没问题 "Shouldn't be a problem"
On the surface, the speaker calmly asserts that no problem will arise – or at least that no insoluble problem will arise – but she is in fact sleuthily acknowledging that the problem will never, ever be solved. A variation: wèntí bú dà (问题不大 "the problem is not big"). It may not be big, but it will remain a problem. Assume that your *wenti* will most certainly remain a wenti regardless of whether or not it should be.

• Mǎshàng 马上 "Right away"
Its roots in the image of someone getting on a horse, ostensibly to gallop at tremendous speeds toward whatever is in need of immediate attention, might calm one into believing that resolution is close at hand, but beware. When a waitress, in response to your request to cuī yí xià (催一下 hurry up) the lunch you've ordered but haven't yet received, says "mashang jiu hao le," you do, despite her protestations to the contrary, still have time to cancel it and/or walk home, shower, watch some TV and return to the restaurant for dinner, where your dish will be hot off the wok.

• Zài lù shàng 在路上 "On the road"
One is supposed to be calmed, knowing that the speaker is on the way and will arrive imminently. But the image should, in fact, bring to mind Kerouac and the Beats: Think of Dean and Sal heading west with no fear or concept of time, space, destination or state of mind. "Zai lu shang" is anywhere from just getting out of the shower to stuck in what will certainly be an hours-long traffic jam to just outside the door. Keys to decoding the actual ETA of the person you're waiting for are those unspoken: toilets flushing, the sound of a voice ripped from (over)sleep, or the recording signalling that the taxi's flag has just been dropped.

• Chà bù duō 差不多 "More or less"
A wily way of feigning to be in complete agreement. "So it'll cost me 5,000 kuai?" "Cha bu duo," will come the response from the guy about to charge you no less than RMB 8,000. "So," asks the businessman to the company with whom he'd like to do business, "we're agreed then?" A "cha bu duo" here might mean anything from "Absolutely" to "Sure, on everything except where we give you any money, spend any of our money or get off our asses in any way, shape or form."

7 Opinions and judgments

看法和判断 Kànfǎ hé pànduàn

Sentences

- Which do you (like) prefer? 你喜欢哪个？ Nǐ xǐhuan něi gè?
- What do you think (of this)? 你觉得（这个）怎么样？
  Nǐ júede (zhèi gè) zěnmeyàng?
- You've gone too far 你太过分了 Nǐ tài guòfèn le
- What a pity / shame 太可惜了 Tài kěxī le
- I don't mind / Whatever 我无所谓 Wǒ wúsuǒwèi
- Well done 干得好 Gàn de hǎo
- How awful / horrible 太讨厌了 Tài tǎoyàn le
- This is not what I expected 这跟我想象的不一样
  Zhè gēn wǒ xiǎngxiàng de bù yíyàng
- What's your opinion? 你有什么看法？ Nǐ yǒu shénme kànfǎ?

Listen for this

- háihǎo 还好 not bad
- tàibàng le 太棒了 great / excellent
- bèir bàng 倍儿棒 spectacular / wicked
- shuǎng 爽 awesome ("feels so good")
- hái kěyǐ 还可以 from "good enough" to "OK!"
- tài chàjìn le 太差劲了 terrible
- ěxin 恶心 disgusting
- bièniu 别扭 awkward
- Nǐ zhēn kělián 你真可怜 Poor you!

8 Feelings 感觉 Gǎnjué

- happy 高兴 gāoxìng
- sad 难过 nánguò
- annoyed 烦恼 fánnǎo
- depressed 沮丧 jǔsàng
- disappointed 失望 shīwàng
- embarrassed 尴尬 gāngà
- busy 忙 máng
- surprised 惊讶 jīngyà
- worried 担心 dānxīn
- proud 自豪 zìháo
- hot 热 rè
- cold 冷 lěng
- hungry 饿 è
- thirsty 渴 kě
- drunk 醉 zuì
- shy 害羞 hàixiū
- outgoing 开朗 kāilǎng
- lucky 幸运 xìngyùn
- unlucky 不幸 búxìng
- oppressed 压抑 yāyì
- angry 生气 shēngqì
- lonely 孤单 gūdān
- missing home 想家 xiǎngjiā
- scared 害怕 hàipà
- energetic 精力旺盛 jīnglì wàngshèng
- tired 累 lèi
- sleepy 困 kùn
- confused 糊涂 hútu
- sick 病 bìng
- dizzy (out of it) 头晕 tóuyūn

Sentences

To express feelings, emotions and physical states, the verb "to be" is unnessesary. Substitute any of the above adjectives like this:

- I'm (not) ... 我(很/不/没)... Wǒ (hěn/bú/méi) ...

(1) I'm not drunk 我没醉 Wǒ méi zuì
(2) I'm not tired 我不累 Wǒ bú lèi
(3) I'm hot 我很热 Wǒ hěn rè
(4) I'm shy 我很害羞 Wǒ hěn hàixiū

9 Goodbyes 道别 Dàobié

- Ok, I've got to get going 那，我得走了/那我先走了 Nà, wǒ děi zǒu le / Nà wǒ xiān zǒu le

- Goodbye (formal) 再见 Zàijiàn

- Goodbye (informal) 回见 Huíjiàn

- It was great meeting you. 很高兴和您见面 Hěn gāoxìng hé nín jiànmiàn.

- What's your ... phone / address / email 你的．．．电话／地址／电子邮箱是什么？ Nǐ de diànhuà/dìzhǐ/diànzǐ yóuxiāng shì shénme?

- Will you write / call me? 你会给我写信/打电话吗？ Nǐ huì gěi wǒ xiě xìn/dǎ diànhuà ma?

- Here's my ... phone / address / email 这是我的．．．电话／地址／电子邮箱 Zhè shì wǒ de...diànhuà/dìzhǐ/diànzǐ yóuxiāng

- See you ...

(1) in a little while 一会儿见 yíhuìr jiàn
(2) tomorrow 明儿见 míngr jiàn
(3) later 回头见 huítóu jiàn
(4) next week 下星期见 xià xīngqī jiàn

- I hope we meet again soon 我希望我们很快能再见面 Wǒ xīwàng wǒmen hěnkuài néng zài jiànmiàn

HOUSING & HOTELS ►

If you're bored and a little frisky, may we recommend perusing Beijing's English-language real estate classifieds. They're just as droll as the personals and far less confusing about who's being taken for a ride: you. Whether fair or not, it is commonly held that foreigners who cannot speak Chinese can be induced to pay a "language deficiency tax" in the form of higher prices on just about everything, including property. Mastering some of the vocabulary and phrases below can help you save money by allowing you to read the invariably-cheaper Chinese-language listings, gain access to a far broader property pool and negotiate directly with the landlord.

1 Searching for a home

找房 Zhǎo fáng

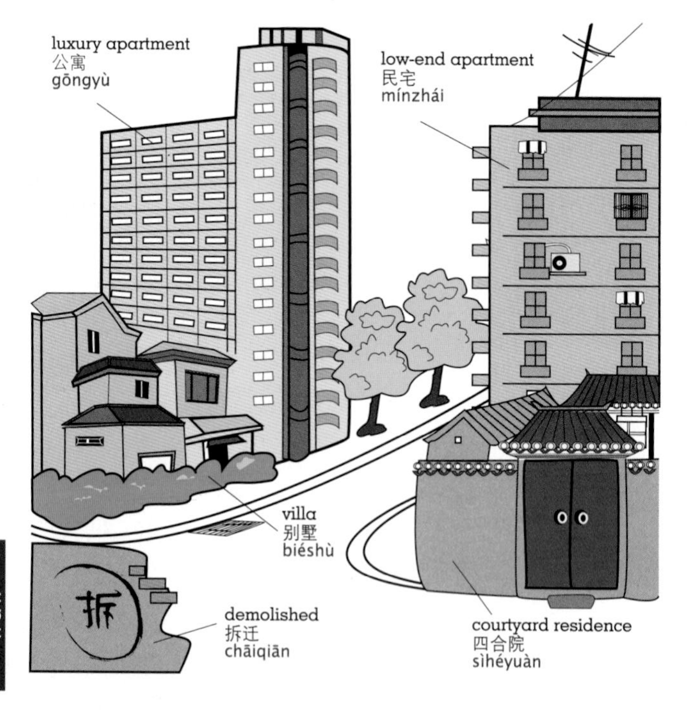

Sentences

• Where is there ... ? 哪儿有 . . . ? nǎr yǒu ... ?

(1) a property agent's office 房地产公司 fángdìchǎn gōngsī

(2) a management company office 物业公司 wùyè gōngsī
(3) an apartment for rent 房子出租 fángzi chūzū

- I am looking for a ... 我在找一间... Wǒ zài zhǎo yìjiān ...

(1) luxury apartment 公寓 gōngyù
(2) mid-level apartment 普通楼房 pǔtōng lóufáng
(3) villa 别墅 biéshù
(4) 2 bedroom, 1 living room place 两室一厅的房子 liǎngshì yìtīng de fángzi
(5) furnished apartment 家具齐全的房子 jiājù qíquán de fángzi

- How many ... ? 有几个...? yǒu jǐ ge ... ?

(1) bedrooms 卧室 wòshì
(2) bathrooms 卫生间 wèishēngjiān

- How many square meters? 有多少平米? Yǒu duōshǎo píngmǐ?

- Are you kidding me? This place is a dump! 你开玩笑呢吧? 这个地方太破啦! Nǐ kāi wánxiào ne ba? Zhèigè dìfang tài pò la!

- I need a place with 24-hour hot water, furnished and fitted out. 我想要一个有24小时热水，家电齐全，精装修的房子。Wǒ xiǎng yào yí ge yǒu èrshísì xiǎoshí rèshuǐ, jiādiàn qíquán, jīng zhuāngxiū de fángzi.

- Is it (furnished / unfurnished)? 这个是(带/不带)家具的吗? Zhèige shì (dài / bú dài) jiājù de ma?

- What furniture does it include? 包括什么家具? Bāokuò shénme jiājù?

Listen for this

- chuáng 床 bed
- shāfā 沙发 sofa
- bìchú 壁橱 closet
- cānzhuō 餐桌 dinner table
- dìtǎn 地毯 rug
- bīngxiāng 冰箱 refrigerator
- zàojù 灶具 stove
- rèshuǐqì 热水器 hot water heater
- xǐyījī 洗衣机 washing machine
- kōngtiáo 空调 air conditioner
- yǒuxiàn diànshì 有线电视 cable TV

(See also Furniture and Electronics pages 148 and 158)

for rent chū zū | seeking to buy qiú shòu

房地产公司

出租 □ 求购 □
求租 □ 出售 □

Property Company fángdìchǎn gōngsī | seeking rental qiúzū | for sale chūshòu

位置: wèizhì ____ address
楼层: lóucéng ____ floor # / out of

朝向: cháoxiàng ____ direction
面积: miànji ____ floor space

jūshì ____ 居室 tīng ____ 厅 bedrooms living rooms
家具水电: jiājù shuǐdiàn ____ furnishings

小区名称: xiǎoqū míngchēng ____ community name
装修: zhuāngxiū ____ fittings

币种: bìzhǒng ____ currency
发布日期: fābù rìqī ____ posted date

价格: jiàgé ____ price
付款方式: fùkuǎn fāngshì ____ payment method

Sentences

• Can you show me (some places) ... 你能不能 . . . 带我去看看
Nǐ néng bùnéng ... dài wǒ qù kànkan

(1) today 今天 jīntiān
(2) right now 现在 xiànzài
(3) tomorrow 明天 míngtiān

• How much is the rent? 房租多少钱? Fángzū duōshao qián?

• I'd have to see the apartment before I can say how much I'd pay for it 我得先看看房子再说能出多少钱 Wǒ děi xiān kànkan fángzi zài shuō néng chū duōshao qián

• This is out of my budget 这个超过我的预算了 Zhèige chāoguò wǒde yùsuàn le

Listen for this

• zhōngjiè 中介 property agent

• jīng zhuāngxiū 精装修 high standard refurbishing

• jìfù / yā yī fù sān 季付 / 押一付三 quarterly payments / one month's deposit, three months' rent

• Nǐ yào huā duōshao qián? 你要花多少钱? How much do you want to spend?

2 Examining an apartment 检查房子 Jiǎnchá fángzi

Sentences

• Am I able to control the temperature (of the room)? 我能控制(室内)温度吗? Wǒ néng kòngzhì (shìnèi) wēndù ma?

• How far away is the nearest subway stop? 最近的地铁站离这儿有多远? Zuìjìn de dìtiězhàn lí zhèr yǒu duōyuǎn?

• The water pressure isn't good enough 水压不够大 Shuǐyā búgòu dà

• Is the elevator 24-hours? 这儿的电梯是24小时的吗? Zhěr de diàntī shì èrshísì xiǎoshí de ma?

• When can I move in? 我什么时候能搬进来? Wǒ shénme shíhou néng bān jìnlái?

• Will you clean it before I move in? 我搬进来之前你能清理一下吗? Wǒ bān jìnlái zhīqián nǐ néng qīnglǐ yíxià ma?

• Does the shower drain well? 淋浴的下水好吗? Línyù de xiàshuǐ hǎo ma?

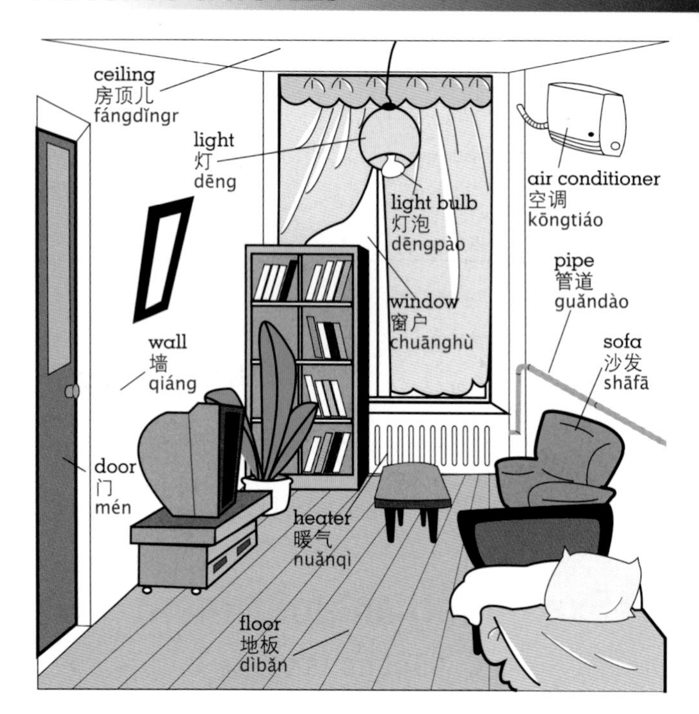

• Who pays the...? 谁交...? Shéijiāo...?

(1) management fee 物业费 wùyèfèi
(2) water bill 水费 shuǐfèi
(3) electricity bill 电费 diànfèi
(4) gas bill 煤气费 méiqìfèi
(5) telephone bill 电话费 diànhuàfèi
(6) heating fee 暖气费 nuǎnqìfèi
(7) parking fee 停车费 tíngchēfèi
(8) gym fee 健身费 jiànshēnfèi
(9) rental tax 房屋租赁税 fángwū zūlìn shuì
(10) cable TV bill 有线电视费 yǒuxiàn diànshì fèi

• How much is the ... per month? ...一个月多少钱? ... Yí gè yuè duōshao qián?

• Who owns the property? 谁是房东? Shéi shì fángdōng?

• Is there a fire detector and fire extinguisher? 有烟感器和灭火器吗? Yǒu yāngǎnqì hé mièhuǒqì ma?

Listen for this

- Zhèige xiǎoqū zhì'ān tèbié hǎo 这个小区治安特别好 This neighborhood is really safe
- Gòuwù jiāotōng dōu fāngbiàn 购物交通都方便 Convenient transportation and shopping
- Yíqiè dōu bāokuò le 一切都包括了 Everything is included

3 Negotiating & signing the lease

谈判与签合同 Tánpàn yǔ qiān hétong

Sentences

- The payment method (period) is ... 付款方式是... Fùkuǎn fāngshi shì...

(1) monthly 月付 yuè fù
(2) quarterly 季付 jì fù
(3) half yearly 半年付 bànnián fù

- deposit 押金 yājīn
- normal wear and tear 正常磨损 zhèngcháng mósǔn
- Can you (remove / take away) the ...? 你能把...(拆了/拿走)吗? Nǐ néng bǎ ... (chāi le / nǎ zóu) ma?
- Can you buy a ... ? 你能买一个...吗? Nǐ néng mǎi yí ge ... ma?
- Can you paint this room? 能刷一下儿这个房间吗? Néng shuā yíxiàr zhèige fángjiān ma ?
- Write it down. Put it in the contract 写下来吧。在合同上标出来 Xiě xiàlái ba. Zài hétong shàng biāo chūlái
- If you charge me an agency fee, I won't sign the lease! 如果你要跟我收中介费, 我不会签这个合同! Rúguǒ nǐ yào gēn wǒ shōu zhōngjièfèi, wǒ búhuì qiān zhèige hétong!
- Your fee is between you and the landlord. It doesn't have anything to do with me 你付的费用是你和房东之间的事儿。 跟我没什么关系 Nǐ fù de fèiyòng shì nǐ hé fángdōng zhījiān de shìr. Gēn wǒ méi shénme guānxi

• Can I sublet? 我能转租给别人吗？Wǒ néng zhuǎnzū gěi biérén ma?

• Can we include a break clause if I have to leave early? 我们能不能加入一条关于中止合同的条款？我有可能得提前搬走。Wǒmen néng bùnéng jiārù yìtiáo guānyú zhōngzhǐ hétong de tiáokuǎn? Wǒ yǒu kěnéng děi tíqián bān zǒu.

• If I sign a longer lease, can you reduce the rent? 如果我签时间长点儿的合同，房租能便宜点儿吗？Rúguǒ wǒ qiān shíjiān cháng diǎnr de hétong, fángzū néng piányi diǎnr ma?

• If the ... breaks, who is responsible for repairs? 如果...坏了，谁负责修理？ Rúguǒ ....huàile, shéi fùzé xiūlǐ ?

• What is the ... meter reading? 现在... 表走了多少个字儿了？Xiànzài .... biǎo zǒule duōshao gè zìr le?

• How much per unit for the ...? ...每个字儿多少钱？... měi gè zìr duōshao qián?

• Where can I pay the ... ? 在哪儿能交 ... ？Zài nǎr néng jiāo...?

(1) water 水费 shuǐfèi
(2) electricity 电费 diànfèi
(3) gas 煤气费 méiqìfèi

• Whose name is on the phone account? 电话账户上是谁的名字？Diànhuà zhànghù shàng shì shéide míngzi?

4 Registering at the PSB
在派出所登记 Zài pàichūsuǒ dēngjì

Sentences

Note: Excluding L visa holders, all foreigners need to register their place of residence with the local Public Security Bureau within 24 hours of moving.

• I need to register for the Temporary Residence Permit 我需要办临时住宿登记 Wǒ xūyào bàn Línshí Zhùsù Dēngjì.

• I just moved in 我刚搬进去 Wǒ gāng bān jìnqù

• I haven't started living there 我现在还没开始在那儿住呢。Wǒ xiànzài hái méi kāishǐ zài nàr zhù ne.

• I don't pay rent; he and I are good buddies. I teach his son/daughter English. 我不用付房租。我和他是好朋友。我教他儿子/女儿英文。Wǒ búyòng fù fángzū. Wǒ hé tā shì hǎo péngyou. Wǒ jiāo tā érzi/nǚ'ér yīngwén.

Listen for this

• Nǐ zhù zài nàr duōjiǔ le? 你住在那儿多久了？How long have you been living there?

• hùzhào 护照 passport

• fángdōng shēnfènzhèng 房东身份证 landlord's ID card

• fángdōng hùkǒuběnr 房东户口本儿 landlord's household registration book

• fángdōng fángchǎnzhèng 房东房产证 landlord's property deed

• Nǐ yào zhù nàr duōcháng shíjiān? 你要住那儿多长时间？How long will you be staying there?

5 Living 日常生活 Rìcháng shēnghuó

Sentences

Note: for ayi-related phrases, see Kids page 75 to 83.

• Where is the mail delivered? 信件都送到哪儿？Xìnjiàn dōu sòng dào nǎr?

• Does the mailbox need a key? 信箱需要钥匙吗？Xìnxiāng xūyào yàoshi ma?

• I need ADSL installed 我需要报装ADSL Wǒ xūyào bàozhuāng ADSL

• Where is the nearest water delivery? 最近的水站在哪儿？Zuì jìn de shuǐzhàn zài nǎr?

• When can you deliver it? 什么时候能送到？ Shénme shíhou néng sòngdào?

• I am not home during the day, you have to deliver it after 6pm or before 9am 我白天不在家，你得在晚上6点之后或早上9点之前给我送 Wǒ báitiān bú zài jiā, nǐ děi zài wǎnshàng liùdiǎn zhīhòu huò zǎoshàng jiǔdiǎn zhīqián gěi wǒ sòng

• I am locked out of my apartment. Can you help me find someone to open the door? 我被锁在门外了，你能不能帮我找个人把门打开？ Wǒ bèi suǒ zài ménwài le, nǐ néng bùnéng bāng wǒ zhǎo gè rén bǎ mén dǎkāi?

• The electricity is off in my apartment. Can you send someone to figure out the problem? 我们家停电了，你能不能派个人来看看什么问题？ Wǒmen jiā tíngdiàn le, nǐ néng bùnéng pài gè rén lái kànkan shì shénme wèntí?

• Please keep the noise down 麻烦小点儿声儿 Máfan xiǎo diǎnr shēngr

• According to regulations, you cannot be doing construction work now 根据规定，你现在不能进行装修 Gēnjù guīdìng, nǐ xiànzài bùnéng jìnxíng zhuāngxiū

• Apartment number ... is making noise. Can you call them for me? ...号的人特别吵。你能帮我给他们打个电话吗？ ... hào de rén tèbié chǎo. Nǐ néng bāng wō gěi tāmen dǎ ge diànhuà ma?

6 Disagreeing with your landlord 和房东有分歧 Hé fángdōng yǒu fēnqí

Sentences

• I need to register with the PSB in order to be able to get my visa renewed 我必须在派出所登记才能续我的签证 Wǒ bìxū zài pàichūsuǒ dēngjì cáinéng xù wǒ de qiānzhèng

• The ... is broken. Could you come and fix it? 那个...坏了。您能过来修一下吗？ Nèige ... huàile, nín néng guòlái xiū yí xià ma?

• I don't know how it broke, I wasn't here at the time 我不知道它怎么坏的。当时我不在 Wǒ bùzhīdào tā zěnme huài de. Dāngshí wǒ búzài

• If you don't fix it, I'm going to have to go to court and file a report 如果你不给我修好， 我就去法院起诉你 Rúguǒ nǐ bù gěiwǒ xiūhǎo, wǒ jiù qù fǎyuàn qǐsù nǐ

• Have you paid the rental tax? 你交房屋租赁税了吗？ Nǐ jiāo fángwū zūlìnshuì le ma?

7 A visit by the police
警察来访 Jǐngchá lái fǎng

Sentences

• I'm coming 来了来了 láile láile

• Hold on for one second, I'm not decent 稍等一下儿，我穿件衣服 Shāo děng yí xiàr, wǒ chuān jiàn yīfu

• I'm sorry it's so messy in here, I've been too busy to clean lately 实在不好意思，我这儿太乱了，最近实在太忙，没时间收拾 Shízài bùhǎoyìsi, wǒ zhèr tài luàn le, zuìjìn shízài tài máng, méi shíjiān shōushi

• I'm sorry; I can't find my housing permit. Can I bring it by the station later? 不好意思，我找不到我的住宿登记证了，我能不能晚点儿带来？ Bùhǎoyìsi, wǒ zhǎo bú dào wǒ de zhùsù dēngjìzhèng le, wǒ néng bùnéng wǎn diǎn dàilái?

• Let me call a friend who speaks Chinese 我给一个会说中文的朋友打个电话 Wǒ gěi yí ge huì shuō zhōngwén de péngyou dǎ ge diànhuà

Listen for this:

• Zhèr yǒu duōshǎo rén zhù? 这儿有多少人住？ How many people live here?

• Nèige fángjiān sheí zhù? 那个房间谁住？ Who lives in that room?

- Nǐ shì něi guó rén? 你是哪国人？ What country are you from?
- Nǐ zài Běijīng zuò shénme? 你在北京做什么？ What are you doing in Beijing?
- Nǐ de hùzhào hé Línshí Zhùsù Dēngjìzhèng zài nǎr? 你的护照和临时住宿登记证在哪儿？ Where is your passport and Temporary Residence Permit?
- Nǐ zài nǎr gōngzuò? 你在哪儿工作？ Who is your employer?
- Míngtiān lái yí tàng pàichūsuǒ, wǒ zài gēn nǐ shuō. 明天来一趟派出所，我再跟你说。Come down to the station tomorrow so we can talk more.

8 Booking a hotel/hostel room

订酒店／旅馆房间

Dìng jiǔdiàn/lǚguǎn fángjiān

Sentences

- Where is there a ... ? 请问哪儿有 . . . ？ Qǐngwèn nǎr yǒu ... ?

(1) hostel 青年旅社 qīngnián lǚshè
(2) mid-range hotel 旅馆 lǚguǎn
(3) luxury hotel 宾馆/酒店 bīnguǎn / jiǔdiàn

- I'd like to make a reservation 我想订一个房间 Wǒ xiǎng dìng yí gè fángjiān
- Do you have a .... ? 你们这儿有没有 . . . ? Nǐmen zhèr yǒu méiyǒu ...?

(1) double room (suite) 套间 tàojiān
(2) single room 单人间 dānrénjiān
(3) twin 双人间 shuāngrénjiān
(4) standard room 标准间 biāozhǔnjiān

- Do you have a room with a bathroom? 你们有没有带卫生间的房间？ Nǐmen yǒu méiyǒu dài wèishēngjiān de fángjiān?

- Can I get a (student / Hostelling International) discount（学生/国际青年旅社组织会员）有优惠吗？(Xuéshēng/Guójì qīngnián lǚshè zǔzhi huìyuán) yǒu yōuhuì ma?

- When is check-out? 结账是什么时候？Jiézhàng shì shénme shíhòu?

- Is there 24-hour hot water? 有24小时热水吗？ Yǒu èrshísì xiǎoshí rèshuǐ ma?

- Can I see the room? 可不可以先看一看房间？ Kě bùkěyǐ xiān kànyíkàn fángjiān?

- slippers 拖鞋 tuōxié

- hot water thermos 暖壶 nuǎnhú

- I have a reservation 我订了房间 Wǒ dìngle fángjiān

- My name is ... 我的名字是. . . Wǒ de míngzi shì ...

Listen for this

- hùzhào 护照 passport
- Jǐ tiān? 几天？How many nights?
- Méiyǒu fángjiān le 没有房间了 We're full
- Suǒyǒu fángjiān dōu yào jiā shōu fúwùfèi 所有房间都要加收服务费 There is a service charge for all rooms

Sentences

- for three nights 三天 sān tiān

- from July 2 to July 6 从七月二号到七月六号 cóng qīyuè èrhào dào qīyuè liùhào

- How much is it per .... ? 多少钱一... ? Duōshǎo qián yì...?

(1)day 天 tiān (2) person 人 rén

9 A knock at the door

敲门 Qiāomén

Sentences

- Who is it? 谁啊？Shéi a?
- Hold on a second 等一下儿 Děng yí xiàr
- Please come back in a bit 请过一会儿再来 Qǐng guò yí huìr zài lái
- Please go away 请走开 Qǐng zǒukāi

FOOD ►

1 Basics 基础词汇 Jīchǔ cíhuì

Words

breakfast 早饭 zǎofàn
lunch 午饭 wǔfàn
dinner 晚饭 wǎnfàn
snack 零食 língshí
late-night meal 宵夜 xiāoyè

Sentences

- I'm hungry 我饿了 Wǒ è le
- I'm starving 我饿死了 Wǒ è sǐ le
- I'm thirsty 我渴了 Wǒ kě le

2 Looking for a place to eat 找地方吃饭 Zhǎo dìfang chīfàn

Sentences

Note: There are many names in Chinese for a restaurant: 餐馆 cānguǎn, 餐厅 cāntīng, 饭店 fàndiàn, 饭馆 fànguǎn, 酒楼 jiǔlóu. The differences between the meaning of these words is slight and they can generably be used interchangeably.

- I'm looking for / can you recommend a... 我想找个/您能不能推荐一个 Wǒ xiǎng zhǎo gè/Nín néng bùnéng tuījiàn yīgè

(1) restaurant 饭馆 fànguǎn
(2) cafe 咖啡厅 kāfēitīng
(3) teahouse 茶馆 cháguǎn
(4) bar 酒吧 jiǔbā
(5) cafeteria 食堂 shítáng
(6) street vendor 路边摊儿 lùbiān tānr
(7) a cheap meal 便宜的吃饭的地儿 piányì de chīfàn de dìr
(8) western food 西餐 xīcān

- Where is the closest place to get something quick? 最近的能简单吃点儿的地方在哪儿? Zuìjìn de néng jiǎndān chī diǎnr de dìfāng zài nǎr?

• The smoke makes me uncomfortable, can you find an area with less smoke? 我闻烟味儿不舒服，你能不能找个烟少点儿的地方？ Wǒ wén yānwèir bù shūfu, nǐ néng bùnéng zhǎo ge yān shǎo diǎnr de dìfang?

• Do you have a non-smoking room? 你们这儿有禁烟区吗？ Nǐmen zhèr yǒu jìnyānqū ma?

3 Making a reservation
预定座位 Yùdìng zuòwèi

Sentences

• I'd like to make a reservation for (tonight at 7.30pm) 我想预定（今天晚上七点半的）座位 Wǒ xiǎng yùdìng (jīntiān wǎnshàng qīdiǎnbàn de) zuòwèi

- We are 6 people 我们一共6个人 Wǒmen yīgòng liù ge rén

- My name is... 我的名字是... Wǒ de míngzi shì...

Listen for this

- Nín jǐ wèi? 您几位？ How many persons?
- Jǐ diǎn? 几点？ What time?
- Xīyān ma? 吸烟吗？ Smoking or non-smoking? (*lit*: Smoke?)
- Guān ménr le / Bú zuòfàn 关门儿了/不做饭 We are closed
- Nín děi děng ... 您得等 ... You have to wait ...
  (1) yì fēnzhōng 一分钟 a minute
  (2) shí fēnzhōng 十分钟 ten minutes

4 At the restaurant

在饭店 Zài fàndiàn

Sentences

- Can we sit here? 我们能坐这儿吗？ Wǒmen néng zuò zhèr ma?

- Do you have a private room? 你们有包间吗？ Nǐmen yǒu bāojiān ma?

- Could you clean this ... 你能把...弄干净吗？ Nǐ néng bǎ ... nòng gānjìng ma?

  (1) table 桌子 zhuōzi
  (2) glass 杯子 bēizi
  (3) dish 小盘子 xiǎo pánzi

- Do these chopsticks and napkins cost extra? 用这种筷子和餐巾要另收钱吗？ Yòng zhè zhǒng kuàizi hé cānjīn yào lìng shōu qián ma?

- How much is the buffet per person? 自助多少钱一位？ Zìzhù duōshao qián yí wèi?

5 Ordering 点菜 Diǎncài

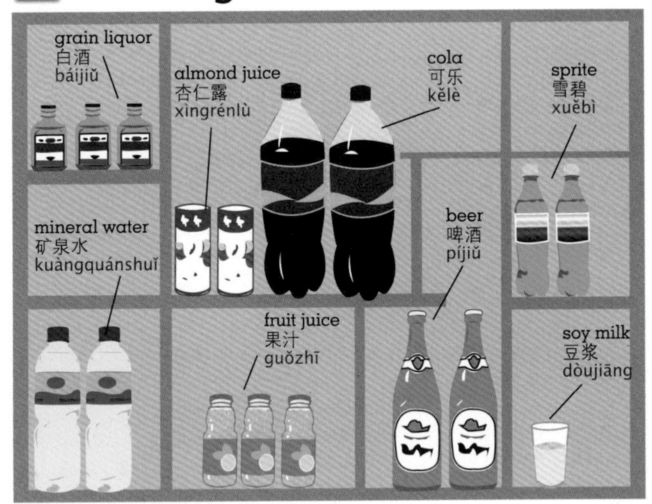

Sentences

- Can I see the menu? 我能看看菜单吗？ Wǒ néng kànkan càidān ma?

- Do you have an English menu? 你们有英文菜单吗？ Nǐmen yǒu yīngwén càidān ma?

- Can you bring another menu? 你能不能再来一份儿菜单？ Nǐ néng bùnéng zài lái yí fènr càidān?

- I (we) haven't decided yet, can you give me (us) a few minutes?我(们)还没决定，您能再等会儿吗？ Wǒ(men) hái méi juédìng, nín néng zài děng huìr ma?

- What is your specialty? 你们有什么特色菜？ Nǐmen yǒu shénme tèsè cài?

- I'll have what those people are having 我要点那些人吃的菜 Wǒ yào diǎn nàxiē rén chī de cài

- Can you recommend a ... 你能推荐个…吗？ Nǐ néng tuījiàn gè … ma?

(1) meat dish 肉菜 ròucài
(2) vegetable dish 素菜 sùcài
(3) tofu dish 有豆腐的菜 yǒu dòufu de cài

- Is this dish ... 这个...吗 Zhège ... ma?

(1) bitter 苦 kǔ
(2) oily 油 yóu
(3) salty 咸 xián
(4) sour 酸 suān
(5) spicy 辣 là
(6) sweet 甜 tián

- Please add (no / less / more)... (不/少/多)放... (Bù / Shǎo / Duō) fàng ...

(1) chili 辣椒 làjiāo
(2) garlic 蒜 suàn
(3) MSG 味精 wèijīng
(4) oil 油 yóu
(5) salt 盐 yán
(6) sauce 酱油 jiàngyóu
(7) sugar 糖 táng

- That's enough 够了/好了 Gòu le / Hǎo le

- Can you bring the rice at the same time? 顺便上米饭吧 Shùnbiàn shàng mǐfàn ba

- Can you bring the ... earlier / later? 能早点/晚点上...吗? Néng zǎodiǎn/wǎndiǎn shàng ... ma?

- I'll have that 我点那个 Wǒ diǎn nèige

- Bring me ... 给我来... Gěi wǒ lái ...

(1) a glass of hot water 一杯开水 yì bēi kāishuǐ
(2) a glass of ice water 一杯冰水 yì bēi bīngshuǐ
(3) a cold beer 瓶凉啤酒 píng liáng píjiǔ
(4) free tea 免费的茶 miǎnfèi de chá
(5) some napkins 一些餐巾纸 xiē cānjīnzhǐ
(6) free chopsticks 双免费的筷子 shuāng miǎnfèi de kuàizi

- Bring another ... 再来一... Zài lái yī ...

Listen for this

- Xiǎng chī diǎnr shénme? 想吃点儿什么? What do you want to have?
- Yào (bīngde/liángde) ma? 要(冰的/凉的)吗? Do you want it cold?
- Duìbùqǐ, mài wán le 对不起,卖完了 Sorry, it's sold out
- Hái yào biéde ma? 还要别的吗? Would you like anything else?

- Yǒu méiyǒu jìkǒu? 有没有忌口？ Anything to avoid (instructions for preparation)?
- Yào dǎkāi ma? 要打开吗？ Should I open it?

6 Dietary restrictions
饮食禁忌 Yǐnshí jìnjì

Sentences

Note: Because of China's Muslim minorities, many Chinese are familiar with halal 清真 qīngzhēn which are the Muslim dietary rules. This phrase can be useful for describing what you want left out of your meal.

- Does this have ... in it? 这里面有...吗？ Zhè lǐmiàn yǒu ... ma?
- I'm allergic to ... 我对...过敏 Wǒ duì ... guòmǐn

(1) dairy 奶制品 nǎizhìpǐn
(2) eggplant 茄子 qiézi
(3) peanuts / nuts 花生/果仁 huāshēng / guǒrén
(4) sugar 糖 táng

- I'm a (vegetarian / vegan) 我是(吃素的 / 严格素食主义者) wǒ shì (chī sù de / yángé sùshí zhǔyì zhě)
- I'm Jewish, I eat only kosher food 我是犹太人，只吃犹太教允许的食物 Wǒ shì yóutài rén, zhǐ chī yóutài jiào yǔnxǔ de shíwù
- I don't eat pork 我不吃猪肉 Wǒ bù chī zhūròu
- Is there any ... in the sauce? 调料里有...吗？ Tiáoliào lǐ yǒu ... ma?
- Are you sure? Not even a little bit? 你确定吗？一点儿都没有吗？ Nǐ quèdìng ma? Yì diǎnr dōu méiyǒu ma?
- Can you please not use any ... 您能不能不用... Nín néng bùnéng bú yòng ...

(1) animal based oil 荤油 hūnyóu
(2) chicken stock 鸡精 jījīng
(3) fish sauce 海鲜调料 hǎixiān tiáoliào

Listen for this

- Méiyǒu 没有 We don't have that
- Zuò bùliǎo 做不了 We can't make it (*lit*: It can't be made)
- Nàge búshì zhūròu, shì jīròu 那个不是猪肉，是鸡肉 It's not pork, it's chicken

7 Eating 吃饭 Chīfàn

Sentences

- How much longer will our food be? 我们的菜还要多长时间？Wǒmen de cài háiyào duōcháng shíjiān?
- Can you hurry it up a bit? 您能催一下儿吗？Nín néng cuī yí xiàr ma?
- Cheers! 干杯！Gānbēi!
- Where's the restroom? 洗手间在哪儿？Xǐshǒujiān zài nǎr?
- This is not what I ordered 这不是我点的 Zhèi búshì wǒ diǎn de
- Are there internal organs in this dish? 这道菜有内脏吗？Zhèi dào cài yǒu nèizàng ma?
- Can you cook it some more? 您能再给做熟点儿吗？Nín néng zài gěi zuò shóu diǎnr ma?
- Can you reheat this rice? 您能把米饭热一下儿吗？Nín néng bǎ mǐfàn rè yí xiàr ma ?
- Can you put it in a doggy bag? 能帮我打包吗？Néng bāng wǒ dǎbāo ma?
- Bill, please! 买单！Mǎidān!
- What is this charge? 这个是什么的钱？zhègè shì shénme de qián?
- Print a receipt 开发票 Kāi fāpiào

Listen for this

- Yào kāi gèrén de háishì dānwèi de? 要开个人的还是单位的？Would you like the receipt made out to an individual or a company?
- Duìbùqǐ, méiyǒu fāpiào 对不起，没有发票 I'm sorry, we're out of receipts

8 Food delivery 送餐 Sòng cān

Sentences

- Do you deliver food? 你们送餐吗？ Nǐmen sòng cān ma ?
- How much is that altogether? 总共多少钱？ Zǒnggòng duōshǎo qián?
- I don't have change, bring change 我没有零钱，带点儿零钱来吧 Wǒ méiyǒu língqián, dài diǎnr língqián lái ba

Listen for this

- (Sòng / Búsòng) cān (送/不送)餐 We (do / don't) deliver
- Nǐ zài shénme dìfang? 你在什么地方？ Where are you?
- Nǐ yǒu méiyǒu língqián? 你有没有零钱？ Do you have small change?

9 At the grocery store

在超市 Zài chāoshì

Sentences

- How much per ... ? 多少钱 ... ？ Duōshǎo qián ... ?

(1) half kilogram 一斤 yì jīn
(2) 100 grams 一百克 yìbǎi kè
(3) each 一个 yí gè

- I'd like 200 grams 我要两百克的 Wǒ yào liángbǎi kè de
- I'd like RMB 20 worth 我要二十块钱的 Wǒ yào èrshí kuài qián de

baking materials 烤面包配料 kǎo miànbāo pèiliào

- cornstarch 淀粉 diànfěn
- baking powder 发酵粉 fājiàofěn
- flour 面粉 miànfěn
- dumpling flour 饺子粉 jiǎozi fěn
- self-rising flour 自发粉 zìfā fěn

vegetables 蔬菜 shūcài

- artichokes 宝塔菜 bǎotǎ cài
- asparagus 芦荀 lúxūn
- bamboo shoots 竹笋 zhúsǔn
- basil 九层塔 jiǔcéngtǎ
- bean sprouts 豆芽儿 dòuyár
- broccoli 西兰花 xīlánhuā
- carrot 胡萝卜 húluóbo
- cauliflower 菜花儿 càihuār
- celery 芹菜 qíncài
- chili pepper 辣椒 làjiāo
- Chinese cabbage 大白菜 dàbáicài
- coriander 香菜 xiāngcài
- corn 玉米 yùmǐ
- cucumber 黄瓜 huángguā
- dill 茴香 huíxiāng
- eggplant / aubergine 茄子 Qiézi
- garlic 蒜 suàn
- ginger 姜 jiāng
- green beans 四季豆 sìjìdòu
- leeks 韭菜 jiǔcài
- lettuce, iceberg 圆生菜 yuán shēngcài
- lettuce, romaine green 罗马生菜 luómǎ shēngcài
- lettuce, romaine red 紫叶生菜 zǐyè shēngcài
- lotus root 莲藕 lián'ǒu
- mint 薄荷 bòhe
- mushrooms 蘑菇 mógu
- onion, red 红洋葱 hóng yángcōng
- onion, white 白洋葱 bái yángcōng
- oregano 牛至 niúzhì
- oyster mushrooms 平菇 píngū
- parsley 香芹 xiāngqín
- peas 豌豆 wāndòu
- pepper, green 青椒 qīngjiāo
- pepper, red 红辣椒 hóng làjiāo
- potato 土豆 tǔdòu
- pumpkin 南瓜 nánguā
- rosemary 迷迭香 mídiéxiāng
- sage, salvia 撒尔维亚干叶 sā'ěrwéiyà gānyè
- shitake 香菇 xiānggū
- snow peas 荷兰豆 héländòu
- spinach 菠菜 bōcài
- spring onions/shallots 葱 cōng
- sweet corn 甜玉米 tián yùmǐ
- sweet potato 白薯，地瓜 báishǔ, dìguā
- tomato cherry 圣女果 shèngnǚ guǒ
- tomato 西红柿 xīhóngshì
- water chestnut 荸荠 bíqì
- white mushrooms 草菇 cǎogū
- zucchini 西葫芦 xīhúlu

meat 肉类 ròulèi

- bacon 培根 péigēn
- beef (ground and steak) 牛肉（绞丝，牛排）niúròu (jiǎosī, niúpái)

- chicken (breast, legs and wings)
  鸡（胸肉，腿，翅） jī (xiōngròu, tuǐ, chì)
- dog 狗肉 gǒuròu
- donkey 驴肉 lǘròu
- ham, sliced thin for sandwich 火腿，适合做三明治的薄片 huǒtuǐ, shìhé zuò sānmíngzhì de báo piàn
- pork (roast, tenderloin and ribs)
  猪肉（烤，里脊，排骨） zhūròu (kǎo, lǐjǐ, páigǔ)
- rabbit 兔肉 tùròu
- salami 萨拉米（蒜味咸辣肠） sālāmǐ (suànwèi xián là cháng)
- sausage 香肠 xiāngcháng
- snake 蛇肉 shéròu
- turkey 火鸡 huǒjī

cheese 奶酪 nǎilào

- blue cheese 蓝奶酪 lán nǎilào
- Brie 布里 bùlǐ
- cheddar 车达 chēdá
- cream cheese 奶油芝士 nǎiyóu zhīshì
- Edam cheese 红球奶酪 hóngqiú nǎilào
- Emmental 瑞士多孔干酪 ruìshì duōkǒng gānlào
- goat cheese 羊奶酪 yáng nǎilào
- Gouda 豪达 háodá
- Monterey Jack 蒙特里杰克干酪 méngtèlǐ jiékè gānlào
- mozzarella 马苏里拉，意大利干酪 mǎsūlǐlā, yìdàlì gānlào
- Parmesan 帕尔马干酪 pà'ěrmǎ gānlào
- Roquefort 羊乳干酪 yángrǔ gānlào

seafood 海鲜 hǎixiān

- abalone 鲍鱼 bàoyú
- crab 螃蟹 pángxiè
- crayfish 小龙虾 xiǎo lóngxiā
- lobster 龙虾 lóngxiā
- mussel 蚌 bàng
- octopus 章鱼 zhāngyú
- salmon 鲑鱼 guìyú
- scallop 扇贝 shànbèi
- shrimp 虾 xiā
- tuna (canned / fresh)
  （罐头，鲜）金枪鱼
  (guàntou, xiān) jīnqiāngyú

dairy 奶制品 nǎizhìpǐn

- sour cream 酸奶油 suānnǎiyóu
- whipping cream 淡奶油 dàn nǎiyóu
- milk 牛奶 niúnǎi
- milk powder 奶粉 nǎifěn
- milk, chocolate 巧克力牛奶 qiǎokèlì niúnǎi
- yoghurt 酸奶 suānnǎi

fruit 水果 shuǐguǒ

- apple 苹果 píngguǒ
- lychee 荔枝 lìzhī

- apple, green 青苹果 qīng píngguǒ
- avocado 油梨 yóulí
- banana 香蕉 xiāngjiāo
- cherry 樱桃 yīngtao
- coconut 椰子 yēzi
- cranberry 蔓越莓 mànyuèméi
- grape 葡萄 pútao
- hawthorn 山楂 shānzhā
- kiwi fruit 猕猴桃 míhóutáo
- lemon 柠檬 níngméng
- lime 酸橙/莱姆 suānchéng/láimǔ
- mango 芒果 mángguǒ
- orange 橙子 chéngzi
- papaya 木瓜 mùguā
- peach 桃 táo
- pear 梨 lí
- pineapple 菠萝 bōluó
- prunes 李子干儿 lǐzi gānr
- raisin 葡萄干儿 pútao gānr
- strawberry 草莓 cǎoméi
- tangerines 柑桔 gānjú
- watermelon 西瓜 xīguā

spices, sugars and syrups 香料 xiāngliào

- basil 九层塔 jiǔcéngtǎ
- bay leaves 干月桂叶 gān yuèguì yè
- brown sugar 红糖 hóngtáng
- cinnamon 肉桂 ròuguì
- curry paste 咖喱糊 gālǐ hú
- curry powder 咖喱粉 gālǐ fěn
- garlic salt 蒜盐 suànyán
- ginger 姜 jiāng
- honey 蜂蜜 fēngmì
- maple syrup 枫糖 fēngtáng
- pepper, black 黑胡椒 hēi hújiāo
- pepper, Sichuan 花椒 huājiāo
- pepper, white 白胡椒 bái hújiāo
- rosemary leaves 迷迭香叶 mídiéxiāng yè
- sugar, cubed 方糖 fāngtáng
- sugar, granulated 粒状糖 lìzhuàng táng
- sugar, powdered 砂糖 shātáng

sauces, dressings and oils 调料 tiáoliào

- BBQ sauce 烤肉酱汁 kǎoròu jiàngzhī
- chili oil 辣椒油 làjiāoyóu
- chili sauce 辣椒酱 làjiāojiàng
- five spice 五香 wǔxiāng
- hoisin sauce 海鲜沙司 hǎixiān shāsī
- honey 蜂蜜 fēngmì
- jam/jelly 果酱 guǒjiàng
- mayonnaise 蛋黄酱 dànhuángjiàng (aka 沙拉酱 shālā jiàng "salad sauce")
- mouth numbing pepper oil 花椒油 huājiāoyóu
- mustard 芥末 jièmo
- olive oil 橄榄油 gǎnlǎnyóu
- oyster sauce 蚝油 háoyóu
- peanut butter 花生酱 huāshēngjiàng
- peanut oil 花生油 huāshēngyóu
- plum sauce 梅子酱 méizijiàng
- rice vinegar 米醋 mǐcù
- salad dressing 沙拉酱 shālājiàng
- sesame oil (aka fragrant oil) 芝麻油（香油） zhīmayóu (xiāngyóu)
- Shanxi vinegar 山西陈醋 Shānxī chéncù
- soy sauce 酱油 jiàngyóu
- sunflower oil 葵花籽油 kuíhuāzǐyóu
- thousand island dressing 千岛酱 qiāndǎojiàng
- white vinegar 白醋 báicù

canned food 罐装食品 guànzhuāng shípǐn

- apple sauce 苹果酱 píngguǒjiàng
- beans (red kidney) 红菜豆 hóngcàidòu
- beef broth 牛肉汤 niúròutāng
- chicken broth 鸡汤 jītāng
- cranberry sauce 越橘酱 yuèjújiàng
- olives 橄榄 gǎnlǎn
- pasta sauce 意大利面酱 yìdàlìmiàn jiàng
- peas 豌豆 wāndòu
- pickle 泡菜 pàocài
- tomato paste 番茄糊 fānqié hú
- tuna 金枪鱼 jīnqiāngyú

nuts 坚果 jiānguǒ

- almond 杏仁 xìngrén
- cashew 腰果 yāoguǒ
- hazlenut 栗子 lìzi
- peanuts 花生 huāshēng
- peanuts, boiled 煮花生 zhǔ huāshēng
- pecans 长寿果 chángshòuguǒ
- pistachio 开心果 kāixīnguǒ
- walnuts 核桃 hétao

snacks 零食 língshí

- candy 糖果 tángguǒ
- dried sweet potato 红薯干儿 hóngshǔgānr
- dried plum 话梅 huàméi
- gum 口香糖 kǒuxiāngtáng
- hawthorn fruit snacks 果丹皮 guǒdānpí
- jelly snacks 果冻 guǒdòng
- jerky (cured meat) 牛肉干儿 niúròu gānr
- snack seeds (usually sunflower) 瓜子 guāzǐ
- popcorn 爆米花 bàomǐhuā
- Oreo cookies 奥力奥饼干 àolì'ào bǐnggān
- Chips Ahoy cookies 趣多多饼干 Qùduōduō bǐnggān
- potato chips 薯条shǔtiáo
- Ritz cracker 乐之饼干 Lèzhī bǐnggān
- sliced dried banana 香蕉片 xiāngjiāopiàn
- tortilla chips 墨西哥玉米脆片 mòxīgē yùmǐ cuìpiàn
- cereal 麦片màipiàn
- cornflakes 玉米片 yùmǐ piàn
- Raisin Bran 葡萄干麦片 pútáogān màipiàn
- muesli 干果燕麦片 gānguǒ yànmàipiàn
- oatmeal (燕)麦片 / (燕)麦粥 (yàn) màipiàn / (yàn) màizhōu

bread 面包 miànbāo

- bagel 焙果 bèiguǒ
- bagel, cinnamon raisin 葡萄干儿肉桂焙果 pútáogānr ròuguì béiguǒ
- baguette 法棒 fǎbàng
- black bread 黑面包 hēi miànbāo
- cake 蛋糕 dàngāo
- loaf 方包 fāngbāo
- muffin 松饼 sōngbǐng
- pancake 薄煎饼 báo jiānbǐng
- pita 皮塔饼 pítābǐng
- scones 司康 sīkāng
- toast bread 吐司面包 tǔsī miànbāo

- cookie 饼干 bǐnggān
- croissant 牛角面包 niújiǎo miànbāo
- walnut bread 胡桃面包 hútao miànbāo
- wheat bread 全麦面包 quánmài miànbāo

deli products 熟食 shúshí

- paté (liver, rabbit, duck, canned) 冻肉(肝, 兔子, 鸭子, 罐装) dòngròu (gān, tùzi, yāzi, guànzhuāng)
- pickles (gherkins, cornichons) 泡菜(腌瓜, 酸瓜) pàocài (yān guā, suān guā)
- pasta 意大利面食 yìdàlì miànshí
  (1) ravioli with meat 肉饺 ròujiǎo
  (2) ravioli with cheese 奶酪饺 nǎilào jiǎo
  (3) ravioli with mushrooms 蘑菇饺 mógū jiǎo
  (4) penne 通心粉 tōngxīnfěn
  (5) fusili 螺丝粉 luósīfěn
  (6) rigatoni 大弯管通心粉 dà wānguǎn tōngxīnfěn
  (7) spaghetti 意大利面 yìdàlì miàn
  (8) linguini 细扁面 xì biǎn miàn
  (9) lasagna 宽面 kuān miàn
- pasta sauce 意大利面酱 yìdàlì miàn jiàng
- tomato sauce 番茄酱 Fānqié jiàng
- pesto sauce九层塔酱 Jiǔcéngtǎ jiàng

10 Eating in 在家吃饭 Zài jiā chīfàn

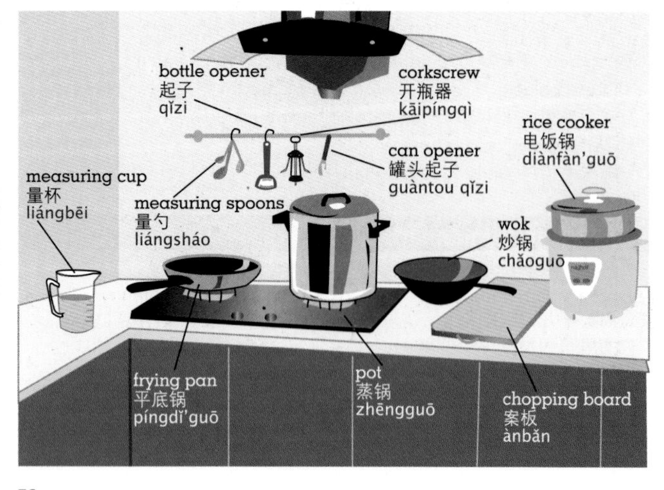

11 Chinese restaurant specialties
家常菜 Jiāchángcài

cold dishes 凉菜 liángcài

- boiled bean curd with leek 小葱拌豆腐 xiǎocōng bàn dòufu
- boiled dried bean milk cream with celery 西芹腐竹 xīqín fǔzhú
- boiled green soybean 煮毛豆 zhǔ máodòu
- Chinese toon shoots and bean curd 香椿拌豆腐 xiāngchūn bàn dòufu
- cold starch noodles 大拉皮儿 dà lāpír
- duck foot with mustard sauce 芥茉鸭掌 jièmò yāzhǎng
- ginger sauce preserved duck egg 姜汁松花 jiāngzhī sōnghuā
- great harvest (sliced fresh vegetables) 大丰收 dà fēngshōu
- jellyfish with vinegar 老醋蛰头 lǎocù zhétóu
- Korean pickles (kimchee) 韩国泡菜 hánguó pàocài
- marinated bitter melon 凉拌苦瓜 liáng bàn kǔguā
- marinated cucumber with garlic 拍黄瓜 pāi huángguā
- marinated seaweed 凉拌海带 liáng bàn hǎidài
- mashed eggplant 茄泥 qiéní
- north Sichuan-style cold vermicelli 川北凉粉 chuānběi liángfěn
- pig ear with spicy oil 红油猪耳朵 hóngyóu zhū ěrduo
- preserved duck egg with bean curd 皮蛋豆腐 pídàn dòufu
- preserved garlic 糖蒜 tángsuàn
- roast suckling pig 烤乳猪 kǎo rǔzhū
- salted duck 盐水鸭 yánshuǐ yā
- salty boiled peanuts 煮花生米zhǔ huāshēngmǐ
- saute tripe with chili 麻辣肚丝 málà dǔsī
- Sichuan pickled vegetables 四川泡菜 Sìchuān pàocài
- sliced beef and tripe in spicy sauce 夫妻肺片 fūqī fèipiàn
- spicy boiled sliced chicken 口水鸡 kǒushuǐ jī
- spicy cold salad 老虎菜 lǎohǔ cài
- spinach with mustard 芥末菠菜 jièmò bōcài
- sweet marinated lotus roots 糖拌藕 táng bàn ǒu
- sweet and sour cucumber 糖醋黄瓜 tángcù huángguā
- tomatoes in sugar 糖拌西红柿 táng bàn xīhóngshì

pork 猪肉类 zhūròu lèi

- braised eggplant with minced pork 猪肉烧茄子 zhūròu shāo qiézi
- braised eggplant with shredded pork and chili sauce 鱼香茄子 yúxiāng qiézi
- braised pork meatballs with brown sauce 红烧狮子头 hóngshāo shīzitóu

- braised pig tendon with brown sauce 红烧蹄筋 hóngshāo tíjīn
- braised pork with brown sauce 红烧肉 hóngshāoròu
- braised pork with salted dried vegetable 梅菜扣肉 méicài kòu ròu
- deep fried pork fillet 软炸里脊 ruǎn zhá lǐjǐ
- deep fried spareribs with spiced salt 椒盐排骨 jiāoyán páigǔ
- diced pork stir fried with red pepper and peanuts 宫保肉丁 gōngbǎo ròudīng
- diced pork with soybean sauce 酱爆肉丁 jiàngbào ròudīng
- fish-flavored sauté pork shreds 鱼香肉丝 yúxiāng ròusī
- four-happiness pork balls 四喜丸子 sìxǐ wánzi
- fried pork kidney with soy sauce 炒腰花 chǎo yāohuā
- fried shredded pork with green pepper 青椒肉丝 qīngjiāo ròusī
- fried sliced pork with haricot beans 肉片炒扁豆 ròupiàn chǎo biǎndòu
- green beans with minced meat 榄菜肉沫四季豆lǎncài ròumò sìjìdòu
- grilled pork 叉烧肉 chāshāoròu
- pork shreds with Beijing soybean paste 京酱肉丝 jīngjiàng ròusī
- sautéed diced pork with cashew nuts 腰果肉丁 yāoguǒ ròudīng
- spiced pork leg slices in brown sauce 酱肘花 jiàng zhǒuhuā
- spicy vermicelli and ground pork (aka ants climbing a tree) 蚂蚁上树 mǎyǐ shàngshù
- steamed boned rib of pork 东坡肉 dōngpō ròu
- steamed meatballs with clear soup 清炖狮子头 qīngdùn shīzitóu
- steamed pork ribs with rice powder 粉蒸排骨 fěnzhēng páigǔ
- steamed pork with spiced rice flour 米粉肉 mǐfěn ròu
- steamed spareribs with brown sauce 红烧排骨 hóngshāo páigǔ
- stewed pig's trotters with peanuts 花生炖猪手 huāshēng dùn zhūshǒu
- stir fried shredded pork with egg, agaric and cucumber / mu shu pork 木须肉 mùxūròu
- stir-fried green beans 干煸四季豆 gānbiān sìjìdòu
- stir-fried spicy pork dices 辣子肉丁 làzi ròudīng
- sweet and sour pork fillet 糖醋里脊 tángcù lǐjǐ
- sweet and sour pork with pineapple 菠萝咕噜肉 bōluó gǔlǎo ròu
- sweet and sour spareribs 糖醋排骨 tángcù páigǔ
- twice-cooked pork, Sichuan style 回锅肉 huíguō ròu
- white boiled pork with mashed garlic 蒜泥白肉 suànní báiròu

beef & mutton 牛羊肉 niú yángròu

- "water" (spicy oil) boiled beef 水煮牛肉 shuǐzhǔ niúròu
- beef in curry sauce 咖喱牛肉 gāli niúròu
- braised beef and potatoes 土豆炖牛肉 tǔdòu dùn niúròu
- braised beef sauté 红烧牛肉 hóngshāo niúròu

- braised beef with radish 萝卜牛腩 luóbo niúnán
- five spice flavored beef 五香牛肉 wǔxiāng niúròu
- mutton sauté leek 葱爆羊肉 cōng bào yángròu
- pan-fried sliced beef with black pepper 黑椒牛柳 hēijiāo niúliǔ
- paper-wrapped deep fried beef 纸包牛肉 zhǐ bāo niúròu
- ribs of lamb 羊羯子 yáng xiēzi
- roast mutton kebabs 烤羊肉串 kǎo yángròuchuàn
- roast mutton, Mongolian-style 烤羊肉 kǎo yángròu
- sizzling iron plate beef tenderloin 铁板牛柳 tiěbǎn niúliǔ
- soft fried sizzling plate beef slices with sauce 铁板牛里脊 tiěbǎn niú lǐjǐ
- spiced beef 酱牛肉 jiàng niúròu
- stewed beef with fresh tomato 番茄牛肉 fānqié niúròu

poultry 禽类 qínlèi

- crispy fried chicken 香酥鸡 xiāngsū jī
- crispy fried pigeon 脆皮乳鸽 cuìpí rǔgē
- curry chicken 咖喱鸡 gāli jī
- deep fried quail 炸鹌鹑 zhá ānchún
- diced chicken with bean sauce 酱爆鸡丁 jiàngbào jīdīng
- diced chicken with cashew nuts 腰果鸡丁 yāoguǒ jīdīng
- fried chicken with chili 辣子鸡 làzi jī
- fried chicken with pepper and peanuts (aka kung pao chicken) 宫保鸡丁 gōngbǎo jīdīng
- peking duck 北京烤鸭 běijīng kǎoyā
- quick-fried spicy diced chicken 辣子鸡丁 làzi jīdīng
- stewed chicken with chestnuts and green pepper 炖栗子鸡 dùn lìzi jī
- stewed duck flavored with camphor leaves and tea 樟茶鸭 zhāngchá yā

fish 鱼 yú

- "water" (spicy oil) boiled fish水煮鱼 shuǐzhǔ yú
- braised hairtail in soy sauce 红烧带鱼 hóngshāo dàiyú
- braised silver carp with garlic 大蒜烧鲢鱼 dàsuàn shāo liányú
- braised white eel / finless eel with garlic sauce 蒜烧白鳝/黄鳝 suàn shāo báishàn/huángshàn
- braised yellow fish 红烧黄鱼 hóngshāo huángyú
- dry-fried hairtail 干炸带鱼 gānzhá dàiyú
- dry-fried yellow croaker 干炸黄花鱼 gānzhá huánghuāyú
- dry-fried mandarin fish 干烧桂鱼 gānshāo guìyú
- endive with dace 豆豉鲮鱼油麦菜 dòuchǐ língyú yóumàicài
- fried carp with sweet and sour sauce 糖醋鲤鱼 tángcù lǐyú
- fried fish in sweet and sour sauce 西湖醋鱼 xīhú cù yú

- fried squirrel-shaped mandarin fish in sweet and sour sauce 松鼠桂鱼 sōngshǔ guìyú
- fried white bait 酥炸银鱼 sūzhá yínyú
- sauerkraut fish 酸菜鱼 suāncài yú
- sautéed sliced dried cuttlefish 干煸鱿鱼 gānbiān yóuyú
- steamed fresh braised carp 清蒸鲤鱼 qīngzhēng lǐyú
- steamed fresh weever 清蒸鲈鱼 qīngzhēng lúyú
- steamed grouper fish 清蒸石斑 qīngzhēng shíbān
- steamed mandarin fish 清蒸桂鱼 qīngzhēng guìyú
- steamed sole 蒸比目鱼 zhēng bǐmùyú
- steamed white eel 清蒸白鳝 qīngzhēng báishàn
- stir fried cuttlefish with celery 西芹鲜鱿 xīqín xiān yóu
- stir fried squid with vegetable 炒鱿鱼 chǎo yóuyú
- stir-fried eels 干煸鳝鱼 gānbiān shànyú

shrimp 虾 xiā

- boiled shrimps with shell in salt-water 盐水虾 yánshuǐ xiā
- braised lobster slices with broccoli 干烧龙虾 gānshāo lóngxiā
- braised prawns in sweet sauce 油焖大虾 yóumèn dàxiā
- braised white gourd and dried shrimps 海米冬瓜 hǎimǐ dōngguā
- drunken fresh shrimps 醉虾 zuì xiā
- poached fresh shrimps 白灼基围虾 báizhuó jīwéixiā
- shelled shrimps with cashew nuts 腰果虾仁 yāoguǒ xiārén
- steamed prawns 清蒸大虾 qīngzhēng dàxiā
- two styles of shrimps (boiled and fried with spiced salt) 一虾两吃（白灼和椒盐） yīxiā liǎngchī (báizhuó hé jiāoyán)

seafood 海鲜 hǎixiān

- abalone 鲍鱼 bàoyú
- braised sea cucumber in vinegar pepper sauce 酸辣海参 suānlà hǎishēn
- braised sea cucumber 红烧海参 hóngshāo hǎishēn
- crab spawn 蟹黄 xièhuáng
- crisp rice with seafood ingredients 三鲜锅巴 sānxiān guōbā
- fresh water crab 河蟹 héxiè
- sautéed conch with garlic 蒜烧海螺 suàn shāo hǎiluó
- sautéed scallop with oyster sauce 蚝油扇贝háoyóu shànbèi
- sautéed scallops 油爆鲜贝 yóu bào xiānbèi
- shark's fin 鱼翅 yúchì
- sliced scallop with yellow leeks 韭黄鲜贝 jiǔhuáng xiānbèi
- steamed fresh water crabs 蒸河蟹 zhēng héxiè
- steamed pork and crabmeat ball 蟹粉狮子头 xièfěn shīzitóu
- steamed sea crabs 蒸梭子蟹 zhēng suōzixiè
- steamed soft-shelled turtle 清蒸甲鱼 qīngzhēng jiǎyú

others 其他 qítā

- "water" (spicy oil) boiled bull frog 水煮牛蛙 shuǐzhǔ niúwā
- bear 熊 xióng
- camel 骆驼 luòtuo
- fried scorpion with spicy salt 椒盐蝎子 jiāoyán xiēzi
- frog 田鸡 tiánjī
- venison 鹿肉 lùròu

egg 蛋 dàn

- egg pancake 摊鸡蛋 tān jīdàn
- poached eggs 荷包蛋 hébāodàn
- quail egg 鹌鹑蛋 ānchun dàn
- sautéed egg with leeks 韭菜鸡蛋 jiǔcài jīdàn
- scrambled egg with bitter melon 苦瓜鸡蛋 kǔguā jīdàn
- scrambled eggs with tomatoes 西红柿鸡蛋 xīhóngshì jīdàn
- scrambled eggs with yellow leeks 韭黄鸡蛋 jiǔhuáng jīdàn

bean curd 豆腐 dòufu

- bean curd with crabmeat 蟹粉豆腐 xièfěn dòufu
- braised bean curd (with mushroom and vegetables) 红烧豆腐 hóngshāo dòufu
- braised bean curd 锅塌豆腐 guōtā dòufu
- crispy "Japanese" tofu 脆皮日本豆腐 cuìpí rìběn dòufu
- home style bean curd 家常豆腐 jiācháng dòufu
- spicy sautéed bean curd with pepper (aka mapo tofu) 麻婆豆腐 mápó dòufu

vegetables 蔬菜 shūcài

- braised eggplants 烧茄子 shāo qiézi
- broad bean 蚕豆 cándòu
- celery with lily bulbs 西芹百合 xīqín bǎihé
- Chinese wolfberries 枸杞 gǒuqí
- fried dry bean curd with celery 熏干炒西芹 xūngān chǎo xīqín
- fried snow peas 清炒荷兰豆 qīng chǎo héléndòu
- fried potato slivers 炸土豆丝 zhá tǔdòusī
- fried sauté mushrooms and bamboo shoots 烧二冬 shāo èrdōng
- garlic sautéed broccoli 蒜茸西兰花 suànróng xīlánhuā
- kelp/seaweed 海带 hǎidài
- onion 洋葱/葱头 yángcōng/cōngtóu
- coriander 香菜xiāngcài
- pine nuts with sweet corn 松仁玉米 sōngrén yùmǐ
- pumpkin 南瓜 nánguā
- sautéed Chinese cabbage with vinegar 醋溜白菜 cùliū báicài

- sautéed lettuce in oyster sauce 蚝油生菜 háoyóu shēngcài
- sautéed cabbage heart with black mushroom 香菇菜心 xiānggū càixīn
- sautéed eggplants, potatoes and green peppers 地三鲜 dì sānxiān
- spicy and sour cabbage 酸辣圆白菜 suānlà yuánbáicài
- spinach 菠菜 bōcài
- spring onion 葱 cōng
- stir-fried cabbage mustard vegetable 清炒芥兰 qīngchǎo jièlán
- stir-fried mungbean sprouts with chives (*lit*: green snakes and white snakes) 韭菜炒绿豆芽（青蛇白蛇）jiǔcài chǎo lǜ dòuyá (qīngshé báishé)
- straw mushroom 草菇 cǎogū
- sweet and sour shredded lotus roots 糖醋炒藕丝 tángcù chǎo ǒu'sī
- sweet potato 白薯 báishǔ
- vermicelli 粉丝 fěnsī
- vinegar stir-fried potato shreds 醋溜土豆丝 cùliū tǔdòusī
- white fungus 银耳 yín'ěr
- winter mushroom 冬菇 dōnggū

pot and casserole 砂锅和煲 shāguō hé bǎo

- bean curd casserole 豆腐煲 dòufu bǎo
- bean curd in casserole with soup 砂锅豆腐 shāguō dòufu
- carp's head in casserole with soup 砂锅鱼头 shāguō yútóu
- mixed meats in casserole with soup 砂锅什锦 shāguō shíjǐn
- stewed minced meat ball in pot 砂锅狮子头 shāguō shīzitóu

soup 汤 tāng

- bird's nest in clear soup 清汤宫燕 qīngtāng gōngyàn
- boiled black chicken with ginseng soup 人参乌鸡汤 rénshēn wūjī tāng
- chicken and sweetcorn soup 鸡茸玉米羹 jīróng yùmǐ gēng
- chicken soup 鸡汤 jītāng
- Chinese cabbage soup with dried shrimps 海米白菜汤 hǎimǐ báicài tāng
- Chinese cabbage soup with minced pork ball 白菜汆丸子汤 báicài cuān wánzi tāng
- Chinese matrimony vine with fungus in soup 枸杞银耳汤 gǒuqí yín'ěr tāng
- clear soupstock 清汤 qīng tāng
- cuttlefish's egg soup 乌鱼蛋汤 wūyúdàn tāng
- flavored soup 鲜汤 xiān tāng

- minced beef soup with egg white (aka West lake beef soup) 西湖牛肉羹 Xīhú niúròu gēng
- shredded pork with spicy pickled vegetable soup 榨菜肉丝汤 zhàcài ròusī tāng
- shrimps and sweet corn soup 鲜虾粟米羹 xiānxiā sùmǐ gēng
- spicy and sour soup 酸辣汤 suānlà tāng
- stewed turtle soup 清炖甲鱼汤 qīngdùn jiǎyú tāng
- thick soup stock 浓汤 nóng tāng
- tomato andegg drop soup 西红柿鸡蛋汤 xīhóngshì jīdàn tāng
- winter melon with pork balls soup 冬瓜丸子汤 dōngguā wánzi tāng

rice, noodles and dumplings 主食 zhǔshí

- barbecued pork buns 猪肉叉烧包 zhūròu chāshāobāo
- beef noodles 牛肉面 niúròu miàn
- boiled dumplings (with various stuffing) 水饺 shuǐjiǎo
- Chinese crepe with egg 煎饼 jiānbǐng
- cold noodles with chicken shreds 鸡丝凉面 jīsī liángmiàn
- egg pancake 鸡蛋饼 jīdàn bǐng
- fried rice with eggs 蛋炒饭 dàn chǎo fàn
- fried dumplings 锅贴 guōtiē
- fried noodles with beef 牛肉炒面 niúròu chǎomiàn
- fried noodles with chicken 鸡丝炒面 jīsī chǎomiàn
- fried noodles with shredded pork 肉丝炒面 ròusī chǎomiàn
- fried rice with shredded pork and egg 肉丝蛋饭 ròusī dàn fàn
- fried thick spring onion pastry with 葱花饼 cōnghuā bǐng
- fried vermicelli 炒米粉 chǎo mǐfěn
- glutinous rice 糯米 nuòmǐ
- home style pan-baked bread 家常饼/大饼 jiācháng bǐng/dàbǐng
- juicy steamed buns 灌汤包 guàntāng bāo
- Korean-style cold noodles 朝鲜冷面 cháoxiǎn lěngmiàn
- noodles and minced pork with soybean sauce 炸酱面 zhájiàng miàn
- noodles with sauce 打卤面 dǎlǔ miàn
- pancake with egg filling 鸡蛋灌饼 jīdàn guàn bǐng
- pan-fried sesame puff 芝麻烧饼 zhīma shāobǐng
- pie 馅儿饼 xiànrbǐng
- quick-boiled mutton noodles 羊肉氽面 yángròu cuān miàn
- rice 米饭 mǐfàn
- sautéed dumpling 水煎包 shuǐjiānbāo
- Sichuan-style noodles with pepper sauce 担担面 dàndàn miàn
- soup noodles with fried spareribs 排骨汤面 páigǔ tāngmiàn
- soup noodles with mixed ingredients 什锦汤面 shíjǐn tāngmiàn
- soup noodles with shredded pork and spicy pickles 榨菜肉丝面 zhàcài ròusī miàn

- soup noodles with shredded pork and vegetable pickles 雪菜肉丝面 xuěcài ròusī miàn
- soup noodles with shredded pork 肉丝汤面 ròusī tāngmiàn
- soup noodles with sliced chicken 鸡丝汤面 jīsī tāngmiàn
- soup noodles with tomatoes and eggs 西红柿鸡蛋面 xīhóngshì jīdàn miàn
- soup noodles with wonton 馄饨面 húntun miàn
- spring rolls 春卷 chūnjuǎn
- steamed bread rolls 花卷 huājuǎn
- steamed buns with filling包子 bāozi
- steamed dumplings 蒸饺 zhēngjiǎo
- steamed pork buns 小笼包 xiǎolóng bāo
- steamed shrimp and pork dumplings 烧麦 shāomài
- steamed shrimp dumplings 虾饺 xiā jiǎo
- steamed sponge cake 丝糕 sīgāo
- steamed sweet bean buns 豆沙包 dòushā bāo
- whittled noodles 刀削面 dāoxiāo miàn
- Yangzhou fried rice 扬州炒饭 yángzhōu chǎofàn

desserts 甜品 tiánpǐn

- "eight-treasure" rice 八宝饭 bābǎo fàn
- black rice gruel with longan pulp 桂圆黑米粥 guìyuán hēimǐ zhōu
- boiled sweet dumplings made of glutinous rice flour 元宵 yuánxiāo
- Chinese almond jelly 杏仁豆腐 xìngrén dòufu
- Chinese wolfberries and white fungus 枸杞银耳 gǒuqí yín'ěr
- Chinese yams in syrup 拔丝山药 básī shānyào
- deep fried dough sticks 油条 yóutiáo
- deep-fried crisp milk 脆皮炸鲜奶 cuìpí zhá xiānnǎi
- fruit pudding 水果布丁 shuǐguǒ bùdīng
- lotus seeds in sugar syrup 冰糖莲子 bīngtáng liánzǐ
- mashed pea cake 豌豆黄 wāndòuhuáng
- multi-layer cake 千层饼 qiāncéng bǐng
- red bean paste with lotus seed 莲子红豆沙 liánzǐ hōngdòushā
- steamed bread of corn flour 窝头 wōtóu
- steamed glutinous rice flour cake with mashed red beans (aka rolling donkey) 驴打滚 lǘdǎgǔn
- steamed glutinous rice wrapped in bamboo leaves 粽子 zòngzi
- sugar fried apple in white syrup 拔丝苹果 básī píngguǒ
- swallow's nest in rock candy 冰糖燕窝 bīngtáng yànwō
- syrup 拔丝 básī
- walnut porridge 核桃酪 hétáo lào
- white fungus soup 清汤银耳 qīngtāng yín'ěr

KIDS & FAMILY LIFE ►

1 Family tree

家族关系图 Jiāzú guānxi tú

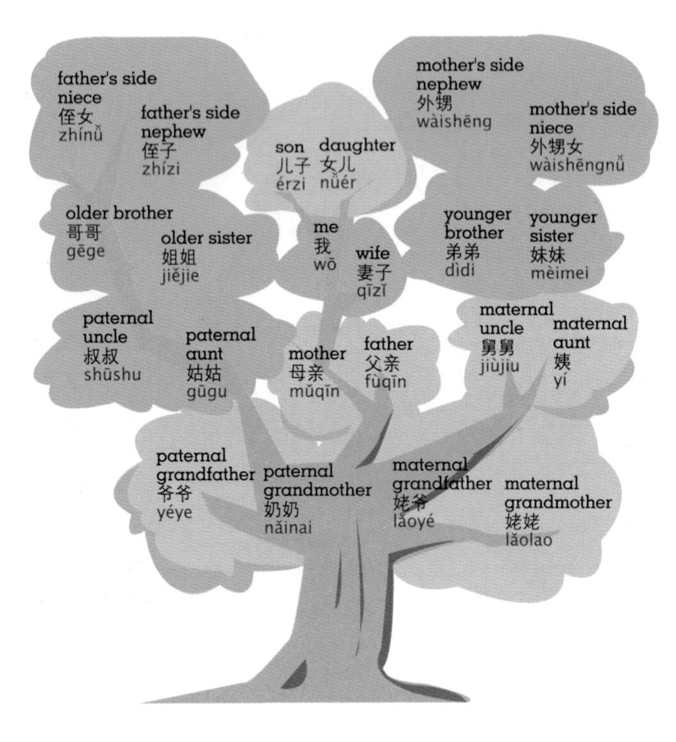

2 Being approached

Kids, especially young and foreign-looking ones, draw a lot of attention in Beijing. Here are some phrases to help you respond to, or politely deflect, such attention.

(For more introductory vocabulary and phrases see Introduction p12 and "Stick to the Script," p14)

Sentences

• My child's name is ... 我的孩子叫... Wǒ dè háizi jiào ...

• Yes you may ... 你可以... Nǐ kéyǐ ...

(1) hold her 抱她 bào tā
(2) take a picture with him 跟他照张相 gēn tā zhào zhāng xiàng

• Excuse me, please don't ... 不好意思，请别... bùhǎo yìsi, qǐng bié ...

(1) touch him / her 碰他/她 pèng tā
(2) give my child food 给我的小孩吃的 gěi wǒ de xiǎohái chīde
(3) stare at him / her 盯着他/她看 dīngzhe tā kàn
(4) wake up my child 吵醒我的孩子 chǎoxǐng wǒ de háizi

• Please be gentle 请轻一点 Qǐng qīng yì diǎn

• I'm sorry, we are late and have to go 对不起，太晚了，我们必须得走了 Duìbùqǐ, tài wǎn lè, wǒmen bìxū děi zǒu le

• I'm sorry, my child is very ... right now 对不起，我的孩子现在很... Duìbùqǐ, wǒ de háizi xiànzài hěn ...

(1) tired 累 lèi
(2) sensitive 敏感 mǐn'gǎn
(3) hyper/excited 兴奋 xīngfèn

• No, my daughter is not cold! Are you a doctor!? 不，我女儿不冷。你难道是医生吗？Bù, wǒ nǚ'er bù lěng. Nǐ nándào shì yīshēng ma?

• She has a / an ... 她有个... Tā yǒu gè ...

(1) older brother 哥哥 gēge
(2) younger sister 妹妹 mèimei

• He is an only child 他是独生子 Tā shì dúshēngzǐ

Listen for this

• Tā jiào shénme míngzi? 他/她叫什么名字？What is his / her name?

• Nǐ duōdà le? 你多大了？How old are you?

• Nǐ cóng nǎr lái? 你从哪儿来？Where are you from?

• Nǐ huì shuō zhōngwén ma? 你会说中文吗？Do you speak Chinese?

- Wòwo shǒu 握握手 Let's shake hands
- Wǒmen néng hé tā zhào zhāng xiàng ma? 我们能和他照张相吗？ Can we take a photo with him?
- Nǐ shì nǎ guó rén? 你是哪国人？ What country are you from?
- Nǐ zài nǎr shàngxué? 你在哪儿上学？ Where do you go to school?
- Wǒ néng bàobao tā ma? 我能抱抱他吗？ Can I hold him/her?
- Tā shì ge xiǎo yángwáwa 他是个小洋娃娃 S/he's a little foreign doll
- Shì nánhái háishì nǚhái? 是男孩还是女孩？Is it a boy or a girl?
- Nǐ shì tā āyí ma? 你是她阿姨吗？Are you her Ayi?
- Tā yǒu xiōngdì jiěmèi ma? 他有兄弟姐妹吗？Does he have siblings?
- Nǐ jiù zhè yí gè háizi ma? 你就这一个孩子吗？Is this your only child?
- Zěnme bú zài yào yí gè háizi? 怎么不再要一个孩子？Why don't you have another child?
- Nǐ bù xiǎng yào gè nánháir/nǚháir ma? 你不想要个男孩儿/女孩儿吗？ Don't you want a boy / girl?
- Nǐ érzi yuànyì hé wǒ nǚ'ér shuōshuo yīngyǔ ma? 你儿子愿意和我女儿说说英语吗？Will your son speak English with my daughter?
- Tā zài Běijīng chūshēng de ma? 她在北京出生的吗？ Was she born in Beijing?
- Tā shuō nǎ guó huà? 她说哪国话？What language does she speak?
- Tā zhōngwén shuōde zhēn hǎo 他中文说得真好 He speaks very good Chinese
- Tā chī shénme? 她吃什么？What does she eat?
- Tā bàba shì zhōngguórén ma? 他爸爸是中国人吗？Is his father Chinese?
- Tā huì zǒulù ma? 她会走路吗？Can she walk?

3 School 学校 Xuéxiào

Vocabulary

art 美术课 měishùkè
bully 恶霸 èbà
Chinese language 语文课 yǔwénkè
classmates 同学 tóngxué
classroom 教室 jiàoshì
dissipated 散漫的 sănmàn de
drama 戏剧课 xìjùkè
English language 英语课 yīngyǔkè
good student 好学生 hǎo xuéshēng
grade 年级 niánjí
hard worker 用功的学生 yònggōng de xuéshēng
high school 高中 gāozhōng
history 历史课 lìshǐkè
homework 家庭作业 jiātíng zuòyè
recess 休息 xiūxi
kindergarten 幼儿园 yòu'éryuán
math 数学 shùxué
middle school 中学 zhōngxué
Montessori 蒙特梭利 méngtèsuōlì
music 音乐课 yīnyuèkè
parent-teacher conference 家长会 jiāzhănghuì
physical education 体育课 tǐyùkè
preschool 学前班 xuéqiánbān
primary school 小学 xiǎoxué
registering for school 入学注册 rùxué zhùcè
science 自然课 zìránkè
summer school 暑期班 shǔqībān
teacher 老师 láoshī
test 测验 cèyàn
textbooks 课本 kèběn
uniform 校服 xiàofú

Sentences

• For what ages do you offer instruction? 你们收哪些年龄的孩子? Nǐmen shōu nǎxiē niánlíng de háizi?

• How much is tuition? 学费多少钱? Xuéfèi duōshǎo qián?

• How many students per class? 每班多少学生? Měi bān duōshǎo xuéshēng?

• Are there other foreign children? 有别的外国孩子吗? Yǒu bié de wàiguó háizi ma?

• How much of the instruction is in ... 有多少课是用...教的? Yǒu duōshǎo kè shì yòng ... jiāo de?

(1) English 英语 Yīngyǔ
(2) Chinese 中文 Zhōngwén

• Do you offer an ... curriculum? 你们有没有...课程? Nǐmen yǒu méiyǒu ... kèchéng?

(1) Advanced Placement 跳级 tiàojí
(2) International Baccalaureate 国际大学预科 guójì dàxué yùkē

- Do you have after school activities / sports? 有没有课外活动？ Yǒu méiyǒu kèwài huódòng?

- report card 成绩单 chéngjìdān

- Chinese College Entrance Exam 中国高考 zhōngguó gāokǎo

4 Shopping 购物 Gòuwù

(For more on shopping, see p141)

Vocabulary

Clothes

baby clothes 婴儿服装 yīng'ér fúzhuāng
baby diapers 尿布 niàobù
baby wipes 婴儿湿巾 yīng'ér shījīn
booties 婴儿毛线鞋 yīng'ér máoxiàn xié
pajamas 睡衣 shuìyī
baby snow suit 婴儿雪服 yīng'ér xuěfú

Food

baby food 婴儿食品 yīng'ér shípǐn
baby formula 婴儿配方奶粉 yīng'ér pèifāng nǎifěn
baby cereal 婴儿麦片 yīng'ér màipiàn

Gear

baby bottles 奶瓶儿 nǎipíngr
baby car seat 婴儿车座 yīng'ér chēzuò
bibs 围嘴儿 wéizuǐr
booster seat 加高座椅 jiā gāo zuòyǐ
bottle warmer 婴儿奶瓶保温器 yīng'ér nǎipíng bǎowēnqì
changing table 换尿片桌 huàn niàopiàn zhuō
children's books 儿童书籍 értóng shūjí
children's clothes 童装 tóngzhuāng
children's shoes 童鞋 tóngxié
crib 婴儿床 yīng'érchuáng
crib sheets 婴儿床床单 yīng'érchuáng chuángdān
crib mattress 婴儿床床垫 yīng'érchuáng chuángdiàn
cradle 摇篮 yáolán

Bilingual Barnyard

Hey kids! Learn to speak to animals in Chinese ...

by Lee Ambrozy

哼哼 hēng hēng
Pig: oink

汪汪 wāng wāng
Dog: ruff

哞哞 mōu mōu
Cow: moo

咝 sī
Snake: hissssss

咴咴 huī huī
Horse: neigh

呱呱 guā guā
Frog: croak

喵喵 miāo miāo
Cat: meow

喔喔 wō wō
Rooster: cock-a-doodle-doo!

吱吱 zhī zhī
Bird: chirp

咪咪 mī mī
Kitten: mew

嗡嗡 wēng wēng
Bee: buzz

嘎嘎 gā gā
Duck: quack

咩咩 miē miē
Sheep: baa

呵呵 hē hē
Monkey: (Song Wukong, the Monkey King's laughter)

嗷 āo
Wolf: aoowww-wooool!!!!

K & F LIFE

growth chart 成长曲线表 chéngzhǎng qūxiàn biǎo
high chair 高脚婴儿椅 gāojiǎo yīng'ér yǐ
pacifier 奶嘴儿 nǎizuǐr
playpen 婴儿围栏 yīng'ér wéilán
sipping cup 婴儿吮杯 yīng'ér shǔnbēi
stroller 幼儿车 yòu'ér chē
swing 秋千 qiūqiān
water-proof mattress 防水床垫 fángshuǐ chuángdiàn

Toys

activity mats 游戏垫 yóuxì diàn
balls 球类 qiúlèi
Barbie 芭比娃娃 Bābǐ wáwa
bath toys 浴室玩具 yùshì wánjù
Batman 蝙蝠侠 Biǎnfúxiá
board games 棋类游戏 qílèi yóuxì
coloring books 填色本 tiánsèběn
crayons 蜡笔 làbǐ
Disney 迪士尼 Díshìní
dolls 洋娃娃 yángwáwa
Fisher Price 费雪牌玩具 Fèixuěpái wánjù
kites 风筝 fēngzhēng
Lego 乐高 Lègāo
mobiles 活动玩具 huódòng wánjù
paint 漆 qī
Playdoh 培乐多 Péilèduō
puzzles 拼图 pīntú
rattles 儿童沙锤 értóng shāchuí
stickers 贴纸 tiēzhǐ
stuffed animals 毛绒动物玩具 máoróng dòngwù wánjù

5 Health 健康 Jiànkāng

Vocabulary

baby thermometer 婴儿体温计 yīng'ér tǐwēnjì
vaccine 疫苗 yìmiáo
pediatrician 儿科医生 érkē yīshēng
baby aspirin 婴儿阿斯匹林 yīng'ér āsīpīlín
children's cold medicine 儿童感冒药 értóng gǎnmàoyào
children's vitamins 儿童维他命 értóng wéitāmìng
children's cough syrup 儿童止咳糖浆 értóng zhǐké tángjiāng
band-aids 邦迪创可贴 bāngdí chuàngkětiē

baby toilet 婴儿厕所 yīng'ér cèsuǒ
baby monitor 婴儿监听器 yīng'ér jiāntīngqì
nasal aspirator 鼻腔吸管 bíqiāng xīguǎn
baby shampoo 婴儿洗发水 yīng'ér xǐfàshuǐ
bath tub 婴儿浴盆 yīng'ér yùpén

breast pads 乳垫 rǔdiàn
breast pump 吸乳器 xīrǔqì
breast milk storage bottles 母乳储存瓶 mǔrǔ chǔcún píng
nursing bras 哺乳内衣 bǔrǔ nèiyī

sterilizer kit 杀菌套装 shājūn tàozhuāng
bottle / nipple brush 奶瓶／奶嘴儿刷 nǎipíng / nǎizuǐr shuā

6 In restaurants 在餐厅 Zài cāntīng

Sentences

• Please do / don't hold my baby 请抱一下／别抱我的孩子 Qǐng bào yíxià/bié bào wǒ de háizi

• Do you have ... ? 你有...吗？ Nǐ yǒu...ma?

(1) a kids' menu 儿童菜单 értóng càidān
(2) a booster chair 加高座椅 jiā gāo zuòyǐ
(3) a baby cup 婴儿杯 yīng'ér bēi
(4) a play area 儿童游乐区 értóng yóulèqū
(5) a non-smoking area 禁烟区 jìnyānqū
(6) a spoon 勺子 sháozi

• Could I get some room temperature water? 能给我点儿常温水吗？ Néng gěi wǒ diǎnr chángwēn shuǐ ma?

• Please don't take her outside the room 别把她带到外面去 Bié bǎ tā dài dào wàimiàn qù

• Could you add hot water to the formula in this bottle? 能拿热水冲一下瓶子里的奶粉吗？ Néng ná rèshuǐ chōng yí xià píngzi lǐ de nǎifěn ma?

7 Fun activities
趣味活动 Qùwèi huódòng

(For more vocabulary and phrases see Sports and Fitness, p167 and Museums, p119)

Vocabulary

bathing cap 游泳帽 yóuyǒng mào
blow-up castle 充气城堡 chōngqì chéngbǎo
bumper cars 碰碰车 pèngpengchē
cars 赛车 sàichē
ferris wheel 大观览车dà guānlǎnchē
fishing 钓鱼 diàoyú
ice chair 冰车 bīng chē
ice skating 滑冰 huábīng
merry-go-round 旋转木马 xuánzhuàn mùmǎ
MiG 米格式飞机 Mǐgéshì fēijī
paddle boat 划船 huáchuán
play area 游乐区 yóulèqū
roller coaster 过山车 guòshānchē
slides 滑梯 huátī
swimming pool 游泳池 yóuyǒngchí
swing 秋千 qiūqiān
trampoline 蹦床 bèngchuáng
water slide 滑水 huáshuǐ

Sentences

- Is there a children's ticket? 有儿童票吗？Yǒu értóngpiào ma?
- What is the height limit? 身高限制是多少？Shēngāo xiànzhì shì duōshǎo?
- How do you pay? 是按什么算的？Shì àn shénme suàn de?

Listen for this

- měicì 每次 per turn
- měi shí fēnzhōng 每十分钟 per ten minutes
- bù xiànshí 不限时 all you want
- Mǎi piào zài nàbiān 买票在那边 Buy tickets over there
- Shèngāo búdào liǎng mǐ de háizi miǎnfèi 身高不到两米的孩子免费 Free for kids under two meters tall
- Qǐng fù yìbǎi kuài qián yājīn 请付一百块钱押金 Please pay a RMB 100 deposit
- Qǐng tuō xié 请脱鞋 Please take off your shoes

Watch for this

- lost child area 走失儿童认领区 zǒushī értóng rènlǐngqū
- don't walk on the grass 别在草地上走 bié zài cǎodì shàng zǒu

8 Finding an ayi 找阿姨 Zhǎo āyí

Ayi, which literally means auntie, is used to describe maids, nannies, caregivers, or anyone else who performs miracles in homes and offices across Beijing.

Sentences

- I'm looking for an ayi, do you know someone that you would recommend?我想找个阿姨，有什么你认识的合适的人可以推荐吗？Wǒ xiǎng zhǎo ge āyí, yǒu shénme nǐ rènshi de héshì de rén kěyǐ tuījiàn ma?

- Can you help me find an ayi? 能帮我找个阿姨吗？Néng bāng wǒ zhǎo gè āyí ma?

- I need an ayi that can ... 我需要一个能...的阿姨 wǒ xūyào yí gè néng...de āyí

(1) speak English 说英语 shuō yīngyǔ
(2) live-in 住我家 zhù wǒ jiā
(3) work full-time 全职工作 quánzhí gōngzuò
(4) work part-time 兼职工作 jiānzhí gōngzuò
(5) cook 做饭 zuòfàn
(6) clean 清洁 qīngjié
(7) care for young children / babies
照顾小孩/婴儿的 zhàogù xiǎohái/yīng'ér de
(8) work weekends 周末工作 zhōumò gōngzuò

- This is my contact information, please have them contact me to arrange an interview 这是我的联系方式，请让她们联系我，安排面试 Zhè shì wǒ de liánxi fāngshì, qǐng ràng tāmen liánxi wǒ, ānpái miànshì

9 Ayi interview

面试阿姨 Miànshì āyí

Sentences

- Are you single or married? 你结婚了吗？Nǐ jiéhūn le ma?
- Do you have children? 你有孩子吗？Nǐ yǒu háizi ma?
- How old are you? 你多大年纪了？Nǐ duōdà niánji le?
- Have you ever been an ayi before? 以前做过阿姨吗？Yǐqián zuò guò āyí ma?
- Have you ever worked with foreigners before?以前给外国人工作过吗？Yǐqián gěi wàiguórén gōngzuò guò ma?
- For how long? What nationalities? 做了多久？哪国人？ Zuò le duōjiǔ? Nǎ guó rén?
- Can you understand Pinyin? 你会拼音吗？Nǐ huì pīnyīn ma?
- Do you know how to do laundry? 你会洗衣服吗？Nǐ huì xǐ yīfu ma?
- Do you know how to iron clothes? 你会熨衣服吗？Nǐ huì yùn yīfu ma?
- Do you know how to cook ... 你会做...吗？Nǐ huì zuò...ma?

(1) Chinese food 中餐 zhōngcān (2) Western food 西餐 xīcān

- Do you have experience with young children or babies? 你有照顾小孩/婴儿的经验吗？Nǐ yǒu zhàogu xiǎohái/yīng'ér de jīngyàn ma?
- Are you familiar with electrical appliances? 你对家用电器熟悉吗？Nǐ duì jiāyòng diànqì shúxi ma?
- Can you provide references? 你有推荐信吗？Nǐ yǒu tuījiànxìn ma?
- We have to talk it over. I will call you 我们还得再谈谈．我会再给你打电话的 Wǒmen hái děi zài tántan. Wǒ huì zài gěi nǐ dǎ diànhuà de

10 Employment details
雇佣细节 Gùyōng xìjié

Sentences

- You will start working for us on ... year ... month ... day 你将在...年...月...日开始在这儿工作 Nǐ jiāng zài ... nián ... yuè ... rì kāishǐ zài zhèr gōngzuò

- Your salary will be RMB ... per month 你的工资是每月...人民币 Nǐ dè gōngzī shì měi yuè ... rénmínbì

- There will be a probation period of ... 试用期是... Shìyòngqī shì ...

- You will work ... 你将会...工作 Nǐ jiāng huì ... gōngzuò

  (1) everyday 每天 měi tiān
  (2) weekdays 周一到周五 zhōuyī dào zhōuwǔ
  (3) weekends 周末 zhōumò
  (4) once a week 一周一次 yì zhōu yí cì

- Your workday will be ... o'clock to ... o'clock 你的工作时间是...点到...点 Nǐ de gōngzuò shíjiān shì ... diǎn dào ... diǎn.

- Your vacation schedule will be ... 你的假期为... Nǐ de jiàqī wéi ...

  (1) (two / four) weeks for Spring Festival
  春节(两/四周) Chūnjié (liǎng/sì zhōu)
  (2) all Chinese national holidays
  所有中国法定节假日 sǔoyǒu Zhōngguó fǎdìng jiéjiàrì
  (3) determined later 以后再定 yǐhòu zài dìng

- We (will / will not) provide health insurance 我们(提供/不提供)健康保险 Wǒmen (tígōng/bù tígōng) jiànkāng bǎoxiǎn.

- You'll receive your salary (taxed / untaxed) 你的工资是税后/税前的 Nǐ de gōngzī shì (shuìhòu/shuìqián) de

Listen for this

- Wǒ jīntiān/míngtiān lái bù liǎo le 我今天/明天来不了了 I can not come in today / tomorrow

• Wǒ chídào lè 我迟到了 I am late

• Wǒ míngtiān huì wǎn diǎnr lái 我明天会晚点儿来 I will be late tomorrow

• Míngtiān wǒ děi zǎo diǎnr zǒu 明天我得早点儿走 I need to leave earlier tomorrow

• Yǒu diǎnr jíshìr, wǒ děi... 有点儿急事儿，我得... I have an emergency, I need to take ...
(1) qǐng yì tiān jià 请一天假 the day off
(2) qǐng yí gè xīngqī jià 请一个星期假 the week off

• Nǐ néng bùnéng zhǎo gè fānyì? Wǒ děi hé nǐ hǎohao tántan zhè shìr 你能不能找个翻译？我得和你好好谈谈这事儿 I need a translator to discuss this with your further. Can you arrange one?

11 Instructions 指示 Zhǐshì

Vocabulary

Time

daily 每天 měitiān
once a day 一天一次 yì tiān yí cì
twice a day 一天两次 yì tiān liǎng cì
every other week 隔周 gézhōu
when needed 需要的时候 xūyào de shíhou
now 现在 xiànzài
all the time 一直 yìzhí
on arrival 到的时候 dào de shíhou
before you leave 走之前 zǒu zhīqián
when it's raining 下雨的时候 xiàyǔ de shíhou
when it's hot 热的时候 rè de shíhou
when it's cold 冷的时候 lěng de shíhou

Chores

straighten up 整理 zhěnglǐ
clean 清洁 qīngjié
change 换 huàn
pick up 接 jiē
drop off 送到 sòngdào
call for delivery 叫人送 Jiào rén sòng
call for repair 找人修理 zhǎo rén xiūlǐ
make 做 zuò
prepare 准备 zhǔnbèi
scrub 刷 shuā
wash 洗 xǐ
throw away 扔掉 rēngdiào
turn on 开 kāi
turn off 关 guān

Sentences

- Please wash the windows and then prepare lunch 请先擦窗户再准备午饭 Qǐng xiān cā chuānghu zài zhǔnbèi wǔfàn
- Be careful to turn off the gas 记住关煤气 Jìzhù guān méiqì
- Please clean the kitchen 请打扫厨房 Qǐng dǎsǎo chúfáng

(for more home vocabulary, see Housing & Hotels, p29)

12 House rules 规矩 Guīju

Sentences

- Please ... 请. . . Qǐng ...

(1) take off your shoes in the house 进屋脱鞋 jìn wū tuō xié
(2) knock before entering an occupied room 进有人的房间前先敲门 jìn yǒurén de fángjiān qián xiān qiāomén
(3) stay home and call us if you are sick 如果你病了就呆在家里，给我们打个电话 rúguǒ nǐ bìng le jìu dāi zài jiā lǐ, gěi wǒmen dǎ ge diànhuà

- Please don't ... 请别. . . Qǐng bié ...

(1) smoke in the house 在屋里吸烟 zài wūlǐ xīyān
(2) give medicine to our children without my approval 不经过我允许给孩子吃药 bù jīngguò wǒ yǔnxǔ gěi háizi chīyào
(3) open the door for strangers 给陌生人开门 gěi mòshēngrén kāimén

13 Cleaning 清洁 Qīngjié

Vocabulary

Cleaning Agents

all-purpose cleaner 多用清洁剂 duōyòng qīngjiéjì
carpet cleaner 地毯清洁剂 dìtǎn qīngjiéjì
clothes detergent 洗衣粉 xǐyīfěn
dish soap 洗涤灵 xǐdílíng
hand soap 香皂 xiāngzào
hot water 热水 rèshuǐ
toilet bowl cleaner 洁厕剂 jiécèjì
window cleaner 擦窗器 cāchuāngqì

Cleaning tools

broom 扫帚 sàozhou
bucket 桶 tǒng
dustpan 簸箕 bòji
mop 拖把 tuōba
paper towel 纸巾 zhǐjīn
rag 抹布 mǒbù
scrub brush 硬毛刷子 yìngmáo shuāzi
sponge 海绵 hǎimián
vacuum 吸尘器 xīchénqì

Sentences

• When cleaning the counters please use ... 擦橱柜的时候请用... Cā chúguì de shíhou qǐng yòng...

hot water 热水，rèshuǐ
all-purpose cleaner 多用清洁剂 duōyòng qīngjiéjì
a sponge 海绵 hǎimián

• When cleaning glass please use ... 擦玻璃的时候请用... Cā bōli de shíhou qǐng yòng ...

window cleaner 擦窗器 cāchuāngqì
paper towels 纸巾 zhǐjīn

• Only clean a room when it is empty 没人的时候再打扫 Méi rén de shíhou zài dǎsǎo

• Make the beds 铺床 Pū chuáng

• Change the sheets 换床单 Huàn chuángdān

• First dust every surface, then vacuum and mop the floor 先擦表面的尘土，再吸尘和拖地 Xiān cā biǎomiàn de chéntǔ, zài xīchén hé tuōdì

• Take out the garbage from each room 把每个屋的垃圾都清出来 Bǎ měige wū de lājī dōu qīng chūlái

• Put away things lying around 把乱扔的东西放好 Bǎ luàn rēng de dōngxi fàng hǎo

• Gather up dirty clothes for laundry 把脏衣服收在一起 Bǎ zāng yīfu shōu zài yìqǐ

- Wipe down and scrub clean all surfaces 擦洗所有表面 Cāxǐ suǒyǒu biǎomiàn

- Keep the plants watered 给花儿浇水 Gěi huār jiāoshuǐ

14 Cooking 做饭 Zuòfàn

(For more vocabulary on food and cooking, see Food p51-56)

Sentences

- Wash your hands before preparing food 做饭前要洗手 Zuòfàn qián yào xǐshǒu

- Do not put any metal items in the microwave 别把金属的东西放在微波炉里 Bié bǎ jīnshǔ de dōngxi fàngzài wēibōlú lǐ

- Use only bottled water for all cooking and drinks 做饭用水和喝的水都只用瓶装水 Zuòfàn yòngshuǐ hé hēde shuǐ dōu zhǐ yòng píngzhuāng shuǐ

- Make dinner for the whole family everyday, unless told otherwise 没特别说明的话，每天都要给全家人准备晚饭 Méi tèbié shuōmíng dehuà, měitiān dōu yào gěi quánjiā rén zhǔnbèi wǎnfàn

- While dinner is cooking, please set the table 做饭的空当可以摆桌子 Zuòfàn de kòngdāng kěyǐ bǎi zhuōzi

- Please make sure all meals include a vegetable dish, a meat dish, and staple dish 保证每顿饭都有一荤一素和主食 Bǎozhèng měi dùn fàn dōu yǒu yì hūn yí sù hé zhǔshí

- Please ... these 请把这些... Qǐng bǎ zhèxiē ...

(1) bake 烤了 kǎo le
(2) boil 煮了 zhǔ le
(3) chop 切了 qiē le
(4) freeze 冻起来 dòng qǐlai
(5) fry 炒了 chǎo le
(6) grill 烧烤 shāokǎo
(7) mix 混合 hùnhé
(8) peel 剥皮 bāo pí
(9) refrigerate 晾凉 liàngliáng
(10) slice 切片 qiē piàn
(11) steam 蒸 zhēng
(12) throw away 扔掉 rēngdiào
(13) wash 洗 xǐ
(14) warm up 热一下 rè yí xià

15 Ayi errands 叮嘱 Dīngzhǔ

Sentences

- You are responsible for replacing cleaning products and food items as necessary 如果清洁用品和食物没了的话你要去买新的 Rúguǒ qīngjié yòngpǐn hé shíwù méi le dehuà nǐ yào qù mǎi xīn de

- Become familiar with the brands we use and try to get the exact same kind at the store 记住我们用过的牌子，最好每次都买一样的 Jìzhù wǒmen yòng guò de páizi, zuìhǎo měicì dōu mǎi yíyàng de

- You can call this number to get these items delivered 你可以打这个电话让他们送货 Nǐ kěyǐ dǎ zhège diànhuà ràng tāmen sòng huò

- You can take the empty packaging with you to the store to be sure you get the right kind 去商店的时候把空瓶子带上，别买错了Qù shāngdiàn de shíhou bǎ kōng píngzi dài shàng, bié mǎi cuò le

- Be sure to keep all receipts from purchases 买东西的收据要收好 Mǎi dōngxi de shōujù yào shōu hǎo

- I will give you money for shopping / petty cash 我会给你买东西的钱/零用钱 Wǒ huì gěi nǐ mǎi dōngxi de qián / língyòngqián

- Let me know if you need more money for shopping 买东西钱不够的话告诉我 Mǎi dōngxi qián búgòu dehuà gàosù wǒ

16 Childcare 带孩子 Dài háizi

Sentences

- This is very important ... 这个很重要... Zhège hěn zhòngyào ...

- You tell me promptly about any issues or concerns you have 如果你有任何想法或问题马上告诉我 Rúguǒ nǐ yǒu rènhé xiǎngfǎ huò wèntí mǎshàng gàosu wǒ

- If my child gets injured, you let me know immediately 如果我的孩子受伤了，马上告诉我 Rúguǒ wǒ de háizi shòushāng le, mǎshàng gàosu wǒ

- The children follow the rules we have set 让孩子遵守我们定的规矩 Ràng háizi zūnshǒu wǒmen dìng de guījù

- You do not spank my child 你不能打孩子 Nǐ bùnéng dǎ háizi

- You do not yell at my child 不许对孩大吼大叫 Bùxǔ duì háizi dàhǒudàjiào

- You are always aware of where the children are and what they are doing 要时刻注意孩子在哪儿，在做些什么 Yào shíkè zhùyì háizi zài nǎr, zài zuò xiē shénme

- If my child is not obedient with you, do not feel frustrated 如果孩子不听你的话，不用烦 Rúguǒ háizi bù tīng nǐ de huà, bù yòng fán

- Let me know, and I will reinforce to my child that you are the authority when I am not around 告诉我，我会让他明白我不在这儿的时候要听你的 Gàosu wǒ, wǒ huì ràng tā míngbai wǒ bù zài zhèr de shíhou yào tīng nǐ de

- Please don't let the children watch more than two hours of television a day 每天别让孩子看电视超过两小时 Měitiān bié ràng háizi kàn diànshì chāoguò liǎng xiǎoshí

17 Babysitting

临时照看 Línshí zhàokàn

Sentences

- We will be going to ... 我们要去... Wǒmen yào qù ...

- And then around ... we will be at ... 然后大概... 我们会去... Ránhòu dàgài ... wǒmen huì qù ...

- We will be back around 11pm 我们晚上十一点左右回来 Wǒmen wǎnshang shíyīdiǎn zuǒyòu huílái

- The number is ... 电话号码是... Diànhuà hàomǎ shì ...

- There is no telephone number, but we will have our mobile phones 那儿没有电话，但我们带着手机 Nàr méiyǒu diànhuà, dàn wǒmen dài zhe shǒujī

Duncan McLiao of the Clan McLiao...

What's in a name?

by Eric Abrahamsen

Consider your typical Chinese application form. The very first box, where you're meant to make your personal mark, is labeled 姓名 (xìngmíng). This term, so commonplace as to be invisible, is a contraction of 姓氏 名字 (xíngshì míngzi), four characters which, taken together, tell a 6,000-year-old tale.

Before the advent of recorded history, China's society traced lineage through maternal lines (the components of the character 姓 xìng mean "born" 生 shēng by a particular "woman" 女 nǚ). Surnames were first used to avoid inbreeding, but this became less useful as clans grew in size – later, entire countries sometimes bore the same surname.

氏 (shì) were used to further differentiate family branches. The 氏 was patrilinear, and generally indicated location, profession, or official title. By the Warring States period (475-221 BC), the difference between 姓 and 氏 was thoroughly blurred, and modern surnames may once have been 姓 (particularly those with the female radical), or they may have been 氏.

The ancient Chinese were name-happy. Everyone started out with a 名 (míng), to which their parents added a 字 (zì) when the boy or girl came of age. 名 were used when speaking to inferiors; equals or superiors were always addressed by their 字. One's 字 and 名 were often related in meaning – someone called 明 míng (bright) might be given 亮 liàng (shine) as their 字, for instance. Family patriarchs planned out family trees several generations in advance, sometimes specifying the full names of potential children, sometimes just the radical, or the first of the two characters. This systematic approach sometimes extended to boys being named numerically, by the order of their birth. This practice hasn't entirely died out, though it is losing significance with the advent of one-child families.

Another colorful naming tradition was the giving of grotesque monikers to very young children, in the hopes that evil spirits would be dissuaded from harming them. After all, what self-respecting demon would prey on a child named "Dog Turd" (狗蛋 Gǒudàn)? In rural families, fathers would rush outside immediately after the birth of a son, and name the child after the first unpleasant thing they saw. Hence names such as 锁柱 Sǔozhù ("tying post") or 狗剩 Gǒushèng ("dog's leftovers") which, if the children were unlucky, could stick with them well into adulthood. This tradition lingered on in rural areas until after the founding of the PRC. One well-known example are Tianjin's famous 狗不理 gǒu bùlǐ ("even dogs won't touch it") *baozi* – referring not to the baozi themselves, but to the man who invented them.

Chinese names have always carried significance, and trends in names often reveal much about the spirit of the times. The ancient Chinese went for aesthetically pleasing names – one character from the Dream of the Red Chamber was named 茗烟 Míngyān, or "the fragrance which rises from excellent tea." Girls have traditionally gotten stuck with flower names or, if particularly unlucky, names indicating that their parents would rather have had a boy: 婷 Tíng (which sounds like "stop", meaning "stop having girls") or 招弟 Zhāodì, meaning "bring along a younger brother." Names in the early twentieth century often incorporated the characters 宝 bǎo (treasure) and 财 cái (riches), indicating a fixation on wealth, while the establishment of the PRC brought a rash of kids named 建国 Jiànguó and 立国 Lìguó (Build the Country and Upright Country). During the Cultural Revolution it was all 防军 Fángjūn (Protect the Army) or 卫东 Wèidōng (Protect the East/Chairman Mao). In recent decades male names have tended towards strength (强 qiáng and 志 zhì), while girls are back with flowers again.

In modern times, the custom of giving names is plagued by a familiar problem: too many people. The three most popular surnames, 李 Lǐ, 王 Wáng and 张 Zhāng, together account for a whopping 21.4 per cent of the population, and the same couple hundred characters are reused over and over again in given names. Name-related bureaucratic snafus are becoming a serious issue, and the government is trying to encourage parents to break away from tradition in naming their children. Four-character names are starting to come into fashion, but it's going to take more than that to tell the teeming multitudes apart.

- This is my mobile number ... 我的手机号码是... Wǒ de shǒujī hàomǎ shì ...

- Put him to bed at 8pm 让他八点睡觉 Ràng tā bā diǎn shuìjiào

- Please feed him/her a little fruit 让他／她吃点儿水果 Ràng tā chī diǎnr shuǐguǒ

- Do not feed him/her junkfood 别让他／她吃零食 Bié ràng tā chī língshí

- She can only watch one DVD 只许她看一部DVD Zhǐ xǔ tā kàn yí bù DVD

- He cannot watch TV 不许他看电视 Bù xǔ tā kàn diànshì

- Call us if anything happens 有什么事儿给我们打电话 Yǒu shénme shìr gěi wǒmen dǎ diànhuà

18 Asking after your child

询问情况 Xúnwèn qíngkuàng

Sentences

- How was he? 他怎么样? Tā zěnme yàng?

- How did she behave? 她表现怎么样? Tā biǎoxiàn zěnme yàng?

- Did he obey you? 他听你的话吗? Tā tīng nǐ de huà ma?

- I'm sorry she made a mess 对不起，她把这儿弄得一团糟 Duìbùqǐ, tā bǎ zhèr nòng de yì tuán zāo

Listen for this

- Tā hěn guāi 他／她很乖 S/he is well behaved
- Chū le diǎnr shìr 出了点儿事儿 Something happened
- Tā... 她... She ...
  (1) fāshāo le 发烧了 had a fever
  (2) tù le 吐了 vomited

19 Laundry 洗衣服 Xǐ yīfu

(For more on laundry and clothes, see Dry cleaning in Useful Info, p262 and Shopping, p144)

Sentences

- Check the labels on clothes carefully to see how to clean them 仔细看衣服上的标签儿再确定怎么洗 Zíxì kàn yīfu shàng de biāoqiānr zài quèdìng zěnme xǐ

- Sort clothes according to ... 衣服按...分类洗 yīfu àn...fēnlèi xǐ

  colors 颜色 yánsè
  cloth material 布料 bùliào
  wash temperature 水洗的温度 shuǐxǐ de wēndù

- To prevent staining, wash new clothes separately 为了不染色，把新衣服分开洗 Wèile bù rǎnsè, bǎ xīn yīfu fēnkāi xǐ.

- Before washing, use a stain remover on any visible stains 洗之前先用去污剂处理一下明显的污渍 Xǐ zhīqián xiān yòng qùwūjì chùlǐ yí xià míngxiǎn de wūzì

Family Information

- Home 家 jiā

(1) Address 住址 zhùzhǐ
(2) Phone 电话 diànhuà

- Husband 丈夫 zhàngfu

(1) Name 姓名 xìngmíng
(2) Cellphone 手机 shǒujī
(3) Office Phone 办公室电话 bàngōngshì diànhuà
(4) Company Name 公司名字 gōngsī mīngzi
(5) Company address 公司地址 gōngsī dìzhǐ

- Wife 妻子 qīzǐ

(1) Name 姓名 xìngmíng
(2) Cellphone 手机 shóujī
(3) Office Phone 办公室电话 bàngōngshì diànhuà
(4) Company Name 公司名字 gōngsī mīngzi
(5) Company address 公司地址 gōngsī dìzhǐ

- Child 孩子 háizi

(1) Name 姓名 xìngmíng
(2) School 学校 xuéxiào

- Emergency Contact 紧急情况联系人 jínjí qíngkuàng liánxirěn

(1) Name 姓名 xìngmíng
(2) Relationship 关系 guānxi
(3) Phone 电话 diànhuà
(4) Other phone 其他电话号码 qítā diànhuà hàomǎ
(5) Doctor 医生 yīshēng
(6) Phone 电话 diànhuà
(7) Other phone 其他电话 qítā diànhuà
(8) Police 警察 jǐngchá
(9) Fire 火警 huójǐng
(10) Ambulance 救护车 jiùhùchē

ART & CULTURE

By familiarizing yourself with some of the phrases and vocabulary in this chapter, you will be able to engage in stimulating verbal intercourse with all manner of artists, musicians, theater buffs and beatniks. Tally ho!

1 Art essentials 艺术基础 Yìshù jīchǔ

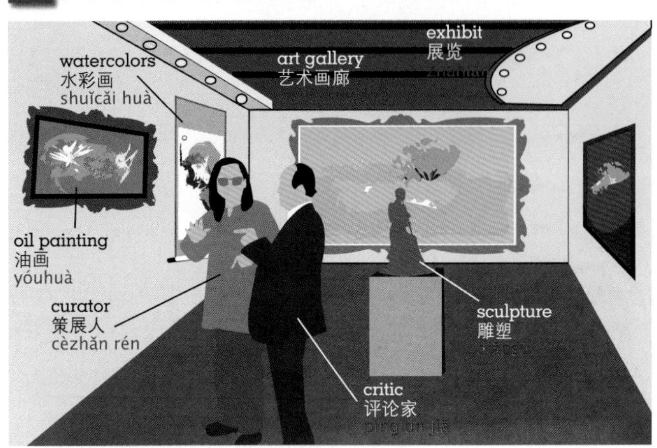

Vocabulary

art gallery 艺术画廊 yìshù huàláng
art museum 美术馆 měishùguǎn
auction 拍卖会 pāimài huì
biennale/triennale 双／三年展 shuāng/sān nián zhǎn
exhibit (solo / group) 展览（个人／联展）zhǎnlǎn (gèrén / liánzhǎn)
opening 开幕式 kāimùshì

oil painting 油画 yóuhuà
paint 绘画 huìhuà
sculpture 雕塑 diāosù
watercolors 水彩画 shuǐcǎi huà

collection 收藏品 shōucáng pǐn
collector 收藏家 shōucáng jiā
critic 评论家 pínglùn jiā
curator 策展人 cèzhǎn rén

artist collective 艺术家群体 yìshùjiā qúntǐ
artist village 画家村 huàjiā cūn
happy in poverty 穷欢乐 qióng huānlè
non-profit 非盈利 fēi yínglì
studio 工作室 gōngzuò shì
utopia 乌托邦 wūtuōbāng

aesthetic 美感 měigǎn
influence 影响 yíngxiǎng
style 风格 fēnggé
technique 技术 jìshù

Sentences

- Can you tell me the way to … ? 请问去…怎么走？ Qǐngwèn qù … zěnme zǒu?

(1) Panorama art gallery 观景廊 Guānjǐngláng
(2) Songzhuang artist village 宋家庄画家村 Sòngjiāzhuāng huàjiā cūn
(3) 798 art district 七九八艺术区 qījiǔbā yìshù qū

- Fang Lijun is showing at the Red Gate Gallery 方力均目前在红门画廊有展览 Fāng Lìjūn mùqián zài hóngmén huàláng yǒu zhǎnlǎn

- I like Ai Wei Wei's early photographic works 我喜欢艾未未的早期摄影作品 Wǒ xǐhuān Aì Wèiwèi de zǎoqī shèyǐng zuòpǐn

- I'm interested in buying this painting 我想买这幅作品 Wǒ xiǎng mǎi zhè fù zuòpǐn

Listen for this

- zhǔliú 主流 mainstream
- luǒlù 裸露 nudity
- dìxià 地下 underground
- xūkōng 虚空 pointless/empty
- qiánwèi 前卫 cutting edge
- lǎotào 老套 it's been done before
- Zhè gè fēnggé kěndìng liúxíng bù qǐlái, tài zhǔliú le 这个风格肯定流行不起来，太主流了 This style can't be popular. It's too mainstream

2 Traditional Chinese arts

中国传统艺术

Zhōngguó chuántǒng yìshù

Vocabulary

bronze 青铜 qīngtóng
dough sculpture 面塑 miàn sù
embroidery 刺绣 cìxiù
five color enamel (wu'tsai) 五彩珐琅 wǔcǎi fǎláng
folk art 民间艺术 mínjiān yìshù
woodcut 木刻 mùkè
calligraphy 书法 shūfǎ
seal script 隶书 lìshū
regular script 楷书 kǎishū
running (semi-cursive) script 行书 xíngshū

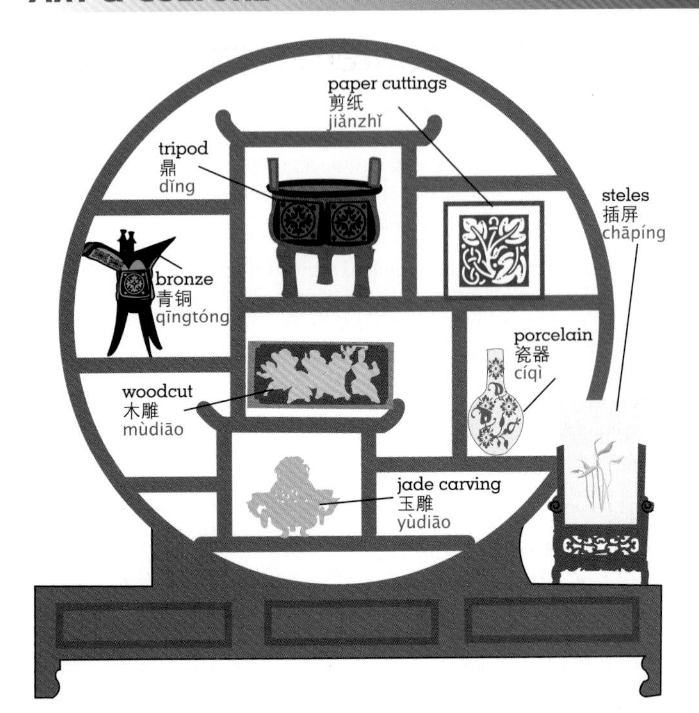

jade carving 玉雕 yù diāo
kite 风筝 fēngzhēng
paper cuttings 剪纸 jiǎn zhǐ
porcelain 瓷器 cíqì
steles 石碑 shí bēi
tripod 鼎 dǐng
woodblock print
套色板画 tàosè bǎnhuà
grass script 草书 cǎoshū
landscape paintings
风景画 fēngjǐng huà
ink & wash 水墨 shuǐmò
calligraphy paper 宣纸 xuānzhǐ
to mount 裱 biǎo
scroll mounting
装裱 zhuāng biǎo

Sentences

- I particularly appreciate art from the ... period 我特别欣赏．．．时期的艺术 Wǒ tèbié xīnshǎng ... shíqī de yìshù

(1) (Xia, Shang, Zhou) dynasty (夏，商，周)代 (Xià, Shāng, Zhōu) dài
(2) (Han, Ming, Qing) dynasty (汉，明，清)朝 (Hàn, Míng, Qīng) cháo
(3) Spring and Autumn/Warring States period
春秋/战国时代 Chūnqiū / Zhànguó shídài

3 Modern/contemporary art

现代／当代艺术

Xiàndài/dāngdài yìshù

Vocabulary

advertising language 广告语言 guǎnggào yǔyán
avant-garde 先锋派／前卫 xiānfēngpài/qiánwèi
collage 拼贴 pīntiē
conceptual art 概念艺术 gàiniàn yìshù
design 设计 shèjì
digital arts 数码艺术 shùmǎ yìshù
experimental art 实验艺术 shíyàn yìshù
graffiti art 涂鸦 túyā
installation art 装制艺术 zhuāngzhì yìshù
multimedia 多媒体 duōméitǐ
new media 新媒体 xīn méitǐ
performance art 行为艺术 xíngwéi yìshù
photography 摄影 shèyǐng
propaganda posters 宣传画 xuānchuán huà
video art 媒介艺术 méijiè yìshù
virtual reality 虚拟世界 xū'nǐ shìjiè

Sentences

• Show me the latest works of oil painting master Liu Xiaodong 给我看看油画大师刘小东近期的作品 Gěi wǒ kànkan yóuhuà dàshī Liú Xiǎodōng jìnqī de zuòpǐn

• Will this be worth something in ten years? 十年后这个作品会值钱吗？ Shí nián hòu zhè gè zuòpǐn huì zhíqián ma?

• Brief me on the artist Yin Qi's style 能给我介绍一下艺术家尹齐的个人风格吗？ Néng gěi wǒ jièshào yí xià yìshùjiā Yǐn Qí de gèrén fēnggé ma?

• Is that an authentic Zhang Dali graffiti scrawl? 这个是张大力的亲笔涂鸦吗？ Zhè gè shì Zhāng Dàlì de qīnbǐ túyā ma?

Primitive Pictographs

The genealogical "tree roots" of ancient characters!

by Lee Ambrozy

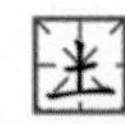

tǔ: primitive for "soil, earth" (the top line is the ground, the bottom is rock, the vertical line represents "all things")

tián: primitive for "furrowed field"

yóu: cause, reason 2) because of, owing to (imagine a sprout coming from a field)

miáo: seedling (see shoots sprouting at the edge of the field)

lǐ: ancient unit of land measurement 2) inside (see a field resting on the character for "earth")

huáng: yellow, like a sunflower (an ancient form of "bright" is anchored by a field)

léi: thunder (rainclouds above a field)

yǔ: primitive for "rain" (according to most scholars' accounts, the dots are drops, the line is heaven, the enclosure symbolizes clouds)

shān: primitive for "mountain" (a horizontal earth line is topped with three tall stones)

mù: primitive for "eye" 2) mesh, hole 3) look (imagine an eye on its side)

gān: primitive "to oppose" 2) offend 3) dry (in the shape of a pestle)

hàn: drought, dry spell (the desiccating effect of the sun, which rests on the pestle)

tīan: sky, heaven (a man with a line symbolizing heaven above)

lì: stand at attention 2) to erect, set something up (a man standing on the ground)

fū: husband, man, person engaged in manual labor (man with a pin in his hair to show he's of age)

yāng: core, center (a man stands in the center of an enclosed space)

jiāo: hand over, turn in 2) settle in 3) meet, join (a man with his legs crossed, intertwined)

shuǎng: bright, clear, crisp 2) straightforward, openhearted 3) comfortable (a man with arms in motion, active and alert)

rén: primitive for "man" 2) humanity, human 3) personality (the profile of a person with two legs in walking motion)

yáng: primitive "sheep or lamb" (as seen from behind, its horns and backside)

měi: beautiful (a "big" under a sheep, beauty is a big sheep)

gōng: primitive for "work" 2) workers and the working class 3) labor

yà: inferior, shabby (a deformed, hunchback version of "work")

mù: primitive for tree, wood (a trunk and branches)

běn: root or stem 2) main, chief, principal 3) original, initial (the line through the trunk denotes earth)

mò: tip, end 2) non-essential (the top horizontal line represents the highest tree branches)

wèi: have not, did not 2) no, not (the highest branches of the tree have been snipped)

gǔo: fruit 2) yield, results (the field on the tree symbolizes a harvest from its branches)

fēng: the primitive "rich, plentiful" (see one very leafy bough)

mǐ: the primitive "grain" 2) glutinous rice (four grains separated in the thrashing represented by the cross in the middle)

wén: the primitive "literary, genteel" 2) character, script, writing 3) culture, rite

dà: the primitive "great, tall" (a grown man with legs and arms outstretched)

gǎo: brightly shining (the sun above the tree tops)

wáng: primitive for "king, monarch" 2) highest rank of feudal times (one vertical line connects three horizontals: heaven, earth and man)

kǒu: primitive for "mouth" 2) taste 3) people, population (imagine our most prominent orifice)

gǔ: ancient times (the character for "ten" sits on a mouth, implying tales passed down for ten generations)

è: evil and terrifying (four mouths crying out loud, ensconced in an ancient form for "attack")

gān: sweet (a mouth happily holding something inside)

fēi: primitive "opposition" 2) wrong, error 3) no, not (an abstract character with two opposite sides reflecting each other)

rì: primitive for "sun" 2) day (a sun pierced by a line representing "time")

dàn: dawn, daybreak (the sun rests on the horizon)

zhōng: primitive "center" (a square target pierced by an arrow)

Modern definitions provided by the illustrious Contemporary Chinese Dictionary, 2003〈现代汉语词典〉汉英版, and etymological explanations courtesy of Dr L. Wieger's Chinese Characters, their origin, etymology, history, classification and signification, first published in 1915.

4 "Made in China" art movements

中国特色的艺术派别

Zhōngguó tèsè de yìshù pàibié

Vocabulary

Apartment Art 公寓艺术 Gōngyù Yìshù
Cynical Realism 玩世现实主义 Wánshì Xiànshí Zhǔyì
Eastern Mysticism 东方神密主义 Dōngfāng Shénmì Zhǔyì
Gaudy Art 艳俗艺术 Yànsú Yìshù
Minimalism 极简主义 Jíjiǎn Zhǔyì
Political Pop 政治波普 Zhèngzhì Bōpǔ
Post '70s Art 七十年代后期艺术 Qīshí Niándài Hòuqī Yìshù
Shock Art 冲击艺术，修克艺术 Chōngjī Yìshù, Xiūkè Yìshù
Socialist Realism
社会主义的现实主义 Shèhuì Zhǔyì de Xiànshí Zhǔyì

Listen for this

- bàoháosī jiànzhù xuépài 鲍豪斯建筑学派 Bauhaus architecture
- shìchǎng dǎoxiàng yìshùjiā 市场导向艺术家 market driven artists
- shìchǎng gǎibiàn zhōngguó hòu de yí dài 市场改变中国后的一代 Post-consumer generation of artists
- yí yè chéngmíng 一夜成名 overnight success

Sentences

- What do you think of this new "cartoon generation"? 你怎么评价新的“卡通一代”？ Nǐ zěnme píngjià xīn de "kǎtōng yí dài"?
- These colorful, fascinating works are by an emerging artist 这些色彩丰富、充满神密感的作品是出自一位新锐艺术家之手Zhè xiē sècǎi fēngfù, chōngmǎn shénmìgǎn de zuòpǐn shì chū zì yí wèi xīnruì yìshùjiā zhī shǒu
- What do you think the artist is trying to say? 你觉得这位艺术家想表达什么？ Nǐ juéde zhè wèi yìshùjiā xiǎng biǎodá shénme?

5 Playing critic 批判 Pīpàn

Amuse and astound with your crippling intellect - and impressively po-mo vocabulary.

Vocabulary

balance 平衡 pínghéng
contextualize 放在上下文中考虑 fàng zài shàngxiàwén zhōng kǎolǜ
deconstruct 解构拆析 jiěgòu chāixī
dialectics 辩证法 biànzhèng fǎ
hegemony 霸权 bàquán
interplay 相互影响 xiānghù yǐngxiǎng
multiculturalism 多元文化主义 duōyuán wénhuà zhǔyì
negative space 实体周围的空间 shítǐ zhōuwéi de kōngjiān
perspective 透视法 tòushìfǎ
post-modern 后现代 hòu xiàndài
post-structuralism 后结构主义 hòu jiégòu zhǔyì
schema (composition) 构图 gòutú

Sentences

- I can't accept the reality this painting projects 我不认同这幅作品所表达的含意 Wǒ bú rèntóng zhè fú zuòpǐn suǒ biǎodá de hányì

- He borrows too heavily from Andy Warhol's aesthetic 他作品的感觉太像沃霍尔的风格了 Tā zuòpǐn de gǎnjué tài xiàng Wóhuò'ěr de fēnggé le

6 At the newsstand

在报刊亭 Zài bàokāntíng

Sentences

- How much for that ... ? . . . 多少钱? ... duōshǎo qián?

(1) Guns and Ammo magazine
那本《枪与军火》nà běn <qiāng yǔ jūnhuǒ>
(2) government funded newspaper
政府投资报纸 zhèngfǔ tóuzī bàozhǐ

A & C

(3) magazine with the fashionable, young, urban woman on the cover 那本封面是个时尚年轻的都市女孩的杂志 nà běn fēngmiàn shì gè shíshàng niánqīng de dūshì nǚhái de zázhì

• Which of these newspapers ... 哪份报纸... Nǎ fèng bàozhǐ ...

(1) is the most interesting? 最有意思? zuì yǒu yìsi?
(2) is the most popular? 卖得最好? mài de zuì hǎo?
(3) is the most fun to read? 读起来最有趣? dú qǐlái zuì yǒuqù?
(4) has the most pictures? 图片最多? túpiàn zuì duō?
(5) has the most UFO news? 飞碟新闻最多? fēidié xīnwén zuì duō?

7 Books 书籍 Shūjí

Sentences

• Where can I find the ... section ...的部分在哪儿? ... de bùfèn zài nǎr?

autobiography 自传 zìzhuàn
cookbook 菜谱 càipǔ
picture books 画册 huàcè
comic books 连环画 liánhuán huà

• Too many books! I'm going to faint 好多书啊!我都要晕倒了 Hǎoduō shū a! Wǒ dōu yào yūn dǎo le

• Could you please help me find me a book? 请问,您能不能帮我找一本书? Qǐngwèn, nín néng bùnéng bāng wǒ zhǎo yì běn shū?

• It's called ... 它叫... Tā jiào ...

• When was it published? 什么时候出版的? Shénme shíhòu chūbǎn de?

author 作者 zuòzhě
biography 传记 zhuànjì
children's book 儿童读物 értóng dúwù
cover 封面 fēngmiàn
dictionary 字典 zìdiǎn
guide 指南 zhǐnán
handbook 手册 shǒucè
hardcover 精装 jīngzhuāng
history 历史 lìshǐ
magazine 杂志 zázhì
map 地图 dìtú
newspaper 报纸 bàozhǐ
novel 小说 xiǎoshuō
page 页 yè
paperback 平装 píngzhuāng
poetry 诗歌 shīgē
publisher 出版商 chūbǎnshāng
translation 翻译 fānyì
travel 旅游 lǚyóu

Test Your Western Art History

Match the artist's name (in Chinese) to the movement they are famous for

1. Cubism:
立体主
Lìtǐ zhǔyì

2. Dadaism (anti-art):
达达主义（反艺术）
Dádá zhǔyì (fǎn yìshù)

3. Surrealism:
超现实主义
Chāo xiànshí zhǔyì

4. Expressionism:
表现主义
Biǎoxiàn zhǔyì

5. Renaissance:
文艺复兴
Wényì fùxīng

6. Impressionism:
印象主义
Yìnxiàng zhǔyì

7. Abstract Expressionism:
抽象表现主义
Chōuxiàng biǎoxiàn zhǔyì

8. Futurism:
未来主义
Wèilái zhǔyì

9. Action Painting:
行动绘画
Xíngdòng huìhuà

10. Pop Art:
波普艺术
Bōpǔ yìshù

11. Post-Modern:
后现代主义
Hòuxiàndài zhǔyì

(A) Monet: 莫奈 Mònài
Renoir: 雷诺阿 Léinuò'ā

(B) Claes Oldenburg:
克拉斯 · 奥尔登堡
Kèlāsī àoěrdēngbǎo
Andy Warhol: 安迪.沃霍尔
āndí Wòhuò'ěr

(C) Marcel Duchamp: 马塞尔 · 杜尚
Mǎsài'ěr dùshàng

(D) Jackson Pollock: 杰克逊 · 波洛克
Jiékèxùn Bōluòkè

(E) Salvador Dali: 萨尔瓦多 · 达利
Sà'ěrwǎduō Dálì

(F) Charles Jencks: 查尔斯 · 詹克斯
Chá'ěrsī Zhānkèsī
Phillip Johnson: 菲利普 · 约翰逊
Fēilìpǔ Yuēhànxùn

(G) Leonardo: 莱奥纳尔多 · 达芬奇
Lái'àonà'ěrduō Dáfēnqí
Raphael: 拉斐尔 Lāfēi'ěr
Michelangelo: 米开朗
Mǐkāilǎngqíluó

(H) Mark Rothko: 马克 · 罗思科
Mǎkè Luósīkē

(I) Giacomo Balla: 贾科莫 · 巴拉
Jiǎkēmò Bālā

(J) Picasso: 毕加索 Bìjiāsuǒ

(K) Edvard Munch: 爱德华 · 蒙克
àidéhuá Méngkè
Vincent Van Gogh: 文森特 · 梵高
Wénsēntè Fángāo

Answers:
1=J; 2=C; 3=E; 4=K; 5=G; 6=A; 7=H; 8=I; 9=D; 10=B; 11=F

library 图书馆 túshūguǎn
linguistic 语言学 yǔyánxué
Chinese learning 汉语学习 hànyǔ xuéxí
foreign language 外语 wàiyǔ

Listen for this

- Sure, it's on 3rd floor. 没问题，这本书在三楼 Méi wèntí, zhè běn shū zài sānlóu

8 Theater 剧场 Jùchǎng

Vocabulary

acrobatics 杂技 zájì
actors 演员 yǎnyuán
backstage 后台 hòutái
behind the scenes/curtain 幕后 mù hòu
box office 售票处 shòupiàochù
costume 演出服 yǎnchūfú
director 导演 dǎoyǎn
modern dance 现代舞 xiàndàiwǔ
modern theater 现代剧院 xiàndài jùyuàn
performance 表演 biǎoyǎn
play 剧本 jùběn
playwright 剧作家 jùzuòjiā
plot 情节 qíngjié
puppet 木偶 mù'ǒu
set 布景 bùjǐng

Sentences

- When is the performance of (Shaolin Warriors)? （少林武僧）的表演什么时候开始？(Shàolín Wǔsēng) de biǎoyǎn shénme shíhòu kāishǐ?

- What nights are there performances? 哪天晚上有表演？Nǎ tiān wǎnshàng yǒu biǎoyǎn?

- Where can you buy tickets? 在哪儿买票？ Zài nǎr mǎi piào?

- Can the tickets be delivered? 能送票吗？Néng sòng piào ma?

- Can you hold the tickets for me at the box office? 能在售票处给我预留点儿票吗？ Néng zài shòupiàochù gěi wǒ yùliú diǎnr piào ma?

- How long is the performance? 表演多长时间？ Biǎoyǎn duō cháng shíjiān?

- Is there an intermission? 有中场休息吗？Yǒu zhōngchǎng xiūxi ma?

- Are there subtitles? 有字幕吗？Yǒu zìmù ma?

- boring 无聊 wúliáo

- Brilliant! 精彩！Jīngcǎi!

9 Peking Opera 京剧 Jīngjù

Vocabulary

triangular flag 靠旗 kàoqí
opening 开场 kāichǎng
pheasant or peacock feathers on top of a warrior's helmet 翎子 língzi
speculative reselling of tickets 倒票 dǎopiào
clown 丑角 chǒujué
villain 奸臣 jiānchén
Monkey King 美猴王 Měihóuwáng

For more music vocabulary, see Nightlife p130-134 and Shopping, p156.

10 Classical music 古典音乐 Gǔdiǎn yīnyuè

Vocabulary

(For more on musical instruments, see Shopping p161)

brass 铜管乐器 tóngguǎn yuèqì
conductor 指挥 zhǐhuī
horn 号 hào
orchestra 管弦乐 guǎnxiányuè
percussion 打击乐 dǎjīyuè
string 弦乐 xiányuè
wind 吹奏乐器 chuīzòu yuèqì

Sentences

- Shh! Please don't talk; I'm trying to listen 嘘！别说话；我在听呢 Xū! Bié shuōhuà; wǒ zài tīng ne

• The sound from the horn section isn't bright enough 号的声音不够大 Hào de shēngyīn bú gòu dà

11 Cinema/film 电影 Diànyǐng

Sentences

• Is (Harry Potter) playing at your theater? 哈利波特在你那儿上映了吗？Hālì Bōtè zài nǐ nàr shàngyìng le ma?

• Is it dubbed in Chinese or is it in the original language? 是中文配音的还是原声？Shì zhōngwén pèiyīn de háishì yuánshēng?

• Are there English subtitles? 有英文字幕吗？ Yǒu yīngwén zìmù ma?

• When is it playing? 几点开演？Jǐ diǎn kāiyǎn?

• Is there an earlier/later show? 有早点儿/晚点儿的场次吗？Yǒu zǎodiǎnr/wǎndiǎnr de chǎngcì ma?

• How much is a ticket? 票价多少？Piàojià duōshǎo?

• Do you have student discounts? 有学生票吗？Yǒu xuéshēngpiào ma?

• Who's in it? 谁演的？ Shéi yǎn de?

• Is it any good? 好看吗？Hǎo kàn ma?

Listen for this

• ...yǎn de ...演的 It stars ...

• Wánquán méi qíngjié 完全没情节 It has absolutely no plot

(For more film vocabulary, see Shopping p156)

13 Television 电视 Diànshì

Vocabulary

BTV 北京台 Běijīngtái
cable 有线 yǒuxiàn
CCTV 中央台 Zhōngyāngtái
channel 频道 píndào
game show 娱乐节目 yúlè jiémù
host 主持人 zhǔchírén
news 新闻 xīnwén
program 节目 jiémù
satellite 卫星 wèixīng
sitcom/soap 连续剧 liánxùjù
television in English 英语的电视 yīngyǔ de diànshì
television series 电视剧 diànshìjù
variety show 综艺节目 zōngyì jiémù

Sentences

• She's pretty 她很漂亮 Tā hěn piàoliàng

• He's handsome 他很帅 Tā hěn shuài

• That host is too ... 那个主持人太... Nà gè zhǔchírén tài ...

arrogant 自大了 zìdà le
flamboyant 妖艳了 yāoyàn le
clever for his/her britches 爱耍小聪明了 ài shuǎ xiǎo cōngmíng le

• Oh, this show is so funny! 啊，这个节目真逗！ A, zhèi gè jiémù zhēn dòu!

• Do you think F4 will stay together? 你觉得F4会单飞吗？ Nǐ juéde Fsì huì dānfēi ma?

Notes

SIGHTSEEING ►

From the Great Wall to the parks at dawn and bustling markets, you don't need to know Chinese to take away a sense of energy and amazement while enjoying all that Beijing has to offer. However, with a little brush up on history and terminology as well as a few choice phrases, the Beijing sightseeing experience can be that much more rewarding. Some mysteries can be solved with a simple question, and history can come alive through the human echoes all around you ...

1 Basics 基础词汇 Jīchǔ cíhuì

Sentences

- Please take me to ... 麻烦送我去... Máfan sòng wǒ qù ...

(1) White Cloud Temple 白云观 Báiyúnguàn
(2) the Ancient Observatory 古观象台 Gǔ Guānxiàngtái
(3) Ya'er Hutong alley 鸦儿胡同 Yā'ér Hútòng
(4) the Ming dynasty city wall 明城墙遗址 Míng chéngqiáng yízhǐ

- I'd like to visit ... 我想去参观... Wǒ xiǎng qù cānguān ...

(1) the Forbidden City 故宫 Gùgōng
(2) the National Art Museum 美术馆 Měishùguǎn
(3) the Great Wall at Mutianyu 慕田峪长城 Mùtiányù Chángchéng

(For a full list of sights, see pages 118, 120 and 122)

- What time does (the Old Summer Palace) open? (圆明园)什么时候开放? (Yuánmíngyuán) shénme shíhou kāifàng?

- What time does (the Temple of Heaven) close? (天坛公园)什么时候关门? (Tiāntán Gōngyuán) shénme shíhou guān mén?

- Which days of the week is (Prince Gong's Mansion) open? (恭王府)星期几开? (Gōngwángfǔ) xīngqī jǐ kāi?

- How much is a / an ... ? ...多少钱? ... duōshǎo qián?

(1) ticket 门票 ménpiào
(2) postcard 明信片 míngxìnpiàn
(3) map 地图 dìtú
(4) "I climbed the Great Wall" T-shirt “我登上了长城”T恤衫 "Wǒ dēng shàng le Chángchéng" T-xùshān

• Do you have English-language ... 你这儿有英文...吗？Nǐ zhèr yǒu yīngwén ... ma?

(1) tour guides 导游 dǎoyóu
(2) audio guides 语音导游 yǔyīn dǎoyóu
(3) guidebooks 指南 zhǐnán

• Where can I find ... ? 哪儿有...？ Nǎr yǒu ... ?

(1) a tourist information booth 游客问讯处 yóukè wènxùnchù
(2) a bathroom 厕所 cèsuǒ
(3) a place to rest 休息的地方 xiūxi de dìfang
(4) something to eat / drink 吃的/喝的 chīde / hēde
(5) the entrance / exit 入口/出口 rùkǒu / chūkǒu
(6) the Forbidden Starbucks 星巴克故宫店 Xīngbākè Gùgōng diàn

• Can I watch you ... ? 我能看你...吗？Wǒ néng kàn nǐ ... ma?

(1) do the fan dance 表演扇子舞 biǎoyǎn shànzi wǔ
(2) make *baozi* 做包子 zuò bāozi
(3) breakdance 跳霹雳舞 tiào pīlìwǔ
(4) play 玩 wánr

• Could I join you? 我能跟你们一起吗？Wǒ néng gēn nǐmen yìqǐ ma?

• How do I do it? 怎么做？Zěnme zuò?

Listen for this

• Wǒmen xiàwǔ sì diǎn tíngzhǐ shòu piào 我们下午4点停止售票 We stop selling tickets at 4pm

• Yíhéyuán wǎnshang bā diǎn guānmén 颐和园晚上8点关门 The Summer Palace closes at 8pm

• Wǒmen yǒu ... yǔyīn dǎoyóu 我们有...语音导游 We have audio guides in ...

(1) Yīngyǔ 英语 English
(2) Fǎyǔ 法语 French
(3) Déyǔ 德语 German
(4) Yìdàlìyǔ 意大利语 Italian
(5) Xībānyáyǔ 西班牙语 Spanish
(6) Rìyǔ 日语 Japanese
(7) Hányǔ 韩语 Korean
(8) éyǔ 俄语 Russian

• Qǐng bǎ yǔyīn dǎoyóu shèbèi huán dào běi chūkǒu 请把语音导游设备还到北出口 Return the audio guide device at the north exit

2 Image appropriation

拍照 Pāizhào

Sentences

• Can I take a picture of that? 我能把它拍下来吗？ Wǒ néng bǎ tā pāi xiàlai ma?

• Can I take a picture of you? 我能给你照张相吗？ Wǒ néng gěi nǐ zhào zhāng xiàng ma?

• Can you take a picture of us? 你能给我们照张相吗？ Nǐ néng gěi wǒmen zhào zhāng xiàng ma?

• Press the button down halfway and hold it to focus and then push it the rest of the way to take the picture 半按快门对焦，对好了之后全按下去就拍好了 Bàn àn kuàimén duìjiāo, duì hǎo le zhīhòu quán àn xiàqu jiù pāi hǎo le

• Don't leave too much space above our heads 上边儿别留太多 Shàngbiānr bié liú tài duō

• Try to get the ... in the picture 最好把这个...照进去 Zuìhǎo bǎ zhèi gè ... zhào jìnqù

(1) scenery 风景 fēngjǐng
(2) mountain 山 shān
(3) police/soldiers 警察/军人 jǐngchá/jūnrén
(4) building 楼 lóu

• I'm sorry, I'd rather not be in the picture, but I'd be happy to take a picture of you 对不起，我不想照相，但我很乐意给你照一张 Duìbùqǐ, wǒ bù xiǎng zhàoxiàng, dàn wǒ hěn lèyì gěi nǐ zhào yì zhāng

Listen for this

• Wǒ néng gěi nǐ zhào zhāng xiàng ma? 我能给你照张相吗？May I take picture of you?

• Nǐ néng hé wǒmen hé gè yǐng ma? 你能和我们合个影吗？Will you be in a picture with us?

• Bāng wǒ bào yí xià háizi, wǒ zhào zhāng xiàng 帮我抱一下孩子，我照张相 Hold my child so I can take a picture

3 Asking about sights

询问景点情况

Xúnwèn jǐngdiǎn qíngkuàng

Sentences

• How old is this place? 这儿有多少年历史了? Zhèr yǒu duōshao nián lìshǐ le?

• Who built this place? 这个地方是谁建的? Zhèi gè dìfang shì shéi jiàn de?

• Why here? 为什么要在这儿? Wèishénme yào zài zhèr?

• What is that? 那是什么? Nà shì shénme?

• What is this used for? 这是干什么用的? Zhèi shì gàn shénme yòng de?

• What does that mean? 那是什么意思? Nà shì shénme yìsi?

• Why is it like this? 这个为什么是这样的? Zhèigè wèishénme shì zhèyàng de?

Listen for this

• Yìqiān nián qián sēngrénmen xiūjiàn le zhè zuò miào 一千年前僧人们修建了这座庙 Monks built this temple a thousand years ago

• Tā zhīsuǒyǐ zhèyàng shì gēnjù Zhōngguó de ... 它之所以这样是根据中国的... It's like this because of Chinese ...

(1) fēngshuǐ 风水 geomancy (Fengshui)

(2) chuántǒng 传统 tradition

(3) xísú 习俗 customs

(4) qìngdiǎn 庆典 ceremony

• Zhīsuǒyǐ zài zhèr jiàn shì yīnwéi zhèr de fēngshuǐ hǎo 之所以在这儿建是因为这儿的风水好 This place was chosen because it has good Fengshui

• Jiàn qǔqiáo shì wèile hǒngpiàn guǐshén 建曲桥是为了哄骗鬼神 The zigzag bridge is meant to trick ghosts (who can only move in a straight line)

4 Hutongs (alleyways) 胡同 Hútòng

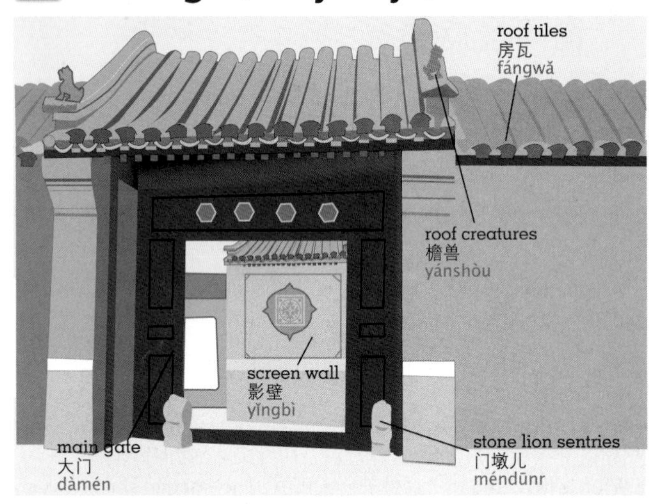

5 Houhai 后海 Hòuhǎi

Vocabulary

bar 酒吧 jiǔbā
Beihai Park 北海公园
Běihǎi Gōngyuán
cafe 咖啡厅 kāfēitīng
carefree atmosphere
愉快气氛 yúkuài qìfèn
Former Residence of
Song Qingling 宋庆龄故居
Sòng Qìnglíng Gùjū
Grand Canal 大运河 Dà Yùnhé
Houhai 后海 Hòuhǎi
hutong tours 胡同游 hútòng yóu
ice skating 滑冰 huábīng
Jishuitan 积水潭 Jīshuǐtán
Mei Lanfang Memorial Hall
梅兰芳纪念馆
Méi Lánfāng Jìniànguǎn
pedicab driver 蹬三轮儿的
dēng sānlúnr de
Qianhai 前海 Qiánhǎi
River Romance (boat tour)
好梦江南 Hǎomèng Jiāngnán
Shichahai 什刹海 Shíchàhǎi
winter swimming 冬泳 dōngyǒng
Xihai 西海 Xīhǎi
Yinding Bridge 银锭桥
Yíndìng Qiáo

Sentences

- No thanks, I like walking 谢谢，不用了，我喜欢走路 Xièxie, búyòng le, wǒ xǐhuan zǒulù
- Houhai is so romantic! 后海太浪漫了！Hòuhǎi tài làngmàn le!
- How much for the River Romance boat rental? 在好梦江南租船多少钱？Zài Hǎomèng Jiāngnán zū chuán duōshao qián?

6 Aural history

聆听历史 Língtīng lìshǐ

Vocabulary

gong 锣 luó
drum 鼓 gǔ
bell 钟 zhōng
chimes 编钟 biānzhōng
Drum Tower 鼓楼 Gǔlóu
Bell Tower 钟楼 Zhōnglóu
Big Bell Temple 大钟寺 Dàzhōngsì
Ancient Music Center 文博交流馆 Wénbó Jiāoliúguǎn

Sentences

- When will the next performance be? 下一场表演几点开始？Xià yì chǎng biǎoyǎn jǐdiǎn kāishǐ?
- I would like to reserve a ticket for the musical performance 我想预定音乐会的票 Wǒ xiǎng yùdìng yīnyuèhuì de piào
- Can I videotape it? 我能录下来吗？Wǒ néng lù xiàlái ma?
- I am a professional (bell ringer / drummer) in my country, may I give it a try? 我在我们那儿是敲(钟/鼓)专家，我能试试吗？Wǒ zài wǒmen nàr shì qiāo (zhōng / gǔ) zhuānjiā, wǒ néng shìshi ma?

7 "Humble" abodes

"寒舍" Hánshè

Vocabulary

Palace Museum 故宫博物院 Gùgōng Bówùyuàn
Forbidden City, 紫禁城 Zǐjìnchéng
Tian'anmen Gate 天安门 Tiān'ānmén
Meridian Gate 午门 Wǔmén
Watch Tower 角楼 Jiǎolóu

Humble cast

eunuch 太监 tàijian
emperor 皇帝 huángdì
son of heaven 天子 tiānzǐ
empress 皇后 huánghòu
concubine 妃嫔 fēipín
Celestial Empire 天朝大国 Tiāncháo Dàguó

Sentences

• Wow, a "Chinese art exhibition" today? This is indeed fortuitous. 啊，今天有 "中国艺术展"？太走运了 ā, jīntiān yǒu "Zhōngguó yìshù zhǎn"? Tài zǒuyùn le

Summer Palace 颐和园 Yíhéyuán

Marble boat 石舫 Shífǎng
foreign aggression 外国侵略 wàiguó qīnlüè
Eight Power Allied Army 八国联军 Bāguóliánjūn
Hall of Jade Ripples玉澜堂 Yùlántáng
Garden of Harmonious Virtue 谐趣园 Xiéqùyuán
Long Corridor 长廊 Chángláng
Hall of Benevolence and Longevity 仁寿殿 Rénshòudiàn
Longevity Hill 万寿山 Wànshòushān
extravagances 奢华 shēhuá
Empress Dowager Cixi 慈禧太后 Cíxǐ Tàihòu

• When does the park close? 公园几点关门？Gōngyuán jǐ diǎn guānmén?

• What bus can I take to the light rail station? 坐几路车能去轻轨？Zuò jǐ lù chē néng qù qīngguǐ?

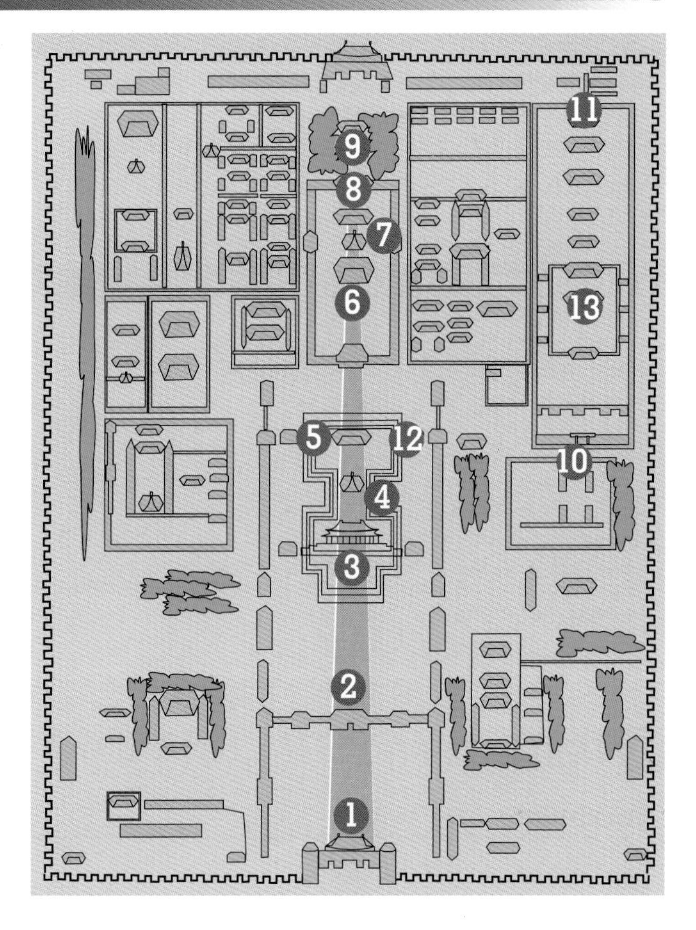

(1) Wu Gate 午门 Wǔmén
(2) Gate of Supreme Harmony 太和门 Tàihémén
(3) Hall of Supreme Harmony 太和殿 Tàihédiàn
(4) Hall of Medium Harmony 中和殿 Zhōnghédiàn
(5) Hall of Protective Harmony 保和殿 Bǎohédiàn
(6) Hall of Heavenly Purity 乾清宫 Qiánqīnggōng
(7) Hall of Union and Peace 交泰殿 Jiāotàidiàn
(8) Hall of Earthly Peace坤宁宫 Kūnnínggōng
(9) Imperial Gardens 御花园 Yùhuāyuán
(10) Nine Dragon Well 九龙壁 Jiǔlóngbì
(11) Well of the Pearl Concubine 珍妃井 Zhēnfēijǐng
(12) Hall of Clocks 钟表馆 Zhōngbiǎoguǎn
(13) Hall of Jewelry 珠宝馆 Zhūbǎoguǎn

Prince Gong's mansion 恭王府 Gōngwángfǔ

Heshen 和绅 Hé Shēn
Strange Rock Garden 怪石园 Guàishíyuán
lotus pond 荷花池 héhuāchí

• When is the Peking Opera performance? 什么时候有京剧表演? Shénme shíhou yǒu Jīngjù biǎoyǎn?

Yuanmingyuan 圆明园 Yuánmíngyuán

Opium Wars 鸦片战争 Yāpiàn Zhànzhēng
unequal treaties 不平等条约 bù píngděng tiáoyuē
Great Fountain ruins 大水法遗址 Dàshuǐfǎ yízhǐ
maze 迷宫 mígōng
canals 运河 yùnhé
lakes 湖 hú
lotus flowers 莲花 liánhuā
national humiliation 国耻 guóchǐ
amorous rendezvous 私会 sīhuì

• I'll meet you in the maze at midnight 我午夜在迷宫等你 Wǒ wǔyè zài mígōng děng nǐ

8 Tian'anmen 天安门 Tiān'ānmén

Vocabulary

flag raising ceremony 升旗仪式 shēngqí yíshì
flag lowering ceremony 降旗仪式 jiàngqí yíshì
May Fourth Movement 五四运动 Wǔsì Yùndòng
Liberation 解放 Jiěfàng
Founding of the People's Republic of China
中华人民共和国成立 Zhōnghuá Rénmín Gònghéguó chénglì
The Chinese people have stood up!
中国人民站起来了! Zhōngguó rénmín zhàn qǐlái le!
kite flying 放风筝 fàng fēngzheng
Mao portrait 毛主席像 Máo Zhǔxí xiàng

Sentences

- I'll meet you by the portrait of Mao Zedong 我在毛主席像前等你 Wǒ zài Máo Zhǔxí xiàng qián děng nǐ

- What time is the flag (raising / lowering) ceremony? (升旗/降旗)仪式几点开始? (Shēngqí / jiàngqí) yíshì jǐdiǎn kāishǐ?

- Slogans 口号 Kǒuhào

  (1) Long Live the People's Republic of China
  中华人民共和国万岁 Zhōnghuá Rénmín Gònghéguó wànsuì
  (2) Long Live the Unity of the Peoples of the World
  世界人民大团结万岁 Shìjiè rénmín dà tuánjié wànsuì

- Great Hall of the People: 人民大会堂 Rénmín Dàhuìtáng

  (1) Socialism with Chinese characteristics
  有中国特色的社会主义 yǒu Zhōngguó tèsè de shèhuìzhǔyì
  (2) National People's Congress 人民代表大会 Rénmín Dàibiǎo Dàhuì
  (3) Communist Party 共产党 Gòngchǎndǎng
  (4) State Council 国务院 Guówùyuàn

- China National Museum 中国国家博物馆 Zhōngguó Guójiā Bówùguǎn

  (1) Museum of Chinese Revolution
  中国革命博物馆 Zhōngguó Gémìng Bówùguǎn
  (2) Museum of Chinese History
  中国历史博物馆 Zhōngguó Lìshǐ Bówùguǎn

- Chairman Mao Mausoleum, 毛主席纪念堂 Máozhǔxí Jìniàntáng

  (1) Great Helmsman 伟大舵手 Wěidà Duòshǒu
  (2) dead body 遗体 yítǐ
  (3) security check 安全检查 ānquán jiǎnchá
  (4) embalm 防腐处理 fángfǔ chùlǐ
  (5) revolution 革命 gémìng
  (6) military genius 军事天才 jūnshì tiāncái

- Monument to the People's Heroes 人民英雄纪念碑 Rénmín Yīngxióng Jìniànbēi

  (1) oppressed masses
  被压迫的劳苦大众 bèi yāpò de láokǔ dàzhòng
  (2) British opium 英国鸦片 Yīngguó yāpiàn
  (3) Struggle to the bitter end! 奋斗到底! Fèngdòu dàodǐ!

9 Temple talk 寺庙 Sìmiào

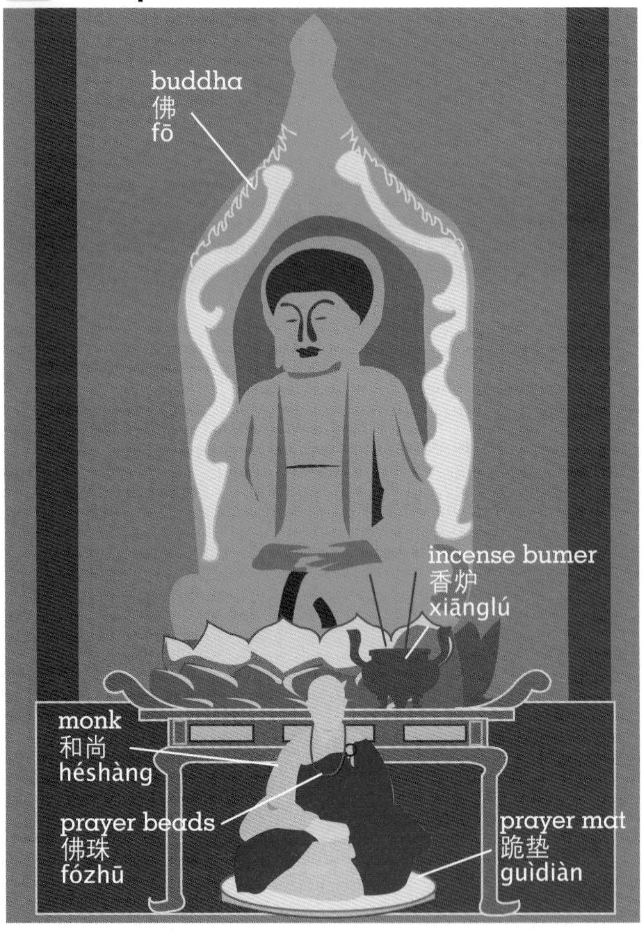

Vocabulary

altar 祭坛 jìtán
incense burner 香炉 xiānglú
prayer beads 佛珠 fózhū
prayer mat (祈祷时的)跪垫 (qídǎo shí de) guìdiàn
prayer wheel 法轮 fǎlún
monk 和尚/道士 héshang/dàoshi
nun 修女/尼姑 xiūnǚ/nígū

Buddha 佛 fó

Religious vocabulary 宗教词汇 Zōngjiào cíhuì

Taoism 道教 Dàojiào
Buddhism 佛教 Fójiào
Islam 伊斯兰教 Yīsīlánjiào
imam 阿訇 āhòng
sacrifices 祭品 jìpǐn
religion/s 宗教 zōngjiào
rituals 仪式 yíshì
temple fair 庙会 miàohuì
numerology 生辰八字占卜 shēngchénbāzì zhānbǔ
annual report to heaven 祭天 jì tiān
kowtow / genuflect 磕头 kētóu
fasting 斋戒 zhāijiè
pray 祈祷 qǐdǎo
prayers 祷告词 dǎogàocí
priest 牧师 mùshī
burn incense 烧香 shāo xiāng
devil dances 驱魔舞 qūmówǔ
Taoist clinic 道教慈济义诊诊所 Dàojiào cíjì yìzhěn zhěnsuǒ
Laozi 老子 Lǎozǐ
Layers of Hell 地狱层数 Dìyù céngshù

- Department of Resurrection 掌放生司 Zhǎng Fàngshēng Sī
- Department of Birds and Animals
  掌飞禽走兽司 Zhǎng Fēiqín Zǒushòu Sī
- Department of Morality for Officials 掌官职司 Zhǎng Guānzhí Sī

Sentences

- May I burn incense? 我能烧香吗？ Wǒ néng shāo xiāng ma?

- I am a ... 我是... Wǒ shì ...

(1) Christian 基督徒 Jīdūtú
(2) Muslim 穆斯林 Mùsīlín
(3) Buddhist 佛教徒 Fójiàotú
(4) Jew 犹太教徒 Yóutàijiàotú
(5) Catholic 天主教徒 Tiānzhǔjiàotú

- I am an atheist 我是无神论者 Wǒ shì wùshénlùnzhě

- To get rich, who should I pray to? 想发财要拜哪个神？ Xiǎng fācái yào bài něigè shén?

- Where is the nearest mosque? 最近的清真寺在哪儿？ Zuìjìn de qīngzhēnsì zài nǎr?

- What religion are you? 你信什么教？ Nǐ xìn shénme jiào?

- Can you teach me the devil dance? 你能教我跳驱魔舞吗？ Nǐ néng jiāo wǒ tiào qūmówǔ ma?

- How would the emperor pray for good harvest? 皇帝是怎么祈求风调雨顺的？ Huángdì shì zěnme qǐqiú fēngtiáoyǔshùn de?

Listen for this

- Qù Huíyīngbì nàr chànggēr bǐjiào hǎo 去回音壁那儿唱歌儿比较好 The Echo wall is good for singing
- jìpǐn 祭品 sacrifice
- Zhù nǐ hǎoyùn 祝你好运 Good luck
- zhùfú 祝福 blessing
- Wǒ shì fójiàotú 我是佛教徒 I am a Buddhist

Temples 寺庙 Sìmiào

Azure Cloud Temple碧云寺 Bìyún Sì
Baitasi 白塔寺 Báitǎ Sì
Confucius Temple 孔庙 Kǒng Miào
Dongyue Miao 东岳庙 Dōngyuè Miào
Guanghua Temple 广化寺 Guǎnghuà Sì
Guozijian 国子监 Guózǐjiān
Lama Temple 雍和宫 Yōnghégōng
Niujie Mosque 牛街清真寺 Niújiē Qīngzhēnsi
Reclining Buddha Temple 卧佛寺Wòfó Sì
St Michael's Cathedral 东郊民巷教堂 Dōngjiāomínxiàng Jiàotáng
Temple of Heaven 天坛 Tiāntán
Temple of the Origin of the Dharma 法源寺 Fǎyuán Sì
White Cloud Temple 白云观 Báiyún Guàn

10 Tombs 陵墓 Língmù

Vocabulary

Ming Tombs 十三陵 Shísānlíng
spirit way 神路 shénlù
stone statues 石像生 Shíxiàngshēng

Changling 长陵 Chánglíng
Dingling 定陵 Dìnglíng
Zhaoling 昭陵 Zhāolíng
Jesuit 耶酥 Yēsū
Beijing Administrative College 北京行政学院 Běijīng Xíngzhèng Xuéyuàn
astronomy wiz 天文学专家 tiānwénxué zhuānjiā
trigonometry 三角几何 sānjiǎo jǐhé
Euclid 欧几里得 ōujīlǐdé
Eastern Qing Tombs清东陵 Qīng Dōng Líng
Western Qing Tombs清西陵 Qīng Xī Líng
Dabaotai Xi Han Dynasty Tomb 大葆台西汉墓 Dàbǎotái Xīhàn mù
Matteo Ricci 利玛窦 Lìmǎdòu

Sentences

- Which tombs are the best? 哪些陵墓是最好的? Nǎxiē língmù shì zuìhǎo de?

- Why can't we visit the other tombs? 我们干嘛不去别的陵墓看看? Wǒmen gànmá bú qù bié de língmù kànkan?

Watch for this

- Tíngyè zhěngxiū 停业整修 Closed for renovation

11 Museums 博物馆 Bówùguǎn

Vocabulary

(For art and art museum vocabulary, see Art and Culture, p90)

museum pass 博物馆通票 bówùguǎn tōngpiào
painting 绘画 huìhuà
calligraphy 书法 shūfǎ
Buddhist statue 佛像 fóxiàng
AK 47 AK47步枪 AK sìqī bùqiāng
tank 坦克 tǎnkè
Korean War 朝鲜战争 Cháoxiǎn Zhànzhēng
War of Resistance Against Japanese Aggression 抗日战争 Kàngrì Zhànzhēng

Sentences

• Where is the Museum of Ancient Architechture? 古代建筑博物馆在哪儿？ Gǔdài Jiànzhù Bówùguǎn zài nǎr?

• Where is the calligraphy? 看书法在哪儿？ Kàn shūfǎ zài nǎr?

• Are there any events at the observatory tonight? 古观象台今天晚上有什么活动吗？ Gǔ Guānxiàngtái jīntiān wǎnshàng yǒu shénme huódòng ma?

Listen for this

• Gǔdài Jiànzhù Bówùguǎn zài Xiānnóngtán 古代建筑博物馆在先农坛
The Museum of Ancient Architecture is at the Xiannong Temple

• Gǔ Qiánbì Bówùguǎn zài Déshèngmén 古钱币博物馆在德胜门
The Ancient Coin Museum is at Deshengmen

Museums

• Ancient Coin Museum 古钱币博物馆 Gǔ Qiánbì Bówùguǎn
• Ancient Observatory 古观象台 Gǔ Guānxiàngtái
• Arthur Sackler Museum
赛克勒考古与艺术博物馆 Sàikèlè Kǎogǔ yǔ Yìshù Bówùguǎn
• Beijing Folk Arts Museum
北京民间艺术博物馆 Běijīng Mínjiān Yìshù Bówùguǎn
• Beijing Police Museum 北京警察博物馆 Běijīng Jǐngchá Bówùguǎn
• Cao Xueqin Memorial Hall 曹雪芹纪念馆 Cáo Xuěqín Jìniànguǎn
• Chinese Military History Museum
中国军事历史博物馆 Zhōngguó Jūnshì Lìshǐ Bówùguǎn
• Dragon Bone Hill 龙骨山 Lónggǔ Shān
• Former Residence of Mao Dun 茅盾故居 Máo Dùn Gùjū
• Guo Moruo Museum郭沫若纪念馆 Guō Mòruò Jìniànguǎn
• Huguang Huiguan: Peking Opera Museum
湖广会馆：京剧博物馆 Húguǎng Huìguǎn: Jīngjù Bówùguǎn
• Lao She Former Residence and Museum
老舍故居和博物馆 Lǎo Shě Gùjū hé Bówùguǎn
• Lu Xun Museum 鲁迅纪念馆 Lǔ Xùn Jìniànguǎn
• Museum of Ancient Architecture
古代建筑博物馆 Gǔdài Jiànzhù Bówùguǎn
• National Art Museum 中国美术馆 Zhōngguó Měishùguǎn
• National Museum of Modern Chinese Literature
中国现代文学馆 Zhōngguó Xiàndài Wénxué Guǎn

- Peking Man Museum 北京人博物馆 Běijīngrén Bówùguǎn
- Poly Art Museum 保利艺术博物馆 Bǎolì Yìshù Bówùguǎn
- Xu Beihong Museum 徐悲鸿纪念馆 Xú Bēihóng Jìniànguǎn

12 Parks 公园 Gōngyuán

Vocabulary

grass 草地 cǎodì
tree 树 shù
flower 花 huā
leaf 叶子 yèzi
hill 山 shān
lake 湖 hú
island 岛 dǎo
play area 游乐区 yóulè qū
taichi 太极拳 tàijíquán
trampoline 蹦蹦床 bèngbèngchuáng
bonsai tree 盆景 pénjǐng
orchid 兰花 lánhuā
lotus 荷花 héhuā

Sentences

- Why is this called the "Guilty" Scholar Tree? 为什么这棵树叫"有罪"槐树？ Wèishénme zhè kē shù jiào "Yǒu zuì" Huáishù?
- Who is IM Pei? 贝聿铭是谁？ Bèi Lǜmíng shì shéi?
- When will the lotuses bloom? 荷花什么时候开？ Héhuā shénme shíhòu kāi?
- Am I too big to bounce on the trampoline? 我这么大的人能不能玩蹦蹦床？ Wǒ zhème dà de rén néng bùnéng wánr bèngbèngchuáng?
- How do I get down the hill? 我怎么下山？ Wǒ zěnme xià shān?
- Now that's what I call a dagoba! 这才是真正的舍利塔！ Zhè cái shì zhēnzhèng de shělìtǎ!

Listen for this

- Míngcháo zuìhòu yí wèi huángdì jiùshì zài nèi kē shù shàng diào sǐ de 明朝最后一位皇帝就是在那棵树上吊死的 The last Ming emperor hung himself on that tree

• Bèi Lǜmíng shì yí wèi shìjiè zhīmíng de jiànzhùshī 贝聿铭是一位世界知名的建筑师 IM Pei is a world famous architect

• Héhuā huì zài xiàtiān shèngkāi 荷花会在夏天盛开 The lotuses bloom in the summer

• lǎnchē 缆车 chairlift/cable car

Parks

Beihai Park 北海公园 Běihǎi Gōngyuán
Botanical Garden 植物园 Zhíwùyuán
Chaoyang Park 朝阳公园 Cháoyáng Gōngyuán
Ditan 地坛 Dìtán
Fragrant Hills Park 香山公园 Xiāngshān Gōngyuán
Grand View Garden 大观园 Dàguānyuán
Guanyuan Park 官园 Guānyuán
Honglingjin Park 红领巾公园 Hónglǐngjīn Gōngyuán
Longtanhu Park 龙潭湖公园 Lóngtánhú Gōngyuán
Prospect Hill 景山公园 Jǐngshān Gōngyuán
Qingnianhu Park 青年湖公园 Qīngniánhú Gōngyuán
Ritan 日坛 Rìtán
Taoranting Park 陶然亭公园 Táorántíng Gōngyuán
Temple of Heaven 天坛 Tiāntán
Tuanjiehu Park 团结湖公园 Tuánjiéhú Gōngyuán
Xinglong Park 兴隆公园 Xīnglóng Gōngyuán
Yuyuantan 玉渊潭公园 Yùyuāntán Gōngyuán
Zhongshan Park 中山公园 Zhōngshān Gōngyuán
Zizhuyuan 紫竹院公园 Zǐzhúyuàn Gōngyuán

13 The Great Wall 长城 Chángchéng

Vocabulary

Oy, the humanity! 天啊！ Tiān a!
trinket seller 卖小玩意儿的 mài xiǎo wányìr de
Great Wall T-shirt 长城T恤衫 Chángchéng T-xùshān
Qin Shihuang 秦始皇 Qínshǐhuáng
twisted ankle 脚崴了 jiǎo wǎi le
steep climb 陡坡 dǒupō
toboggan ride 滑道 huádào
porter 挑夫 tiāofū

watchtower 烽火台 fēnghuǒtái
wild Great Wall 野长城 yě Chángchéng

Sentences

- Gee, the Great Wall sure is magnificent! 哇！长城真伟大！ Wā! Chángchéng zhēn wěidà!

- The Great Wall is NOT visible from the moon 在月球上是看不到长城的 Zài yuèqiú shàng shì kàn bú dào Chángchéng de

Listen for this

- Xiūjiàn Chángchéng shì wèile fángyù wàidí rùqīn 修建长城是为了防御外敌入侵 The wall was built to keep the invaders out

- Dàn xiànzài wǒmen hé wàiguórén yìqǐ xīnshǎng tā 但现在我们和外国人一起欣赏它 But now we enjoy it with foreigners together

- Great Wall locales

Bādálǐng 八达岭 Badaling
Jūyōngguān 居庸关 Juyongguan
Mùtiányù慕田峪 Mutianyu
Huánghuāchéng 黄花城 Huanghuacheng
Sīmǎtái 司马台 Simatai
Jīnshānlǐng 金山岭 Jinshanling

Notes

NIGHTLIFE ►

1 Going out 外出 Wàichū

Sentences

- Where can I go for some fun? 哪儿有好玩儿的可以去？ Nǎr yǒu hǎowánr de kěyǐ qù?
- Is there anything close by? 附近有地儿吗？ Fùjìn yǒu dìr ma?
- Where can I find a ... ? / I want to go to a ... 哪儿有...？ ／我想去... Nǎr yǒu...? / wǒ xiǎng qù...

(1) bar / pub 酒吧／酒馆 jiǔbā / jiǔguǎn
(2) club / disco 夜总会／迪厅 yèzǒnghuì / dītīng
(3) café 咖啡厅 kāfēitīng
(4) Karaoke 卡拉OK/KTV kǎlā OK / KTV
(5) live music venue 音乐现场演出的地方 yīnyuè xiànchǎng yǎnchū de dìfāng
(6) cinema 电影院 diànyǐngyuàn
(7) theater 剧场 jùchǎng
(8) pool hall 台球厅 táiqiútīng
(9) bowling alley 保龄球馆 bǎolíngqiúguǎn
(10) bathhouse 洗浴中心 xǐyù zhōngxīn

• Are you doing anything tonight? 你今天晚上有事吗？ Nǐ jīntiān wǎnshàng yǒushì ma?

• Do you have any plans for (today/this afternoon/tonight)? 你（今天/今天下午/今天晚上）有安排吗？ Nǐ (jīntiān/jīntiān xiàwǔ/jīntiān wǎnshàng) yǒu ānpái ma?

• Would you like to go out with me? (formal) 您愿意和我一起出去吗？ Nín xiǎng hé wǒ yìqǐ chūqù ma?

• Would you like to go out with me? (informal) 想跟我出去遛一圈儿吗？ Xiǎng gēn wǒ chūqù liū yìquānr ma?

• Would you like to have a dinner with me? 你愿意和我一起吃晚饭吗？ Nǐ yuànyì hé wǒ yìqǐ chī wǎnfàn ma ?

Listen for this

• Hǎo a 好啊 Yeah / alright

• Hǎo, méi wèntí 好，没问题 Sure, no problem

• Bù le, xièxie 不了，谢谢 No thanks

• Kǒngpà bùxíng 恐怕不行 I'm afraid I can't

• Wǒ bù xiǎng qù 我不想去 I don't want to go

• Wǒ bú huì ... 我不会... I can't ...
(1) dance 跳舞 tiàowǔ
(2) bowl 打保龄 dǎ bǎolíng
(3) sing 唱歌 chànggē

2 Meeting up 见面 Jiànmiàn

Sentences

• What time should we meet? 我们几点见面？ Wǒmen jǐdiǎn jiànmiàn?

• Where will we meet? 我们在哪儿见面？ Wǒmen zài nǎr jiànmiàn?

• Let's meet ... 我们...见面 Wǒmén ... jiànmiàn

(1) at eight o' clock 八点 bādiǎn
(2) at the entrance 在门口 zài ménkǒu
(3) at your place 在你那儿 zài nǐ nàr
(4) at the Wudaokou subway station
在五道口城铁站 zài Wǔdàokǒu chéngtiě zhàn

• I'll pick you up 我去接你 Wǒ qù jiē nǐ

• Are you ready? 你准备好了吗？ Nǐ zhǔnbèi hǎo le ma?

• I'm ready 我准备好了 Wǒ zhǔnbèi hǎo le

• I'm running a little late 我有点儿晚了 Wǒ yǒudiǎnr wǎn le

• Where will you be? 你会在哪儿？ Nǐ huì zài nǎr?

• How will I find you? 我怎么找你？ Wǒ zěnmè zhǎo nǐ?

• If I'm not there by 10 o'clock, don't wait for me 如果我10点还没到的话就别等我了 Rúguǒ wǒ shídiǎn hái méi dào de huà jiù bié děng wǒ le

• I have to be home by ... 我得...前回家 Wǒ děi ... qián huíjiā

• OK 好的 Hǎode

• I'll see you then (in a little while) 待会儿见 Dāi huìr jiàn

• I'm looking forward to it 我很期待 Wǒ hěn qīdài

• Sorry I'm late 不好意思，我迟到了 Bùhǎoyìsi, wǒ chídào le

3 Out on the town

在外面玩 Zai waimiàn wan

Sentences

• When do you (open / close)? 几点（开门/关门）？ Jǐdiǎn (kāimén / guānmén)?

• When does the band actually start playing? 乐队什么时候开始演出？ Yuèduì shénme shíhou kāishǐ yǎnchū?

Barroom Basics

Handy phrases for all the fresh faces

by Eric Abrahamsen

September brings waves of new foreign students to the capital, eager to be initiated into the mysteries of the Chinese tongue, and more or less doomed to the drink-sodden study habits of their predecessors. The average liúxuéshēng (留学生 exchange student) tends to make local bars a pivotal part of the curriculum, and we provide the following not to condone student drinking, but to help you get more out of your evening than a headache. And if a few long-term expats who still haven't progressed beyond "ni hao" (you know who you are) benefit as well, then that's all the better.

- Is there a quiet corner in here where I can study? 这儿有没有比较安静的地方我可以学习的？Zhèr yǒu méiyǒu bǐjiào ānjìng de dìfāng wǒ kěyǐ xuéxí de?
- I need to leave now, I have classes at eight in the morning 我现在必须要走了，早上8点我有课 Wǒ xiànzài bìxū yào zǒu le, zǎoshàng bā diǎn wǒ yǒu kè
- Oh, all right, I'll have another 好，我再要一杯 Hǎo, wǒ zài yào yì bēi
- I think *baijiu* is absolutely foul 我觉得白酒真的太难喝了 Wǒ juéde báijiǔ zhēn de tài nán hē le
- I am a drooling fool for baijiu 我特爱喝白酒 Wǒ tè ài hē báijiǔ
- I'll teach you English in exchange for beer 我教你英语，你请我喝免费啤酒，怎么样？Wǒ jiāo nǐ yīngyǔ, nǐ qǐng wǒ hē miǎnfèi píjiǔ, zěnme yàng?
- I feel sick 我觉得难受 Wǒ juéde nánshòu
- My friend feels sick 我朋友觉得难受 Wǒ péngyǒu juéde nánshòu
- Can you help me call a cab? 你能帮我叫一辆出租车吗？Nǐ néng bāng wǒ jiào yí liàng chūzūchē ma?
- Can you please help me lift him up? 你能帮我把他扶起来吗？Nǐ néng bāng wǒ bǎ tā fú qǐlái ma?
- The music in here is awful 这儿的音乐实在难听 Zhèr de yīnyuè shízài nántīng
- My drink is watery/too small 我的酒酒劲儿不够/太小了 Wǒde jiǔ jiǔjìnr bú gòu/tài xiǎo le
- Please don't clap at me 不，请别招呼我 Bù, qǐng bié zhāohu wǒ
- No, I don't want ... 不，我不想(要) Bù, wǒ bù xiǎng (yào)
  (1) a massage 按摩 àn mó
  (2) DVDs
  (3) to go to a lady bar 去女士酒吧 qù nǚshì jiǔbā

• When is happy hour? 欢乐时光是什么时候？Huānlè shíguāng shì shénme shíhou?

• I want a drink 我想来杯喝的 Wǒ xiǎng lái bēi hē de

• Is there a service charge? 有没有服务费？Yǒu méiyǒu fúwùfèi?

• What's the cover charge? 门票多少钱？Ménpiào duōshǎo qián?

• Is there minimum consumption charge? 有没有最低消费？Yǒu méiyǒu zuìdī xiāofèi?

• security guard 保安 bǎo'ān

• Hey, calm down 嘿，冷静点儿 Hèi, lěngjìng diǎnr

• Where's the manager? 经理在哪儿？Jīnglǐ zài nǎr?

• I was just roughed up by your security guards 我刚才被你们的保安打了 Wǒ gāngcái bèi nǐmen de bǎo'ān dǎ le

• Make it stiff 要烈一点儿 Yào liè yìdiǎnr

• Chivas and green tea 芝华士和绿茶 Zhīhuáshì hé lǜchá

• Do we pay for drinks now or at the end? 我们是现在给酒钱还是最后结？Wǒmen shì xiànzài gěi jiǔqián háishì zuìhòu jié?

• Can I see the bill? 我能看看账单吗？Wǒ néng kànkan zhàngdān ma?

4 Cutting a rug 跳舞 Tiàowǔ

Sentences

• Can I have this dance? 你想跟我跳舞吗？Nǐ xiǎng gēn wǒ tiàowǔ ma?

• Let's dance! 咱们跳舞吧！Zánmen tiàowǔ ba!

• Dancing is good exercise 跳舞是个很好的运动 Tiàowǔ shì gè hěnhǎo de yùndòng

• Don't be shy 别害羞 Bié hàixiū

• I bet you're a good dancer 我估计你很会跳舞 Wǒ gūjì nǐ hěn huì tiàowǔ

• As soon as we start dancing everyone else will too 只要我们开始跳舞，大家就会跟着跳起来 Zhǐyào wǒmen kāishǐ tiàowǔ, dàjiā jiù huì gēn zhe tiào qǐlái

• Shake your booty! 扭扭屁股啊！ Niǔniǔ pìgu a!

• What's your favorite kind of dance? 你最喜欢跳什么舞？ Nǐ zuì xǐhuān tiào shénme wǔ?

- African (traditional) dance 非洲（传统）舞 Fēizhōu (chuántǒng) wǔ
- ballet 芭蕾舞 bāléiwǔ
- belly dancing 肚皮舞 dùpíwǔ
- bhangra (Indian) 印度舞 Yìndù wǔ
- bounce 蹦 bèng
- break dancing 霹雳舞 pīlìwǔ
- chacha 恰恰 qiàqià
- Chinese traditional folk dance 中国传统民族舞 Zhōngguó chuántǒng mínzúwǔ
- disco 迪斯科 dísīkē
- electronic music 电子音乐 diànzǐ yīnyuè
- jazz 爵士 juéshì
- lambada ("the forbidden dance") 伦巴达舞 lúnbādáwǔ
- latin dance 拉丁舞 lādīngwǔ
- macarena 玛卡莲娜 mǎkǎliánnà
- mambo 曼波 mànbō
- modern dance 现代舞 xiàndàiwǔ
- reggae 雷鬼 léiguǐ
- rhumba 伦巴 lúnbā
- salsa 萨尔萨/莎莎 sà-ěr-sà/shāshā
- samba 桑巴 sāngbā
- street dancing 街舞 jiēwǔ
- tap 踢踏舞 tītāwǔ
- tango 探戈 tāngē

Listen for this

• Xiǎoxīn, bié cǎi wǒ jiǎo! 小心，别踩我脚！ Be careful! Don't step on my feet!

Sentences

• You're a very skillful dancer 你跳得很好 Nǐ tiào de hěn hǎo

• I've got no rhythm 我没有节奏感 Wǒ méiyǒu jiézòugǎn

• What kind of music do you like to listen to? 你喜欢听什么音乐？ Nǐ xǐhuan tīng shénme yīnyuè?

For those about to rock ...

by Jon Campbell

You don't have to master musical Mandarin to get a gig in Beijing, but surviving the sound check will be easier with choice bits of rock (摇滚 yáogǔn) lingo.

To strike the right attitude, drop the "*qing wen*"s (请问, pardon me) and address everyone as *gemenr* (哥们儿 bro, buddy, dude). For complements, we can't emphasize enough the importance of the word "cow" (牛 niú), whether in punk (朋克儿 péngkèr), post-punk (后朋克儿 hòu péngkèr), new wave (新浪 xīn làng), nu metal (新金属 xīn jīnshǔ), black metal (黑金属 hēi jīnshǔ), death metal (死亡金属 sǐwǎng jīnshǔ), speed metal (速度金属 sùdù jīnshǔ), or post-rock (后摇 hòu yáo) situations.

wèi 喂 check

It is essential to choose carefully the words you use to test the mic so as to maximize the effect thereupon. When uttering your first amplified words, pretend you're a pot-bellied manager with a pleather clutch purse answering his phone after two full rounds of its pop song ringtone. Repeat *wei* as question and exclamation until drummer gets upset and starts bashing.

huíxiǎng 回响 reverb

Thanks to the popularity of karaoke, no speaker in town is safe from the horrors of reverb. To avoid a vocal style that sounds as if it were coming from within a 10-story soup can inside an oversized treasure chest on the ocean floor, simply say: "Gē'menr, wǒmen bù shì zài Màilèdí chàng gēr ne. Bǎ huíxiǎng guān xiǎo" (哥们儿我们不是在麦乐迪唱歌儿呢。把回响关小 Buddy, this ain't freakin' Melody KTV, turn the reverb down).

xiàoguǒqì 效果器 effects pedals

While there are proper Chinese words for each effect pedal, one can get away with Sinicizing their English names. Thus, "wah" becomes 哇 wā and "delay" becomes 低瑞 dīruì. *Zàoyīn* (噪音 distortion), a lovely word also meaning "noise," will come in handy to describe your pedal and the sonic soup emanating from the speakers.

yīnxiǎng 音响 amplifier (and speaker)

Use this term in such sentences as, "Why does my bass amp fart every time I play a note?" (为什么这个贝司音响每次弹都出放屁声儿? Wéishènme zhè gè bèisī yīnxiǎng měi cì tán dōu chū fàngpì shēngr?) or "When will you guys fix this speaker?" (你们什么时候会把这个音响修好了? Nǐmen shénme shíhòu huì bǎ zhè gè yīnxiǎng xiū hǎo le?). The answer will invariably be "*méi shìr*!" (没事儿 No big deal!).

tiáoyīnshī 调音师 sound technician

The character 师 shī (scholar) implies that the technician is schooled in the art of sound. Don't be fooled. The dude behind the desk (tiáoyīn tái 调音台) is unlikely to have earned his title: hints include his use of the verb "play" (wánr 玩儿) in reference to his duties, an overabundance of reverb, and his inability to figure out the source of the feedback (回响 huíxiǎng).

shèbèi 设备 equipment

Refers to everything from mixing desk (调音台 tiáoyīntái) to drum kit (架子鼓 jiàzigǔ) to microphones (麦克风 màikèfēng) to cable (线 xiàn, measure word: 根 gēnr). The venue will say, "Wǒmen yǒu sǔoyǒu xūyào de shèbèi" (我们有所有需要的设备 we have all the equipment necessary), to which a common response might be, "Nǐ yǒu méiyǒu méi bèi yǎo guò de chǎpiàn?" (你有没有没被咬过的镲片? Do you have any cymbals without bite-sized chunks missing?)

Other useful phrases:

- So sorry, but we don't know how to play ... 不好意思我们不知道怎么弹... Bù hǎo yìsi, wǒmen bù zhīdào zěnme tán ...

(1) Hotel California 加州宾馆 jiāzhōu bīnguǎn
(2) Country Roads 乡村公路 xiāngcūn gōnglù

- Shut up! We don't play requests, this ain't freakin' Melody KTV 闭嘴! 我们不弹那个，这不是你该死的麦乐迪卡啦OK! Bì zuì! Yāoqiú bù xíng, zhè bú shì nǐ gāisǐde Màilèdí kǎlā OK!

- No, I don't pay cover ... 我不买门票... Wǒ bù mǎi ménpiào ...

(1) I'm in a rock band
我是摇滚乐队的成员 Wǒ shì yáogǔn yuèduì de chéngyuán
(2) I'm too cool 我太牛了 Wǒ tài niú le
(3) I'm friends with the guitarist / manager
我是吉他手/经理的朋友 ... Wǒ shì jítāshǒu / jīnglǐ de péngyǒu
(4) Don't you know who I am?
难道你不知道我是谁? ... Nándào nǐ bù zhīdào wǒ shì shéi?

"alternative" 非主流 fēi zhǔliú
caribbean 加勒比海音乐 jiālèbǐhǎi yīnyuè
classical 古典 gǔdiǎn
experimental 试验音乐 shìyàn yīnyuè
Indian 印度音乐 Yìndù yīnyuè
rock and roll 摇滚 yáogǔn
pop 流行 liúxíng
punk 朋克 péngkè
rap 说唱 shuōchàng

• You can really ... 你很会... Nǐ hěn huì ...

spin转 zhuàn
lead 带 dài
follow 跟 gēn
wiggle 扭 niǔ

• Everybody in the crowd (all together) ... 大家一起来... Dàjiā yìqǐ lái ...

holla 叫好 jiàohǎo
scream! 喝彩 hècǎi
shake everything you got 摇摆 yáobǎi
nod your head 点点头 diǎndiǎn tóu

• Dude, this band rocks! 哥们儿，这乐队真牛！Gēménr, zhèi yuèduì zhēn niú!

• They push the boundaries of music, and taste 他们让广大群众的耳朵经受了一次考验 Tāmen ràng guǎndà qúnzhòng de ěrduo jīngshòu le yícì kǎoyàn

• That's my jam 这是我的歌儿 Zhèi shì wǒ de gēr

Listen for this

• dance partner 舞伴 wǔbàn

• tacit / secret understanding 默契 mòqì

• You dance like ... 你跳得很像... Nǐ tiào de hěn xiàng ...
(1) a seal 海豹 hǎibào
(2) a top / dradle / dervish 陀螺 tuóluó
(3) Michael Jackson 麦克.杰克逊 Màikè Jiékèxùn
(4) a professional 专业舞蹈演员 zhuānyè wǔdǎo yǎnyuán
(5) a penguin 企鹅 qǐ'é
(6) a plank of wood 木板 mùbǎn

• Your dance style is fun to watch 你跳舞的风格很有意思 Nǐ tiàowǔ de fēnggé hěn yǒu yìsi

5 Romance 恋爱 Liàn'ài

Pick up lines

- Can I sit here? 我能坐这儿吗？Wǒ néng zuò zhèr ma?

- Can I get you something to drink? 我能给你点杯喝的吗？Wǒ néng gěi nǐ diǎn bēi hēde ma?

- Need a light? 要打火机吗？Yào dǎhuǒjī ma?

- How about a dance? 可以跳个舞吗？Kěyǐ tiào gè wǔ ma?

- Want to get out of here? 想出去吗？Xiǎng chūqù ma?

- Where should we go? 我们去哪儿？Wǒmen qù nǎr?

- Can I get your phone number? 能把你的电话给我吗？Néng bǎ nǐ de diànhuà gěi wǒ ma?

Rejections

- Sorry, I already have a (boyfriend / girlfriend) 对不起，我已经有(男朋友/女朋友了 Duìbùqǐ, wǒ yǐjīng yǒu (nánpéngyou/nǚpéngyou) le

- I'm here with my boyfriend / girlfriend 我跟我男朋友/女朋友一起来的 Wǒ gēn wǒ nánpéngyou / nǚpéngyou yìqǐ lái de

- No thank you 不用了，谢谢 Búyòng le, xièxie

- How dare you!? 你敢！？ Nǐ gǎn!?

- Leave me alone 别烦我 Bié fán wǒ

Listen for this

- Zěnme kěnéng? 怎么可能？As if?

Compliments

- You look pretty / handsome 你真漂亮/帅 Nǐ zhēn piàoliàng/shuài

- You look (cute/sexy) 你很（可爱/性感） Nǐ hěn (kě'ài/xìnggǎn)
- You're so cool! 你真酷 Nǐ zhēn kù
- You're really nice (a good person) 你真是个好人 Nǐ zhēn shì gè hǎorén
- You can really dance! 你真会跳舞！Nǐ zhēn huì tiàowǔ!
- You have such a sweet smile 你笑起来很甜 Nǐ xiào qǐlái hěn tián
- You have such beautiful eyes 你的眼睛很美 Nǐ de yǎnjing hěn měi
- You're smart/clever 你很聪明 Nǐ hěn cōngming
- You're fantastic/formidable 你很厉害 Nǐ hěn lìhai
- You're really interesting 你很有意思 Nǐ hěn yǒu yìsi
- You're different from the others 你和他们不一样 Nǐ hé tāmen bù yíyàng
- You're body is kickin'! 你的身材倍儿棒！Nǐ de shēncái bèir bàng!
- I've never met someone as ... as you 我从来没有见过像你这么...的人 Wǒ cónglái méiyǒu jiànguò xiàng nǐ zhème ... de rén

(1) wise 有智慧 yǒu zhìhuì
(2) tasteful 有品味 yǒu pǐnwèi
(3) interesting (great personality) 有个性 yǒu gèxìng
(4) curious 好奇 hàoqí
(5) funny / humorous 幽默 yōumò
(6) elegant / graceful 优雅 yōuyǎ
(7) savvy 懂事儿 dǒngshìr
(8) fun 好玩儿 hǎowánr

- You're really special 你真特别 Nǐ zhēn tèbié

Receiving a compliment

- No, not really (modest, literally "where? where?") 哪里哪里 Nǎlǐ nǎlǐ
- You flatter me / I don't deserve it 不敢当 Bù gǎn dāng
- I have my ... to thank 我要谢谢我的... Wǒ yào xièxie wǒ de ...

(1) mother 妈妈 māma
(2) master 师傅 shīfu
(3) hair stylist 理发师 lǐfàshī
(4) good luck 好运气 hǎo yùnqì
(5) coach 教练 jiàoliàn

Teasing

- Stop teasing me 别逗我 Bié dòu wǒ
- I'm joking 我开玩笑 Wǒ kāi wánxiào
- Don't make fun of me me 别笑我 Bié xiào wǒ
- Why don't you laugh? 你怎么不笑？ Nǐ zěnme bú xiào?
- Too much / gone too far 太过分了 Tài guòfèn le
- I'm furious! 气死我了！ Qì sǐ wǒ le!
- Please! Oh I beg you! 拜托！ Bàituō!
- Stop freaking me out! 别吓我！ Bié xià wǒ!
- Seriously? 真的吗？ Zhēn de ma?
- Don't talk nonsense / bullshit 别胡说 Bié húshuō

Getting closer

- I like being with you 我喜欢和你在一起 Wǒ xǐhuān hé nǐ zài yìqǐ
- I've missed you so much (missed you to death) 我想死你了 Wǒ xiǎng sǐ nǐ le
- I dreamt about you 我梦见你了 Wǒ mèng jiàn nǐ le
- I think about you all day 我整天都想你 Wǒ zhěngtiān dōu xiǎng nǐ
- I've been thinking about you all day 我一直都在想你 Wǒ yìzhí dōu zài xiǎng nǐ
- I really like you 我真的很喜欢你 Wǒ zhēnde hěn xǐhuān nǐ
- When will I see you again? 我什么时候能再见到你？ Wǒ shénme shíhòu néng zài jiàn dào nǐ?
- I fancy you 我看上你了 Wǒ kàn shàng nǐ le
- I've fallen in love with you 我爱上你了 Wǒ ài shàng nǐ le

That thing called ...

Talking love in a modern era

by Lee Ambrozy

迷恋 mílìàn infatuation

虐恋 nüèliàn sadomasochism

暗恋 ànliàn to have a crush on

网恋 wǎngliàn internet love

热恋 rèliàn to be in the honeymoon phase, or head over heels

宠恋 chǒngliàn doting love, to be sweet on

苦恋 kǔliàn bitter love

婚外恋 hūnwàiliàn extramarital love

师生恋 shīshēngliàn teacher-student love

姐弟恋 jiědìliàn love between an older woman and her younger boyfriend

双性恋 shuāngxìngliàn bisexuality

同性恋 tóngxìngliàn homosexuality

老少恋 lǎoshàoliàn inter-generational love

移情别恋 yíqíngbiéliàn a change of heart

忘年恋 wàngniánliàn being in love despite age differences

精神恋爱 jīngshén liàn'ài platonic love

两地恋 liǎngdìliàn a long-distance relationship

跨国恋 kuàguóliàn a long-distance relationship (of the international variety)

人鬼恋 rénguǐliàn supernatural love (referring to classics, where ghosts often seduce the living)

夕阳恋 xīyángliàn sunset love, two elderly people falling in love

三角恋 sānjiǎoliàn a love triangle

榜肩 bàngjiān an extramarital "friend"

相好儿 xiānghǎor "friend" of the opposite sex

心碎 xīnsuì to be broken hearted

两小无猜 liǎngxiǎowúcāi two innocent child playmates (puppy love)

青梅竹马 qīngméi-zhúmǎ green plums and a bamboo horse (sweethearts from a very young age)

爱恨交加 àihènjiāojiā a love-hate relationship

举案齐眉 jǔ'ànqíméi holding the dish at brow level (equality between the sexes)

堕入情网 duòrù qíngwǎng to sink into love's net (love sick)

心心相印 xīnxīnxiāngyìn to have mutual affinities

相敬如宾 xiāngjìngrúbīn a mutually respectful relationship

反目成仇 fǎnmùchéngchóu a thorough hatred after a break up

心灰意冷 xīnhuīyìlěng an ashen and cold heart (despondent)

心如死水 xīnrúsǐshuǐ a heart like still water (woebegone)

Sex

- Do you want to go back to my place for a drink? 想不想跟我回家喝一杯？ Xiǎng bùxiǎng gēn wǒ huíjiā hē yì bèi?

- Do you want to come up for some coffee? 要不要上去喝杯咖啡？ Yào búyào shàngqù hē bēi kāfēi?

- Do you want a massage? 要不要我给你按摩？ Yào búyào wǒ gěi nǐ ànmó?

- Will you spend the night with me? 想不想跟我共度良宵？ Xiǎng bùxiǎng gēn wǒ gòngdù liángxiāo?

- Kiss me 吻我 Wěn wǒ

- Don't speak 别说话 Bié shuō huà

Love

- I love you 我爱你 Wǒ ài nǐ

- I love you, too 我也爱你 Wǒ yě ài nǐ

- Love at first sight 一见钟情 yíjiànzhōngqíng

- I think we're a good match 我觉得我们在一起很合适 Wǒ juéde wǒmen zài yìqǐ hěn héshì

- fate 缘分 yuánfen

- Will you ... 你想. . . Nǐ xiǎng ...

(1) be my (boy / girl) friend? 当我的（男 / 女）朋友吗？
dāng wǒ de (nán / nǚ) péngyou ma?
(2) elope with me? 跟我私奔吗？ gēn wǒ sībēn ma?
(3) live with me? 跟我住吗？ gēn wǒ zhù ma?
(4) marry me? 跟我结婚吗？ gēn wǒ jiéhūn ma?

- Let's have a baby 我们生个孩子吧 Wǒmen shēng gè háizi ba

Problems

- I think you're great, but I don't feel that strongly about you 我觉得你很好，但是我对你没什么感觉 Wǒ juéde nǐ hěn hǎo, dànshì wǒ duì nǐ méi shénme gǎnjué

- I don't love you 我不爱你 Wǒ bú ài nǐ

- Are you seeing someone else? 你是不是在和别人约会？Nǐ shì búshì zài hé biérén yuēhuì?

- He/she is just a friend 他/她只是个朋友 Tā zhǐshì ge péngyou

- We'll work it out 我们会好的 Wǒmen huì hǎo de

- I don't think it's working out (we haven't solved the problem) 我不觉得问题解决了 Wǒ bù juéde wèntí jiějué le

- You don't care about me 你不关心我 Nǐ bù guānxīn wǒ

- There are too many problems 问题太多了 Wèntí tài duō le

- I can't stand you 我受不了你 Wo shòubùliǎo nǐ

- You're too greedy 你太贪心了 Nǐ tài tānxīn le

- You're too selfish 你太自私了 Nǐ tài zìsī le

- You're insensitive 你太冷漠了 Nǐ tài lěngmòu le

- You don't understand me 你不了解我 Nǐ bù liáojiě wǒ

- I want to break up 我想分手 Wǒ xiǎng fēnshǒu

- I never want to see you again 我永远都不想再见到你 Wǒ yǒngyuǎn dōu bùxiǎng zài jiàndào nǐ

- Tomorrow is my last day here 明天是我在这儿的最后一天 Míngtiān shì wǒ zài zhèr de zuìhòu yìtiān

- See you in cyberspace! 网上见！Wǎng shàng jiàn!

SHOPPING

Mastering the art of shopping in Beijing is certainly one of the most rewarding ways to make your Chinese pay off. With a little spiritual and linguistic preparation, your bargaining battles will yield victory after victory. You will reap a singularly satisfying accruement: loads of cheap, wonderful stuff!

1 Quick tips:

- Never say a price.
- Act like you are in a hurry and that you are incredibly bored buying this stuff because you do it all the time.
- Never buy something at the first place you go. Always take that price somewhere else and see if they will go cheaper.
- Don't carry too much money. If you have a lot of money you might end up spending more than you should. It doesn't hurt to come back to get something later if you really like it. You might avoid wasting money if you let your consumer frenzy passions cool down for a few days/hours.
- Walk away after you have made your best offer. This is the ceremonial ritual for "closing the deal."

Sentences

- How (much) do you sell this (for)? 这个怎么卖？ Zhèige zěnme mài?
- How much is it? 这个多少钱？ Zhèi ge duōshao qián?
- What is the lowest price you can offer? 最低多少钱？ Zuì dī duōshao qián?
- Too expensive! 太贵了！ Tài guì le!
- No no no no 不不不不 Bùbùbùbù (with "stop" hand-waving motion)
- Can't it be a little cheaper? 不能再便宜点儿了吗？ Bùnéng zài piányi diǎnr le ma?
- Is there a discount for buying bulk? 多买点儿能打折吗？ Duō mǎi diǎnr néng dǎzhé ma?

Listen for this

- Nǐ shuō ge jiàr 你说个价儿 Say a price / name your price
- Kāi wánxiào ba! 开玩笑吧！You must be joking!
- kǎnjiàr / jiǎngjiàr 砍价儿/讲价儿 bargain / haggle
- zhuànqián 赚钱 make money
- We don't bargain – said in a few ways

(1) Bù kǎnjiàr 不砍价儿 We don't "cut down the price" (like cutting off someone's head or cutting down a tree)
(2) Bù jiǎngjiàr 不讲价儿 We don't bargain
(3) Bù dǎzhé / méi yōuhuì 不打折/没优惠 No discount
(4) Zhè shì pīfā jià 这是批发价 This is the wholesale price
(5) Bùnéng zài piányi le 不能再便宜了 It can't get any cheaper
(6) Wǒ gāi péiqián le 我该赔钱了 I'll be losing money

Sentences

- I'll wait for you to say (your price) 还是你说吧 Háishì nǐ shuō ba
- You say! 你说！Nǐ shuō!
- You need to make it cheaper 你得再便宜点儿 Nǐ děi zài piányi diǎnr
- It's still not enough 还是不够（便宜）Háishì bú gòu (piányi)
- It's like this, I'll wander around and we'll discuss it more when I get back 这样吧，我再转转，回头再说 Zhè yàng ba, wǒ zài zhuànzhuan, húitóu zài shuō
- Over there their price is a lot cheaper than yours 他们那边卖的比你们便宜多了 Tāmen nèibiān mài de bǐ nǐmen piányi duō le
- Your (price) should be a little bit cheaper than theirs 你的价得比他们再便宜点儿 Nǐ de jià děi bǐ tāmen zài piányi diǎnr
- Just make it a little bit cheaper 再便宜一点点 Zài piányi yì diǎndiǎn
- I'll pay no more than RMB 30 我最多给30 Wǒ zuìduō gěi sānshí

• Just a bit cheaper and that settles it, right? 再便宜一点儿不就行了吗，对不对？ Zài piányi yì diǎnr bú jiù xíng le ma, duì búduì?

• Isn't that the end of it? 这就完了？ Zhè jiù wán le?

• I don't really like it 我不是特别喜欢 Wǒ búshì tèbié xǐhuan

• Forget it 算了吧 Suàn le ba

• Anyway, I don't need it 反正我也不需要 Fǎnzheng wǒ yě bù xūyào

• I don't care 我无所谓 Wǒ wúsuǒwèi

• I'm leaving 我走了 Wǒ zǒu le

Listen for:

• Piányi bùliǎo 便宜不了 I can't go any cheaper

• Hǎo, gěi nǐ ná ba! 好，给你拿吧！ Fine, take it! (at your price)

• Nǐ zhēn huì kǎnjiàr! 你真会砍价儿！ You really are a good bargainer!

2 Buying clothes 买衣服 Mǎi yīfu

Sentences

• Can I take a look at that? 我能看看那个吗？ Wǒ néng kànkan nèige ma?

• Can you bring it down? 能把这个拿下来吗？ Néng bǎ zhèige ná xiàlái ma?

• Can I try this on? 我能试试那件吗？ Wǒ néng shìshi nèijiàn ma?

• Do you have a larger size? 有没有大一号的？ Yǒu méiyǒu dà yí hào de?

• Is this the largest size you have? 这个是你们这儿最大号的吗？Zhèige shì nǐmen zhèr zuìdà hào de ma?

• Do you have anything smaller? 有没有小点儿的？Yǒu méiyǒu xiǎo diǎnr de?

• What fabric is this? 这个是什么料子的？Zhèige shì shénme liàozi de?

• Do you have this in another color? 这个有其他颜色的吗？Zhèige yǒu qítā yánsè de ma?

• Is this *really* a brand name? 这件真的是名牌儿吗？Zhèi jiàn *zhēn de* shì míngpáir ma?

Listen for this

• Dāngrán kěyǐ, shìyījiān zài nàbiān 当然可以，试衣间在那边 Sure, go ahead, the fitting room is over there

• Bùhǎoyìsī, nèi jiàn shì zhǎnpǐn, bú mài 不好意思，那件是展品不卖 Sorry, that is the item on display, not for sale

Clothing 服装 Fúzhuāng

bell bottoms 喇叭裤 lǎba kù
belt 腰带 yāodài
blouse 女式衬衫 nǚshì chènshān
cardigan (button-up sweater) 开身毛衣 kāishēn máoyī
cheongsam (long dress) 旗袍 qípáo
down coat 羽绒服 yǔróngfú
earmuffs 耳罩 ěrzhào
fur coat 毛皮上衣 máopí shàngyī
jacket 夹克 jiáke
jeans 牛仔裤 niúzǎikù
Mandarin jacket (Chinese short coat) 马褂儿 mǎguàr
overcoat 大衣 dàyī
overalls 背带裤 bēidàikù
pants 裤子 kùzi
raincoat 雨衣 yǔyī
scarf 围巾 wéijīn
shirt 衬衫 chènshān
shorts 短裤 duǎnkù
skirt 短裙 duǎnqún
sportswear 运动衣 yùndòngyī
suit 套装 tàozhuāng
Mao suit (Sun Yatsen's uniform) 中山装 zhōngshānzhuāng
tuxedo 小礼服 xiǎolǐfú
sweater 毛衣 máoyī
sweatshirt 卫衣 wèiyī
Tang Dynasty suit (traditional Chinese style) 唐装 tángzhuāng
tie 领带 lǐngdài
T-shirt T恤衫 tìxùshān
turtleneck 高领衫 gāolǐngshān
waistcoat 马甲 mǎjiǎ

Underwear 内衣 Nèiyī

bathrobe 浴袍 yùpáo
bra 胸罩 xiōngzhào
long underwear 秋衣，秋裤 qiūyī, qiūkù
nightie 睡衣 shuìyī
pantyhose 连裤袜 liánkùwà
socks 袜子 wàzi
tank top / partner beater 吊带背心儿/跨栏背心儿 diàodài bèixīnr / kuàlán bèixīnr
tights 裤袜 kùwà
thong 丁字裤 dīngzìkù

Headgear 帽子 Màozi

beret 贝雷帽 bèiléimào
baseball cap 棒球帽 bàngqiúmào
one size fits all 均码 jūnmǎ
cowboy hat 牛仔帽 niúzǎimào
getting cheated on by your wife 带绿帽子 dài lǜmàozi (lit: "wearing a green hat")

Accessories 配饰 Pèishì

backpack 双肩背包 shuāngjiān bēibāo
handbag 手提包 shǒutíbāo
leather handbag/briefcase 皮包／公文包 píbāo/gōngwénbāo
scarf 围巾 wéijīn
sunglasses 太阳眼镜 tàiyáng yǎnjìng
suitcase 手提箱 shǒutíxiāng
wallet 钱包 qiánbāo

Sentences

• In total, how much? 一共多少钱？ Yígòng duōshao qián?

• I don't like this (these) ... 我不喜欢这(些)... Wǒ bù xǐhuan zhèi (xiē) ...

(1) button 扣子 kòuzi
(2) collar / lapel 领子 lǐngzi
(3) embroidery 刺绣 cìxiù
(4) pleats 褶子 zhězi
(5) pocket 口袋 kǒudài
(6) sleeve 袖子 xiùzi
(7) zipper 拉锁 lāsuǒ
(8) elastic pull cords 弹力拉绳 tánlì lāshéng

• I need something a little ... 我想要稍微…一点儿的 Wǒ xiǎng yào shāowēi ... yì diǎnr de

(1) casual 休闲 xiūxián
(2) fashionable 时尚 shíshàng
(3) trendy 流行 liúxíng
(4) formal 正式 zhèngshì

• It's too ... 太...了 Tài ... le

(1) loose 松 sōng
(2) long 长 cháng
(3) narrow 窄 zhǎi
(4) short 短 duǎn
(5) tight 紧 jǐn
(6) wide 宽 kuān

3 Tailoring 裁缝 Cáifeng

Sentences

- Do you have anything ... 有没有 . . . 的 Yǒu méiyǒu ... de

(1) shinier 亮点儿 liàng diǎnr
(2) softer 软点儿 ruǎn diǎnr
(3) thicker/thinner 厚点儿/薄点儿 hòu diǎnr / báo diǎnr

- What fabric is this? 这是什么布料? Zhè shì shénme bùliào?

Fabrics 布料 Bùliào

blend 混纺 hùnfǎng
cashmere 羊绒 yángróng
chemical fiber 化纤 huàxiān
corduroy 灯芯绒 dēngxīnróng
cotton 棉 mián
down 羽绒 yǔróng
fur 皮草 pícǎo
lace 蕾丝 léisī
leather 皮革 pígé
linen 亚麻 yàmá
nylon 尼龙 nílóng
plastic 塑料 sùliào
pleather 人造革 rénzàogé
polyester 涤纶 dílún
silk 丝绸 sīchóu
suede 翻毛皮 fānmáopí
rattan matting 藤席 téng xí
rubber 橡胶 xiàngjiāo
wool 毛 máo

Measurements 量尺寸 Liáng chǐcùn

chest 胸围 xiōngwéi
hip 臀围 túnwéi
neck 颈围 jìngwéi
shoulder 肩宽 jiānkuān
size 尺寸 chǐcùn
thick 厚 hòu
thin 薄 báo
waist 腰围 yāowéi

Listen for this

- measure your waist circumference 量腰围 liáng yāowéi
- measure from your shoulder to your ankle 量一下从你的肩膀到脚踝之间的距离 liáng yí xià cóng nǐde jiānbǎng dào jiǎohuái zhījiān de jùlí

4 Antiques and furniture

古玩和家具 Gǔwán hé jiājù

Sentences

- Is this genuine or a fake? 这个是真的还是赝品？ Zhèi ge shì zhēnde háishì yànpǐn?
- How old is it? 这个是哪年的？ Zhèige shì nǎ nián de?

Listen for this

- Dāngrán shì zhēnde, wǒ cónglái bú mài jiǎhuò 当然是真的，我从来不卖假货 Of course it's genuine, I never sell fake antiques
- Xiǎo shēng diǎnr, zhèi ge shì jiǎ de ... 小声点儿，这个是假的... Be quiet, this is fake ...
- Dànshì nǐ bǎ zhèi ge mǎi huí jiā, nǐ kěyǐ gàosù suǒyǒu rén zhèi ge shì zhēnde 但是你把这个买回家，你可以告诉所有人这个是真的 But when you take it back home, you can tell everybody it's real
- Méi rén néng fēn de chūlái 没人能分得出来 No one can tell the difference
- yànpǐn 赝品 counterfeit
- gǔwán 古玩 curio
- fǎnggǔpǐn 仿古品 antique reproductions
- wénwù jiàndìng 文物鉴定 relics certification
- lǎomù xīnzuò 老木新作 salvaged wood reproduction

Types of wood 木材种类 Mùcaí zhǒnglèi

boxwood 黄杨木 huángyángmù
camphor 樟木 zhāngmù
cherry 樱桃木 yīngtáomù
ebony 乌木 wūmù
lacquer 漆器 qīqì
mahogany 红木 hóngmù
rosewood 红木（黑檀，紫檀） hóngmù (hēitán, zǐtán)
sandalwood 檀木 tánmù
walnut 胡桃木 hútáomù

Furniture 家具 Jiājù

armoire 大衣柜 dàyīguì
footrest 脚凳 jiǎodèng

bed 床 chuáng
bench 长凳 chángdèng
bookcase 书柜 shūguì
Buddhist statue 佛像 fóxiàng
cabinet 柜子 guìzi
tibetan carpet 西藏地毯 xīzàng dìtǎn
handmade 手工 shǒugōng
chair 椅子 yǐzi
clock 钟 zhōng
couch/sofa 沙发 shāfā
curtain 窗帘 chuānglián
lamp 灯 dēng
mirror 镜子 jìngzi
painting 画 huà
screen 屏风 píngfēng
stool 凳子 dèngzi
table 桌子 zhuōzi
dining table 餐桌 cānzhuō
coffee table 茶几儿 chájīr
desk 书桌/写字台 shūzhuō/xiězìtái
tapestry 挂毯 guàtǎn
vase 花瓶 huāpíng

Bedding 床上用品 Chuángshàng yòngpǐn

bed sheet 床单 chuángdān
pillow 枕头 zhěntou
quilt (cover) 被子(罩) bèizi(zhào)
towel 毛巾 máojīn

Sentences

- How long is this carpet? 这个地毯多长? Zhèi ge dìtǎn duō cháng?
- How wide? 多宽? Duō kuān?
- This table is too heavy 这个桌子太重了 Zhèi ge zhuōzi tài zhòng le
- This sofa sure is comfy 这个沙发真舒服 Zhèi ge shāfā zhēn shūfu

5 Organizing delivery

送货 Sònghuò

Sentences

- Do you deliver? 你们送货吗? Nǐmen sònghuò ma?
- How much is the delivery charge? 送货费多少钱? Sònghuòfèi duōshǎo qián?
- Can I export this? 我能把这个带出国吗? Wǒ néng bǎ zhèi ge dài chū guó ma?

- Can I mail it internationally? 可以寄到国外吗？ Kěyǐ jì dào guówài ma?

- Can I get delivery insurance? 可以保价吗？ Kěyǐ bǎojià ma?

Listen for this

- Nǐ xiǎng shénme shíhòu sòng dào? 你想什么时候送到？ When do you need it by?
- yājīn 押金 deposit
- diàntī / lóutī 电梯/楼梯 elevator / stairs
- Nǐmen jiā (diàntī/mén) duō dà? 你们家（电梯/门）多大？ What are the dimensions of your (elevator / door frame)?

6 Art & art supplies

艺术和美术用品

Yìshù hé měishù yòngpǐn

Sentences

- Do you have ... ? 请问您这儿有...吗？ Qǐngwèn nín zhèr yǒu ... ma?

(1) calligraphy supplies 书法用品 shūfǎ yòngpǐn
(2) calligrapher's ink 墨 mò
(3) canvas 画布 huàbù
(4) chisel 凿子 záozi
(5) charcoal 炭笔 tànbǐ
(6) chalk 粉笔 fěnbǐ
(7) clay 陶土 táotǔ
(8) colored pencils 彩色铅笔 cǎisè qiānbǐ
(9) crayons 蜡笔 làbǐ
(10) easel 画架 huàjià
(11) glue 胶水 jiāoshuǐ
(12) ink stone 砚台 yàntai
(13) paint 颜料 yánliào
acrylic 压克力yākèlì
oil 油性yóuxìng
brush 毛笔 máobǐ
thinner 稀料 xīliào
(14) pastels 彩色粉笔 cǎisè fěnbǐ
(15) pencils 铅笔 qiānbǐ
(16) pottery wheel 制陶转台 zhìtáo zhuàntái
(17) rice paper 宣纸 xuānzhǐ
(18) ruler 尺子 chǐzi
(19) sketchbook 写生簿 xiěshēng bù
(20) scissors 剪子 jiǎnzi

Listen for this

- Bùhǎoyìsī, wǒmen zhèlǐ méiyǒu 不好意思，我们这里没有 Sorry, we don't have it
- Nǐ piàn bù liǎo wǒ, nǐ búshì yìshùjiā 你骗不了我，你不是艺术家 You can't fool me, you're not an artist
- frame 画框 huàkuàng
- matting 卡纸 kǎzhǐ

7 Bicycles & motorcycles

自行车和摩托车

Zìxíngchē hé mótuōchē

For more information about fixing/enhancing bikes and bike parts, *see Transportation p214.*

Sentences

- I want to buy a ... 我想买一辆... Wǒ xiǎng mǎi yí liàng ...
  (1) new bike 新自行车 xīn zìxíngchē
  (2) used bike 旧自行车 jiù zìxíngchē
  (3) electric bike 电动自行车 diàndòng zìxíngchē
  (4) scooter 迷你摩托车 mínǐ mótuōchē
  (5) folding bike 折叠自行车 zhédié zìxíngchē
  (6) motorcycle 摩托车 mótuōchē
  (7) mountain bike 山地车 shāndìchē
  (8) racing bike 赛车 sàichē
  (9) woman's bike 女车 nǚchē
  (10) men's bike男车 nánchē
- Can I take it for a test ride? 我能骑一圈儿试试吗？ Wǒ néng qí yì quānr shìshi ma?
- How many gears does it have? 有几个档？ Yǒu jǐ ge dǎng?
- How long is the warranty? 保修多长时间？ Bǎoxiū duō cháng shíjiān?

Brands 品牌 Pǐnpái

Giant 捷安特 Jié'āntè
Flying Pigeon飞鸽 Fēigē
Forever永久 Yǒngjiǔ

Gear 装备 Zhuāngbèi

- Do you sell locks? 你们卖锁吗？ Nǐmen mài suǒ ma?

- I need ... 我要. . . Wǒ yào...

(1) a U lock 一个"U"型锁 yí gè U xíng suǒ
(2) a long lock 一个长点儿的锁 yí gè cháng diǎnr de suǒ
(3) a thicker lock 一个粗点儿的锁 yí gè cū diǎnr de suǒ
(4) a helmet 头盔 tóukuī
(5) a racing jersey 骑行服 qíxíng fú
(6) a bell 一个车铃 yí ge chēlíng
(7) a basket 一个车筐 yí ge chēkuāng
(8) a light 一个车灯 yí ge chēdēng

Electric bikes 电动自行车 Diàndòng zìxíngchē

- How long will the battery last? 这个电池能用多长时间？ Zhè ge diànchí néng yòng duō cháng shíjiān?

- How long does it take to charge it up? 充电要多长时间？ Chōngdiàn yào duō cháng shíjiān?

Scooters 迷你摩托车 Mínǐ mótuōchē

- How large is the engine? 发动机排量是多大的？ Fādòngjī páiliàng shì duō dà de?

- What's the maximum speed? 最快能开到多少？ Zuì kuài néng kāi dào duōshao?

- What is the fuel consumption (km/L)? 油耗多少(一升油多少公里)？ Yóuhào duōshǎo (yì shēng yóu duōshǎo gōnglǐ)?

8 Cosmetics 化妆品 Huàzhuāngpǐn

Vocabulary

blush 腮红 sāihóng
eyeliner 眼线笔 yǎnxiànbǐ
eyeshadow 眼影 yǎnyǐng
foundation 粉底 fěndǐ
lipgloss 唇彩 chúncǎi
lipstick 唇膏 chúngāo
mascara 睫毛膏 jiémáogāo
nailpolish 指甲油 zhǐjia yóu
nailpolish remover 洗甲水 xǐjiǎshuǐ

9 Camera & photo equipment 照相机和摄影设备 Zhàoxiàngjī hé shèyǐng shèbèi

Sentences

• How much per print? 一张多少钱？ Yì zhāng duōshao qián?

• Can you develop photos if I bring in a ... ? 如果我带...来能洗吗？ Rúguǒ wǒ dài ... lái néng xǐ ma?

USB drive 优盘 yōupán
floppy disk 软盘 ruǎnpán
CD
CD ROM 光盘 guāngpán

• Can you develop photos if they are in an email attachment? 邮件附件里的照片能洗吗？ Yóujiàn fùjiàn lǐ de zhàopiàn néng xǐ ma?

• Can you put my photos on a disk? 你能把我的相片拷在一张盘上吗？ Nǐ néng bǎ wǒ de xiàngpiān kǎo zài yì zhāng pán shàng ma?

• Is this 500 megapixels? 这个是500万像素的吗？ Zhèi ge shì wǔbǎiwàn xiàngsù de ma?

• I'd like to enlarge this print 我要把这张放大 Wǒ yào bǎ zhèi zhāng fàngdà

• I need passport-sized photos 我需要证件照 Wǒ xūyào zhèngjiàn zhào

Listen for this

- ... cùn ...寸 ... inch
- Xǐ duōshao zhāng? 洗多少张？How many copies?
- xiàngkuàng 相框 frames
- báibiān 白边 backing
- Zhèi ge túpiàn wénjiàn tài xiǎo le, rúguǒ fàngdà dehuà xiàoguǒ bùhǎo 这个图片文件太小了，如果放大的话效果不好 The file of the photo is too small, it won't look good blown up
- Zhèi ge shì jiāopiàn xiàngjī, búshì shùmǎ de 这个是胶片相机，不是数码的 It's a film camera, not a digital one
- róng miàn 绒面 matt
- dǐpiàn zāng le 底片脏了 smudged negatives

Photography 摄影 Shèyǐng

aperture 光圈 guāngquān
(lithium) battery (锂) 电池 (lǐ) diànchí
black and white 黑白 hēibái
camera 相机 xiàngjī
color 颜色 yánsè
composition 构图 gòutú
contrast 对比 duìbǐ
develop 冲印/冲洗 chōngyìn/chōngxǐ
digital (video) camera 数码(摄) 相机 shùmǎ (shè) xiàngjī
film 胶卷 jiāojuǎn
flash 闪光灯 shǎnguāngdēng
focus 焦点 jiāodiǎn
focusing 对焦 duìjiāo
LCD monitor 液晶屏 yèjīng píng
lens 镜头 jìngtóu
light meter 测光表 céguāngbiǎo
negative 底片 dǐpiàn
photography 摄影 shèyǐng
pixel 像素 xiàngsù
shutter 快门 kuàimén
storage card 存储卡 cúnchǔkǎ
tripod 三脚架 sānjiǎojià
white balance 白平衡 báipínghéng
wide angle 广角 guǎngjiǎo
zoom 变焦 biànjiāo

Sentences

- Nice contrast 对比好 Duìbǐ hǎo
- This picture has excellent composition 这张照片的构图特别好 Zhè zhāng zhàopiàn de gòutú tèbié hǎo

10 Computers and software
电脑和软件 Diànnǎo hé ruǎnjiàn

Sentences

• Can you build me a computer? 你能帮我攒个电脑吗？Nǐ néng bāng wǒ cuán gè diànnǎo ma?

• What is the speed of this burner? 这个刻录机几倍速的？Zhèi gè kèlùjī jǐ bèi sù de?

• Do you have an English version (of this software)? （这个软件）有英文版吗？(Zhè gè ruǎnjiàn) yǒu yīngwénbǎn ma?

• Which is better, an electric brain (computer) or a human brain? 人脑和电脑，哪一个好？ Rénnǎo hé diànnǎo, nǎ yí gè hǎo?

• My computer ... 我的电脑... Wǒ de diànnǎo ...

(1) won't start 不能开机 bùnéng kāijī
(2) can't get online 不能上网 bùnéng shàngwǎng
(3) is busted 坏了 huài le
(4) has a problem 有毛病 yǒu máobìng

• I need to replace my ... 我要换我的... Wǒ yào huàn wǒ de ...

audio card 声卡 shēngkǎ
blue tooth 蓝牙 lányá
CD/DVD ROM 光驱 guāngqū
CD/DVD-RW 刻录机 kèlùjī
COM port 通讯端口 tōngxùn duānkǒu
CPU 中央处理器 zhōngyāng chùlǐqì
ethernet adaptor 网络适配器 wǎngluò shìpèiqì
floppy drive 软驱 ruǎnqū
hard drive 硬盘 yìngpán
hub 集线器 jíxiànqì
LPT port 打印机端口 dǎyìnjī duānkǒu
infrared device 红外设备 hóngwài shèbèi
internet 互联网 hùliánwǎng
memory (slot) 内存（槽）nèicún (cáo)
modem 调制解调器／猫 tiáozhìjiětiáoqì / māo
monitor 显示器 xiǎnshìqì
mouse 鼠标 shǔbiāo
motherboard 主板 zhǔbǎn
operating system 操作系统 cāozuò xìtǒng
power supply电源 diànyuán
router 路由器 lùyóuqì
server 服务器 fúwùqì
software 软件 ruǎnjiàn
surge protector 保护插座 bǎohù chāzuò
tower 机箱 jīxiāng
video card 显卡 xiǎnkǎ
wi-fi 无线网络 wúxiàn wǎngluò

keyboard 键盘 jiànpán
LAN 局域网 júyùwǎng
(LCD) monitor (液晶) 显示器 (yèjīng) xiǎnshìqì
wireless (card)
无线（卡）wúxiàn (kǎ)

Listen for this

Zhè gè xiū bù liǎo 这个修不了 This can't be fixed

Bùnéng huàn 不能换 It can't be exchanged

Nǐ děi mǎi xīnde 你得买新的 You have to buy a new one

ruǎnjiàn de wèntí 软件的问题 software problem

11 Decorating companies & materials 装修公司和建材

Zhuāngxiū gōngsī hé jiàncái

Vocabulary

bathtub 浴缸 yùgāng
cabinets 橱柜 chúguì
light fixtures 灯座 dēngzuò
environmentally safe
环保 huánbǎo
faucet 水龙头 shuǐlóngtóu
flooring 地板 dìbǎn
formaldehyde 甲醛 jiǎquán
hinges 合页 héyè
pipes 管道 guǎndào
paint 粉刷 fěnshuā
plaster 石膏 shígāo
plywood 大芯板 dàxīnbǎn
power outlets 电源插座
diànyuán chāzuò
renovation 翻修 fānxiū
sink 水盆 shuǐpén
shower 淋浴 línyù
tiles 瓷砖 cízhuān
wiring 布线 bù xiàn
wood screws 木螺丝 mù luósī

12 DVDs & CDs DVD 和 CD DVD hé CD

Vocabulary

DVDs

action 动作 dòngzuò
love/romance 爱情 àiqíng

actor/actress 演员 yǎnyuán
animation 动画 dònghuà
bilingual 双语 shuāngyǔ
comedy 喜剧 xǐjù
director 导演 dǎoyǎn
documentary 纪录 jìlù
horror 恐怖 kǒngbù
science fiction 科幻 kēhuàn
subtitle 字幕 zìmù
tragedy 悲剧 bēijù
TV series 电视连续剧 diànshì liánxùjù
movie 电影 diànyǐng
war 战争 zhànzhēng

Sentences

• Is this a Chinese movie? 这是中国电影吗？Zhè shì zhōngguó diànyǐng ma?

• Is this film in English? 这部电影是英文的吗？Zhè bù diànyǐng shì yīngwén de ma?

• Does it have (English / Chinese) subtitles? 有（英文/中文）字幕吗？ Yǒu (yīngwén/zhōngwén) zìmù ma?

• Is this DVD made from a real DVD or is it made from someone secretly videotaping the movie? 这是碟版还是枪版？ Zhè shì diébǎn háishì qiāngbǎn?

• Does this DVD work in foreign DVD players? 国外的DVD机能读吗？ Guówài de DVD jī néng dú ma?

• Have you seen it? 你看过吗？Nǐ kàn guò ma?

• Do you have ... 你有没有... Nǐ yǒu méiyǒu ...

• If I find out the Chinese name of the movie I'm thinking of, can you get it for me? 我要是想起来电影的中文名字，你能帮我找到这个片子吗？ Wǒ yào shì xiǎng qǐlái diànyǐng de zhōngwén míngzi, nǐ néng bāng wǒ zhǎo dào zhè ge piànzi ma?

• Who's in it (what actors)? 谁演的？Shéi yǎn de?

• If it doesn't work, can I bring it back and get a refund? 要是盘不行，能回来退吗？Yàoshì pán bùxíng, néng huílái tuì ma?

•Can I try it out to check ... ? 我能不能试一下儿看看...怎么样？Wǒ néng bùnéng shì yí xiàr kànkan ... zěnmeyàng?

(1) the subtitles 字幕 zìmù
(2) the picture quality 画质 huàzhì

Listen for this

- Kěyǐ huàn, dàn bùnéng tuì 可以换，但不能退 You can't get a refund, but you can exchange it
- Yǒu ... 有... It stars ...
- wàiguó 外国 foreign
- Xiānggǎng diànyǐng 香港电影 Hong Kong film

CDs

band 乐队 yuèduì
classical music 古典音乐 gǔdiǎn yīnyuè
country 乡村 xiāngcūn
compilation 合辑 héjí
folk 民谣 mínyáo
live 现场 xiànchǎng
score 乐谱 yuèpǔ
singer 歌手 gēshǒu
symphony 交响乐 jiāoxiǎngyuè

For more on music genre vocabulary see Nightlife p131

Sentences

- Is this CD the band's new album? 这是不是那个乐队的新专辑？ Zhèi shì búshì nèi gè yuèduì de xīn zhuānjí?

13 Electronics & home appliances

电子产品和家电

Diànzǐ chǎnpǐn hé jiādiàn

Vocabulary

air conditioning unit 空调 kōngtiáo
blender 搅拌机 jiǎobànjī
clothes dryer 烘干机 hōnggānjī
dishwasher 洗碗机 xǐwǎnjī
DVD player DVD机 DVD jī
headphones 耳机 ěrjī
microwave 微波炉 wēibōlú
oven (or toaster oven) 烤箱 kǎoxiāng
refrigerator 冰箱 bīngxiāng
speakers 音箱 yīnxiāng
stereo 立体声音响 lìtǐshēng yīnxiǎng
stove 炉灶 lúzào
television 电视 diànshì
vacuum cleaner 吸尘器 xīchénqì
walkman 随身听 suíshēntīng
washing machine 洗衣机 xǐyījī

14 Glasses 眼镜 Yǎnjìng

Vocabulary

See also Health and Beauty p187

cleaning liquid 清洗液 qīngxǐyè
contact lenses 隐形眼镜 yǐnxíng yǎnjìng
crystal 水晶 shuǐjīng
disposable 抛弃型 pāoqì xíng
eyesight 视力 shìlì
frame 镜架 jìngjià
hypermetropia 远视 yuǎnshì
lens 镜片 jìngpiàn
myopia 近视 jìnshì
optometry 验光 yànguāng
sunglasses 太阳眼镜 tàiyáng yǎnjìng

Sentences

• Can you put those lenses in these frames? 能把这种镜片装到这个镜框上吗？ Néng bǎ zhèi zhǒng jìngpiàn zhuāng dào zhèi gè jìngkuàng shàng ma?

• Can you fix these glasses? 能修这副眼镜吗？ Néng xiū zhèi fù yǎnjìng ma?

• Here's my prescription 这是我的验光报告 Zhè shì wǒ de yànguāng bàogào

• I am nearsighted/farsighted 我近视/远视 Wǒ jìnshì/yuǎnshì

15 Jewelry 珠宝 Zhūbǎo

Sentences

• Is this (a) real ...? 这个是真的...吗？ Zhè gè shì zhēn de ... ma?

amber 琥珀 hǔpò
amethyst 紫水晶 zǐ shuǐjīng
coral 珊瑚 shānhú
crystal 水晶 shuǐjīng
cubic zirconium 锆石 gàoshí
diamond 钻石 zuànshí
emerald 玛瑙/绿宝石 mǎnǎo/lǜbǎoshí
gold 黄金 huángjīn
gold plated 镀金 dùjīn
jade 玉 yù
opal 猫眼石 māoyǎnshí
pearls 珍珠 zhēnzhū
platinum 铂金 bójīn
ruby 红宝石 hóngbǎoshí
sapphire 蓝宝石 lánbǎoshí
silver 白银 báiyín
turquoise 绿松石 lǜsōngshí

- I really like this ... 我特别喜欢这个... Wǒ tèbié xǐhuan zhège ...

bracelet 手链/手镯 shǒuliàn/shǒuzhuó
brooch 胸针 xiōngzhēn
earring 耳环 ěrhuán
engagement ring 订婚戒指 dìnghūn jièzhǐ
necklace 项链 xiàngliàn
nose ring 鼻环 bíhuán
ring 戒指 jièzhǐ
toe ring 趾戒 zhǐjiè

- How many carats? 几克拉? Jǐ kèlā?

- Is this pearl ... ? 这个珍珠是...的吗? Zhèi ge zhēnzhū shì ... de ma?

(1) cultured 养殖 yǎngzhí
(2) seawater 海水 hǎishuǐ
(3) freshwater 淡水 dànshuǐ

Listen for this

- qiēgōng 切工 cut
- yánsè 颜色 color
- jìngdù 净度 clarity
- chúndù 纯度 purity
- shìchǎng jià 市场价 market price
- èrshǒu 二手 second hand / used
- pīfā jià 批发价 wholesale price

16 Mobile phones 手机 Shǒujī

Vocabulary

built-in Bluetooth 内置蓝牙 nèizhì lányá
built-in infrared 内置红外 nèizhì hóngwài
charger 充电器 chōngdiànqì
China Unicom 中国联通 Zhōngguó Liántōng
China Mobile 中国移动 Zhōngguó Yídòng
chord 和弦 héxián
earphone 耳机 ěrjī
model 型号 xínghào
multimedia message 彩信 cǎixìn
phone fee 话费 huàfèi
refill card 充值卡 chōngzhíkǎ
ring tone 铃声 língshēng
screen 屏幕 píngmù
SMS (text messaging) 短信 duǎnxìn
storage capacity 存储容量 cúnchǔ róngliàng
user guide 说明书 shuōmíngshū
voice recorder 录音器 lùyīnqì
volume 音量 yīnliàng
weight 重量 zhòngliàng

Sentences

- How long is the warranty? 保修多长时间？ Bǎoxiū duō cháng shíjiān?

- Can I buy a SIM card here? 我能在这儿买SIM卡吗？ Wǒ néng zài zhèr mǎi SIM kǎ ma?

- Can this one ... ? 这个能...吗？ Zhèi ge néng ... ma?

  (1) (receive/make) international calls （接/打）国际长途 (jiē/dǎ) guójì chángtú
  (2) go online 上网 shàngwǎng
  (3) take pictures 拍照 pāizhào
  (4) record movies 摄像 shèxiàng
  (5) play games 打游戏 dǎ yóuxì

- What is the rate per minute? 一分钟多少钱？ Yì fēnzhōng duōshao qián?

Listen for this

- shìnèi tōnghuà 市内通话 local call
- chángtú (guónèi) 长途（国内） long distance (domestic)
- guójì 国际 international
- tōnghuà shíjiān 通话时间 call duration

17 Musical instruments 乐器 Yuèqì

Vocabulary

bagpipes 风笛 fēngdí
(electric) bass (电)贝斯 (diàn) bèisi
bongos 手鼓 shǒugǔ
cello 大提琴 dàtíqín
clarinet 单簧管 dānhuángguǎn
cymbal 镲 chǎ
drum 鼓 gǔ
dulcimer 扬琴 yángqín
erhu 二胡 èrhú
keyboard 键盘 jiànpán
organ 风琴 fēngqín
pandean pipe 笙 shēng
percussion 打击乐器 dǎjī yuèqì
piano 钢琴 gāngqín
pipa (Chinese lute) 琵琶 pípa
saxophone 萨克斯 sàkèsī
suona (trumpet-like Chinese instrument) 唢呐 suǒnà

flute 长笛 chángdí
gong 锣 luó
guitar (acoustic) 箱琴 xiāngqín
guitar (electric) (电)吉他 (diàn) jítā
trumpet 小号 xiǎohào
violin 小提琴 xiǎotíqín
zheng (Chinese zither with 25 strings) 古筝 gǔzhēng

Equipment & effects 设备和效果 Shèbèi hé xiàoguǒ

amplifier (AMP) 放大器 fàngdàqì
chorus 合唱效果器 héchàng xiàoguǒqì
delay 延时效果器 yánshí xiàoguǒqì
distortion (dist) 失真效果器 shīzhēn xiàoguǒqì
drumstick 鼓槌 gǔchuí
echo 回声 huí shēng
effects pedals 效果器 xiàoguǒqì
feedback 反馈 fǎnkuì
flanger 弗兰格效果器 fúlángé xiàoguǒqì
gain 增益 zēngyì
guitar pick 吉他拨片 jítā bōpiàn
lead 超载音 chāozǎiyīn
microphone 麦克风 màikèfēng
musical score 乐谱 yuèpǔ
over drive 过载guòzǎi
parametric EQ 参数均衡器 cānshù jūnhéngqì
string 琴弦 qínxián
treble 高音 gāoyīn
tuner 调音器 tiáoyīnqì

18 Plants 植物 Zhíwù

Sentences

• How often should I water this? 我应该多长时间浇一次水？Wǒ yīnggāi duō cháng shíjiān jiāo yí cì shuǐ?

• How fast does this grow? 这个长得有多快？Zhèi ge zhǎng de yǒu duō kuài?

• How long can this survive without water? 不浇水的话，这个能活多长时间？Bù jiāoshuǐ de huà, zhèi ge néng huó duō cháng shíjiān?

• Do cats like to eat this? 这东西猫爱吃吗？Zhèi dōngxī māo ài chī ma?

• What meaning do these flowers convey? 这些花儿表达什么意思？Zhè xiē huār biǎodá shénme yìsi?

Listen for this

- Zhè xiē huār biǎoshì ... 这些花儿表示 . . . This flower expresses ...
  (1) àiqíng 爱情 love
  (2) zhùhè 祝贺 congratulations
  (3) hǎoyùn 好运 good luck
  (4) yǒuyì 友谊 friendship
  (5) zhì'āi 致哀 sympathy
  (6) dàoniàn 悼念 mourning
- bā kuài yì zhī 8 块一枝 RMB 8 per stem
- bā kuài yì duǒ 8 块一朵 RMB 8 per flower
- bā kuài yí shù 8 块一束 RMB 8 per bunch

The Flower Shop 花店 Huādiàn

bamboo 竹子 zhúzi
cactus 仙人掌 xiānrénzhǎng
carnation 康乃馨 kāngnǎixīn
China rose 月季 yuèji
chrysanthemum 菊花 júhuā
flowerpot 花盆 huāpén
greenhouse 温室 wēnshì
lavender 薰衣草 xūnyīcǎo
lily 百合 bǎihé
Miniascape (bonsai) 盆景 pénjǐng
"spinal arch bamboo" (Monstera deliciosa) 龟背竹 guībèizhú
"get rich tree" (Pachira macrocarpa) 发财树 fācái shù
peony 牡丹/芍药 mǔdān/sháoyào
rose 玫瑰 méiguī
rosemary 迷迭香 mídiéxiāng
sunflower 向日葵xiàngrìkuí
tulip 郁金香 yùjīnxiāng

19 Religious paraphernalia

宗教用品 Zōngjiào yòngpǐn

Vocabulary

Buddha statue 佛像 fóxiàng
consecration 开光 kāiguāng
incense (burner) 香 (炉) xiāng (lú)
Guanyin statue 观音像 guānyīn xiàng
home altar 家用小祭台 jiāyòng xiǎo jìtái
joss sticks and candles 香烛 xiāngzhú
prayer cushion 跪垫 guìdiàn
scripture/bible 圣经 shèngjīng
shrine 神殿 shéndiàn

20 Shoes and shoe repair

鞋和修鞋 Xié hé xiū xié

Vocabulary

athletic shoes 田径鞋 tiánjìngxié
boots 靴子 xuēzi
chinese cloth shoes 布鞋 bùxié
dress shoes 正装鞋 zhèngzhuāng xié
flats 平底鞋 píngdǐ xié
high heels 高跟鞋 gāogēnxié
hiking shoes 登山鞋 dēngshān xié
kungfu shoes 功夫鞋 gōngfu xié
loafers 无带皮鞋 wúdài píxié
snow boots 雪靴 xuěxuē
sandals 凉鞋 liángxié
slippers 拖鞋 tuōxié
sneakers 运动鞋 yùndòngxié
shoe shine oil 鞋油 xiéyóu
shoe sole 鞋底 xiédǐ
shoe laces 鞋带 xiédài

Sentences

• I'd like ... 我想要... Wǒ xiǎng yào ...

(1) a shoeshine 擦皮鞋 cā píxié
(2) to stitch up this hole 把这个洞补上 bǎ zhè gè dòng bǔ shàng
(3) to repair my sole 修一下鞋底 xiū yí xià xiédǐ

• Can these shoes be salvaged? 这双鞋还能修吗? Zhèi shuāng xié hái néng xiū ma?

• Yo dog, my dogs are dogged 嗳，哥们儿，我的脚很酸啊 ài, gēmenr, wǒ de jiǎo hěn suān a

21 Tattoos and piercings

纹身和穿孔 Wénshēn hé chuānkǒng

Sentences

• I want to pierce my ... 我想在...上打孔 Wǒ xiǎng zài ... shàng dǎkǒng

(1) ear 耳朵 ěrduo
(2) eyebrow 眉毛 méimao
(5) navel 肚脐 dùqí
(6) nose 鼻子 bízi

(3) librette 唇下 chúnxià
(4) lip 嘴唇 zuǐchún
(7) tongue 舌头 shétou

• I want a tattoo on my ... 我想在...纹身 Wǒ xiǎng zài ... wénshēn
(for more body parts see Health and Beauty p180)

• What designs do you have? 你这里有什么图案？ Nǐ zhèlǐ yǒu shénme tú'àn?

• Can you tattoo my own design? 我自己设计的图案可以纹吗？ Wǒ zìjǐ shèjì de tú'àn kěyǐ wén ma?

• Please tattoo Beijing Olympics 2008 on my forehead 麻烦你在我额头上纹一个北京奥运2008 Máfan nǐ zài wǒ étóu shàng wén yí gè Běijīng àoyùn èrlínglíngbā

22 Tea 茶 Chá

Vocabulary

black tea 红茶 hóngchá
brick tea 砖茶 zhuānchá
bubble tea (aka pearl milk tea) 珍珠奶茶 zhēnzhū nǎichá
chrysanthemum tea 菊花茶 júhuāchá
diet tea 减肥茶 jiǎnféichá
English tea 英国茶 yīngguóchá
green tea 绿茶 lǜchá
iced tea 冰茶 bīngchá
jasmine tea 茉莉花茶 mòlìhuāchá
kung fu tea 功夫茶 gōngfuchá
loose tea 茶叶 cháyè
oolong tea 乌龙茶 wūlóngchá
scented tea 花茶 huāchá
teabag 袋泡茶 dài pào chá
tea ceremony 茶道 chádào
tea set 茶具 chájù
teapot 茶壶 cháhú
white tea 白茶 báichá

23 Tobacco products 烟草 Yāncǎo

Vocabulary

ashtray 烟灰缸 yānhuīgāng
blend 混合型 hùnhéxíng
carbon monoxide 一氧化碳 yīyǎnghuàtàn
jet flame lighter 防风打火机 fángfēng dǎhuǒjī
lighter 打火机 dǎhuǒjī
match 火柴 huǒchái

cigar 雪茄 xuějiā
cigarette 香烟 xiāngyān
cured tobacco 烤烟 kǎoyān
cut tobacco 烟丝 yānsī
filter 过滤嘴儿 guòlǜzuǐr
humidor 雪茄盒儿 xuějiā hér
nicotine 烟碱 yānjiǎn
pipe 烟斗 yāndǒu
smoke 吸烟 xīyān
rolling paper 卷烟纸 juǎnyān zhǐ
tar 焦油 jiāoyóu
tobacco leaf 烟叶 yānyè

24 T-shirt printing

T恤衫喷绘 T-xùshān pēnhuì

See also "Buying clothes," p144 for fabrics and measurement vocabulary.

Sentences

- How much are the base shirts? 白底儿T恤衫多少钱？Báidǐr T-xùshān duōshǎo qián?

- Can you show me a few base shirt options? 能给我看看其他样子的白底儿T恤衫吗？Néng gěi wǒ kànkan qítā yàngzi de báidǐr Txùshān ma?

- How much will the printing cost? 印这个样子多少钱？Yìn zhèi ge yàngzi duōshǎo qián?

- What is the minimum number of shirts I need to order? 最少要买多少件？Zuìshǎo yào mǎi duōshǎo jiàn?

- Can I email you the design pattern? 我能把设计方案发电子邮件给你吗？Wǒ néng bǎ shèjì fāng'àn fā diànzǐ yóujiàn gěi nǐ ma?

Listen for this

- Do you want ... 你想要...的吗？Nǐ xiǎng yào ... de ma?
  (1) single color 单色 dānsè
  (2) dual color 双色 shuāngsè
  (3) multicolor 彩色 cǎisè

- We only sell to government organizations 我们只卖给政府机关 Wǒmen zhǐ mài gěi zhèngfǔ jīguān

SPORTS & FITNESS ►

1 Striking up a game
比赛开始 Bǐsài kāishǐ

Sentences

- Can I play? 我能玩儿吗？Wǒ néng wánr ma?
- Nice / Good ball 好球 Hǎo qíu
- My bad 我的，我的 Wǒ de, wǒ de
- Good game 打得好 Dǎ de hǎo
- You played well 你玩儿的不错 Nǐ wánr de búcuò
- I'm sweating like a dog 我浑身上下都溻了 Wǒ húnshēn shàngxià dōu tā le
- I need to rest 我得休息一下儿 Wǒ děi xiūxi yí xiàr
- I like to watch ... 我喜欢看... Wǒ xǐhuan kàn ...

(1) football (soccer) 足球 zúqiú
(2) basketball 篮球 lánqiú
(3) volleyball 排球 páiqiú
(4) billiards 台球 táiqiú

2 Sports chat 运动 Yùndòng

As is the case in English, different sports take different verbs in Chinese.

Sentences

- The following sports take the verb "to hit" 打 dǎ

I like to play ... 我喜欢打... Wǒ xǐhuan dǎ ...
(1) American football 美式足球 měishì zúqiú
(2) badminton 羽毛球 yǔmáoqiú
(3) baseball 棒球 bàngqiú
(4) basketball 篮球 lánqiú
(5) billiards 台球 táiqiú
(6) bowling 保龄球 bǎolíngqiú
(9) ice hockey 冰球 bīngqiú
(10) lacrosse 长曲棍球 cháng qūgùnqiú
(11) ping pong 乒乓球 pīngpāngqiú
(12) rugby 橄榄球 gǎnlǎnqiú
(13) softball 垒球 lěiqiú

(7) boxing 拳击 quánjī
(8) golf 高尔夫 gāo'ěrfū
(14) tennis 网球 wǎngqiú

• The following sports take the verb "to kick" 踢 tī

I like to play ... 我喜欢踢. . . Wǒ xǐhuan tī ...
(1) football (soccer) 足球 zúqiú
(2) shuttlecock 毽子 jiànzi

• The following sports take the verb 'to practice' 练 liàn

I like to practice ... 我喜欢练. . . Wǒ xǐhuan liàn ...
(1) drunken style boxing 醉拳 zuìquán
(2) martial arts 武术 wǔshù
(3) yoga 瑜珈 yújiā

• The following sports take the verb "to ride" 骑 qǐ

I like to ride ... 我喜欢骑. . . Wǒ xǐhuan qí ...
(1) bikes 自行车 zìxíngchē
(2) horses 马 mǎ

• The following sports take the verb 'to play' 玩儿 wánr

I like to play ... 我喜欢玩儿. . . Wǒ xǐhuan wán'r ...
(1) Aussie rules football 澳式橄榄球 ào shì gǎnlǎnqiú
(2) Gaelic football 爱尔兰式足球 ài'erlán shì zúqiú
(3) microlight 动力伞 dònglì sǎn
(4) paraglide 滑翔伞 huáxiángsǎn
(5) frisbee 飞盘 fēipán

• The following sports don't take a specific verb

I like ... 我喜欢⋯ Wǒ xǐhuan ...
(1) boating 划船 huáchuán
(2) bungee jumping 蹦极 bèngjí
(3) camping 野营 yěyíng
(4) climbing 登山 dēngshān
(5) dancing 跳舞 tiàowǔ
(6) dragon boating 划龙舟 huá lóngzhōu
(7) driving & motor sports 赛车 sàichē
(8) fencing 击剑 jījiàn
(9) fishing 钓鱼 diàoyú
(10) flying 飞行运动 fēixíng yùndòng
(11) hiking 徒步旅行 túbù lǚxíng
(12) ice skating 滑冰 huábīng
(13) parachute 跳伞 tiàosǎn
(14) Pilates 普拉提 pǔlātí
(15) running 跑步 pǎobù
(16) sailing 帆船 fānchuán
(17) scuba diving 潜水 qiánshuǐ
(18) shooting 射击 shèjī
(19) skiing 滑雪 huáxuě
(20) snowboarding 滑单板 huá dānbǎn
(21) swimming 游泳 yóuyǒng
(22) wind-surfing 帆板 fānbǎn

3 Gyms & fitness centers
体育馆和健身中心
Tǐyùguǎn hé jiànshēn zhōngxīn

Vocabulary

gym 体育馆 tǐyùguǎn
stadium 体育场 tǐyùchǎng
basketball court 篮球场 lánqiúchǎng
billiard hall 台球厅 táiqiútīng
football field 足球场 zúqiúchǎng
golf course 高尔夫球场 gāo'ěrfūqiúchǎng
ice hockey rink 冰球场 bīngqiúchǎng
ice skating rink 滑冰场 huábīngchǎng
race track 赛车场 sàichēchǎng
skate park 滑板公园 huábǎn gōngyuán
ski resort 滑雪场 huáxuěchǎng
swimming pool 游泳池 yóuyǒngchí

Sentences

• How much is a ... membership? ...的会员费多少钱？ ... de huìyuán fèi duōshao qián?

(1) 3 months 三个月 sānge yuè
(2) 6 months 六个月 liùge yuè
(3) one year 一年 yì nián

• Do you have ... 你们这儿有…吗？ Nǐmen zhèr yǒu ... ma?

(1) treadmills 跑步机 pǎobùjī
(2) free weights 自由重量 zìyóu zhòngliàng
(3) mat (for yoga) (练瑜珈用的)垫子 (liàn yújiā yòng de) diànzi
(4) showers 洗浴的地方 xǐyù de dìfang
(5) stationary bikes 健身车 jiànshēnchē
(6) a pool 游泳池 yóuyǒngchí
(7) dumbbells 哑铃 yǎlíng

• Can I pay per visit? 我能按次交费吗？ Wǒ néng àn cì jiāofèi ma?

• Can I bring a guest? 我能再带一个人来吗？ Wǒ néng zài dài yí gè rén lái ma?

• What kinds of classes do you have? 你们提供什么课程？ Nǐmen tígòng shénme kèchéng?

• Are classes included or do they cost extra? 这些包括课程在内吗，还是需要另外收钱？ Zhèxiē bāokuò kèchéng zài nèi ma, háishì xūyào lìngwài shōu qián?

Listen for this

- Wǒmen tígòng ... 我们提供... We offer ...
  (1) dònggǎn dānchē 动感单车 spinning
  (2) dùpíwǔ 肚皮舞 belly dancing
  (3) gāowēn yújiā 高温瑜珈 hot yoga
  (4) lādīngwǔ 拉丁舞 latin dance
  (5) pǔlātí 普拉提 pilates
  (6) tàbǎn 踏板 step

4 Skiing and Snowboarding
滑雪 huáxuě

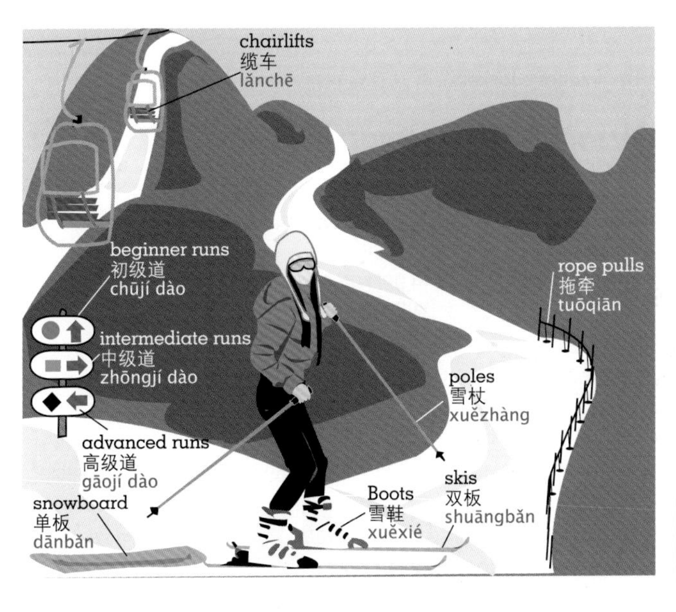

(1) bindings 固定器 gùdìngqì
(2) gloves 手套 shǒutào
(3) goofy foot (right foot first) 右脚前 yòujiǎo qián
(4) regular foot 左脚前 zuǒjiǎo qián
(5) ski goggles 雪镜 xuějìng
(6) ski hat 滑雪帽 huáxuěmào
(7) ski mask 护脸 hùliǎn
(8) ski suit 滑雪服 huáxuěfú
(9) snowboarding 滑单板 huá dānbǎn
(10) tight, loose 紧，松 jǐn, sōng

Sentences

• How many trails do you have? 你们这儿有多少雪道？ Nǐmen zhèr yǒu duōshao xuědào?

• What is total length of trails at your resort? 你们雪场的雪道总长度是多少？ Nǐmen xuěchǎng de xuědào zǒng chángdù shì duōshao?

• How much is a … ? …多少钱？ … duōshao qián?

(1) full-day ticket 全天滑雪票 quántiān huáxuě piào
(2) Half-day ticket 半天滑雪票 bàntiān huáxuě piào
(3) 2-hour ticket 2小时滑雪票 liǎng xiǎoshí huáxuě piào

• Does it include ski or snowboard rental? 包含租雪具吗？ Bāohán zū xuějù ma?

• Does it include snowsuit rental? 包含租雪服吗？ Bāohán zū xuěfú ma?

• Do you have lockers? 有没有更衣柜？ Yǒu méiyǒu gēngyīguì?

• Do you have (ski / snowboard) lessons? 有没有（双板 / 单板）培训？ Yǒu méiyǒu (shuāngbǎn/dānbǎn) péixùn?

• No cutting in line 别插队 bié chāduì

• Is there a place we could get some warm drinks near here? 这附近有没有卖热饮的？ Zhè fùjìn yǒu méiyǒu mài rèyǐn de?

Listen for this

• Nǐ duō gāo? 你多高？ How tall are you?

• Nǐ chuān duō dà hào de xié? 你穿多大号的鞋？ What shoe size are you?

• Nǐ zuǒjiǎo qián háishì yòujiǎo qián? 你左脚前还是右脚前？ Are you left or right footed?

• Nǐ yào gùdìngqì jǐn yìdiǎnr háishì sōng yìdiǎnr? 你要固定器紧一点儿还是松一点儿？ Do you want your bindings tight or loose?

• Tài jǐn le? Tài sōng le? 太紧了？ 太松了？ Too tight? Too loose?

5 Swimming 游泳 Yóuyǒng

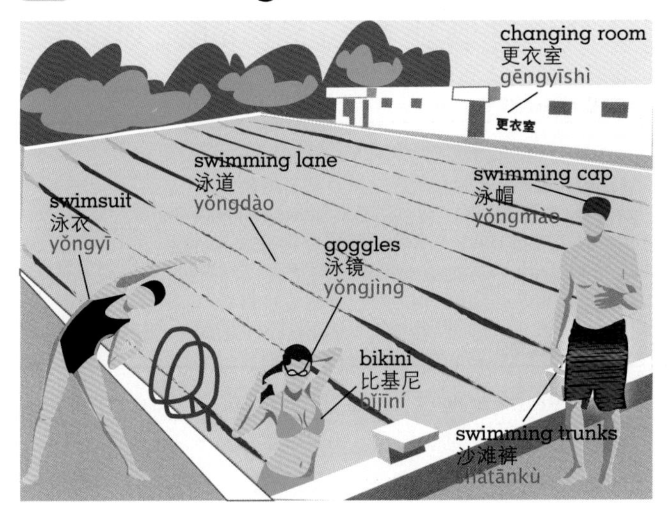

Sentences

- How much to swim? 游泳多少钱？Yóuyǒng duōshao qián?
- What time can I start swimming? 我什么时候可以开始游？Wǒ shénme shíhou kěyǐ kāishǐ yóu?
- What is the pool temperature? 水温多少度？Shuǐwēn duōshao dù?
- Where are the changing rooms? 更衣室在哪儿？Gēngyīshì zài nǎr?

Listen for this

- Nǐ děi dài yǒngmào 你得戴泳帽 You need to wear a swim cap
- Nǐ kěyǐ cóng liǎngdiǎn yóu dào sìdiǎn 你可以从两点游到四点 You can swim from two to four
- Liǎ xiǎoshí sānshí kuài qián 两小时三十块钱 RMB 30 for two hours
- èrshísì dù 二十四度 24 degrees

6 Watching sports

观看体育比赛 Guānkàn tǐyù bǐsài

Vocabulary

foul 犯规 fànguī
game/match 比赛 bǐsài
penalty 判罚 pànfá
player 运动员 yùndòngyuán
to win 赢 yíng
team 队 duì
to lose 输 shū
to score 得分 défēn
to tie 平局 píngjú

Sentences

• Where are these seats? 这几个座位在哪儿？ Zhè jǐge zuòwèi zài nǎr?

• What teams are playing? 哪些队在比赛？ Nǎxiē duì zài bǐsaì?

• What's the score? 比分是多少？ Bǐfēn shì duōshao?

• Who (is winning / won)? 谁（领先/赢了）？ Shéi (lǐngxiān/yíng le)?

Listen for this

• Zhōngguó duì Rìběn 中国对日本 China versus Japan

• Fànguī! 犯规！ Foul!

• (Hóng / Huáng) pái jǐngào! （红 / 黄）牌警告！ (Red / Yellow) card!

• Běijīng Shǒugāng duì yǐ sān bǐ yī lǐngxiān Shànghǎi Shāyú duì 北京首钢队以3比1领先上海鲨鱼队 Beijing Capital Steel (team) is beating Shanghai Sharks 3-1

• Běijīng xiàndài duì gāng shū le 北京现代队刚输了 Beijing Hyundai just lost

• Kuàlán yùndòngyuán Liú Xiáng yíngdé le jīnpái 跨栏运动员刘翔赢得了金牌 Hurdler Liu Xiang wins the gold medal

• Zhōngguó duì, jiāyóu! 中国队加油！ Go, China!

7 More games and sports

其他体育项目 Qítā tǐyǔ xiàngmù

Billiards 台球 táiqiú

billiard table 台球桌 táiqiú zhuō
cue 球杆 qiúgān
chalk 滑石粉 huáshífěn
snooker 斯诺克 sīnuòkè
cue ball 白球 báiqiú
Just like I planned it (said after a tricky shot made accidentally)
就是这么设计的 Jiùshì zhème shèji de

Boating, sailing and wind-surfing

水上运动 Shuǐshàng yùndòng

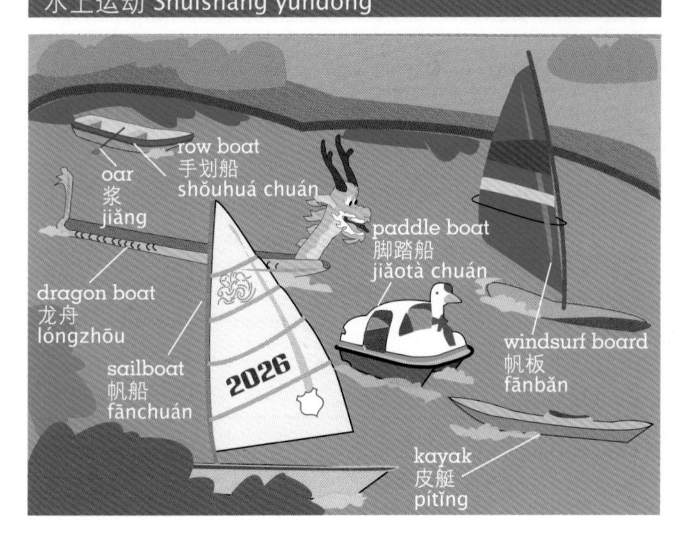

Bowling 保龄球 Bǎolíngqiú

bowling alley 保龄球馆 bǎolíngqiú guǎn
lane 球道 qiúdào
How much is it per game? 每局多少钱？ Měijú duōshǎo qián?
How much is shoe rental? 租鞋多少钱？ Zū xié duōshǎo qián?
Are there any heavier bowling balls?
有没有重一点儿的球？ Yǒu méiyǒu zhòng yìdiǎnr de qiú?

Bungee jumping 蹦极 Bèngjí

Sentences

- How much does it cost? 多少钱？Duōshao qián?
- How high is the drop? 这个有多高？Zhèi ge yǒu duō gāo?
- Is there a weight limit? 有没有体重限制？Yǒu méiyǒu tǐzhòng xiànzhì?
- Is it safe? 安全吗？ānquán ma?

Climbing 攀岩 Pānyán

Vocabulary

climbing wall 攀岩墙 pānyánqiáng
climbing shoes 攀爬鞋 pānpá xié
bolts 岩石拴 yánshí shuān
come down 下来 xiàlái
go up 向上 xiàngshàng
grip 岩点 yándiǎn
harness 保险绳 bǎoxiǎnshéng
helmet 头盔 tóukuī
knee pads 护膝 hùxī
knot 绳结 shéngjié
magnesium powder 镁粉 měifěn
rope/line 绳子 shéngzi
safety harness 安全吊带 ānquán diàodài
wristguard 护腕 hùwàn

Sentences

- Give me some slack 把绳子松一点儿 Bǎ shéngzi sōng yìdiǎnr
- I'm getting tired 我累了 Wǒ lèi le
- Lower me down 把我放低点儿 Bǎ wǒ fàng dī diǎnr

Listen for this

- reach for the next grip 到下一个岩点 dào xià yí gè yándiǎn
- sport (bolted) 运动攀岩（打好螺栓的路线）yùndòng pānyán (dǎ hǎo luóshuān de lùxiàn)
- traditional climbing 传统攀岩 chuántǒng pānyán

Football (soccer) 足球 Zúqiú

corner 角球 jiǎoqiú
free kick 任意球 rènyìqiú
goal 进球 jìnqiú
good ball 好球 hǎo qiú
hand ball 手球 shǒuqiú
kick 踢 tī
penalty kick 点球 diǎnqiú
throw-in 界外球 jièwàiqiú
yellow / red card 黄/红牌 huáng / hóng pái

Golf 高尔夫 Gāo'ěrfū

a bucket of balls 一筐球 yīkuāng qiú
caddie 球童 qiútóng
caddie fee 球童费 qiútóng fèi
cart 球车 qiúchē
club 球杆 qiúgān
driver 1号木杆 yīhào mùgān
iron 铁杆 tiěgān
putter 推杆 tuīgān
course 球场 qiúchǎng
driving range 练习场 liànxíchǎng
entrance fee 入场费 rùchǎngfèi
golf ball 高尔夫球 gāo'ěrfū qiú
golf shoes 高尔夫球鞋 gāo'ěrfūqiúxié
tee 球钉 qiúdīng

Sentences

• How much for a bucket of balls? 一筐球多少钱？Yīkuāng qiú duōshao qián?

• How much per round? 每局多少钱？Měijú duōshao qián?

• Can non-members play? 非会员可以打吗？Fēi huìyuán kěyǐ dǎ ma?

• How much is membership? 会费多少钱？Huìfèi duōshao qián?

• Do you rent clubs? 你们出租球杆吗？Nǐmen chūzū qiúgān ma?

Listen for this

• píngrì měijú qībǎi yuán, zhōumò yìqiān yuán 平日每局700元，周末1000元 RMB 700 per round on weekdays, RMB 1,000 on weekends

• fēi huìyuán bù kěyǐ 非会员不可以 non-members can't play

Hiking & camping
徒步旅游和露营 Túbù lǚyóu hé lùyíng

alpenstock 登山杖 dēngshānzhàng
backpack 背包 bēibāo
compass 指南针 zhǐnánzhēn
first-aid kit 急救包 jíjiù bāo
flashlight 手电 shǒudiàn
gas 煤油 méiyóu
headlight 头灯 tóudēng
hiking boots 登山鞋 dēngshānxié
sleeping bag 睡袋 shuìdài
stove 炉子 lúzi
tarp 防雨布 fángyǔ bù
tent 帐篷 zhàngpeng
topographical map 地形图 dìxíngtú
walking stick 手杖 shǒuzhàng
water bottle 水壶 shuǐhú

For more hiking and camping vocabulary and phrases, see Excursions p230.

Ice skating 滑冰 Huábīng

- Where can I rent ice skates? 去哪儿租冰鞋？ Qù nǎr zū bīngxié?
- Do you have (figure skates / speed skates / hockey skates)? 你们这儿有(花样鞋/速滑鞋/冰球鞋)吗？ Nǐmen zhèr yǒu (huāyàng xié / sùhuá xié / bīngqiú xié) ma?
- How much per hour? 每小时多少钱？ Měi xiǎoshí duōshao qián?
- Is it safe to skate in this ice? 在这个冰面上滑安全吗？ Zài zhèi ge bīngmiàn shàng huá ānquán ma?

Martial arts 武术 Wǔshù

ape form 猿形 yuánxíng
armed combat 器械对练 qìxiè duìliàn
at eye level 与眼平 yǔ yǎn píng
at nose level 与鼻平 yǔ bí píng
balance 平衡 pínghéng
broadsword 刀 dāo
cudgel 棍 gùn
dagger 匕首 bǐshǒu
fork 叉 chā
free combat 散打 sǎndǎ
hook 钩 gōu
sword 剑 jiàn
Shaolin style 少林功夫 Shàolín gōngfu
shield 盾 dùn
taichi 太极拳 tàijí quán
Tiger and crane double style 虎鹤双型 hǔhè shuāngxíng
Wutang style 武当功夫 Wǔdāng gōngfu

HEALTH & BEAUTY ►

Body Parts

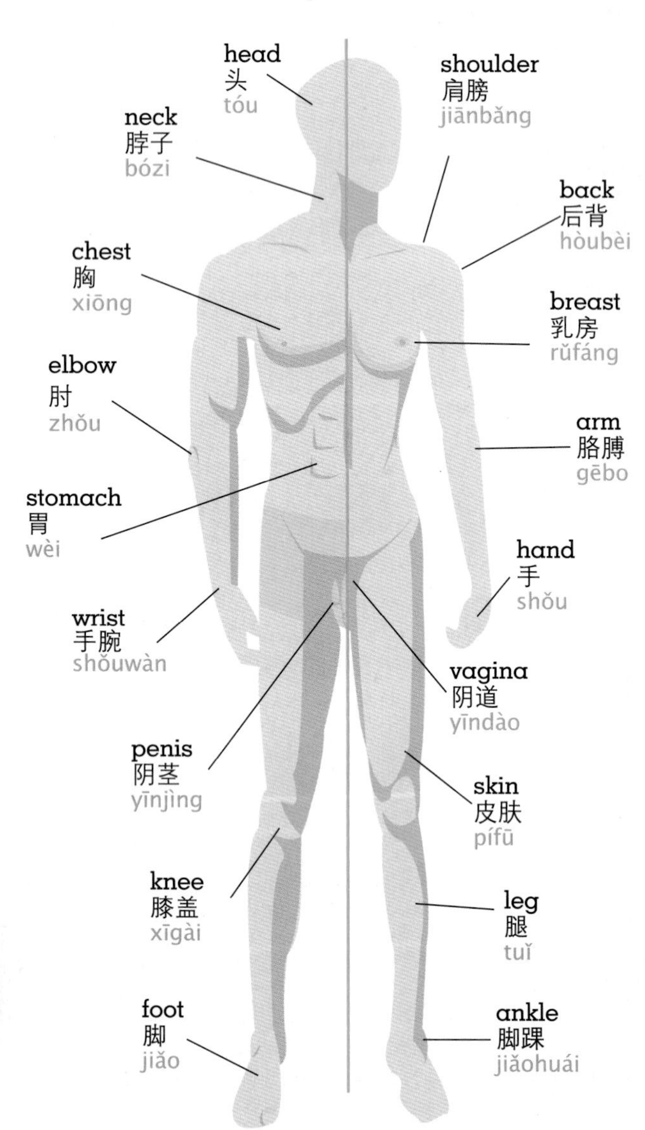
head
头
tóu
shoulder
肩膀
jiānbǎng
neck
脖子
bózi
back
后背
hòubèi
chest
胸
xiōng
breast
乳房
rǔfáng
elbow
肘
zhǒu
arm
胳膊
gēbo
stomach
胃
wèi
hand
手
shǒu
wrist
手腕
shǒuwàn
vagina
阴道
yīndào
penis
阴茎
yīnjìng
skin
皮肤
pífū
knee
膝盖
xīgài
leg
腿
tuǐ
foot
脚
jiǎo
ankle
脚踝
jiǎohuái

1 Emergencies 急救 Jíjiù

Sentences

• Help! 救命！ Jiùmìng!

• Call an ambulance 叫救护车 Jiào jiùhùchē!

• Get a doctor! 叫医生！ Jiào yīshēng!

• Take me to the nearest international hospital 送我到最近的国际医院 Sòng wǒ dào zuìjìn de guójì yīyuàn

• Take me to Beijing Emergency Medical Center 送我到北京市急救中心 Sòng wǒ dào Běijīngshì Jíjiù Zhōngxīn

• Call my ... 打电话给我的... Dǎ diànhuà gěi wǒ de ...

(1) boss 老板 lǎobǎn
(2) company 公司 gōngsī
(3) husband 丈夫 zhàngfu
(4) wife 妻子 qīzǐ
(5) spouse 爱人 àiren

2 Basics 基础词汇 Jīchǔ cíhuì

Sentences

• Where is the nearest 最近的...在哪儿？ Zuìjìn de...zài nǎr?

(1) emergency room 急救室 jíjiùshì
(2) pharmacy 药房 yàofáng
(3) optometrist 眼镜店 yǎnjìng diàn

• Is there an English-speaking physician here? 这儿有会说英语的医生吗？ Zhèr yǒu huì shuō yīngyǔ de yīshēng ma?

• Is there a 24-hour hotline? 有24小时热线电话吗？ Yǒu èrshísì xiǎoshí rèxiàn diànhuà ma?

• I would like to find an English-speaking doctor 我想要一个会讲英语的医生 Wǒ xiǎng yào yí gè huì jiǎng yīngyǔ de yīshēng

• I have health insurance 我有医疗保险 Wǒ yǒu yīliáo bǎoxiǎn

• I have BUPA insurance 我有BUPA保险 Wǒ yǒu BUPA bǎoxiǎn

• I work for ... company 我在...公司 Wǒ zài ... gōngsī

• My company will pay for the costs 我的公司会负责医疗费 Wǒ de gōngsī huì fùzé yīliáofèi

3 Making an appointment

预约 Yùyuē

Sentences

• I need to make an appointment for a ... 我想预约... Wǒ xiǎng yùyuē ...

(1) general checkup 综合体检 zōnghé tǐjiǎn
(2) dentist 牙医 yáyī
(3) pediatrician 儿科医生 érkē yīshēng
(4) gynecologist 妇科医生 fùkē yīshēng
(5) obstetrician 产科医生 chǎnkē yīshēng
(6) female doctor 女医生 nǚ yīshēng
(7) psychologist 心理医生 xīnlǐ yīshēng
(8) traditional Chinese Medicine doctor 中医大夫 zhōngyī dàifū
(9) acupuncturist 针灸师 zhēnjiūshī
(10) specialist 专家 zhuānjiā
(11) x-ray 照X光 zhào x guāng

• Can the doctor make a house call? 医生可以出诊吗？Yīshēng kěyǐ chū zhěn ma?

• Do I need ... ? 我需不需要... Wǒ xū bù xūyào...

(1) to pay with cash 付现金 fù xiànjīn
(2) a credit card 信用卡 xìnyòngkǎ
(3) insurance 买保险 mǎi bǎoxiǎn

• How much is the registration fee? 挂号费多少钱？Guàhàofèi duōshao qián?

4 Seeing the doctor

看医生 Kàn yīshēng

Listen for this

- Nǐ nǎr bù shūfu? 你哪儿不舒服？ What's the problem?
- Nǎr téng? 哪儿疼？ Where does it hurt?
- Zhèyàng duōjiǔ le? 这样多久了？ How long have you had this condition?
- Yǐqián yǒuguò zhèzhǒng qíngkuàng ma? 以前有过这种情况吗？ Have you had this before?

Sentences

- I think I have ... 我觉得我（得了）... Wǒ juéde wǒ (dé le) ...

(1) the flu 感冒 gǎnmào
(2) pneumonia 肺炎 fèiyán
(3) avian flu 禽流感 qínliúgǎn
(4) constipation 便秘 biànmì
(5) malaria 疟疾 nuèji
(6) Japanese encephalitis 乙型脑炎 yǐxíng nǎoyán
(7) a sexually transmitted disease 性病 xìngbìng
(8) sand in my eye 眼睛里进沙子了 yǎnjīng lǐ jìn shāzi le
(9) a broken bone 骨头断了 gǔtou duàn le

- Here are my symptoms: 我有这些症状：Wǒ yǒu zhèxiē zhèng zhuàng:

(1) dizziness 头晕 tóuyūn
(2) fever 发烧 fāshāo
(3) stomach problems 胃不好 wèi bù hǎo
(4) dry skin 皮肤干燥 pífū gānzào
(5) excess phlegm 多痰 duō tán
(6) diarrhea 拉肚子 lādùzi

- I ... 我... Wǒ ...

(1) was stung by a bee 被蜜蜂蜇了 bèi mìfēng zhē le
(2) was in a fight 跟人打架了 gēn rén dǎjià le
(3) have asthma 有哮喘 yǒu xiàochuǎn
(4) am diabetic 有糖尿病 yǒu tángniàobìng
(5) am on medications 在接受药物治疗 zài jiēshòu yàowù zhìliáo
(6) (think I) am pregnant （想我）怀孕了 (xiǎng wǒ) huáiyùn le

- I am allergic to ... 我对...过敏 Wǒ duì ... guòmǐn

(1) anti-inflammatories 消炎药 xiāoyányào
(2) antibiotics 抗生素 kàngshēngsù
(3) bee stings 蜜蜂蜇 mìfēng zhē
(4) codeine 可待因 kědàiyīn
(5) eggs 鸡蛋 jīdàn
(6) nuts 坚果 jiānguǒ
(7) opiates 安眠药 ānmiányào
(8) pain killers 止疼药 zhǐténgyào
(9) penicillin 青霉素 qīngméisù
(10) shellfish 贝类 bèilèi
(11) sulfa drugs 磺胺药 huáng'ānyào

- I've been vaccinated against ... 我已经打过...预防针了 Wǒ yǐjīng dǎ guò ... yùfángzhēn le

(1) hepatitis 肝炎 gānyán
(2) rabies 狂犬病 kuángquǎnbìng
(3) tetanus 破伤风 pòshāngfēng
(4) typhoid 伤寒 shānghán
(5) Japanese encephalitis 乙型脑炎 yǐxíng nǎoyán
(6) malaria 疟疾 nuèji

Listen for this

- Fāshāo ma? 发烧吗？ Do you have a fever?
- Nǐ ... ma? 你...吗？ Do you ...
  (1) hējiǔ 喝酒 drink
  (2) chōuyān 抽烟 smoke
  (3) xīdú 吸毒 take illegal drugs
- Nǐ ... 你... Are you ...
  (1) duì shénme guòmǐn ma? 对什么过敏吗？ allergic to anything?
  (2) zài jiēshòu yàowù zhìliáo ma? 在接受药物治疗吗？ on medication?
  (3) xìngshēnghuó zhèngcháng ma? 性生活正常吗？ sexually active?
  (4) lái lìjià le ma? 来例假了吗？ on your period?
- Qǐng tuō diào ... 请脱掉... Please remove your ...
  (1) shàngyī 上衣 top
  (2) kùzi 裤子 pants
- Qǐng tǎng zhèr 请躺这儿 Please lie down here
- Shēn hūxī 深呼吸 Breathe deeply
- Niǔtóu késòu 扭头咳嗽 Turn your head and cough
- Wǒ děi kàn nǐ de ... 我得看你的... I need to take your ...
  (1) X guāng piàn X光片 X-ray
  (2) dàbiàn yàngběn 大便样本 stool sample
  (3) xuěyàng 血样 blood sample
  (4) niàoyàng 尿样 urine sample
  (5) biǎntáotǐ 扁桃体 tonsil sample
- Nǐ děi zuò jìnyíbù jiǎnchá 你得做进一步检查 You need further tests

• Wǒ yào bǎ nǐ zhuǎn gěi zhuānjiā yīshī 我要把你转给专家医师
I'm going to refer you to a specialist

Watch for this

- emergency ward 急救病房 jíjiù bìngfáng
- internal medicine 内服药 nèifú yào
- external medicine 外用药 wàiyòng yào
- surgery 外科 waìkē
- dermatology 皮肤科 pífūkē
- dentistry 牙科 yákē
- radiology 放射科 fàngshèkē
- traditional Chinese medicine 中医 zhōngyī
- moxibustion 艾灸 àizhì
- acupuncture 针灸 zhēnjiū
- orthodontics 畸齿矫正 jīchǐ jiàozhèng
- psychiatric care 精神病科 jīngshénbìngkē
- obstetrics 产科 chǎnkē
- gynecology 妇科 fùkē
- pediatrics 儿科 érkē
- optometry 验光 yànguāng
- operating (room) 手术（手术室）shǒushù (shǒushùshì)

5 At the pharmacy

在药店 Zài yàodiàn

Sentences

• Do you have ... 你们有没有 . . . Nǐmen yǒu méiyǒu ...

(1) Chinese medicine 中药 zhōngyào
(2) Western medicine 西药 xīyào
(3) Herbal medicine 草药 cǎoyào

• I need a refill of this medication 我要换药 Wǒ yào huàn yào

• I need something for my ... 我要开点治 . . . 的药 Wǒ yào kāi diǎn zhì ... de yào

(1) stomach ache 胃疼 wèi téng
(2) diarrhea 拉肚子 lādùzi
(3) constipation 便秘 biànmì
(4) flu 流感 liúgǎn
(5) cold 感冒 gǎnmào
(6) dry skin 皮肤干燥 pífū gānzào
(7) headache 头疼 tóu téng

• How often should I take it? 多久吃一次？Duōjiǔ chī yí cì?

• For how long should I take it? 要吃多久？Yào chī duōjiǔ?

• Can I drink alcohol while on this medication? 吃药期间能喝酒吗？Chī yào qījiān néng hē jiǔ ma?

• How do I take this? 这个药怎么用？Zhègè yào zěnme yòng?

Listen for this

• kǒufú 口服 take orally

• wàiyòng 外用 external remedy

• Nǐ yǒu chǔfāng ma? 你有处方吗？Do you have a prescription?

• Mǎi zhègè yào xūyào yǒu chǔfāng 买这个药需要有处方 You need a prescription to buy this medicine

6 Medicine and medical tools

药品和医疗器械 Yàopǐn hé yīliáo qìxiè

Vocabulary

Acetaminophen (a replacement for aspirin) 退热净 tuìrèjìng
antacid 抗酸剂 kàngsuānjì
antibiotics 抗生素 kàngshēngsù
antiseptic 消毒剂 xiāodújì
aspirin 阿司匹林 āsīpīlín
band aid 创可贴(邦迪) chuàngkětiē (bāngdí)
birth control pills 避孕药 bìyùnyào
calamine lotion 炉甘石液 lúgānshí yè
condoms 避孕套 bìyùntào
contact lens / eyeglass fluid 隐形眼镜/眼镜药水 yǐnxíng yǎnjìng / yǎnjìng yàoshuǐ
hand moisturizer 护手霜 hùshǒushuāng
ibuprofen 布洛芬 bùluòfēn
Immodium 易蒙停 yìméngtíng
inhaler 吸入器 xīrùqì
injector 注射器 zhùshèqì
iodine 碘酒 diǎnjiǔ
laxative 泻药 xièyào
lip balm 润唇膏 rùnchúngāo
lomotil 止泻宁 zhǐxièníng
malaria tablets 疟疾药 nuèjiyào
pregnancy test 妊娠测试 rènshēn cèshì
re-hydration salts 盐水 yánshuǐ
rubbing alcohol 外用酒精 wàiyòng jiǔjīng

cough medicine 止咳药 zhǐkéyào
deodorant 除臭剂 chúchòujì
dramamine 晕海宁 yūnhǎiníng
eye drops 眼药水 yǎnyàoshuǐ
floss 牙线 yáxiàn
Golden Throat (throat losenge) 金嗓子喉宝 jīnsǎngzi hóubǎo
sanitary pads 卫生巾 wèishēngjīn
sleeping pill/s 安眠药 ānmiányào
sun cream 防晒霜 fángshàishuāng
syringe 注射器 zhùshèqì
tampons 棉球 miánqiú
thermometer 体温计 tǐwēnjì
Tylenol 泰诺 Tàinuò
vitamin/s 维他命 wéitāmìng

7 At the optometrist

验光配镜 Yànguāng pèijìng

Sentences

- I need new ... 我想要一副新的. . . Wǒ xiǎng yào yī fù xīnde ...
  (1) glasses 眼镜 yǎnjìng
  (2) contact lenses 隐型眼镜 yǐnxíng yǎnjìng
  (3) frames 眼镜框 yǎnjìng kuàng
  (4) prescriptions 镜片 jìngpiàn

- My prescription is 150 我的验光报告是150度 Wǒ de yànguāng bàogào shì yìbǎiwǔshí dù

- Can I take an eye test? 我能测一下视力吗? Wǒ néng cè yí xià shìlì ma?

- How much will it cost? 多少钱? Duōshǎo qián?

- When can I pick them up? 我什么时候来取? Wǒ shénme shíhou lái qǔ?

- Can I have a receipt for my insurance? 能给我一张保险的发票吗? Néng gěi wǒ yì zhāng bǎoxiǎn de fāpiào ma?

Listen for this

- Zuǒbiān hǎo hái shì yòubiān hǎo? 左边好还是右边好? Which one is better, left or right?
- sǎnguāng 散光 astigmatism

Bodily Emotions

Breathe life into your speech with body-related onomatopoeias

by Lee Ambrozy

• 嗷 áo exclamation of pain
Ao! Gāi sǐ de gǒu! 嗷！该死的狗！Ow! Damned dog!

• 咕噜 gūlū stomach grumbling
Wǒ méiyǒu yī fēn qián, dùzi tiāntiān gūlū jiào 我没有一分钱，肚子天天咕噜叫 I don't have a penny, everyday my tummy rumbles

• 嘣嘣 bēngbēng heart beating
Kàndào tā jiù liǎnhóng xīn bēngbēng tiào 看到她就脸红心嘣嘣跳 When I see her I blush and my heart starts pounding

• 怦怦 pēngpēng heart throbbing with emotion
Lǎobǎn yī ràngràng wǒ xīnlǐ jiù pēngpēng tiào 老板一嚷嚷我心里就怦怦跳 When the boss shouts, my heart throbs with anxiety

• 呜呜 wūwū whimpering
Wūwūwū, huózhè shì wèile shénme ya? 呜呜呜，活着是为了什么呀！Boo hoo hoo, what's the use of living?

• 哇哇 wāwā wailing
Tā bú yào nǐ, wāwā di kū yě méi yòng 她不要你，哇哇地哭也没用 She doesn't want you, it's no use wailing all day

• 噗噜 pulu a flood of tears
Yǎnlèi pulupulu diào zài dì shàng 眼泪噗噜噗噜掉是在地上 Her tears gushed to the ground

• 哼 hèng a grunt, a snort
Hèng! Nǐ suǎn lǎo jǐ? 哼！你算老几？Hmmph! Who do you think you are?

• 哧哧 chīchī snickering
Chīchī, kān tā de kùchǎ lòu chū lái le! 哧哧，看她的裤衩露出来了！Chichichi (heeheehee), look at her panties peeking out!

• 嘿嘿 hēihēi cackling
Hēihēihēi! Kàn nǐ wǎng nǎr pǎo! 嘿嘿嘿！看你往哪儿跑！Hahaha! Where you gonna run to?

• 呵呵哈哈 hēhēhāhā hearty laughter
Hēhēhāhā, wǒ fācái le! 呵呵哈哈，我发财了！ Heehee haha! I've struck it rich!

• 哄哄 hōnghōng guffaws
Hōnghōnghōng, zài lái yī bēi jiǔ 哄哄哄，再来一杯酒 Hohohoho! Let's have another round of drinks!

• 哆嗦 duōsuo trembling from fear, cold or anger
Tā shuō wǒ pàng, qì de wǒ zhí duōsuo! 她说我胖，气的我直哆嗦！ She said I was fat. Got me so mad I'm "duosuo" FURIOUS!

• 嗝 gé hiccupping
Chī le shí gè mántou shéi dōu huì dǎ gé de ma? 吃了十个馒头谁都会打嗝的吗？ After eating ten steamed buns, wouldn't anybody hiccup?

• 啐 cuì spitting
Nǐ shuō huà néng bùnéng bù cuì wǒ yī liǎn ma? 你说话能不能不啐我一脸吗？ You think you could speak without spitting in my face?

• 喀 kā coughing, vomiting
Tā gǎnmào le, kākā di késou 他感冒了，喀喀地咳嗽 He's got the flu, hacking and coughing

• 噗 pū farting
Sījī de zuòwèi tūrán pū le yī shēng ma? 司机的坐位突然噗了一声？ Was that a sudden "pu" sound from the driver's seat?

• 吁吁 xūxū wheezing
Zhēn méi yòng! Cái jǐ cì jiù xūxū de chuǎn 真没用！才几次就吁吁地喘 Useless! After only a couple times it was wheezing like "xuxu"

• 呼哧 hūchī panting
Hē wán jiǔ kàn dào shuàigē wǒ rěn bú zhù hūchīhūchī de 喝完酒看到帅哥我忍不住呼哧呼哧的 After a few drinks I can't resist "huchihuchi" panting when I see a hottie

• 呼噜 hūlu snoring
Jiù yīnwéi lǎo dǎ hūlu wǒmén jiù yào líhūn le 就因为老打呼噜我们就要离婚了 Due to the frequent snoring, we must get a divorce

• 嗡嗡 wēngwēng a buzzing headache
Zuówǎn hē duō le, zǎoshàng tóu wēngwēng xiǎng 昨晚喝多了，早上头嗡嗡响 Tied one on last night. This morning my head is buzzing like a jackhammer

H & B

8 At the dentist 看牙医 Kàn yáyī

Sentences

- My tooth hurts 我牙疼 Wǒ yá téng
- I want my teeth cleaned 我想洗牙 Wǒ xiǎng xǐ yá
- I want my teeth whitened 我想美白牙齿 Wǒ xiǎng měibái yáchǐ
- I think I need a filling 我可能得补牙 Wǒ kěnéng děi bǔ yá
- Can I get ... ? 我能用...吗？ Wǒ néng yòng ... ma?

(1) anesthetic 麻醉 mázuì
(2) novocaine 局部麻醉 júbù mázuì
(3) nitrous (oxide) 笑气(一氧化二氮) xiàoqì (yīyǎnghuà'èrdàn)
(4) a porcelain filling 陶瓷补牙 táocí bǔ yá

- It hurts / doesn't hurt 好疼！/一点儿也不疼 Hǎo téng!/Yì diǎnr yě bù téng
- Stop! 停一下！ Tíng yí xià!

Listen for this

- Wǎng hòu tǎng 往后躺 Lie back
- Shùkǒu 漱口 Rinse and spit
- Tóu wǎng hòu yǎng 头往后仰 Tilt your head back
- Zhāng dà diǎnr 张大点儿 Open wider
- Yǎo hé 咬合 Bite down
- Wǒmen lái zhào zhāng X guāng piàn 我们来照张X光片 We need to take an x-ray
- Rúguǒ téng de huà gàosu wǒ 如果疼的话告诉我 Let me know if it hurts
- Nǐ hái děi zài lái yí cì 你还得再来一次 You need to come back again (for another appointment)

9 Medical clinics and hospitals

- Bayley & Jackson Medical Center
庇利积臣医疗中心 Bìlìjīchén Yīliáo Zhōngxīn
7 Ritan Donglu, Chaoyang District 朝阳区日坛东路7号
(8562 9998, after hours 8562 9990)

- Beijing Children's Hospital 北京儿童医院 Běijīng értóng Yīyuàn
56 Nanlishi Lu, Xicheng District 西城区南礼士路56号 (6802 8401)

- Beijing Emergency Medical Center
北京市急救中心 Běijīngshì Jíjiù Zhōngxīn
103 Qianmen Xidajie, Xuanwu District 宣武区前门西大街103号
(6609 8114)

- Beijing Friendship Hospital 北京友谊医院 Běijīng Yǒuyí Yīyuàn
95 Yong'an Lu, Xuanwu District 宣武区永安路95号
(6301 4411 ext 3482)

- Beijing Intech Eye Hospital 英智眼科医院 Yīngzhì Yǎnkē Yīyuàn
1/4/5/F, Panjiayuan Mansion, 12 Panjiayuan Nanli, Chaoyang District
朝阳区潘家园南里12号潘家园大厦1/4/5层(6771 5558, fax 6775 8429)

- Beijing International SOS Clinic
北京国际救援中心 Běijīng Guójì Jiùyuán Zhōngxīn
Building C Beixin Jingyi Mansion, Sanlitun Xiwujie, Chaoyang District
朝阳区三里屯西五街北信京谊大厦C 座 (6462 9112, 24hrs 6462 9100)

- Beijing Maternity Hospital 北京妇产医院 Běijīng Fùchǎn Yīyuàn
17 Qihelou, Dongcheng District 东城区骑河楼17号 (6525 0731)

- Beijing Obstetrics and Gynecology Hospital
北京妇产医院 Běijīng fùchǎn yīyuàn
251 Yaojiayuan Lu, Chaoyang District 朝阳区姚家园路251号
(8597 6699)

- Beijing United Family Clinics
北京和睦家医院诊所 Běijīng Hémùjiā Yīyuàn Zhěnsuǒ
1）Unit 818, Pinnacle Plaza, Tianzhu Developing Zone,
Shunyi District 顺义区天竺开发区日祥广场818单元；
2）B/1 St.Regis Apartment Building, 21 Jianguomenwai Dajie,
Chaoyang District
朝阳区建国门外大街21号北京国际俱乐部饭店公寓楼地下一层
(8532 1221)

- Beijing United Family Hospital 北京和睦家医院 Běijīng Hémùjiā Yīyuàn
  2 Jiangtai Lu, Chaoyang District 朝阳区将台路2号
  (6433 3960/2345, fax 6433 3963)

- Beijing Vista Clinic 维世达诊所 Wéishìdá Zhěnsuǒ
  B29 Kerry Center, 1 Guanghua Lu, Chaoyang District
  朝阳区光华路1号嘉里中心B29
  (8529 6618, fax 8529 6615)

- Cancer Institute and Hospital 中国医学科学院肿瘤医院
  Zhōngguó Yīxué Kēxuéyuàn Zhǒngliú Yīyuàn
  17 Panjiayuan Nanli, Chaoyang District 朝阳区潘家园南里17号
  (6778 1331)

- Hong Kong International Medical Clinic
  香港国际医务诊所 Xiānggǎng Guójì Yīwù Zhěnsuǒ
  9/F Office Tower, Hong Kong Macau Center, 2 Chaoyangmen Beidajie, Chaoyang District 朝阳门北大街2号港澳中心办公楼9层
  (6501 4260/ 2288 ext 2346)

- International Medical Center (IMC)
  北京国际医疗中心 Běijīng Guójì Yīliáo Zhōngxīn
  S106, 1/F Lufthansa Office Building, 50 Liangmahe Lu, Chaoyang District 朝阳区亮马河路50号北京燕莎中心写字楼1层S106
  (6465 1561/ 2/ 3)

- Peking Union Medical College Hospital
  北京协和医院 Běijīng Xiéhé Yīyuàn
  53 Dongdan Beidajie,Dongcheng District 东城区东单北大街53号
  (6529 5284)

- Sino-Japanese Friendship Hospital
  北京中日友好医院 Běijīng Zhōngrì Yǒuhǎo Yīyuàn
  Yinghua Donglu, Heping Jie, Chaoyang District
  朝阳区和平街樱花东路
  (6422 2952)

- Tongren Hospital 北京同仁医院 Běijīng Tóngrén Yīyuàn
  2 Chongnei Dajie, Dongcheng District 东城区崇内大街2号
  (6512 9911)

Emergency Card

(Please fill out and photocopy as needed)

(1) My name is ______________________

我叫 ______________________

Wǒ jiào ______________________

(2) My home telephone number is ______________________

我家电话是 ______________________

Wǒ jiā diànhuà shì ______________________

(3) In an emergency, take me to ______________________

I am affiliated with ______________________

(company, school, or organization)

如遇紧急情况请送我到______________________

我是______________________（公司，学校或组织）成员

Rú yù jǐnjí qíngkuàng qǐng sòng wǒ dào______________________

Wǒ shì______________ (gōngsī, xuéxiào huò zǔzhī) chéngyuán

(4) My insurance provider is ______________________

我购买了______________________的保险

Wǒ gòumǎi lè______________________dè bǎoxiǎn

(5) Policy number______________, and they will pay all my bills

保险号码为______________，他们会支付所有费用

Bǎoxiǎn hàomǎ wéi __________, tāmen huì zhīfù suǒyǒu fèiyòng

(6) I have allergies to ______________________

I am currently on ______________________ medications

我对______________过敏。我现在在服用______________药

Wǒ duì______________guòmǐn. Wǒ xiànzài zài fúyòng__________yào

10 At the hair salon

在美发厅 Zài měifàtīng

Vocabulary

bangs 刘海儿 liúhǎir
barrettes 条形发卡 tiáoxíng fàqiǎ
beard 连鬓胡子 liánbìn húzi
black hair 黑发 hēifà
blonde 金(黄色头)发的 jīn(huángsè tóu)fa de
brunette 深褐色头发的 shènhèsè tóufa de
clips 夹子 jiāzi
curlers 卷发夹子 juǎnfà jiāzi
curls 卷发 juǎnfà
extensions 接发 jiē fà
goatee 山羊胡 shānyánghú
mustache 小胡子 xiǎohúzi
part 头发分界 tóufà fēnjiè
red head 红褐色头发的 hónghèsè tóufa de
sideburns 鬓角 bìnjiǎo
split ends 发尾分岔 fàwěi fēnchà
tips 发梢 fàshāo

Sentences

• Can I get ... 我想（要）... Wǒ xiǎng (yào) ...

(1) a hair cut 剪发 jiǎnfà
(2) a hair wash 洗头 xǐtóu
(3) "the works" (wash/cut/blowdry) 洗剪吹 xǐ jiǎn chuī
(4) a solid-color hair dye 单色染 dānsè rǎn
(5) highlights 挑染 tiǎo rǎn
(6) a rinse (light color to hide some gray) 焗油 jūyóu
(7) a perm 烫发 tàngfà
(8) my hair straightened 拉直 lā zhí
(9) braids 梳辫子 shū biànzi
(10) dreadlocks 骇人发咎 hàirén fàjiū
(11) cornrows 玉米辫子头 yùmǐ biànzi tóu
(12) a combover 地方支持中央式发型 dìfāng zhīchí zhōngyāng shì fàxíng
(13) a shag 蓬乱一团的头发 péngluànyītuán de tóufà
(14) my head shaved bald 剃光头 tì guāngtóu
(15) a handcut, long with varying lengths (common haircut) 手剪长碎 shǒujiǎn chángsuì
(16) steaming treatment 蒸汽加热 zhēngqì jiārè

• Do you have books or magazines I can look through to find the style I want? 你有没有书或者杂志？我可以在里面找找喜欢的发型 Nǐ yǒu méiyǒu shū huòzhě zázhì? Wǒ kěyǐ zài lǐmiàn zhǎozhao xǐhuan de fàxíng

• Do you have foreign hair stylists? 你们有外国发型师吗？Nǐmen yǒu wàiguó fàxíngshī ma?

• Just take a little off the top 把上面稍微剪掉一些就行 Bǎ shàngmiàn shāowēi jiǎn diào yīxiē jiù xíng

• Don't ... 别. . . Bié ...

(1) thin it out too much 打得太薄 dǎ de tài báo
(2) cut it too short 剪得太短 jiǎn de tài duǎn

• Can you make it ... ? 能不能把它弄成. . . néng bùnéng bǎ tā nòng chéng...

(1) shorter on the back and sides
后面和两边短一点 hòumiàn hé liǎngbiān duǎn yī diǎn
(2) look like this picture
像这个图里的一样 xiàng zhège túlǐ de yīyàng
(3) hip/fashionable 时尚一点 shíshàng yì diǎn
(4) curly 卷一点儿 juǎn yī diǎnr
(5) mullet (aka business in front, party in back)
前短后长的发型 qián duǎn hòu cháng de fàxíng

• Can you make the back ... 能不能把后面剪得. . . Néng bùnéng bǎ hòumian jiǎn de ...

(1) very short 很短 hěn duǎn
(2) square 齐一点儿 qí yìdiǎnr
(3) round 圆一点儿 yuán yìdiǎnr

• I have ... 我的头发. . . Wǒ de tóufa ...

(1) oily hair 很油 hěn yóu
(2) dry hair 很干 hěn gān
(3) split ends 发梢分岔了 fàshāo fēnchà le
(4) dandruff 有头皮屑 yǒu tóupíxiè
(5) lice 有虱子 yǒu shīzi

• Please, do not use the razor/clippers 请别用剃刀/大剪刀 Qǐng bié (yòng tìdāo/dà jiǎndāo)

• I don't want my hair to be uneven all over 我不想让我的头发分得这么偏 Wǒ bù xiǎng ràng wǒ de tóufa fēn dé zhème piān

• Do you have a DVD player so I can watch a DVD while I wait? 你这儿有DVD机吗？我想边等边看DVD Nǐ zhèr yǒu DVD jī ma? Wǒ xiǎng biān děng biān kàn DVD

• I only want a haircut, no massage please 我只想剪头，不要按摩 Wǒ zhǐ xiǎng jiǎntóu, bú yào ànmó

• I'm in a hurry, can you make it a quickie? 我赶时间，你能不能快点儿？Wǒ gǎn shíjiān, nǐ néng bùnéng kuài diǎnr?

Listen for this

- Nǐ xiǎng liú ... 你想留... ... do you want it?
  (1) duōduǎn? 多短? How short (2) duōcháng? 多长? How long
- Shénme yàngshì? 什么样式? What style?
- Cóng zhè běn shū lǐ tiāo yí gè ba 从这本书里挑一个吧 Pick one from this book
- Nǐ yào xǐtóu ma? 你要洗头吗? Do you want your hair washed?
- Zhè shì nǐ tóufà de běnsè ma? 这是你头发的本色吗? Is that your natural hair color?
- Nǐ rǎn guò fà ma? 你染过发吗? Have you dyed your hair?
- Nǐ xiǎng ...ma ? 你想...吗? Do you want your hair ...
  (1) piǎo fà 漂发 bleached? (2) juǎn fà 卷发 permed?
- Nǐ yào yòng ... ma? 你要用...吗? Do you want us to use ... ?
  (1) xǐfàshuǐ 洗发水 shampoo
  (2) hùfàsù 护发素 conditioner
  (3) mósī 摩丝 hair mousse
  (4) zhělì 啫喱 hair gel
  (5) fàjiāo 发胶 hair spray
  (6) ruǎnhuà jì 软化剂 softener
  (7) yíngyǎng hùlǐ 营养护理 nutrient protection

11 At the beauty salon

在美容院 Zài měiróngyuàn

Vocabulary

slimming treatments 减肥疗程 jiǎnféi liáochéng
aromatherapy 芳香疗法 fāngxiāng liáofǎ
all-natural 全自然 quán zìrán
tanning bed 日光浴床 rìguāngyù chuáng
self-tanning spray 美黑喷雾 měihēi pēnwù
acrylic nails 水晶指甲 shuǐjīng zhījiǎ
facial 面部护理 miànbù húlǐ

Sentences

- Can you ... 你会...吗? Nǐ huì ... ma ?

(1) push my cuticles back 去死皮 qù sǐpí
(2) pluck my eyebrows 修眉毛 xiū méimao

- A little harder 重一点儿 Zhòng yì diǎnr
- A little softer 轻一点儿 Qīng yì diǎnr
- That hurts 好疼啊 Hǎo téng a
- That feels good 很舒服 Hěn shūfu
- Can you wax my ... 你能给我...脱毛吗? Nǐ néng gěi wǒ ... tuōmáo ma?

(1) legs 腿部 tuǐbù
(2) bikini area 比基尼区 bǐjīní qū
(3) back 后背 hòubèi
(4) chest 胸部 xiōngbù

Listen for this

- Nǐ xiǎng ... ma? 你想...吗? Do you want ...
  (1) xiū zhǐjia 修指甲 manicure
  (2) xiū jiǎo 修脚 pedicure
  (3) zuò miànbù hùlǐ 做面部护理 facial
  (4) zǐwàixiàn rìguāngyù 紫外线日光浴 a UV tan
  (5) měiróng hùlǐ 美容护理 a beauty treatment
  (6) rìguāngyù 日光浴 a tanning session
  (7) fǎshì xiū zhījiǎ 法式修指甲 French manicure
  (8) qù jiǎozhì 去角质 cream buffing
  (9) zhòng jiémáo 种睫毛 your eyelashes lengthed

For cosmetics, see Shopping p153.

12 At the spa 在 Spa Zài Spa

Sentences

- I would like ... 我想做... Wǒ xiǎng zuò ...

(1) blind person massage 盲人按摩 mángrén ànmó
(2) cupping / moxibustation 拔火罐儿 bá huǒguànr
(3) deep tissue massage
深层肌肉放松按摩 shēncéng jīròu fàngsōng ànmó
(4) foot massage 足底/足疗 zúdǐ / zúliáo
(5) ear candles 耳烛疗法 ěrzhú liáofǎ
(6) grabbing the flesh 推拿 tuīná
(7) health-care 保健 bǎojiàn
(8) hot stone 热石疗法 rèshí liáofǎ
(9) milk and honey 奶蜜 nǎi mì

(10) salt and milk 盐奶 yán nǎi
(11) Swedish massage 瑞典式按摩 ruìdiǎnshì ànmó
(12) Thai massage 泰式按摩 tàishì ànmó
(13) traditional Chinese massage
传统中式按摩 chuántǒng zhōngshì ànmó

• Do you have ... 你们有没有... Nǐmen yǒu méiyǒu ...

(1) body scrubs 搓澡 cuōzǎo
(2) Chinese herbal medicine foot soak 中药泡脚 zhōngyào pàojiǎo
(3) clay packs 黏土护理 niántǔ hùlǐ
(4) cold pool 冷水池 lěngshuǐchí
(5) hot mud spa 火山泥温泉浴 huǒshānní wēnquán yù
(6) hot springs 温泉 wēnquán
(7) hot tub 热浴盆 rè yùpén
(8) milk baths 牛奶浴 niúnǎiyù
(9) sauna 桑拿 sāngná
(10) seaweed and mud wrap 深海泥体膜 shēnhǎiní tǐmó
(11) steam room 蒸汽浴房 zhēngqì yùfáng
(12) resting room 休息厅 xiūxitīng

13 Plastic surgery 整形外科手术
Zhěngxíng wàikē shǒushù

Sentences

• Do you offer ... 你们做...吗? Nǐmen zuò ... ma?

(1) electrolysis 电子除痣 diànzǐ chú zhì
(2) botox 肉毒杆菌除皱 ròudúgǎnjūn chúzhòu
(3) liposuction 抽脂手术 chōuzhǐ shǒushù
(4) collagen (fat injections) lips 嘴唇增厚术 zuǐchún zēnghòu zhù
(5) nose job 鼻子整形 bízi zhěngxíng
(6) breast enlargement 隆胸 lóngxiōng
(7) penis enlargement 阴茎增长术 yīnjīng zēngcháng shù
(8) tummy tuck 腹部整形术 fùbù zhěngxíng shù
(9) facelift 面部整容 miànbù zhěngróng
(10) chemical peel 化学脱皮术 huàxué tuōpí shù
(11) eyelid 眼睑手术 yǎnjiǎn shǒushù

• How much is it? 多少钱? Duōshǎo qián?

• Has the doctor had any training outside of China? 医生有没有出国受过培训? Yīshēng yǒu méiyǒu chūguó shòuguò péixùn?

TRANSPORTATION ►

1 Orientation & direction
方位和方向 Fāngwèi hé fāngxiàng

Vocabulary

north 北 běi	⟷	south 南 nán
east 东 dōng	⟷	west 西 xī
on 上 shàng	⟷	above 上面 shàngmiàn
under 下 xià	⟷	below 下面 xiàmiàn
left 左 zuǒ	⟷	right 右 yòu
ahead 前头 qiántou	⟷	behind 后头 hòutou
front 前面 qiánmiàn	⟷	back 后面 hòumiàn
inside 里面 lǐmiàn	⟷	outside 外面 wàimiàn
entrance 入口 rùkǒu	⟷	exit 出口 chūkǒu
enter 进入 jìnrù	⟷	exit 出去 chūqù
beside 在旁边 zài pángbiān	⟷	between 在中间 zài zhōngjiān
near 近 jìn	⟷	far 远 yuǎn
nearest 最近的 zuìjìn de	⟷	furthest 最远的 zuìyuǎn de
straight 直走 zhí zǒu	⟷	turn 转弯 zhuǎnwān
faster 快点儿 kuài diǎnr	⟷	slower 慢点儿 màn diǎn'r
fastest 最快的 zuìkuài de	⟷	slowest 最慢的 zuìmàn de

2 Getting directions 问路 Wènlù

Sentences

• Sorry to bother you. I'm lost. Can you help me? 麻烦你一下，我迷路了。能帮帮我吗？ Máfán nǐ yí xià, wǒ mílù le. Néng bāngbang wǒ ma?

• Can you tell me how to get to ... ? 我怎么去...？ Wǒ zěnme qù...?

(1) the nearest subway 最近的地铁口 zuìjìn de dìtiě kǒu
(2) Liqun Roast Duck Restaurant 利群烤鸭店 Lìqún Kǎoyā Diàn

• About how far is it? 大概有多远？ Dàgài yǒu duōyuǎn?

• Do you know where I can find an English language street map? 哪儿有英文的地图？ Nǎr yǒu yīngwén de dìtú?

• Would you please show me where the Lama Temple is on the map? 麻烦你在地图上给我指出来雍和宫在哪儿？Máfan nǐ zài dìtú shàng gěi wǒ zhǐ chūlái Yōnghégōng zài nǎr?

Listen for this

• Zài Yǒuyì Shāngdiàn hé ā'ěrjílìyà dàshǐguǎn zhōngjiān 在友谊商店和阿尔及利亚大使馆中间 It's between the Freindship store and the Algerian embassy

• Guò Yíndìng Qiáo zài yòu guǎi 过银锭桥再右拐 Cross Yinding Bridge and take a right

• Yúnshàng zài Kǎoròujì pángbiānr 云上在烤肉季旁边儿 Club Nuage is next to Kaorouji Restaurant

3 Taking a cab

坐出租车 Zuò chūzūchē

Sentences

• Can you call a cab for me? 帮我叫辆出租车好吗？ Bāng wǒ jiào liàng chūzūchē hǎo ma?

• Are you working right now? 你走吗？ Nǐ zǒu ma?

• I'm going to ... 我去... Wǒ qù ...

(1) the airport 机场 jīchǎng
(2) Sanlitun 三里屯 Sānlǐtún
(3) the International School of Beijing 北京国际学校 Běijīng Guójì Xuéxiào
(4) Beijing Railway Station 北京站 Běijīng Zhàn
(5) the Lusongyuan Hotel 侣淞园宾馆 Lǚsōngyuán Bīnguǎn

• First we will go to ... , then we will go to ... 我们先去...，再去... Wǒmen xiān qù ..., zài qù ...

• We are sharing this taxi: we'll drop her off first then me 我们一起打车，先送她再送我 Wǒmen yìqǐ dǎ chē, xiān sòng tā zài sòng wǒ

- Do you know this place? 这个地方你认识吗？Zhèigè dìfang, nǐ rènshi ma?

- Are you absolutely sure? 你确定知道吗？Nǐ quèdìng zhīdao ma?

- Drive straight ahead 一直往前开 Yìzhí wǎng qián kāi

- Use the meter 打表 Dǎ biǎo

- Take the Airport Expressway 走机场高速 Zǒu Jīchǎng Gāosù

- Avoid (Third Ring Road / Jingshun Lu) 别走（三环/京顺路）Bié zǒu (Sānhuán / Jīngshùn Lù)

- Never take Jianguomenwai at rush hour 高峰时间千万别走建国门外 Gāofēng shíjiān qiānwàn bié zǒu Jiànguóménwài

- What route do you suggest? 你说怎么走好？Nǐ shuō zěnme zǒu hǎo?

- Is this the slowest traffic light in Beijing? 这个红绿灯是不是北京最慢的？Zhèige hónglǜdēng shì búshì Běijīng zuì màn de?

- It's Friday night. No matter where we go, there will be traffic 周五晚上甭管走哪儿都得堵车 Zhōuwǔ wǎnshàng béng guǎn zǒu nǎr dōu děi dǔchē

- I know your way is fine, but please take my way 我知道你那条路没问题，但还是走我这条吧 Wǒ zhīdào nǐ nèitiáo lù méi wèntí, dàn háishì zǒu wǒ zhèitiáo ba

- Take whichever way will be fastest 哪儿快走哪儿 Nǎr kuài zǒu nǎr

- About how long will it take to get there? 到那儿大概多长时间？Dào nàr dàgài duōcháng shíjiān?

- At the... make a (left/right) 在...（左/右）转 Zài... (zuǒ/yòu) zhuǎn

(1) intersection 十字路口 shízì lùkǒu
(2) stoplight 红绿灯 hónglǜdēng
(3) building 楼 lóu
(4) road entrance 路口 lùkǒu
(5) little hutong 小胡同 xiǎo hútòng
(6) compound 小区 xiǎoqū

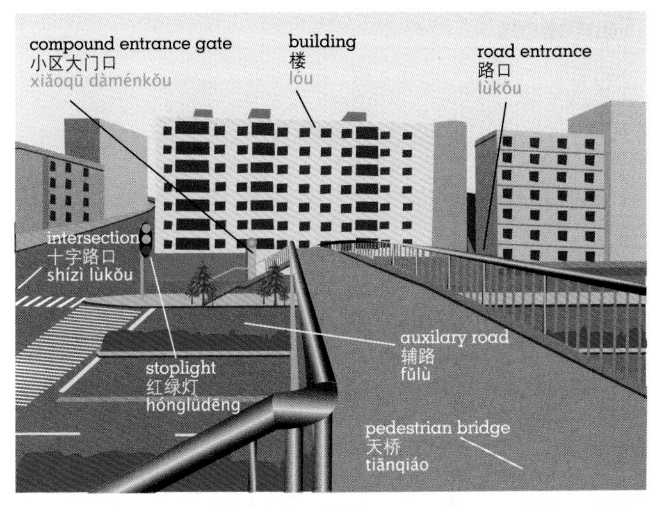

- Go ... 往 . . . 走 Wǎng ... zǒu

  (1) north 北 běi
  (2) south 南 nán
  (3) east 东 dōng
  (4) west 西 xī

- Turn ... 往 . . . 转 Wǎng ... zhuǎn

  (1) right / left 右/左 yòu / zuǒ
  (2) that way 那边 nèibiān

- Turn around (U-turn) 调头 Diàotóu

- Keep going 继续走 Jìxù zǒu

- Go straight 直走 Zhí zǒu

- Go to the end 走到头 Zǒu dào tóu

- Exit here 从这儿出去 Cóng zhèr chūqù

Listen for this

- Qù nǎr? 去哪儿? Where are we going?
- Hǎo lei! 好嘞! OK!
- Dǔ chē ya! 堵车呀! What a traffic jam!

Sentences

- Where is the seatbelt? 安全带在哪儿？ ānquándài zài nǎr?

- Could you (turn on / turn off) ... 把...（打开/关上）好吗？ Bǎ... (dǎkāi / guānshàng) hǎo ma?

  (1) the heater 暖风 nuǎnfēng (2) the A/C 空调 kōngtiáo

- Please, do you mind not smoking? 你能把烟灭了吗？ Nǐ néng bǎ yān miè le ma?

- Can I smoke in your taxi? 车里能抽烟吗？ Chē lǐ néng chōuyān ma?

- Could you (turn down / up) the radio? 把收音机（关小/开大）点儿好吗？ Bǎ shōuyīnjī (guān xiǎo / kāi dà) diānr hǎo ma?

- Where are we ? 我们到哪儿了？ Wǒmen dào nǎr le?

- How far from ... are we? 离...还有多远？ Lí ... háiyǒu duōyuǎn?

- Please ask someone for directions 问问路吧 Wènwen lù ba

- Drive (faster/slower) 开（快/慢）点儿 Kāi (kuài/màn) diǎnr

- Take the auxiliary road (bike lane) 走辅路 Zǒu fǔlù

- We just passed it. Make the next possible U-turn 刚开过了.前面能调头的地方调头吧 Gāng kāi guò le. Qiánmiàn néng diàotóu de dìfāng diàotóu ba

- It's on the other side of the street 在马路对面 Zài mǎlù duìmiàn

- Stop at the gate on the right 在右边的大门停下 Zài yòubiān de dàmén tíng xià

- Enter the compound 进小区里面 Jìn xiǎoqū lǐmiàn

- Stop here, but don't hit the meter 就停这儿，先别停表 Jiù tíng zhèr, xiān bié tíng biǎo

- He will get off, but I will keep going 他下车，我接着走 Tā xiàchè, wǒ jiēzhe zǒu

- Please wait here, I will be back in a little bit 请等一会儿，我马上回来 Qǐng děng yìhuǐr, wǒ mǎshàng huílái

- We're picking someone up 我们去接个人 Wǒmen qù jiē ge rén

- Stop here 停这儿吧 Tíng zhèr ba

- I'm getting off 我在这儿下 Wǒ zài zhèr xià

- Please give me the receipt 麻烦把票给我 Máfan bǎ piào gěi wǒ

- Please open the trunk 请打开后备箱 Qǐng dǎkāi hòubèixiāng

- Do you have change? 你有零钱吗？ Nǐ yǒu língqián ma?

- All I have is a hundred 我只有一百的 Wǒ zhǐyǒu yìbǎi de

- If you don't have change, that is your problem, not mine 你没零钱那是你的问题，不关我的事儿 Nǐ méi língqián nà shì nǐ de wèntí, bù guān wǒ de shìr

- We can get change at that convenience store 我们可以去便利店里换零钱 Wǒmen kěyǐ qù biànlìdiàn lǐ huàn língqián

Listen for this

- Yǒu língde ma? 有零的吗？Do you have small change?
- Wǒ zhǎo bù kāi 我找不开 I can't find any change
- Zhèr bú ràng zǒu 这儿不让走 It's not permitted to drive this way
- Zhèr bú ràng yòu guǎi 这儿不让右拐 We can't take a right here
- Yǒu jǐngchá! 有警察！ There is a cop!
- Dǔ chē! 堵车！Traffic jam!
- chēhuò 车祸 accident

4 Your own driver

私人司机 Sīrén sījī

Sentences

• I'm looking for a driver 我想找个司机 Wǒ xiǎng zhǎo ge sījī

• Please show me your driver's license 请给我看看你的驾照 Qǐng gěi wǒ kànkan nǐ de jiàzhào

• Do you have your own car? 你自己有车吗？Nǐ zìjǐ yǒu chē ma?

• What kind of car do you have? (for a list of models see p217) 你的是什么车？ Nǐ de shì shénme chē?

• What do you charge by the... ? 每. . . 多少钱？ Měi...duōshǎo qián?

(1) hour 小时 xiǎoshí
(2) day 天 tiān
(3) month 月 yuè

• How many hours a week can you work? 你一周可以工作几小时？ Nǐ yì zhōu kěyǐ gōngzuò jǐ xiǎoshí?

• Can you work weekends? 周末能工作吗？ Zhōumò néng gōngzuò ma?

• How long have you worked as a driver? 你干司机这行多长时间了？ Nǐ gàn sījī zhè háng duōcháng shíjiān le?

• Do you know how to fix cars? 你会修车吗？ Nǐ huì xiū chē ma?

• Have you worked with a foreign family before? 以前给外国家庭开过车吗？ Yǐqián gěi wàiguó jiātíng kāi guò chē ma?

• Have you had any accidents? 出过交通事故吗？ Chū guò jiāotōng shìgù ma?

• Do you have auto insurance? 你的车上保险了吗？ Nǐ de chē shàng bǎoxiǎn le ma?

• Can you pick up my daughter at her school? 你能去学校接一下我女儿吗？ Nǐ néng qù xuéxiào jiē yí xià wǒ nǚ'ér ma?

• Please return to pick me up here at 3pm 麻烦下午三点回这儿来接我 Máfan xiàwǔ sāndiǎn huí zhèr lái jiē wǒ

- I will need you to work on Sunday at 9pm 我星期天晚上九点要用车 Wǒ xīngqītiān wǎnshàng jiǔdiǎn yào yòng chē

- Please get the car washed 把车洗洗去吧 Bǎ chē xǐxi qù ba

Listen for this

- Wǒ (měi xiǎoshí / měi gè yuè) shōu ... rénmínbì 我(每小时/每个月)收...人民币 I charge RMB ... (per hour / per month)

- Zhèr dǔchē le, wǒ wǎn diǎnr dào 这儿堵车了，我晚点儿到 I'm stuck in traffic and will be a bit late

- Chē ... 车... The car has ...

(1) bàotāi le 爆胎了 a flat tire
(2) fēngshàn pídài duàn le 风扇皮带断了 a broken fan belt
(3) lòu shuǐ le 漏水了 leaking fluid
(4) méi yóu le 没油了 no gas

5 Airplanes 坐飞机 Zuò fēijī

Sentences

- I want to make a reservation 我想订票 Wǒ xiǎng dìng piào

- For this Friday returning Sunday night 周五去，周日回 Zhōuwǔ qù. zhōurì huí

- From Beijing to ... 从北京到... Cóng Běijīng dào ...

(1) Bangkok 曼谷 Màngǔ
(2) Hanoi 河内 Hénèi
(3) Hong Kong 香港 Xiānggǎng
(4) Manila 马尼拉 Mǎnílā
(5) Osaka 大阪 Dàbǎn
(6) Seoul 首尔 Shǒu'ěr
(7) Singapore 新加坡 Xīnjiāpō
(8) Tokyo 东京 Dōngjīng

- I would like a / an ... 我想要... Wǒ xiǎng yào ...

(1) roundtrip ticket 往返票 wǎngfǎn piào
(2) one-way ticket 单程票 dānchéng piào
(3) economy ticket 经济仓票 jīngjìcāng piào
(4) business class ticket 商务仓票 shāngwùcāng piào

(5) first class ticket 头等仓票 tóuděngcāng piào
(6) aisle seat 过道座 guòdào zuò
(7) window seat 窗口座 chuāngkǒu zuò
(8) child meal 儿童餐 értóng cān
(9) vegetarian meal 素食餐 sùshí cān

• What time is departure? 几点起飞？Jǐdiǎn qǐfēi?

• I need something that leaves ... 我想要...起飞的票 Wǒ xiǎng yào ... qǐfēi de piào

(1) sooner 早点儿 zǎo diǎnr (2) later 晚点儿 wǎn diǎnr

• And what time does it arrive? 几点到？Jǐdiǎn dào?

• Is it non-stop? 是直飞的吗？Shì zhífēi de ma?

• How many bags am I allowed? 我能带几个包儿？Wǒ néng dài jǐ gè bāor?

• What are the weight and size restrictions?有什么重量和体积限制？Yǒu shénme zhòngliàng hé tǐjī xiànzhì?

• Do you have any special (air & hotel) package deals? 有什么优惠的（机票和酒店）套票吗？Yǒu shénme yōuhuì de (jīpiào hé jiǔdiàn) tàopiào ma?

Listen for this

• Qǐng nín pīn yí xià nínde míngzi 请您拼一下您的名字 Could you spell your name please?

• Nǐ xiǎng jǐhào zǒu? 你想几号走？What dates would you like to travel?

• Nǐ xiǎng zuò nǎgè hángkōng gōngsī de fēijī? 你想坐哪个航空公司的飞机？Do you have a preferred airline?

• Nà tiān méiyǒu bānjī 那天没有班机 There are no flights on that day

• Zhège hángbān méi kōngwèi le 这个航班没空位了 The flight is fully booked

• Nǐ děi zài ... zhuǎn jī 你得在...转机 You have to change planes in ...

• Yí jiàn shǒutí xíngli, liǎng jiàn tuōyùn xíngli. 一件手提行李，两件托运行李 One carry-on, two checked bags

• Měi jiàn sānshíwǔ gōngjīn, zǒnggòng bù chāoguò liùshísì gōngjī. 每件35公斤，总共不超过64公斤 35 kilograms per bag, no more than 64 kilograms total

• Měijiàn cháng kuān gāo jiā qǐlái bùnéng chāoguò yī diǎn wǔ mǐ 每件长宽高加起来不能超过1.5米 The length plus width plus height of each piece must not exceed 1.5 meters

6 Checking (departure / arrival) time 查询（出发／到达）时间

Cháxún (chūfā/dàodá) shíjiān

Sentences

• Can you tell me if Air China flight 612 is on time or is delayed? 请问国航的612次航班准时起飞还是有延误？Qǐngwèn Guóháng de liùyīèr cì hángbān zhǔnshí qǐfēi háishì yǒu yánwù?

• Please (fill out / show the)... 请（填／出示）... Qǐng (tián/chūshì) ...

(1) customs card 海关申报卡 hǎnguān shēnbào kǎ
(2) health card 健康申报卡 jiànkāng shēnbào kǎ
(3) departure card 登机牌 dēngjīpái

• Where is the airport Starbucks? 机场里的星巴克咖啡在哪儿？Jīchǎng lǐ de Xīngbākè Kāfēi zài nǎr?

• Where can I change money? 去哪儿换钱？Qù nǎr huàn qián?

Listen for this

• Zhǔnshí qǐfēi 准时起飞 On time departure

• Yánwù liǎng ge xiǎoshí 延误两个小时 It's delayed two hours

• Hángbān qǔxiāo le 航班取消了 The flight is cancelled

• Nǐ de qiānzhèng guòqī le 你的签证过期了 Your visa has expired

7 Getting to the airport

去机场 Qù jīchǎng

Sentences

- Is this a stop for the airport bus? 机场大巴在这儿有站吗? Jīchǎng dàbā zài zhèr yǒu zhàn ma?

- When will the next bus arrive? 下一班车什么时候来? Xià yì bān chē shénme shíhou lái?

- When does the airport bus leave from ... ? 机场大巴几点从...发车? Jīchǎng dàbā jǐdiǎn cóng ... fā chē?

(1) Xidan 西单 Xīdān
(2) Dongzhimenwai 东直门外 Dōngzhíménwài
(3) the Friendship Hotel 友谊宾馆 Yǒuyì Bīnguǎn

8 Taking the subway

坐地铁 Zuò dìtiě

(Note: tickets for lines 1, 2 and 13 cost RMB 3, while combined tickets for these lines and the Batong line cost RMB 4 and 5 respectively.)

- Line One (straight line) 一号线(直线) Yī hào xiàn (zhí xiàn)
- Line Two (ring line) 二号线(环线) èr hào xiàn (huán xiàn)
- Line Thirteen (light rail) 十三号线(轻轨) Shísān hào xiàn (qīngguǐ)
- Batong Line 八通线 Bātōng xiàn

Sentences

- Hey buddy, no hurry 哥们儿, 别挤 Gēmenr, bié jǐ

- Two tickets, please 两张 Liǎng zhāng

- One ... ticket, please 一张...的 Yì zhāng ... de

(1) RMB 3 三块 sān kuài
(2) RMB 4 四块 sì kuài
(3) RMB 5 五块 wǔ kuài

• Is there still a subway car headed to Dongzhimen? 还有去东直门的车吗? Háiyǒu qù Dōngzhímén de chē ma?

• I'm getting off 我要下车 Wǒ yào xià chē

• Are you getting off? 你下吗? Nǐ xià ma?

Listen For this

• Xiān xià hòu shàng 先下后上 Please, let people get off first then get on

• Xià yí zhàn shì ...下一站是 The next stop is ...

9 Taking the train

坐火车 Zuò huǒchē

Sentences

• Where is the ticket booth? 售票口在哪? Shòupiàokǒu zài nǎr?

• Is there a ticket booth for foreigners? 有外宾售票口吗? Yǒu wàibīn shòupiàokǒu ma?

• I need a ticket for tomorrow night for Qingdao 我想买一张明天晚上去青岛的票 Wǒ xiǎng mǎi yì zhāng míngtiān wǎnshàng qù Qīngdǎo de piào

• I want a ... 我想要... Wǒ xiǎng yào ...

(1) hard sleeper 硬卧 yìngwò
(2) hard seat 硬座儿 yìngzuòr
(3) soft sleeper 软卧 ruǎnwò
(4) soft seat 软座儿 ruǎnzuòr

• What times does the train arrive? 几点到? Jǐ diǎn dào?

• Does the train leave from Beijing Railway Station, Beijing West Station, Beijing North Station, or Beijing South Station? 火车从哪发车? 北京站，北京西站，北京北站还是北京南站? Huǒchē cóng nǎr fāchā? Běijīng Zhàn, Běijīng Xī Zhàn, Běijīng Běi Zhàn hàishì Běijīng Nán Zhàn?

• From what platform is this train boarding? 从哪个站台上车？Cóng năge zhàntái shàng chē?

• What time can we board? 几点可以上车？ Jĭdiăn kĕyĭ shàng chē?

• Is there a VIP waiting room? 有贵宾休息室吗？Yŏu guìbīn xiūxishì ma?

• Is there a (snack shop / restaurant)? 有（小吃店/餐厅）吗？ Yŏu (xiăochīdiàn / cāntīng) ma?

• Where is the left-luggage room? 行李寄存处在哪儿？Xínglĭ jìcúnchù zài năr?

Listen for this

• Nĭ yào shàngpù, zhōngpù háishì xiàpù? 你要上铺，中铺还是下铺？Do you want a top bunk, middle bunk or bottom bunk?

• Wŭ kuài qián fúwùfèi 五块钱服务费 There is a five renminbi service fee

• Huŏchēpiào tíqián sì tiān fāshòu 火车票提前四天发售 Train tickets start being sold four days in advance

• Zhè tàng chē piào mài wán le 这趟车票卖完了 That train is sold out

10 Taking the bus

坐公交车 Zuò gōngjiāochē

Sentences

• I'm going to the Summer Palace. Am I on the right bus? 我要去颐和园，没坐错车吧？Wŏ yào qù Yíhéyuán, méi zuò cuò chē ba ?

• I'm getting off 我要下车 Wŏ yào xià chē

Listen for this

- Xià ma? 下吗？Are you getting off?
- Zài ... dǎo chē zuò ... lù 在...倒车坐...路 At ... change to bus number ...
- ... lù chē ...路车 bus No. ...

Watch for this

- Lǎo, yòu, bìng, cán, yùn zhuān zuò 老，幼，病，残，孕专座 Reserved seats for seniors, children, the sick, the disabled and pregnant women

11 Pedicabs 三轮车 Sānlúnchē

Sentences

- How much to Ghost Street? 到簋街多少钱？Dào Guǐjiē duōshao qián?

• What? That's not the right price. I take this trip everyday and it's always five kuai 什么?价儿不对啊，我天天坐才五块钱 Shénme? Jiàr bú duì a, wǒ tiāntiān zuò cái wǔ kuài qián

• How long is the hutong tour? 胡同游一次多长时间? Hútòng yóu yí cì duōcháng shíjiān?

• Does the price include entry tickets? 价钱包括门票吗? Jiàqián bāokuò ménpiào ma?

12 Bikes 自行车 Zìxíngchē

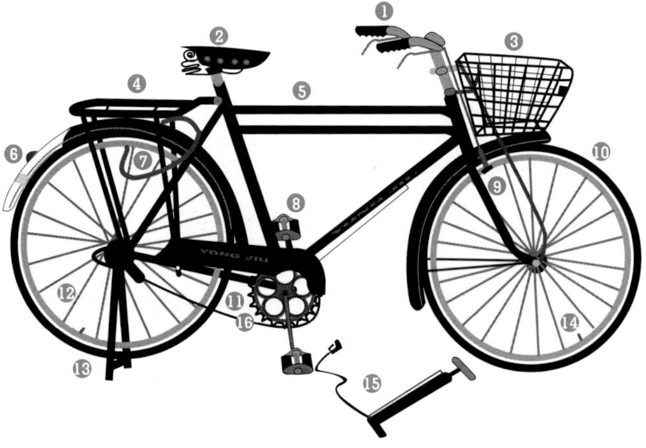

For phrases and vocabulary about buying bikes, see Shopping, p151.

(1) handlebar 车把 chēbǎ
(2) seat 车座 chēzuò
(3) basket 车筐 chēkuāng
(4) rear platform 后车架 hòuchējià
(5) frame 车架子 chējiàzi
(6) light 车灯 chēdēng
(7) lock 车锁 chēsuǒ
(8) pedal 脚蹬子 jiǎodēngzi
(9) brakes 车闸 chēzhá
(10) wheel 车轮 chēlún
(11) gears 齿轮 chǐlún
(12) spokes 车条 chētiáo
(13) kickstand 车支子 chēzhīzi
(14) inner tube air nozzle 气门芯儿 qìménxīngr
(15) tire pump 打气筒 dǎqìtǒng
(16) chain 车链子 chēliànzi

Sentences

- Do you fix bikes? 这儿能修车吗？ Zhèr néng xiū chē ma?

- Do you have an air pump? 你有气筒子吗？ Nǐ yǒu qìtǒngzi ma?

- Can I pump the tires? 我能打点儿气吗？ Wǒ néng dǎ diǎnr qì ma?

- Can you (raise / lower) the seat? 能把车座调(高/低)点儿吗？ Néng bǎ chēzuò tiáo (gāo / dī) diǎnr ma?

- Can you install a ... 能不能装一个... Néng bùnéng zhuāng yí gē ...

- Look, this ... 看，这个... Kàn, zhèigè ...

  (1) tire is flat 车胎爆了 chētāi bào le
  (2) wheel is bent 车轮变形了 chēlún biànxíng le
  (3) breaks are busted 刹车不灵了 shāchē bù líng le
  (4) chain has fallen off 车链子掉了 chē liànzi diào le
  (5) part is broken 零件坏了 língjiàn huài le

- Do you have a replacement? 你有零件替换吗？ Nǐ yǒu língjiàn tìhuàn ma?

- How long will it take to fix? How much will it cost? 修这个要等多长时间，多少钱？ Xiū zhèigè yào děng duōcháng shíjiān, duōshǎo qián?

- I'm gonna go, but I'll be back in half an hour. Will it be done then? 我得走了，半小时后回来。到时候能修好吗？ Wǒ děi zǒu le, bàn xiǎoshí hòu huílái. Dào shíhou néng xiū hǎo ma?

Listen for this

- Zhèi chē děi huàn gè xīn zhápí 这车得换个新闸皮 You need new break pads

- Chāzi huài le 叉子坏了 The fork is broken

- Zhèigè nèitāi děi huàn 这个内胎得换 This inner tube should be changed

- Zhèi zhǒng chē wǒ xiū bù liǎo 这种车我修不了 I can't fix this kind of bike

- Wǒ méiyǒu zhèigè língjiàn 我没有这个零件 I don't have this part

13 Getting your driver's license 获取驾照 Huòqǔ jiàzhào

Sentences

- Where can I take the exam? 在哪儿考试？Zài nǎr kǎoshì?
- When can I take the exam? 什么时候考试？Shénme shíhou kǎoshì?
- Is the exam offered in English? 是用英语考试吗？Shì yòng yīngyǔ kǎoshì ma?
- Do you have English-language study materials for the exam? 考试复习材料有英文的吗？Kǎoshì fùxí cáiliào yǒu yīngwén de ma?

Listen for this

- Nǐ děi ... 你得... You need to ...
  (1) tōngguò bǐshì 通过笔试 pass the written test
  (2) tōngguò lù kǎo 通过路考 pass the road test
  (3) fānyì nǐ běnguó de jiàzhào
  翻译你本国的驾照 translate your home country license
  (4) zài ... yiyuàn tǐjiǎn.
  在...医院体检 take the physical exam at ... hospital
  (5) bǎ hùzhào hé běnguó jiàzhào dài lai 把护照和本国驾照带来
  bring your passport and home country license
  (6) jiāo wǔ zhāng zhèngjiànzhào
  交五张证件照 provide five passport photos
  (7) jiāo fèi 交费 pay the fee
- Nǐ (méi tōngguò / tōngguò le) kǎoshì 你(没通过/通过了)考试 You (failed / passed) the test
- Nǐ liǎng zhōu hòu kěyǐ zài kǎo yí cì 你两周后可以再考一次 You can take the test again in two weeks
- Nǐ jiāng ... shōudào nǐ de jiàzhào 你将...收到你的驾照 You'll receive your license ...
  (1) tōngguò yóujiàn 通过邮件 in the mail
  (2) dàgài yí gè yuè hòu 大概一个月后 in about a month

Watch for this

- Automobile Administrative Office Foreign Affairs' Branch 交管局外事科 Jiāoguǎnjú Wàishìkē

14 Driving 驾驶 Jiàshǐ

AUTO REPAIR
qìchē xiūlǐ

FUEL REFILLING STATION
jiāyóu zhàn

SUBWAY STATION
dìtiě zhàn

TRAIN STATION
huǒchē zhàn

SLOW SLOWLY MOVING CARS
màn chēliàng mànxíng

ROAD WORK AHEAD 300m
qiánfāng shīgōng

15 Buying a car 买车 Mǎi chē

Vocabulary

price 价格 jiàgé
engine capacity 排量 páiliàng
horsepower 马力 mǎlì
fuel consumption 油耗 yóuhào
warranty 保修 bǎoxiū
turbo charge 涡轮增压 wōlún zēngyā

- List of car models

(1) Audi 奥迪 àodí
(2) Beijing Jeep 北京吉普 Běijīng Jípǔ
(3) BMW 宝马 Bǎomǎ
(4) Buick (Century, Sail, Regal)
别克（世纪，赛欧，君威）Biékè (Shìjì, Sài'ōu, Jūnwēi)
(5) Chery QQ 奇瑞QQ Qíruì QQ

(6) Citroen (Fukang, Elysee)
雪铁龙（富康，爱丽舍）Xuětiělóng (Fùkāng, àilìshè)
(7) Fiat (Palio, Siena)
菲亚特（派力奥，西耶那）Fēiyàtè (Pàilì'ào, Xīyēnà)
(8) Ford (Mondeo, Focus)
福特（蒙迪欧，福克斯）Fútè (Méngdí'ōu, Fúkèsī)
(9) Geely 吉利 Jílì
(10) Honda (Accord, Odyssey, Fit)
本田（雅阁，奥德赛，飞度）Běntián (Yǎgé, àodésài, Fēidù)
(11) Hyundai (Sonata, Elantra)
现代（索纳塔，伊兰特）Xiàndài (Suǒnàtǎ, Yīlántè)
(12) Mercedes Benz 奔驰 Bēnchí
(13) Nissan (Paladin, Teana, Sunny) 尼桑（帕拉丁，天籁，阳光）
Nísāng (Pàlādīng, Tiānlài, Yángguāng)
(14) Peugeot (307, 206)
标致（307，206）Biāozhì (Sānlíngqī, èrlíngliù)
(15) Red Flag 红旗 Hóngqí
(16) VW (Passat, Jetta, Bora, Golf, Polo, Gol)
大众（帕萨特，捷达，宝来，高尔夫，波罗，高尔）
Dàzhòng (Pàsàtè, Jiédá, Bǎolái, Gāo'ěrfū, Bōluó, Gāo'ěr)

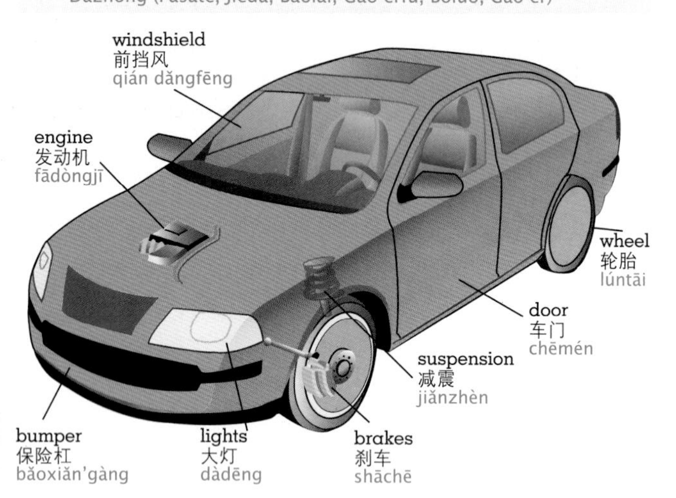

Sentences

- I'm looking for a ... 我想要一辆. . . Wǒ xiǎng yào yí liàng ...

(1) new car 新车 xīn chē
(2) used car 二手车 èrshǒu chē

- Can I take it for a test drive? 我能试驾吗？Wǒ néng shìjià ma?

• Do you have this model in different colors? 这种型号有别的颜色吗？ Zhèzhǒng xínghào yǒu bié de yánsè ma?

• What warranty do you offer? 你们有什么保修服务？ Nǐmen yǒu shénme bǎoxiū fúwù?

• Does it have air bags? 有安全气囊吗？ Yǒu ānquán qìnáng ma?

• Is it standard or automatic transmission? 是手动档的还是自动档的？ Shì shǒudòngdǎng de háishì zìdòngdǎng de?

• What is the ... ? . . . 是多少？ ... shì duōshǎo?

(1) fuel consumption 耗油量 hàoyóuliàng
(2) top speed 最高车速 zuì gāo chēsù
(3) engine size 发动机排量 fādòngjī páiliàng

Listen for this

• Bǎi gōnglǐ bā gè yóu 百公里8个油 8 liters per 100km

• Líng dào bǎi gōnglǐ jiāsù jiǔ diǎn bā miǎo 零到百公里加速9.8秒 0-100kmh acceleration in 9.8 seconds

• Yī diǎn liù de (páiliàng) 1.6的（排量） 1.6 liters (pneumatic exhaust capability)

• ōu sān biāozhǔn 欧三标准 EURO Three standard

• Guó sān biāozhǔn 国三标准 National (China) Three standard

16 Accessories

车用饰品 Chē yòng shìpǐn

Vocabulary

fuzzy dice 绒毛骰子 róngmáo shǎizi
Chairman Mao pendant 毛主席挂像 Máo Zhǔxí guàxiàng
golden tissue box 金纸巾盒 jīn zhǐjīn hé
air freshner 空气清新剂 kōngqì qīngxīn jì
bullet hole sticker 弹孔贴纸 dànkǒng tiēzhǐ
seven dwarves 七个小矮人 qī gè xiǎo ǎirén

17 New car registration

新车注册 Xīn chē zhùcè

Watch for this

- safety and emissions test 安全和尾气检测 ānquán hé wěiqì jiǎncè
- proof of ownership (bill of sale) 购车证明（购车大票）gòuchē zhèngmíng (gòuchē dà piào)
- purchase tax 购置税 gòuzhì shuì
- license plate 牌照 páizhào
- road tax 养路费 yǎnglù fèi
- motor vehicles user tax 机动车车船使用税 jīdòngchē chēchuán shǐyòng shuì
- third party liability coverage 第三者责任险 dìsānzhě zérèn xiǎn

18 Accident 事故 Shìgù

Sentences

- Dial 122 and get help 打122求救 Dǎ yāo èr èr qiú jiù
- I had an accident. I'm at … (road/street) 我出了事故，我在…（路/大街）Wǒ chū le shìgù, wǒ zài … (lù/dàjiē)
- It was just a rear-ending, nobody was hurt 只是追尾，没有人受伤 Zhǐshì zhuīwěi, méiyǒu rén shòu shāng
- Please come fast, there's been a terrible accident and people are grievously injured 请快点儿来，这儿有严重事故，有人受重伤 Qǐng kuài diǎnr lái, zhèr yǒu yánzhòng shìgù, yǒu rén shòu zhòngshāng
- I can't drive the car. Please send a tow truck 我车开不了了，请派辆拖车来 Wǒ chē kāi bù liǎo le, qǐng pài liàng tuōchē lái

19 At the scene

现场处理 Xiànchăng chùlĭ

Sentences

• My car was rear-ended, so it's totally your responsibility 你追尾了，应该是你全责 Nĭ zhuīwĕi le, yīnggāi shì nĭ quánzé

• I'm sorry, I didn't see you 对不起，我刚才没看见你 Duìbùqĭ, wŏ gāngcái méi kànjiàn nĭ

• The light was (red / yellow / green) 刚才是（红/黄/绿）灯 Gāngcái shì (hóng / huáng / lǜ) dēng.

• The damage is (minor / major) 损伤（不严重/很严重）Sŭnshāng (bú yánzhòng / hĕn yánzhòng)

• Do you think we could settle this privately? 咱们能私了吗？Zánmen néng sīliăo ma?

• How much will it cost to fix your car? 你修车要多少钱？Nĭ xiū chē yào duōshao qián?

20 Talking to the police

与交警谈话 Yŭ jiāojĭng tánhuà

Sentences

• Here is my driving license 这是我的驾照 Zhè shì wŏ de jiàzhào

• I need the accident report, so that I can get refunded by my insurance company. 您得给我开事故处理单，这样才能走保险。Nín dĕi gĕi wŏ kāi shìgù chùlĭ dān, zhèyàng cái néng zŏu băoxiăn

Listen for this

• Bă nĭ jiàzhào hé băoxiăn kă gĕi wŏ kànkan 把你驾照和保险卡给我看看 Show me your license and insurance card

• Zĕnme huíshìr? 怎么回事儿？What happened?

21 Insurance 保险 Bǎoxiǎn

Sentences

• Do you sell auto insurance to foreigners? 你们这儿能给外国人的车上保险吗？ Nǐmen zhèr néng gěi wàiguórén de chē shàng bǎoxiǎn ma?

• What are the different plans? 都有什么险种啊？ Dōu yǒu shénme xiǎnzhǒng a?

• What is the deductible? 免赔多少？ Miǎn péi duōshǎo?

• I have a '94 VW Jetta 我有一辆九四年的捷达 Wǒ yǒu yí liàng jiǔsì nián de Jiédá

Listen for this

• Nín de chē shì něi nián shēngchǎn de? 您的车是哪年生产的？ What is the manufacture year of your car?

• Nín zuìshǎo yě yào shàng gè dìsānzhě zérèn xiǎn 您最少也要上个第三者责任险 At a minimum, you need third party liability coverage

• Miǎn péi jīn'é shì rénmínbì ... 免赔金额是人民币... The deductible is RMB ...

22 Renting your own car 自己租车 Zìjǐ zū chē

(For more on renting a car and driver, see also Excursions, p228)

Sentences

• I want to rent a ... with a driver 我想租一辆... 车，带司机 Wǒ xiǎng zū yí liàng... chē, dài sījī

• These are my driving license, passport, resident permit 这是我的驾照，护照和外国人居留证 Zhè shì wǒ de jiàzhào, hùzhào hé wàiguórén jūliúzhèng

• How much does it cost per day? 一天的租金多少钱? Yìtiān de zūjīn yào duōshao qián?

• Do I have to leave a deposit? 要付押金吗？Yào fù yājīn ma?

• Can I pay by credit card? 能用信用卡支付吗？Néng yòng xìnyòngkǎ zhīfù ma?

Listen for this

• Nǐ xūyào dānbǎorén 你需要担保人 You need a guarantor

• Nǐ méiyǒu zhōngguó jiàzhào de huà, bù néng kāi chē 你没有中国驾照的话不能开车 You can't drive without a Chinese driver's license

• Zū yí liàng Fùkāng měitiān sānbǎi èrshí kuài qián 租一辆富康每天320块钱 You can rent a citroen Fukang for RMB 320 per day

• Jiā wǔqiān kuài qián yājīn 加5000块钱押金 With a RMB 5,000 deposit

Notes

EXCURSIONS ►

1 Basics 基础词汇 Jīchǔ cíhuì

Sentences

• I'm going for a .... 我要去... Wǒ yào qù ...

(1) daytrip 一日游 yírìyóu
(2) weekend getaway 度周末 dù zhōumò
(3) holiday excursion 度假 dùjià

• I'm going to get some fresh air 我去呼吸点儿新鲜空气 Wǒ qù hūxī diǎnr xīnxīan kōngqì

• I want to get away from the hustle and bustle of the city 我想远离城市的喧嚣 Wǒ xiǎng yuǎnlí chéngshì de xuānxiāo

2 Planning a trip 计划出行 Jìhuà chūxíng

Sentences

• Where can you recommend to go for ... 您觉得...到哪儿比较好? Nín juéde ... dào nár bǐjiào hǎo?

(1) hiking 徒步旅行 túbù lǚxíng
(2) fishing 钓鱼 diàoyú
(3) camping 露营 lùyíng
(4) some sunshine 晒太阳 shài tàiyáng
(5) rock climbing 攀岩 pānyán
(6) seeing a temple 参观寺庙 cānguān sìmiào
(7) climbing the Great Wall 蹬长城 dēng chángchéng
(8) horseback riding 骑马 qímǎ
(9) bungee jumping 蹦极 bèngjí
(10) swimming 游泳 yóuyǒng
(11) eating barbequed fish 吃烤鱼 chī kǎoyú

• How long does it take to get there? 去那儿要花多长时间? Qù nàr yào huā duōcháng shíjiān?

• Do you have a map? 您有地图吗? Nín yǒu dìtú ma?

3 Calling ahead

提前打电话 Tíqián dǎ diànhuà

A lot of Beijing's excursion trips are seasonal; opening around April and shutting down around October. It's a good idea to call ahead to prevent taking a six-hour bus tour of the Badaling Expressway.

Sentences

• Are you open now? 现在开放吗？ Xiànzài kāifàng ma?

• What time of the year are you open? 每年什么时候开放？ Měi nián shénme shíhou kāifàng?

• What are your daily hours? 每天什么时候开放？ Měi tiān shénme shíhou kāifàng?

• How do I get there? 我怎么去那儿？ Wǒ zěnme qù nàr?

• I will be ... 我要. . . Wǒ yào ...

(1) driving 开车去 kāi chē qù
(2) riding in a cab 打车去 dǎ chē qù
(3) taking a bus 坐公交车去 zuò gōngjiāochē qù

Listen for this

• Nín kāichē háishì zuò gōngjiāochē? 您开车还是坐公交车？ Will you be driving or taking a bus?

• Zǒu Jīngshùn Lù dào Huáiróu, ránhòu kàn lùbiāo dào Hóngluósì 走京顺路到怀柔，然后看路标到红螺寺 Take Jingshun Lu to Huairou, then follow the signs to Hongluo Temple

• Cóng Dōngzhímén zuò jiǔyāoliù lù dào Huáiróu. Xiàchē dǎ dī 从东直门坐916路到怀柔。下车打的 Take Bus 916 from Dongzhimen to Huairou and then take a taxi

4 Asking about the weather

问天气 Wèn tiānqì

Sentences

- What is the temperature there? 那儿几度？Nàr jǐ dù?

- Will it ... tomorrow ? 明天会不会...？ Míngtiān huì búhuì ... ?

(1) rain 下雨 xiàyǔ
(2) snow 下雪 xiàxuě
(3) be windy 刮风 guāfēng
(4) be really hot 特别热 tèbié rè
(5) be really cold 特别冷 tèbié lěng

5 Renting a car 租车 Zū chē

Sentences

- I need a car and driver for a one-day trip to the Great Wall 我想租一辆带司机的车去长城一日游 Wǒ xiǎng zū yí liàng dài sījī de chē qù chángchéng yírìyóu

- There will be four people 我们有四个人 Wǒmen yǒu sì ge rén

- Can the driver drop us off at Jinshanling and then pick us up at Simatai? 司机能不能把我们放在金山岭然后在司马台接我们？ Sījī néng bùnéng bǎ wǒmen fàng zài Jīnshānlǐng ránhòu zài Sīmǎtái jiē wǒmen?

- Does the driver have a cell phone? 司机有手机吗？ Sījī yǒu shǒujī ma?

- How long will it take to drive there? 开车去那儿要花多长时间？ Kāichē qù nàr yào huā duōcháng shíjiān?

- We'd like to leave at 7am and be back by 8pm 我们想早7点出发，晚8点回来 Wǒmen xiǎng zǎo qīdiǎn chūfā, wǎn bādiǎn huílái

- Is that enough time? 时间够吗？ Shíjiān gòu ma?

• How much will it cost? 多少钱？ Duōshǎo qián?

• Is gas included? 包括油费吗？ Bāokuò yóufèi ma?

• I'd like a car and driver for a multi-day trip. How much will it cost per day? 我想要辆带司机的车出去玩儿几天，平均每天多少钱？ Wǒ xiǎng yào liàng dài sījī de chē chūqù wánr jǐtiān, píngjūn měitiān duōshǎo qián?

• Who is responsible for the driver's food and lodging? 谁安排司机的吃住？ Shéi ānpái sījī de chīzhù?

• I need a large van for about 10 people 我想要一辆能坐十个人的面包车 Wǒ xiǎng yào yí liàng néng zuò shí ge rén de miànbāochē

• I need an RV 我想要一辆房车 Wǒ xiǎng yào yí liàng fángchē

• Can you come back and pick us up at the same spot ... ? 您...还在这个地方接我们成吗？ Nín ... hái zài zhèige dìfāng jiē wǒmen chéng ma?

(1) in three hours 三个小时后 sāngè xiǎoshí hòu
(2) tomorrow morning 明天早上 míngtiān zǎoshàng

Listen for this

• Qù shénme dìfang? 去什么地方？ Where are you going?

• Nǐ shénme shíhou xūyào? 你什么时候需要？When do you need it?

• Rúguǒ bù dǔchē liǎng xǐaoshí, dǔchē dehuà jiù shuō bùhǎo le 如果不堵车两小时，堵车的话就说不好了 If there's no traffic, two hours, but with traffic, god knows.

• Bāokuò bǎoxiǎn he sījī de fànfèi 包括保险和司机的饭费 Includes insurance and driver's food

• Bù bāokuò guòlùfèi, qìyóu, sījī de zhùsù 不包括过路费，汽油，司机的住宿 Road tolls, gas and driver's lodgings are not included

• Wǒ shénme shíhou lái jiē nǐ? 我什么时候来接你？ When shall I pick you up?

6 Hiking and camping 徒步旅行和露营 Túbù lǚxíng hé lùyíng

(For equipment, see the Sports, p178)

Sentences

• Can you recommend a place to go hiking? 你能给我推荐个徒步旅行的好地方吗？Nǐ néng gěi wǒ tuījiàn ge túbù lǚxíng de hǎo dìfang ma?

• Does this route go out and back or is there a circle route? 往返是同一条路还是绕一个圈儿？Wǎngfǎn shì tóng yì tiáo lù háishì rào yí ge quānr?

• How long is the trail? 这条路多长？ Zhèi tiáo lù duōcháng?

• Is it overgrown or clear? 路上是杂草丛生吗？Lùshàng shì zácǎo-cóngshēng ma?

• How long will it take to get to the top? 到顶要多久？Dào dǐng yào duōjiǔ?

• On the trail is/are there... ? 路上有没有...？ Lùshàng yǒu méiyǒu ... ?

(1) a cable car 缆车 lǎnchē
(2) sedan chairs 轿子 jiàozi
(3) vista points 景点 jǐngdiǎn
(4) someone selling water 卖水的 mài shuǐ de
(5) a place to pick fruit 采摘的地方 cǎizhāi de dìfang
(6) somewhere to swim 游泳的地方 yóuyǒng de dìfang

• Is there a good vista point near here? 这附近有没有好景点？Zhè fùjìn yǒu méiyǒu hǎo jǐngdiǎn?

• What is the elevation? 海拔多高？Hǎibá duōgāo?

• Can you recommend a place to camp for the night? 最好在哪儿露营过夜？Zuìhǎo zài nǎr lùyíng guòyè?

• Can we camp near here? 我们能在附近露营吗？ Wǒmen néng zài fùjìn lùyíng ma?

• Are we allowed to start a fire here? 这儿能生火吗？ Zhèr néng shēng huǒ ma?

• Can we use a small stove to cook food? 我们能用小炉子做饭吗？ Wǒmen néng yòng xiǎo lúzi zuò fàn ma?

• Can we drink this water? 这儿的水能喝吗？ Zhèr de shuǐ néng hē ma?

(1) lake 湖 hú
(2) waterfall 瀑布 pùbù
(3) vista point 景点 jǐngdiǎn
(4) cave 洞穴 dòngxuè
(5) gorge 峡谷 xiágǔ
(6) forest 森林 sēnlín
(7) grassland 草地 cǎodì
(8) mountain 山 shān
(9) beach 海滩 hǎitān
(10) wild Wall 野长城 yě Chángchéng
(11) Great Wall 长城 Chángchéng
(12) cable car 缆车 lǎnchē
(13) temple 寺庙 sìmiào
(14) river 河 hé

7 Fishing 钓鱼 Diàoyú

Sentences

• Do you rent fishing poles? 您出租鱼竿儿吗？Nín chūzū yúgānr ma?

• Do you sell ...? 您卖…吗？Nín mài ... ma?

(1) bait 鱼饵 yú'ěr
(2) creel 鱼篓 yúlǒu
(3) fishing line 渔线 yúxiàn
(4) fishing pole 鱼竿儿 yúgānr
(5) fishing stool 马扎儿 mǎzhár
(6) float 鱼漂儿 yúpiāor
(7) hook 鱼钩儿 yúgōur
(8) reel 渔线轮 yúxiànlún
(9) tackle 渔具 yújù

• Is there an entrance fee? 要门票吗？Yào ménpiào ma?

• What is the maximum I can catch? 我最多能钓多少？Wǒ zuìduō néng diào duōshǎo?

• What is the minimum size? 最小的鱼多大？Zuìxiǎo de yú duō dà?

• Do you charge ... ? 您是按…收费吗？Nín shì àn ... shōu fèi ma?

(1) per fish 每条鱼 měi tiáo yú
(2) per half kilogram 每斤 měi jīn

• What kind of fish are these? 这些都是什么鱼？Zhè xiē dōu shì shénme yú?

• guìyú 鲑鱼 trout
• lúyú 鲈鱼 weever
• lǐyú 鲤鱼 carp
• jìyú 鲫鱼 crucian carp
• cǎoyú 草鱼 grass carp
• shànyú 鳝鱼 eel

• What works well for bait? 用什么做饵好？Yòng shénme zùo ěr hǎo?

• How much does this fish weigh? 这条鱼多重？Zhè tiáo yú duōzhòng?

• Is there someone here who can clean these fish? 有人拾掇这些鱼吗？Yǒu rén shíduo zhèixiē yú ma?

•Can someone barbeque these fish? 有人会烤鱼吗？Yǒu rén huì kǎo yú ma?

8 Going to the beach

去海边 Qù hǎibiān

Sentences

- What is the temperature of the water? 水温多少度？Shuǐwēn duōshǎo dù?

- Are there changing rooms near here? 附近有更衣室吗？Fùjìn yǒu gēngyīshì ma?

- Do you sell sunscreen? 你们这儿卖防晒霜吗？Nǐmen zhèr mài fángshàishuāng ma?

9 Common travel routes

常见出行路线

Chángjìan chūxíng lùxiàn

Watch for this

Badaling Expressway 八达岭高速公路 Bādálǐng Gāosù Gōnglù
Jingshi Expressway 京石高速公路 Jīngshí Gāosù Gōnglù
Jingshun Lu 京顺路 Jīngshùn Lù
Airport Expressway 机场高速公路 Jīchǎng Gāosù Gōnglù
Jingmi Lu 京密路 Jīngmì Lù
Jingcheng Lu 京承路 Jīngchéng Lù
101 National Road 101国道 Yāolíngyāo Guódào
Jingzhang Lu 京张路 Jīngzhāng Lù
Yanqing Roundabout 延庆环岛 Yánqìng Húandǎo
Beigao Exit 北皋出口 Běigāo Chūkǒu
Bei'anhe Exit 北安河出口 Běi'ānhé Chūkǒu
Fangshan Exit 房山出口 Fángshān Chūkǒu
Yancun Exit 阎村出口 Yáncūn Chūkǒu
Sanyuanqiao Overpass 三元桥 Sānyuánqiáo
Kuliushu Roundabout 枯柳树环岛 Kūliǔshù Huándǎo
Fushi Lu 阜石路 Fǔshí Lù
Jingshen Expressway 京沈高速公路 Jīngshěn Gāosù Gōnglù
Jingjintang Expressway 京津塘高速公路 Jīngjīntáng Gāosù Gōnglù

Common starting locations
常见始发站 Chángjiàn shǐ fā zhàn

(1) Dongzhimen long distance bus station 东直门长途汽车站 Dōngzhímén Chángtú Qìchēzhàn
(2) Summer Palace 颐和园 Yíhéyuán
(3) Tianqiao (near Tiantan) 天桥（天坛附近） Tiānqiáo (Tiāntán fùjìn)
(4) Qianmen 前门 Qiánmén
(5) Pingguoyuan 苹果园 Píngguǒyuán

10 sentences to get away from Great Wall postcard/book guy

• I don't want anything you're selling 你卖的东西，我都不要 nǐ mài de dōngxi, wo dōu bú yào

• My mother died from buying too many postcards 我母亲就是因为买了太多的名信片而去世的 Wǒ mǔqīn jìu shì yīnwéi mǎi le tài duō de míngxìnpiàn ér qùshì de

• I'll buy something on my way back 等我回来再买 Děng wǒ huílái zài mǎi

• I've lost my wallet and my patience; get the hell out of my way! 我已经丢了我的钱包，也没耐心了，你滚开！ Wǒ yǐjìng diū le wǒ de qiánbāo, ye méi nàixīn le, nǐ gǔn kāi!

• I'm allergic to postcards 我对明信片过敏 Wǒ duì míngxìnpiàn guòmǐn

• Stay away from me, I have bird flu! 别靠近我，我有禽流感！ Bié kàojìn wǒ, wǒ yǒu qínlíugǎn

• No matter how far you follow me, I will not buy it 无论你跟我走多远，我都不会买 Wúlùn nǐ gēn wǒ zǒu dūoyǔan, wǒ dōu bú huì mǎi

• If you buy my Costa Rica postcards for $48.88, I will take your Great Wall cards 如果你花48.88美元买我的哥斯达黎加的明信片，我就买你的长城明信片 Rúgǔo nǐ huā sìshíbā dǐan bābā měiyūan mǎi wǒ de Gēsīdálíjiā de míngxìnpian, wǒ jìu mǎi nǐ de Chángchéng míngxìnpiàn

• Sorry, I can only speak Romanian 对不起，我只会讲罗马尼亚语 Dùibùqǐ, wǒ zhǐ huì jiǎng Luómǎníyà yǔ

• Do you take credit cards? I don't have cash 你收信用卡吗？我没现金 Nǐ shōu xìnyòngkǎ ma? Wǒ méi xiànjīn

BUSINESS & WORK

1 Basics 基础词汇 Jīchǔ cíhuì

Vocabulary

job 工作 gōngzuò
career 职业 zhíyè
salary 薪水 xīnshuǐ
client 客户 kèhù
guest 来宾 láibīn
honored guest 嘉宾 jiābīn

Sentences

• Where is the ... ? . . .在哪儿? ... zài nǎr?

(1) business center 商务中心 shāngwù zhōngxīn
(2) conference 大会 dàhuì
(3) office 办公室 bàngōngshì
(4) trade fair 商品交易会 shāngpǐn jiāoyìhuì

• I need ... 我需要. . . Wǒ xūyào ...

(1) an interpreter 一个翻译 yí gè fānyì
(2) to send a fax 发传真 fā chuánzhēn
(3) a computer 一台电脑 yì tái diànnǎo
(4) an Internet connection 互联网络连接 hùlián wǎngluò liánjiē
(5) to print 打印 dǎyìn
(6) to make some copies 复印几份 fùyìn jǐ fèn

2 Networking 关系 Guānxi

Sentences

• I am a ... 我是一个. . . Wǒ shì yí gè ...

(1) teacher 教师 jiàoshī
(2) journalist 记者 jìzhě
(3) manager 经理 jīnglǐ
(4) engineer 工程师 gōngchéngshī
(5) consultant 顾问 gùwèn
(6) diplomat 外交官 wàijiāoguān
(7) writer 作家 zuòjiā
(8) homemaker 家庭主妇 jiātíng zhǔfù
(9) artist 艺术家 yìshùjiā
(10) freelance photographer 自由摄影师 zìyóu shèyǐngshī
(11) doctor 医生 yīshēng
(12) bartender 调酒师 tiáojiǔshī
(13) lawyer 律师 lǜshī

• I am ... 我… Wǒ...

(1) unemployed 下岗了 xiàgǎng le
(2) looking for a job 正在找工作 zhèngzài zhǎo gōngzuò

(3) currently weighing offers 正在权衡各种机会的利弊
zhèngzài quánhéng gèzhǒng jīhuì de lìbì

- I work at .... 我在...工作 Wǒ zài ... gōngzuò

(1) CBD 中央商务区 zhōngyāng shāngwù qū
(2) the Canadian embassy 加拿大大使馆 jiānádà dàshǐguǎn
(3) home 家 jiā
(4) a university 大学 dàxué

- I am in the ... industry 我是...行业的 Wǒ shì ... hángyè de

(1) telecommunications 电讯 diànxùn
(2) advertising 广告 guǎnggào
(3) manufacturing 制造 zhìzào
(4) accounting 会计 kuàijì
(5) entertainment 娱乐 yúlè
(6) Information Technology IT
(7) pharmaceutical 制药 zhìyào
(8) import / export 进口 / 出口 jìnkǒu / chūkǒu
(9) tourism 旅游 lǚyóu

- I work for ... 我为...工作 Wǒ wèi ... gōngzuò

(1) a small company 一家小公司 yì jiā xiǎo gōngsī
(2) a large corporation 一家大集团 yì jiā dà jítuán
(3) myself 我自己 wǒ zìji

- I work for "the man" 我就是一打杂儿的 Wǒ jiù shì yí dǎzár de

- S/he is my colleague 他是我的同事 Tā shì wǒ de tóngshì

- Do you have a name card? 您有名片吗？Nín yǒu míngpiàn ma?

- I would like to meet with you 我想跟你见个面 Wǒ xiǎng gēn nǐ jiàn gè miàn

- Here is my name card 这是我的名片 Zhèshì wǒ de míngpiàn

- I have an appointment 我有个约会 Wǒ yǒu ge yuēhuì

- Thank you for your precious time 谢谢您抽出宝贵时间 Xièxie nín chōuchū bǎoguì shíjiān.

Listen for this

- Nǐ zài nǎr gōngzuò? 你在哪儿工作？Where do you work?
- Nǐ zuò shénme gōngzuò? 你做什么工作？What do you do?

3 Around the office

办公室环境 Bàngōngshì huánjìng

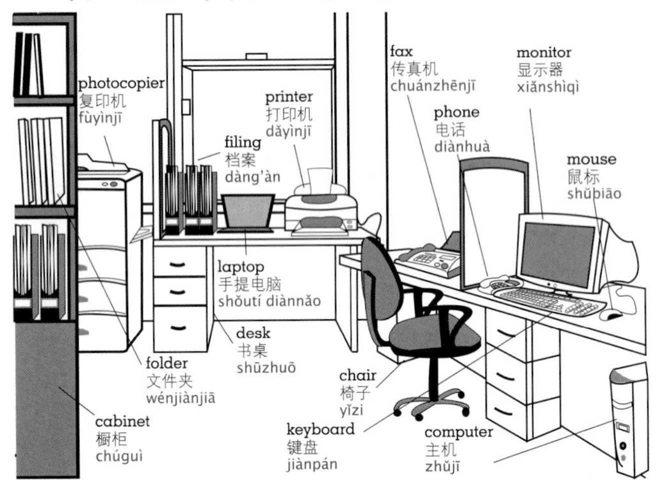

Sentences

- I need to use the ... 我得用那个 . . . Wǒ děi yòng nèige ...

(1) printer 打印机 dǎyìnjī
(2) fax machine 传真机 chuánzhēnjī
(3) meeting room 会议室 huìyìshì
(4) overhead projector 投影仪 tóuyǐngyí
(5) scanner 扫描仪 sǎomiáoyí
(6) paper shredder 碎纸机 sùizhǐjī

- The ... is broken 那个 . . . 坏了 Nèige ... huài le

(1) photocopier 复印机 fùyìnjī
(2) coffee machine 咖啡机 kāfēijī
(3) chair 椅子 yǐzi

- I need some ... 我需要 . . . Wǒ xūyào ...

(1) paperclips 别针 biézhēn
(2) sticky notes 便条 biàntiáo
(3) printer paper 打印纸 dǎyìn zhǐ
(4) pens 笔 bǐ
(5) tape 胶条 jiāotiáo

- What is the problem? 怎么回事儿? Zěnme huí shìr?

Listen for this

- Yǒu rén zhǎo nǐ 有人找你 Somebody is looking for you

- Zhèi dōngxi huài le 这东西坏了 This thing is broken
- zǎocāo 早操 morning exercises
- Tā bèi chǎo le 他被炒了 He was fired
- Tā lízhí le 她离职了 She quit

4 Answering the phone
接电话 Jiē diànhuà

Sentences

- Hello? 喂？ Wèi?
- Who are you looking for? 你找谁？ Nǐ zhǎo shéi?
- Who are you? 你是谁？ Nǐ shì shéi?
- Wrong number! 打错了！ Dǎ cuò le!
- May I have your name? 请问您的名字是？ Qǐngwèn nín de míngzi shì?
- S/he is in a meeting 他正在开会 Tā zhèngzài kāihuì
- S/he is on a business trip 他出差了 Tā chūchāi le
- S/he doesn't work here anymore 他已经不在这里工作了 Tā yǐjīng bú zài zhèlǐ gōngzuò le
- Can you call back in one hour? 你可以过一个小时再打过来吗？ Nǐ kěyǐ guò yígè xiǎoshí zài dǎ guòlai ma?
- Hold on 稍等一下 Shāoděng yí xià
- Let me find someone who speaks Chinese 我去找一个会讲中文的 Wǒ qù zhǎo yí ge huì jiǎng zhōngwén de
- Let me transfer you to ... 我给您转到… Wǒ gěi nín zhuǎndào...

5 Making calls 打电话 Dǎ diànhuà

Sentences

- I'm calling for extension number 611 帮我转到611分机 Bāng wǒ zhuǎndào liù-yāo-yāo fēnjī

- Is there someone there that speaks English? 您那里有人会说英文吗？ Nín nàlǐ yǒurén huì shuō yīngwén ma?

- Could I speak with the (manager/boss)? 我可以跟（经理/老板）谈谈吗？ Wǒ kěyǐ gēn (jīnglǐ/lǎobǎn) tántan ma?

- I was just transferred to you. Please connect me with someone who speaks English 我刚才就被转到你这里来了，请你给我转一个会说英文的 Wǒ gāngcái jiù bèi zhuǎndào nǐ zhèlǐ lái le, qǐng nǐ gěi wǒ zhuǎn yí ge huì shuō yīngwén de

- I will find someone who speaks Chinese to call you back in a little bit 我去找一个会说中文的，待会儿再打给你 Wǒ qù zhǎo yígè huì shuō zhōngwén de, dāihuǐr zài dǎ gěi nǐ

Listen for this

- Nín zhǎo shéi? 您找谁？ Who are you looking for?
- Nǐ shì nǎ wèi? 你是哪位？ Who are you?
- Shāo děng 稍等 Hold on a minute
- Tā bú zài 他不在 He's not in

6 Starting your own company 创建公司 Chuàngjiàn gōngsī

Sentences

- I want to register ... 我想注册... Wǒ xiǎng zhùcè ...

(1) a JV (joint venture) 一家合资公司 yì jiā hézī gōngsī
(2) a WFOE (wholly foreign-owned enterprise) 一家外资公司 yi jia wàizī gōngsī

(3) a representative office 一个驻京代表处 yí gè zhùjīng dàibiǎochù
(4) a trademark 一个商标 yí gè shāngbiāo

• What documents do I need? 我需要准备什么文件？Wǒ xūyào zhǔnbèi shénme wénjiàn?

• I want to rent an office 我想租一间办公室 Wǒ xiǎng zū yì jiān bāngōngshì

• I want to rent a serviced office 我想租用一间商务服务中心 Wǒ xiǎng zūyòng yì jiān shāngwù fúwù zhōngxīn

• I am looking for ... 我在寻找... Wǒ zài xúnzhǎo ...

(1) a local partner to cooperate with
一个本土合作伙伴 yí gè běntǔ hézuò huǒbàn
(2) an accountant 一个会计 kuàijì
(3) a secretary 一个秘书 mìshū
(4) business lawyer 一名商务律师 shāngwù lǜshī
(5) financial advisor 一名财务咨询 cáiwù zīxún
(6) consultant 一位顾问 gùwèn
(7) tech support 一个技术支持 jìshù zhīchí

• How do I repatriate profits? 怎么才能遣返利润？Zěnme cái néng qiǎnfǎn lìrùn?

7 Looking for a job 求职 Qiúzhí

Sentences

• I have ... years of experience 我有...年的经验 Wǒ yǒu ... nián de jīngyàn

• I am a university graduate 我是大学毕业生 Wǒ shì dàxué bíyèshēng

• Can you provide a visa? 你们能提供签证吗？Nǐmen néng tígōng qiānzhèng ma?

• Is housing provided? 提供住处吗？Tígòng zhùchù ma?

• How many vacation days are there a year? 每年有多少天假期？Měi nián yǒu duōshao tiān jiàqī?

In So Many Words ...

Professional translators are called on to perform linguistic alchemy

by Eric Abrahamsen

Learning to translate foreign languages, like learning to speak foreign languages, is an endless process of stages. Today you are perplexed by sentences with no grammatical subject. Tomorrow it will be all the different ways to say "carry." Translation is a booming business, but promises booming headaches. The following issues are quite common, bound to be encountered by the aspiring linguist ...

An immediate and persistent problem is the Chinese language's many forms of address. Chinese students will already have drilled the difference between 叔叔 shūshu (uncle, father's side) and 舅舅 jiùjiu (uncle, mother's side), but the use of complex kinship terms for direct address also creates havoc for the translator. Calling a family member 三姑夫 sān gūfū creates a comfortable air of intimate familiarity; addressing him as "father's-third-sister's-husband" has precisely the opposite effect. But leave it out or gloss it over, and a potentially important detail is lost.

Pronouns of all sorts cause difficulties. English, for example, has "I" (with the plausible additions of the royal "we" and "yours truly"). Chinese, besides 我 wǒ, sports 俺 ǎn, 人家 rénjiā, 老子 lǎozi, 本人 běnrén and 在下 zàixià (that's not even dipping into dialects or ancient Chinese), all with their own special flavors that you'd love to convey in English. How will you translate these terms? The answer is: you probably won't.

In more literary Chinese, one runs up against the problem of 成语 chéngyǔ (idiom). In general, Chinese is relatively forgiving of cliche, and turning 成语 into good English is particularly sticky. 成语 derive from ancient Chinese literature or history, and are much richer in flavor than your average "look a gift horse in the mouth," or "let sleeping dogs lie." But rendering a 成语 into vivid, original English loses the sense of historical reference. If you employ an equivalent English saying, it may come across as stale and tired. Translate it directly, in quotation marks, and chances are it won't make sense at all.

A related issue is the problem of dialect. China has countless different dialects, some of them verging on full-fledged languages. Translating the speech of someone from the Hebei countryside into an Appalachian drawl might be defensible (in moderation), but what if you're dealing with several dialects? You could represent different Chinese dialects with different styles of English, mapping one onto the other, but when you get right down to it, there's just no justification for a Gansu peasant to speak like a Scottish Highlander.

The above may make translation seem like a dreary parade of insurmountable hurdles – and sometimes it is. But these problems all have something in common: they are primarily issues of culture. More than most languages, translating Chinese into English involves the translation of ideas, beliefs and preconceptions, as much as grammar and style. That makes for some grueling challenges, but also satisfying successes, and the rewards are more than just words on a page.

• I need time to consider. Can I get back to you in a couple days? 我需要点儿时间考虑一下儿，我能过两天再给您个答复吗？ Wǒ xūyào diǎnr shíjiān kǎolǜ yí xiàr, wǒ néng guò liǎngtiān zài gěi nín ge dáfu ma?

8 Looking for a teaching job

找教师工作 Zhǎo jiàoshī gōngzuò

Sentences

• I am a certified teacher 我有教师证书 Wǒ yǒu jiàoshī zhèngshū

• How many students per class? 每个班有多少个学生？ Měi ge bān yǒu duōshao ge xuésheng?

• Are the students ... ? 这些学生是...吗？ Zhèxiē xuésheng shì ... ma?

(1) young children 儿童 értóng
(2) teenagers 年轻人 niánqīngrén
(3) college kids 大学生 dàxuéshēng
(4) adults 成人 chéngrén
(5) businesspeople 商务人士 shāngwù rénshì

• Are materials provided? 您提供材料吗？ Nín tígōng cáiliào ma?

• Is the pay monthly, per classroom hour, or per class? 计酬方式是按月薪，课时，还是每一个班付费？ Jìchóu fāngshì shì àn yuèxīn, kèshí hái shì měi yí gè bān fùfèi?

• How many teaching hours per week? 每礼拜几个课时？ Měi lǐbài jǐ ge kèshí?

• Do you need me to work on weekends? 需要我周末工作吗？ Xūyào wǒ zhōumò gōngzuò ma?

• Will you pay for the tickets for a trip home? 可以报销我回国的机票吗？ Kěyǐ bàoxiāo wǒ huíguó de jīpiào ma?

• Do you refund commuting expenses? 能报销车费吗？ Néng bàoxiāo chēfèi ma?

9 In class with kids
儿童课堂 értóng kètáng

Sentences

• Be quiet 安静一下儿 ānjìng yí xiàr

• Sit down 请坐 Qǐng zuò

• We're taking a break now 我们现在休息一下 Wǒmen xiànzài xiūxi yí xià

• Ok, come back 好，回来吧 Hǎo, huílái ba

• No talking 别说话 Bié shuōhuà

• Be good or I'll talk to your parents 听话，否则请家长 Tīnghuà, fǒuzé qǐng jiāzhǎng

10 Dealing with an accountant
处理财务事宜 Chùlǐ cáiwù shìyí

Sentences

• When will I get paid? 什么时候发工资？ Shénme shíhou fā gōngzī?

• Can you send the payment to me via courier? 能不能把工资快递给我？ Néng bùnéng bǎ gōngzī kuàidì gěi wǒ?

• How can I get reimbursed? 怎么报销？ Zěnme bàoxiāo?

Do you take taxes out of my salary? 我的工资扣税吗？ Wǒ de gōngzī kòushuì ma?

• What is the rate? 税率是多少？ Shuìlǜ shì duōshao?

• How can I reduce my taxes? 怎么才能减免税？ Zěnme cáinéng jiǎnmiǎn shuì?

Listen for this

- zhíjiē dǎrù gèrén zhànghù 直接打入个人账户 direct deposit
- Yídìng yào ná yí ge zhèngshì fāpiào 一定要拿一个正式发票 Make sure to collect a tax reciept

11 Chinese language resume

中文简历 Zhōngwén jiǎnlì

Vocabulary

name 姓名 xìngmíng
sex 性别 xìngbié
birthdate 出生日期 chūshēng rìqī
telephone 电话 diànhuà
email 电子邮箱 diànzǐ yóuxiāng
address 地址 dìzhǐ

personal information 个人信息 gèrén xìnxī

educational background 教育背景 jiàoyù bèijǐng
degree 学位 xuéwèi
honors & awards 荣誉与奖励 róngyù yǔ jiǎnglì
work experience 工作经历 gōngzuò jīnglì
working responsibilities 工作职责 gōngzuò zhízé
specialties & abilities 特长与能力 tècháng yǔ nénglì
community groups 社会活动 shèhuì huódòng

Sentences

- Responsible for ... duties 担任...职务 Dānrèn ... zhíwù
- Carried out .... work 完成...工作 Wánchéng ... gōngzuò
- Familiar with MS Office 熟悉 MS Office shúxi MS Office
- I can speak fluent Mandarin and have strong Chinese reading and writing ability 普通话流利，有很强的中文阅读及写作能力 Pǔtōnghuà liúlì, yǒu hěn qiáng de zhōngwén yuèdú jí xiězuò nénglì

12 Email and fax

邮件与传真 Yóujiàn yǔ chuánzhēn

Sentences

- Dear ... 尊敬的... Zūnjìng de ...
- I hereby respectfully (close this letter) 此致敬礼 Cǐzhì jìnglǐ
- Reply 回复 Huífù
- To 致 Zhì
- From 自 Zì
- '@' - At symbol 圈儿A Quān'r A
- '.' - Dot 点儿 Diǎn'r
- '_' - Underscore 下划线 Xiàhuáxiàn
- ' ' - Blank space 空格 Kōnggé
- '-' - Hyphen 破折号 Pòzhéhào
- '/' - Foward slash 右斜线 Yòuxiéxiàn
- '\' - Back slash 左斜线 Zuǒxiéxiàn
- Unrecognizably formatted characters 乱码 Luànmá

Notes

ADULT EDUCATION

1 Learning Chinese

学中文 Xué Zhōngwén

Sentences

• What is (this / that) called in Chinese? (这个/那个)中文叫什么? (Zhèige/nèige) zhōngwén jiào shénme?

• How do you say that in Chinese? 那个用中文怎么说? Nèige yòng zhōngwén zěnme shuō?

• Could you write that down for me? 您能帮我写下来吗? Nín néng bāng wǒ xiě xiàlai ma?

• Could you write it a little more clearly? 您能写清楚点儿吗? Nín néng xiě qīngchu diǎnr ma?

• How do you pronounce that character? 这个字怎么念 Zhèige zì zěnme niàn?

• What tone is it? 是几声? Shì jǐ shēng?

• Could you say that one more time? 您能再说一遍吗? Nín néng zài shuō yí biàn ma?

• Can you speak more slowly? 您能说得再慢点儿吗? Nín néng shuō de zài màn diǎnr ma?

• I'm sorry, I don't understand 对不起，我不太明白 Duìbùqǐ, wǒ bú tài míngbai

Listen for this

• Wǒ yě bù zhīdào! 我也不知道! I don't know either!

Sharpen Your Tongue

Chinese tongue twisters 绕口令 ràokǒulìng

by Gabriel Monroe

Many Chinese words sound the same, particularly to the English speaker's ear. Among the following group of tongue twisters, several challenge the speaker to distinguish tonal differences, others muck around with juǎnshé 卷舌 (distinctions between sh and s, zh and z, ch and c), and some are accent traps, the bane of any lisp-inclined Chinese southerner. Give them a try! Watch those tones and don't mix up your n's and l's or your dingdongs. Once you've mastered a couple of these, the legends of your lingual agility will open doors high and low! Giggle doors, that is ...

Māma qǐ mǎ, mǎ màn, māma mà mǎ 妈妈骑马，马慢，妈妈骂马 Mommy rides a horse. The horse is slow. Mommy curses the horse. (Or literally "Mommy ride horse. Horse slow. Mommy curse horse.")

Sìshísì zhī shí shīzi chī sìshísì zhī shí shīzi 四十四只石狮子吃四十四只石虱子 44 stone lions eat 44 stone lice (Luckily, you probably won't have to say this very often)

Fēng tíng téng tíng tónglíng tíng 风停藤停铜铃停 The wind stops, the vine stops (waving in the wind), the bell stops (ringing)

Chū xīmén zǒu qī bù, jiàn kuàir jī pír bǔ pí kù 出西门走七步，见块儿鸡皮儿补皮裤 Exit the west gate and walk seven steps, see a piece of chicken skin and use it to patch up your leather pants (If you can master this one you'll never be short on advice for someone with a hole in their pants ...)

Niúláng niánnián niàn liúniáng 牛郎年年念刘娘 Year after year, the cowboy pines for Miss Liu (based on a Chinese legend)

Tóng jiā, dǒng jiā dōu dǒngde zhòng dōngguā. Tóng, dǒng liǎng jiā de dōngguā bǐ tǒng dà 童家、董家都懂得种冬瓜.童、董两家的冬瓜比桶大 The Tong family and the Dong family both understand how to grow winter melons. The melons of these two families are bigger than buckets! (This one proves once and for all that melons are worth their weight in giggles ...)

2 Around campus
在校园 Zài xiàoyuán

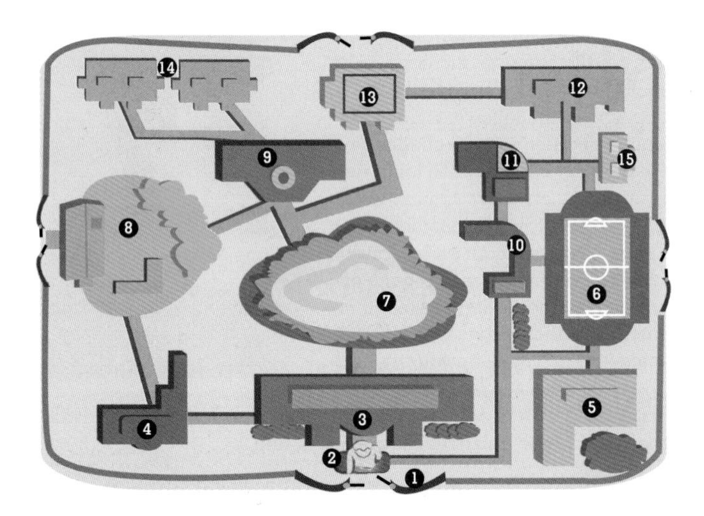

(1) south gate 南门 nánmén
(2) Mao statue 毛主席雕像 Máo zhǔxí diāoxiàng
(3) classroom / teaching building 教室/教学楼 jiàoshì / jiàoxuélóu
(4) science and technology building 科技楼 kējìlóu
(5) basketball courts 篮球场 lánqiúchǎng
(6) gym / track / tennis courts 体育馆/田径场/网球场 tǐyùguǎn / tiánjìngchǎng / wǎngqiúchǎng
(7) park / lake 公园/湖 gōngyuán / hú
(8) kindergarten 幼儿园 yòu'éryuán
(9) library图书馆 túshūguǎn
(10) electronics building 电子楼 diànzǐlóu
(11) foreign students' dorms 留学生宿舍楼 liúxuéshēng sùshèlóu
(12) foreign experts' building 外国专家楼 wàiguó zhuānjiā lóu
(13) cafeteria / canteen 自助餐厅/食堂 zìzhù cāntīng / shítáng
(14) (male/female) student dorms (男生/女生)宿舍 (nánshēng/nǚshēng) sùshè
(15) foreign students' office 留学生办公室 liúxuéshēng bàngōngshì

Sentences

• Where can I get a cafeteria card? 我到哪儿去买饭卡？Wǒ dào nǎr qù mǎi fànkǎ?

• How do I add money? 我怎么加钱？Wǒ zěnme jiāqián?

• Where can I find a good place to study? 哪儿有适合自习的地方？Nǎr yǒu shìhé zìxí de dìfang?

3 Studying at university
在大学进修 Zài dàxué jìnxiū

Sentences

• How do I apply? 我怎么申请？Wǒ zěnme shēnqǐng?

• When is the application deadline? 申请截止日期是什么时候？Shēnqǐng jiézhǐ rìqī shì shénme shíhou?

• Is there an application fee? 有没有报名费？Yǒu méiyǒu bàomíngfèi?

• How much is tuition? 学费多少钱？Xuéfèi duōshao qián?

• Can I audit a class? 能不能试听一节课？Néng bùnéng shìtīng yì jié kè?

• Do you offer degree programs? 有攻读学位的课程吗？Yǒu gōngdú xuéwèi de kèchéng ma?

• What are my on-campus housing options? 学校提供什么样的住宿方式？Xuéxǐao tígòng shénmeyàng de zhùsù fāngshì?

• How much is it per day? 一天多少钱？Yì tiān duōshao qián?

• Where can I find the place to sign up for classes? 请问去哪儿可以报道？Qǐngwèn qù nǎr kěyǐ bàodào?

• What classes are available? 哪些课可以选？ Nǎxiē kè kěyǐ xuǎn?

• Where can I see a schedule of classes? 在哪儿能看到课程表？ Zài nǎr néng kàndào kèchéngbiǎo?

• How many levels do you have? 你们一共有多少级？ Nǐmen yígòng yǒu duōshǎo jí?

• Is there a placement exam? 有没有入学考试？ Yǒu méiyǒu rùxué kǎoshì?

• student ID card 学生证 xuéshēngzhèng

• What are your entry requirements? 你们的入学条件是什么？ Nǐmen de rùxué tiáojiàn shì shénme?

• Do I need to have a score on the Test of Chinese Language Level (HSK)? 我需要提供汉语水平考试的分数吗？ Wǒ xūyào tígōng Hányǔ Shuǐpíng Kǎoshì de fēnshù ma?

Listen for this

• bìnglì dàngàn 病历档案 medical records
• tīnglìkè 听力课 listening comprehension class
• yuèdúkè 阅读课 reading comprehension class
• bàokānkè 报刊课 newspaper reading class
• huìhuàkè 会话课 conversation class
• kǒuyǔ 口语 oral Chinese
• fǔdǎo 辅导 tutor
• shūfǎkè 书法课 calligraphy class
• tàijíquán 太极拳 tai chi
• dānrén fángjiān 单人房间 single room
• shuāngrén fángjiān 双人房间 double room

4 In class 课堂上 Kètáng shàng

Vocabulary

- classmate 同学 tóngxué
- test 考试 kǎoshì
- grade 成绩 chéngjì
- pass 及格 jígé
- fail 不及格 bùjígé

Sentences

- You're such a suckup! 你真是个马屁精！ Nǐ zhēn shì ge mǎpìjīng!

- I did my homework, but I forgot to bring it in 我的作业做了，但是忘带了 Wǒ de zuòyè zuòle, dànshì wàng dài le

- I'm late because my bike broke 我迟到是因为我的自行车坏了 Wǒ chídào shì yīnwéi wǒ de zìxíngchē huài le

Listen for this

- Jiāo zuòyè 交作业 Turn in your homework
- Bǎ shū fāndào ... yè 把书翻到...页 Open your books to page ...
- Jǔ yí gè lìzi 举一个例子 Give an example
- Chóngfù 重复 Repeat

- Dàshēng dú 大声读 Read aloud
- Duì 对 Correct
- Cuò 错 Incorrect
- Fēicháng hǎo! 非常好！Excellent!
- tīngxiě cèyàn 听写测验 dictation exam

5 Private learning center

私立学校 Sīlì xuéxiào

Sentences

- Where are you located? 学校在哪儿？Xuéxiào zài nǎr?
- What's your hourly rate? 你们每小时收多少钱？ Nǐmen měixiǎoshí shōu duōshao qián?
- Do you offer ... classes? 你们有没有. . . 的课程？Nǐmen yǒu méiyǒu ... de kèchéng?

(1) absolute beginners 零基础 língjīchǔ
(2) beginners 初级 chūjí
(3) intermediate 中级 zhōngjí
(3) business Chinese 商务汉语 shāngwù hànyǔ

- How many students per class? 每个班有多少学生？Měi ge bān yǒu duōshao xuésheng?
- How many times a week? 一个星期几次课？Yí ge xīngqī jǐ cì kè?
- How long for each day? 每天多长时间？Měitiān duōcháng shíjiān?
- I want to come in and check it out, is that ok? 我想过来看看，行吗？Wǒ xiǎng guòlái kànkan, xíng ma?
- Can I sit in on a lesson? 我能试听一节课吗？ Wǒ néng shìtīng yì jié kè ma?
- Do you offer one-on-one classes? 你们有没有一对一授课？Nǐmen yǒu méiyǒu yīduìyī shòukè?

• Can I change (classes/teachers)? 我能换(课／老师）吗？Wǒ néng huàn (kè/lǎoshī) ma ?

• Can a teacher come to my house? 老师能来我家吗？Lǎoshī néng lái wǒ jiā ma?

Listen for this

• Liùshíwǔ kuài qián yí ge xiǎoshí 65块钱一个小时 65 yuan per hour

• Měi bān bù chāoguò shíge xuésheng 每班不超过10个学生 Less than 10 students per class

• Nǐ hànyǔ shuǐpíng zěnmeyàng? 你汉语水平怎么样？ What is your Chinese level?

6 Homework 作业 Zuòyè

Watch for this

• liànxí 练习exercises

• tìhuàn 替换 substitution

• tiánkòng 填空 fill in the blanks

• xuǎncí tiánkòng 选词填空 choose the right words to fill in the blanks

• mófǎng zàojù 模仿造句 make sentences after the models

• yòng jùxíng huò cíhuì huídá wèntí 用句型或词汇回答问题 answer the quesions with the given sentence pattern or vocabulary

• wánchéng duìhuà 完成对话 complete the dialogues

• gǎi cuò jù 改错句 correct the sentences

• xuǎnzé zhèngquè dá'àn 选择正确答案 choose the correct answer

• ànzhào lìjù zuò liànxí 按照例句做练习 practice according to the model

Are You Experienced?

Jimi will expand your horizons

by Gabriel Monroe

The Chinese answer to Dr. Seuss might well be a talented cartoonist from Taiwan named Jimi (幾米 Jǐmǐ aka Jimmy Liao), whose illustrations are as lyrical as they are hypnotic.

Aimed at kids of all ages, Jimi's work can be great "gateway literature" for a beginning Chinese learner. Many of his books are written with one story/image per page, so they're conveniently digestible for an on-the-go student. And with a little help from a dictionary or nearby friend, reading a Jimi book yields high gratification.

Jimi's urban cartoon romance *A Chance of Sunshine* (向右走，向左走 xiàng yòu zǒu, xiàng zuǒ zǒu) is a great book to start with. Featuring simple, elegant text and illustrations, the story of mischievous fate is so engaging that you might want a box of tissues on hand as you read. The language of *A Chance of Sunshine* is sparse and accessible, but rife with poetry. You will run the emotional range of a love story punctuated by weather reports, coming across phrases like:

- dense, dark clouds 浓密的乌云 nóngmì de wūyún
- raining cats and dogs, torrential rain 倾盆大雨 qīngpén dàyǔ
- a bone-piercing, chilly wind 刺骨的冷风 cìgǔ de lěngfēng
- in the distance, pigeons spiral in the sky 远方，鸽子在空中盘旋 yuǎnfāng, gēzi zài kōngzhōng pánxuán.
- the bright red evening sun gradually descends 艳红的夕阳缓缓落下 yànhóng de xīyáng huǎnhuǎn luòxià

as well as sentences like:

- It's possible that two parallel lines will one day connect 两条平行线也可能会有交会的一天 liǎngtiáo píngxíngxiàn yě kěnéng yǒu jiāohuì de yìtiān
- the rain soaked them from head to toe, but their hearts were cozy and warm 大雨将他们淋得湿透，但他们的心却是温暖的 Dàyǔ jiāng tāmen lín de shītòu, dàn tāmen de xīn què shì wēnnuǎn de.
- the string of the kite in your hand can suddenly break 握在手里的风筝也会突然断了线 Wò zài shǒulǐ de fēngzhēng yě huì tūrán duàn le xiàn
- In this familiar, yet strange city ... 在这个熟悉又陌生的城市中 . . . Zài zhègè shúxī yòu mòshēng de chéngshì zhōng ...
- they cannot help searching for that strange, yet familiar silhouette 无助地寻找一个陌生又熟悉的身影 Wúzhù di xúnzhǎo yígè mòshēng yòu shúxì de shēnyǐng

Despite all the big, pretty pictures, Jimi books are perfectly acceptable adult reading, and may earn you a raised eyebrow or two. Now that's face!

7 Foreign students' office

留学生办公室

Liúxuéshēng bàngōngshì

Sentences

• I need to extend my visa 我需要续签证 Wǒ xūyào xù qiānzhèng

• I need help resolving a dispute with my roommate 我需要帮助解决与同屋的矛盾 Wǒ xūyào bāngzhù jiějué yǔ tóngwū de máodùn

• I'd like to move (up/down) a level 我想(跳级／降级) Wǒ xiǎng (tiàojí/jiàngjí)

• Can you help me find a tutor? 能不能帮我找一个辅导老师? Néng bùnéng bāng wǒ zhǎo yí ge fǔdǎo lǎoshī?

• I want to get my tuition back 我想退学费 Wǒ xiǎng tuì xuéfèi

• Is there a withdrawal fee? 会不会扣钱? Huì búhuì kòu qián?

Listen for this

• Nín děi huàn qiānzhèng 您得换签证 You will have to get a new visa

Notes

USEFUL INFO ►

1 Dry cleaning 干洗 Gānxǐ

Vocabulary

(For more clothes vocabulary see Shopping, p144)

business suit 西服 xīfú
carpet 地毯 dìtǎn
corduroy 灯芯绒 dēngxīnróng
cotton 棉 mián
couch covers 沙发套 shāfātào
down feathers 羽绒 yǔróng
dress 连衣裙 liányīqún
embroidery 刺绣 cìxiù
fabric 布料 bùliào
jacket 上衣 shàngyī
label 标签 biāoqiān
leather 皮革 pígé
linen 亚麻 yàmá
nylon 尼龙 nílóng
pants 裤子 kùzi
polyester 化纤 huàxiān
scarf 围巾 wéijīn
seat covers 座椅套 zuòyǐ tào
shirt 衬衫 chènshān
silk 丝绸 sīchóu
skirt 短裙 duǎnqún
tie 领带 lǐngdài
waterproof 防水 fángshuǐ
wool 羊毛 yángmáo

Sentences

• Can you clean this? 你能洗这个吗？ Nǐ néng xǐ zhèige ma ?

• How much is it to clean this? 洗这个多少钱？ Xǐ zhèige duōshao qián?

• Please (don't) ... 请（不要）. . . Qǐng (búyào) ...

(1) use bleach 用漂白剂 yòng piǎobáijì
(2) use starch 上浆 shàngjiāng
(3) iron 熨烫 yùntàng
(4) machine wash 机洗 jīxǐ
(5) tumble dry 滚筒烘干 gǔntǒng hōnggān

• This should be washed at ... temperature 这个要用. . . 水洗 Zhèige yào yòng ... shuǐxǐ.

(1) high 高温 gāowēn
(2) medium 中温 zhōngwēn
(3) low 低温 dīwēn

• Will this shrink in the wash? 这个洗了会缩水吗？ Zhèige xǐ le huì suōshuǐ ma ?

• This stain is probably ... 这个污渍是. . . Zhèigè wūzì shì ...

(1) dirt 土 tǔ
(2) red wine 红酒 hóngjiǔ
(3) oil 油 yóu
(4) bike gear grease 自行车油 zìxíngchē yóu
(5) majiang hot pot sauce 火锅麻酱小料 huǒguō májiàng xiǎoliào

• When will it be ready? 什么时候能洗好？ Shénme shíhou néng xǐ hǎo?

• Can it be ready sooner? 能快点儿吗？ Néng kuàidiǎnr ma ?

• Can you have them ready by tomorrow morning/night? 能不能明天早上/晚上洗好？ Néng bùnéng míngtiān zǎoshang / wǎnshang xǐ hǎo?

Listen for this

• Hòutiān lái qǔ 后天来取 Pick them up the day after tomorrow

• Wǒmén xǐ bùliǎo nèige 我们洗不了那个 We can't get that out

Watch for

• dāntàng 单烫 iron only

• píyī qīngxǐ 皮衣清洗 leather dry cleaning

2 Holidays/festivals 节假日 Jiéjiàrì

Sentences

• Wish you a happy ... ! 祝你...快乐！ Zhù nǐ .... kuàilè!

anniversary 周年纪念日 zhōunián jìniànrì
birthday 生日 shēngrì
New Year's 新年 Xīnnián
Spring Festival 春节 Chūnjié
International Labor Day 五一国际劳动节 Wǔyī guójì láodòngjié
National Day 国庆节 Guóqìngjié
Lantern Festival 元宵节 Yuánxiāojié
Mid-Autumn Festival 中秋节 Zhōngqiūjié
Tomb Sweeping day 清明节 Qīngmíngjié
Dragon Boat Festival 端午节 Duānwǔjié
Int'l Women's Day 三八妇女节 Sānbā Fùnǚjié
Int'l Children's Day 六一儿童节 Liùyī értóngjié
Teacher's Day 教师节 Jiàoshījié
Chinese Valentine's Day 七夕 Qīxī
Easter 复活节 Fùhuójié

Christmas 圣诞节 Shèngdànjié
Hanukkah 光明节 Guāngmíngjié
Yom Kippur 赎罪日 Shúzuìrì
Passover 逾越节 Yúyuèjié
Rosh Hashanah 岁首节 Suìshǒujié
Ramadan 斋月 Zhāiyuè
April Fool's Day 愚人节 Yúrénjié
Valentine's Day 情人节Qíngrénjié
Thanksgiving 感恩节 Găn'ēnjié
Independence Day/National Day 独立日/国庆节 Dúlìrì/Guóqìngjié

3 Internet 网络 Wăngluò

Watch for this

- boot up 启动 qǐdòng
- shut down 关机 guānjī
- ok / agree 好 / 同意 hăo / tóngyì
- cancel 取消 qŭxiāo
- next (step/page) 下一步 / 一页 xià (yí bù / yí yè)
- continue 继续 jìxù
- password 密码 mìmă
- login 登录 dēnglù
- user name 用户名 yònghùmíng
- search 搜索 sōusuǒ

Sentences

- How do I apply for broadband ADSL? 我怎么申请ADSL宽带 ? Wǒ zěnme shēnqǐng ADSL kuāndài?

- What documents do I need? 我需要什么资料? Wǒ xūyào shénme zīliào?

- How much is ...? . . . 多少钱? ... duōshao qián?

  (1) installation 安装费 ānzhuāngfèi
  (2) monthly plan (unlimited use) 包月 bāoyuè
  (3) per hour 每小时 měi xiǎoshí

- how fast is it? 有多快? Yǒu duō kuài?

- When can someone come to install it? 什么时候能来人装? Shénme shíhou néng lái rén zhuāng?

Listen for this

- Nǐ xūyào yí ge zhōngguó jūmín de shēnfènzhèng 你需要一个中国居民的身份证 You need a Chinese citizen's ID card

- Nín děi qù yíngyètīng. 您得去营业厅 You need to go to a service center

- Wǔbǎi yīshí'èr K dàikuān 512k带宽 512K bandwidth

- Yí zhào dàikuān 1兆带宽 1MB bandwidth

- xiàzǎi 下载 download

- shàngchuán 上传 upload

- yùfù kǎ 预付卡 prepaid cards

4 Websites 网站 Wǎngzhàn

Vocabulary

1) homepage 主页 zhǔyè
2) about us 关于我们 guānyú wǒmen
3) contact us 联系我们 liánxi wǒmen
4) forum 论坛 lùntán
5) links 友情链接 yǒuqíng liànjiē
6) english salon 英语沙龙 yīngyǔ shālóng
7) site map 站点地图 zhàndiǎn dìtú

www.that'sbj.com

that's网站

1 主页 2 关于我们 3 联系我们 4 论坛 5 友情链接 6 英语沙龙

搜索

邮箱：用户名：

密码：

注册 登录

JJ: 姐姐 (big sister/girl)
jiějie
PLMM: 漂亮妹妹 (pretty girl)
piàoliàng mèimei
3Q: "三Q"(thank you)
sān Q
PMP:拍马屁 (kiss ass)
pāimǎpì
9494: 就是就是 (that's right!)
jiùshì jiùshì
NB: 牛B (awesome)
niúbī
520: 五二零≈我爱你≈I love you
wǔèrlíng≈wǒàinǐ
886: 八八六≈拜拜了≈bye bye
bābāliù≈báibáile

昵称： 进入

甜甜：我还是FurongJJ，谁是PLMM？
Me or Sister Furong who is prettier?

贝贝：当然是你甜甜！
Of course it's you, Sweety!

甜甜：3Q你真会PMP
Thanks, you really know how to kiss ass

贝贝：9494你真
That's right! You're awsome

甜甜：520 886
I love you! Gotta go!

T

7 站点地图

5 Internet cafe 网吧 Wǎngbā

Sentences

- How much per hour? 每小时多少钱？ Měi xiǎoshí duōshao qián?
- Can I print? 我能打印吗？ Wǒ néng dǎyìn ma ?
- Can I use this (floppy disk / flash drive)? 我能用这个（软驱/优盘）吗？ Wǒ néng yòng zhèige (ruǎnqū / yōupán) ma ?
- Can I burn a CD? 我能刻张盘吗？ Wǒ néng kè zhāng pán ma?
- earphones 耳机 ěrjī
- microphone 麦克风 màikèfēng
- I can't see my email 我看不了邮件 Wǒ kàn bùliǎo yóujiàn
- Computer terms:

to connect / plug in (one thing to another via a wire) 连接/插入 liánjiē / chārù

Apple 苹果 Píngguǒ

Microsoft 微软 Wēiruǎn

desktop computer 台式电脑 táishì diànnǎo

laptop 笔记本电脑 bǐjìběn diànnǎo

For more computer vocabulary, see Shopping, p155.

Sentences

- The ... has a problem ...出问题了 ... chū wèntí le.
- Can you fix it? 你能修吗？ Nǐ néng xiū ma?

6 At the post office 在邮局 Zài yóuju

Vocabulary

- customs declaration 海关申报 hǎiguān shēnbào
- domestic 国内 guónèi
- fragile 易碎 yìsuì
- EMS (express mail service) 特快专递 tèkuài zhuāndì

- international 国际 guójì
- registered mail 挂号 guàhào
- postcode 邮编 yóubiān

Sentences

- I want to send a ... 我想寄 / 发一个.... Wǒ xiǎng jì/fā yí gè ...

(1) fax 传真 chuánzhēn
(2) letter 信 xìn
(3) parcel 包裹 bāoguǒ
(4) postcard 明信片 míngxìnpiàn

- I want to buy ... 我想买... Wǒ xiǎng mǎi ...

(1) a stamp 一张邮票 yì zhāng yóupiào
(2) an envelope 一个信封 yí gè xìnfēng
(3) a box 一个盒子 yí gè hézi

- Am I standing in the right line? 我没排错队吧？Wǒ méi pái cuò duì ba?

- Please send it by (airmail / surface mail) to (Australia) 麻烦寄一个（航空件/水陆路邮件）到（澳大利亚）Máfan jì yígè (hángkōng jiàn / shuǐlùlù yóujiàn) dào (àodàlìyà)

- What's the weight limit? 限重多少？Xiànzhòng duōshao?

- What are the dimension limits? 尺寸限制是多少？Chǐcùn xiànzhì shì duōshao?

- Can I send food? 我能寄食品吗？Wǒ néng jì shípǐn ma?

- Is there any mail for me? 有我的邮件吗？Yǒu wǒde yóujiàn ma?

- I want to find out if a package has arrived for me. My name is ... My address is ... 我想查一下我的包裹到了没有。我的名字是...我的地址是... Wǒ xiǎng chá yí xià wǒde bāoguǒ dàole méiyǒu. Wǒ de míngzi shì ... Wǒ de dìzhǐ shì ...

- I have a parcel notice 我有一个包裹单 Wǒ yǒu yí gè bāoguǒdān

- Where can I pick up my parcel? 我上哪儿取（包裹）? Wǒ shàng nǎr qǔ (bāoguǒ)?

- Where is the main foreign post office? 哪儿有大点儿的国际邮局? Nǎr yǒu dà diǎnr de guójì yóujú?

- Which counter should I go to for ... ? 我要...的话该去哪个柜台? Wǒyào ... dehuà gāi qù nǎgè guìtái?

- What's the postage for (a letter / package) to ... 寄（一封信/包裹）到...要多少钱? Jì (yì fēng xìn / bāoguǒ) dào ... yào duōshǎo qián?

- Using (express mail / regular mail), how long will it take to get there and how much will it cost? 用（快件 / 平邮）要多久到那儿? 多少钱? Yòng (kuàijiàn / píngyóu) yào duōjiǔ dào nàr? Duōshǎo qián?

- What is the next (cheapest / fastest) way? 还有别的（便宜的/快的）吗? Hái yǒu biéde (piányi de / kuài de) ma?

- Where's the glue? 胶水儿在哪儿? Jiāoshuǐr zài nǎr?

Listen for this

- Jì zhīqián wǒmen děi jiǎnchá yí xià nínde bāoguǒ 寄之前我们得检查一下您的包裹 We need to inspect your package before we can mail it

- Bùnéng wǎng guówài jì dàobǎn DVD 不能往国外寄盗版DVD You can't mail pirated DVDs overseas

7 Express delivery 快递 Kuàidì

Sentences

- I'd like to arrange a pickup and delivery 我想安排来取货发货 Wǒ xiǎng ānpái lái qǔhuò fāhuò

- Can you do it today? 你们今天能送吗? Nǐmen jīntiān néng sòng ma?

- How much? 多少钱？ Duōshao qián?

- Pick it up at the following address: 到这个地址来取件：Dào zhèige dìzhǐ lái qǔjiàn:

- Deliver it to the following address: 送到这个地址：Sòngdào zhèige dìzhǐ:

- The recipient will pay 收件人付款 Shōujiànrén fùkuǎn

Listen for this

- Nín zài shénme dìfang? 您在什么地方？ Where are you?
- Sòngdào shénme dìfang?送到什么地方？ Where do you want to send it to?
- Nín yào shénme shíhou sòng?您要什么时候送？ When do you want to send it?
- Zài Wǔhuán lǐ háishì Wǔhuán wài? 在五环里还是五环外？ Is that inside or outside of the Fifth Ring Road?

8 Banking 银行 Yínháng

Sentences

- Where is the closest ATM? 最近的（取款机/ATM）在哪儿？ Zuìjìn de (qǔkuǎnjī/ATM) zài nǎr?

- I need to ... 我要... Wǒ yào ...

(1) withdraw money 取钱 qǔ qián
(2) deposit money 存钱 cún qián
(3) change money 换钱 huàn qián
(4) change a traveler's check 换旅行支票 huàn lǚxíng zhīpiào
(5) transfer money from a foreign account
从国外汇款 cóng guówài huìkuǎn

- I'd like to withdraw RMB (3,000) 我要取（三千块）人民币 Wǒ yào qǔ (sānqiān kuài) rénmínbì

- What's the maximum withdrawal ... ? ...最多能取多少？... zuìduō néng qǔ duōshao?

(1) per day 每天 Měi tiān
(2) per session 每次 Měi cì
(3) per month 每月 Měi yuè

- I lost my card 我的卡丢了 Wǒ de kǎ diū le.

- My card is broken 我的卡坏了 Wǒ de kǎ huài le.

- The machine ate my card 我的卡被机器吞了 Wǒ de kǎ bèi jīqi tūn le.

- What form should I fill out? 我该填哪张表？ Wǒ gāi tián nǎ zhāng biǎo?

- Can I write a check on my home country account? 我能开张我本国账户的支票吗？ Wǒ néng kāi zhāng wǒ běnguó zhànghù de zhīpiào ma?

- How long will it take to arrive in my account? 多久能到我的帐上？ Duōjiǔ néng dào wǒ de zhàng shàng?

- What's the charge for that? 手续费多少钱？ Shǒuxùfèi duōshao qián?

(1) ATM card 取款卡 qǔkuǎnkǎ
(2) cash 现金 xiànjīn
(3) check 支票 zhīpiào
(4) credit card 信用卡 xìnyòngkǎ
(5) checking account 支票帐户 zhīpiào zhànghù
(6) savings account 储蓄帐户 chǔxù zhànghù
(7) password 密码 mìmǎ
(8) bankbook 存折 cúnzhé
(9) foreign bankcard 外国银行卡 wàiguó yínhángkǎ
(10) exchange rate 汇率 huìlǜ
(11) exchange fee 汇费 huìfèi
(12) wire transfer 电汇 diànhuì

Listen for this

- Ná hào 拿号 Take a number
- Qǐng shū mìmǎ 请输密码 Enter your password
- Qǐng qiānmíng 请签名 Sign your name
- Tián zhè zhāng biǎo 填这张表 Fill out this form
- Wǒmen zhèr zuò bùliǎo zhèigè yèwù 我们这儿做不了这个业务 We can't do that here

Watch for

- personal banking 个人业务 gèrén yèwù

Banks 银行 Yínháng

(1) American Express 美国运通 Měiguó Yùntōng
(2) Agricultural Bank of China 中国农业银行/农行 Zhōngguó Nóngyè Yínháng / Nóng-Háng
(3) Bank of China 中国银行 Zhōngguó Yínháng
(4) Bank of Beijing 北京银行 Běijīng Yínháng
(5) China Construction Bank 中国建设银行/建行 Zhōngguó Jiànshè Yínháng / Jiàn-Háng
(6) China Everbright Bank 中国光大银行 Zhōngguó Guāngdà Yínháng
(7) China Merchant's Bank 招商银行 Zhāoshāng Yínháng
(8) China Minsheng Bank 中国民生银行 Zhōngguó Mínshēng Yínháng
(9) Citibank 花旗银行 Huāqí Yínháng
(10) HSBC 汇丰银行 Huìfēng Yínháng
(11) Industrial and Commercial Bank of China 中国工商银行 Zhōngguó Gōngshāng Yínháng
(12) Western Union 西联汇款 Xīlián Huìkuǎn

9 Opening a bank account
开户 Kāihù

(1) account application 开户申请 kāihù shēnqǐng
(2) includes ATM card 附带储蓄卡 fùdài chǔxù kǎ
(3) personal information 个人资料 gèrén zīliào
(4) name 姓名 xìngmíng
(5) sex 性别 xìngbié
(6) nationality 国籍 guójí
(7) birthdate 出生日期 chūshēng rìqī
(8) form of identification 证件类型 zhèngjiàn lèixíng
(9) ID number 证件号码 zhèngjiàn hàomǎ
(10) address 住址 zhùzhǐ
(11) postal code 邮编 yóubiān
(12) depositor (signature) 存款人（签章）cúnkuǎn rén (qiānzhāng)

Sentences

- I'd like to open a bank account 我想开个账户 Wǒ xiǎng kāi ge zhànghù
- I need an ATM card 我要办个储蓄卡 Wǒ yào bàn ge chǔxù kǎ

银行个人结算账户开户/借记卡业务登记表

开户申请 ❶							
开户类型	新开卡 ☐		持卡开存折 ☐				
服务种类	银证转帐 ☐		银券通 ☐		开放式基金 ☐		
开户日期	年 月 日		开户行代码				
开户行名称							
1、新开卡请填写							
申请借记卡类型	有存折卡 ☐ ❷		无存折卡 ☐				
2、持卡开存折请填写							
借记卡号							
3、持存折开卡请填写							
存折账号							
4、存折和卡关联请填写（下面"个人资料"部分只需填"姓名"栏）							
借记卡号			活一本通账号				
普通活期账号			个人支票/信用卡				
个人资料 ❸							
姓名	❹	性别	❺	国籍	❻	出生日期	❼
证件类型	❽	证件号码	❾	电话			
住址	❿			邮编	⓫		
备注							
存款人（签章）⓬ 年 月 日			经办人（签章）		开户银行（签章） 年 月 日		

• Can I deposit foreign currency? 我能存外币吗？Wǒ néng cún wàibì ma?

Listen for this

- hùzhào 护照 passport
- qiānmíng 签名 signature
- Zhèshì mìmǎ 这是密码 This is the password

- Nín kěyǐ dào wàimiàn de qǔkuǎnjī shàng gǎi mìmǎ. 您可以到外面的取款机上改密码 Go outside to the ATM and you can change your password there
- Zhè zhāng kǎ zhǐnéng zài Běijīng yòng 这张卡只能在北京用 This ATM card is only valid in Beijing

10 Moving 搬家 Bānjiā

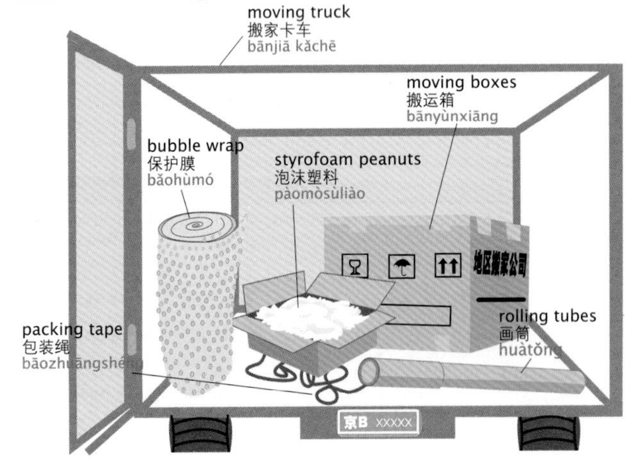

Sentences

- I'd like to arrange a move for this (Saturday) 我想安排这个(星期六)搬家 Wǒ xiǎng ānpái zhèigè (xīngqīliù) bānjiā.
- From (Haidian District) to (Chaoyang District) 从(海淀区)到(朝阳区) Cóng (Hǎidiàn qū) dào (Cháoyáng qū)
- I have a (two) bedroom apartment with ... of furniture and appliances 我有一个（两）居室的房子有...家具和电器 Wǒ yǒu yígè (liǎng) jūshì de fángzi yǒu ... de jiājū hé diànqì

(1) lots 很多的 hěn duō de
(2) some 一些 yìxiē
(3) not a lot 不太多的 bú tài duō de

• What is the maximum load (in cubic meters) and maximum distance (for the price)? （这个价钱）能搬多少立方的东西走多远？(Zhèige jiàqián) Néng bān duōshǎo lìfāng de dōngxi zǒu duōyuǎn?

• How do you charge... ? 你们怎么收费...？ Nǐmen zěnme shōufèi... ?

(1) per load 按车 àn chē
(2) per cubic meter 按立方 àn lìfāng
(3) per km 按公里 àn gōnglǐ
(4) per kg 按公斤 àn gōngjīn

• How much per kilometer? How much per cubic meter? 每公里多少钱？每立方多少钱？ Měi gōnglǐ duōshǎo qián? Měi lìfāng duōshǎo qián?

• What if I exceed the limit? 如果我超过限额了怎么办？Rúguǒ wǒ chāoguò xiàn'é le zěnmebàn?

• The ... needs de- and re-installation. Will that be extra? ...需要拆了再重装上，会有额外的费用吗？ ... xūyào chāi le zài chóng zhuāngshàng, huìyǒu éwài de fèiyòng ma?

• How many guys will there be? Are they from Sichuan? 会来几个人？他们是四川人吗？Huì lái jǐ ge rén? Tāmen shì Sìchuān rén ma?

• These are real antiques from Panjiayuan, so please be careful 这些都是潘家园的古董，你们得小心点儿 Zhèixiē dōushì Pānjiāyuán de gǔdǒng, nǐmen děi xiǎoxīn diǎnr

• Can you come over and give me a written estimate? 你们能过来给我一个书面的估价吗？ Nǐmen néng guòlái gěi wǒ yí gè shūmiàn de gūjià ma?

• My apartment doesn't have an elevator; how much extra per floor? 我的房子没有电梯，每层楼要加多少钱？ Wǒ de fángzi méiyǒu diàntī, měi céng lóu yào jiā duōshǎo qián?

• Can you clean up afterwards? 搬完后你们能帮忙打扫干净吗？Bānwán hòu nǐmen néng bāngmáng dǎsǎo gānjìng ma?

• Can you do the packing? 你们能帮我打包吗？ Nǐmen néng bāng wǒ dǎbāo ma?

• Is there any insurance? 有没有什么保险？ Yǒu méiyǒu shénme bǎoxiǎn?

Listen for this

- Bāndào nǎr? 搬到哪儿？ Where are you moving to?
- Bān shénme dōngxi? 搬什么东西？ What are you moving?
- Yǒu diàntī ma? 有电梯吗？ Is there an elevator?
- Yìchē liǎngbǎi 一车两百 RMB 200 per truckload

11 Getting a pet

领养宠物 Lǐngyǎng chǒngwù

Lost/丢失(Diūshī)

We are **looking for寻找** (xúnzhǎo) our white Pekinese dog - Duoduo. She **disappeared on走失** (zǒushī) April 12th. If you have any information, **please call请致电**(qǐng zhìdiàn) 5555 5555.

Reward if found重酬(zhòngchou)

Sentences

- How old is this ... ? 这...多大了？ Zhèi ... duōdà le?

(1) dog 狗 gǒu	(4) bird 鸟 niǎo
(2) cat 猫 māo	(5) turtle 乌龟 wūguī
(3) fish 鱼 yú	

- Does it have the proper vaccinations? 它有没有打过疫苗？ Tā yǒu méiyǒu dǎguò yìmiáo?

- Do you have any certification (for your dog)? 您（的狗）有证儿吗？ Nín (de gǒu) yǒu zhèngr ma?

- What shots does it need? 它需要打什么针？ Tā xūyào dǎ shénme zhēn?

- This animal looks sick, are you sure it's healthy? 这个家伙看上去好像病了，您肯定它没病吗？ Zhèi ge jiāhuo kànshàngqù hǎoxiàng bìng le, nín kěndìng tā méibìng ma?

- What is this animal's natural fur color? 这个东西的毛本来是什么色儿的？ Zhèigè dōngxi de máo běnlái shì shénme shǎir de ?

- Is it spayed (or neutered)? 它绝育了吗？ Tā juéyù le ma?

- What should I feed it? 我该喂它吃什么？ Wǒ gāi wèi tā chī shénme?

12 Pet grooming

宠物美容 Chǒngwù měiróng

Vocabulary

- comb out 梳毛 shūmáo
- bath 洗澡 xǐzǎo
- nail trim 修指甲 xiū zhǐjia
- fluff dry 吹干 chuī gān
- haircut / shave 剪毛 jiǎn máo
- deflea service 除虱 chú shī

Sentences

- (Disappeared / lost) on ... 在...（不见了/弄丢了）Zài ... (bújiàn le / nòngdiū le)

13 Vets 兽医 Shòuyī

Sentences

• I need to make an appointment for the vet to see my ... 我要和兽医预约一下给我的... 看病。 Wǒ yào hé shòuyī yùyuē yíxià gěi wǒde ...kànbìng.

• My (doggie / queen ant) has been injured 我的（狗狗／蚁王）受伤了 Wǒ de (gǒugǒu / yǐ wáng) shòushāng le

• We need to get vaccinations 需要打防疫针 Xūyào dǎ fángyì zhēn

14 Kenneling 寄养 Jìyǎng

Sentences

• Do you board (cat / fish)? 你们可以寄养（猫／鱼）吗？ Nǐmen kěyi jìyǎng (māo / yú) ma?

• I need to board my pet from ... to ... 我从...到...得把我的宠物寄养在这儿 Wǒ cóng ... dào ... děi bǎ wǒ de chǒngwù jìyǎng zài zhèr

• How much is it per day? 一天多少钱？ Yìtiān duōshao qián?

15 Mobile phones 手机 Shǒujī

Sentences

• I need a ... SIM card 我要一个...的SIM卡 Wǒ yào yígè ... de SIM kǎ

(1) China Mobile中国移动 Zhōngguó Yídòng
(2) China Unicom 中国联通 Zhōngguó Liántōng
(3) Little Smart 小灵通 Xiǎolíngtōng

16 Filling up your account

给手机充值 Gěi shǒujī chōngzhí

Sentences

• I need a mobile phone account refill card 我要一张手机充值卡 Wǒ yào yí zhāng shǒujī chōngzhíkǎ.

• I want to buy a ... card 我想买一张...的卡 Wǒ xiǎng mǎi yìzhāng ... de kǎ

(1) RMB 50 50块 wǔshí kuài
(2) RMB 100 100块 yìbǎi kuài
(3) Shenzhouxing (China Mobile) 神州行 Shénzhōu Xíng
(4) M-Zone 动感地带 Dònggǎn Dìdài
(5) China Mobile card 中国移动 Zhōngguó Yídòng
(6) China Unicom card 中国联通 Zhōngguó Liántōng

17 On the phone 打电话 Dǎ diànhuà

Sentences

• I'm looking for ... 我要找... Wǒ yào zhǎo ...

• Is (Ted) there? (特德)在吗 (Tédé) zài ma?

• This is (Smith) from (IBM) 我是(IBM)的（史密斯） Wǒ shì (IBM) de (shǐmìsī)

• Please tell him/her I called 请转告他我来过电话了 Qǐng zhuǎngào tā wǒ lái guò diànhuà le

• Can I leave a message? 我能留言吗? Wǒ néng liúyán ma?

• My number is ... 我的电话是... Wǒ de diànhuà shì ...

• I'll call back later 我呆会儿再打 Wǒ dāihuǐr zài dǎ

• The connection's bad 信号不好 Xìnhào bùhǎo

• Transfer me to (extension number) 236 给我转(分机)236 Gěi wǒ zhuǎn (fēnjī) èrsānliù

• When is a better time to call? 什么时间打比较好？Shénme shíjiān dă bĭjiào hăo?

• I'd like to make a reservation 我想预定 Wŏ xiăng yùdìng

• Does someone there speak English? 有人会说英语吗？Yŏu rén huì shuō yīngyŭ ma?

Listen for this

• Wèi? 喂？Hello?

• Nĭ zhăo shéi ya? 你找谁呀？Who do you want to speak to?

• Nĭ shì shéi? 你是谁？Who are you?

• Nĭ shénme shìr? 你什么事儿？What's up?

• Nĭ dă cuò le! 你打错了！Wrong number!

• Tā búzài 他不在 He's not in

• Méiyŏu rén jiē 没有人接 No one answered

• Děng yíxiàr 等一下儿 Wait a minute

• Jĭdiăn dào? 几点到？What time will you arrive?

18 Visas 签证 Qiānzhèng

Sentences

• I need a ... 我要办. . . Wŏ yào bàn ...

(1) tourist visa 旅游签证 lǚyóu qiānzhèng
(2) business visa 商务签证 shāngwù qiānzhèng
(3) work visa 工作签证 gōngzuò qiānzhèng
(4) student visa 学生签证 xuéshēng qiānzhèng
(5) multiple entry visa 多次入境签证 duōcì rùjìng qiānzhèng

• I need to extend my visa for another ... days 我要把我的签证再延长. . .天 Wŏ yào bă wŏde qiānzhèng zài yáncháng ... tiān

• I need to change my visa from ... to ... 我要把我的. . .签证换成. . .签证 Wŏ yào bă wŏ de ... qiānzhèng huànchéng ... qiānzhèng

Listen for this

- liǎng zhāng zhèngjiàn zhào 2张证件照 2 passport sized photos
- Nǐ de qiānzhèng dàoqī le 你的签证到期了 Your visa has expired
- Nǐ xūyào yìfēng yāoqǐngxìn 你需要一封邀请信 You need an invitation letter
- Línshí Zhùsù Dēngjìbiǎo 临时住宿登记表 Registration Form of Temporary Residence
- Nín yǒu tǐjiǎn zhèngmíng ma? 您有体检证明吗？Do you have a physical examination certificate?

19 In Trouble 出事儿了 Chū shìr le

Sentences

- Help! 救命啊！ Jiù mìng a!
- Get help quickly 快叫人来帮忙 Kuài jiào rén lái bāngmáng
- Fire! 着火了！ Zháohuǒ le!
- Get a (doctor/ambulance) 叫（医生/救护车）Jiào (yīshēng/jiùhùchē)
- Quick / Hurry 快点儿 Kuài diǎnr
- Watch out / Be Careful 当心/小心 Dāngxīn / Xiǎoxīn
- Stop! 停下！ Tíngxià!
- Get your hands off me 把手拿开 Bǎ shǒu ná kāi
- Let go 放开 Fàngkāi
- Stop thief! 抓小偷！ Zhuā xiǎotōu!
- Could you help me, please 能帮帮我吗？ Néng bāngbang wǒ ma?

• Where's the (police station / emergency exit / fire escape) （派出所/安全出口/消防通道）在哪儿？(Pàichūsuǒ / ānquán chūkǒu / xiāofáng tōngdào) zài nǎr?

• Where's the nearest fire extinguisher 最近的灭火器在哪儿？Zuìjìn de mièhuǒqì zài nǎr?

• Call the fire department 叫消防队 Jiào xiāofángduì

• Call the police! 报警！Bàojǐng!

• Where's the nearest phone? 附近哪儿有电话？Fùjìn nǎr yǒu diànhuà?

• Could I use your phone? 我能用你的电话吗？Wǒ néng yòng nǐ de diànhuà ma?

• What's the emergency number? 急救电话是多少？Jíjiù diànhuà shì duōshao?

• What's the number for the police? 报警电话是多少？Bàojǐng diànhuà shì duōshao?

20 Loss 丢失 Diūshī

Sentences

• I've lost my wallet/purse 我的钱包丢了 Wǒ de qiánbāo diū le

• I lost my ... here yesterday 昨天我的...在这儿丢了 Zuótiān wǒ de ... zài zhèr diū le

• I left my ... here 我把...落这儿了 Wǒ bǎ ... là zhèr le

• Did you find my ... 找到我的...了吗？Zhǎo dào wǒ de ... le ma?

• I was right here 我就在这儿 Wǒ jiù zài zhèr

• It's very valuable 那个十分贵重 Nàgè shífēn guìzhòng

• Where's the lost and found office? 失物招领处在哪儿？Shīwù zhāolǐng chù zài nǎr?

21 Accidents 事故 Shìgù

Sentences

• There's been an accident 出车祸了 Chū chēhuò le

• (Nobody / Someone) has been injured （没/有）人受伤 （Méi / Yǒu) rén shòu shāng

• I want to talk to the police first 我想先跟警察说 Wǒ xiǎng xiān gēn jǐngchá shuō

• May I have your name and phone number? 告诉我你的名字和电话号码 Gàosu wǒ nǐ de míngzi hé diànhuà hàomǎ

• Could I see your (identity card / your insurance papers) 给我看看你的（身份证/保单）Gěi wǒ kànkan nǐ de (shēnfènzhèng / bǎodān)

• Will you act as a witness? 你愿意做目击证人吗？Nǐ yuànyì zuò mùjī zhèngrén ma?

• I need this information for insurance purposes. 我需要这个去申请保险理赔 Wǒ xūyào zhèige qù shēnqǐng bǎoxiǎn lǐpéi

• Are you injured? 你受伤了吗？Nǐ shòushāng le ma?

22 Theft 盗窃 Dàoqiè

Sentences

• I've been robbed 我被抢了 Wǒ bèi qiǎng le

• My ... has been stolen 我的...被偷了 Wǒ de ... bèi tōu le

bike 自行车 zìxíngchē	MP3 player MP3 MPsān
clothes 衣服 yīfu	camera 照相机 zhàoxiàngjī
wallet 钱包 qiánbāo	passport 护照 hùzhào
credit card 信用卡 xìnyòngkǎ	video camera 摄象机 shèxiàngjī

• My car's been broken into 我的车被撬了 Wǒ de chē bèi qiào le

23 Missing person 寻人 Xúnrén

Sentences

- I've lost my child 我的孩子丢了 Wǒ de háizi diū le

- I've become separated from my (spouse / parents / friend) 我和（爱人/父母/朋友）走散了 Wǒ hé (àirén / fùmǔ / péngyǒu) zǒu sàn le

- Could you help me find him/her? 你能帮我找到他/她吗？Nǐ néng bāng wō zhǎodào tā ma?

- Have you seen a lost child? 你看没看见一个走失的小孩儿？Nǐ kàn méi kànjiàn yí gè zǒushī de xiǎoháir?

- S/he's about ... years old 他大约...岁 Tā dàyuē ... suì

- S/he's got ... hair. 他是...头发 Tā shì ... tóufà

short 短 duǎn	black 黑色的 hēisè de
long 长 cháng	grey 灰色的 huīsè de
blond 金黄色的 jīnhuángsè de	curly 卷 juǎn
red 红色的 hóngsè de	straight 直 zhí
brown 棕色的 zōngsè de	frizzy 卷 juǎn

- S/he's wearing ... 他（穿/戴着）... Tā (chuān/dài zhe) ...

swimming trunks 泳裤 yǒngkù
glasses 眼镜 yǎnjìng
red shirt 红色衬衣 hóngsè chènyī
black pants 黑裤子 hēi kùzi

- This is a photo of him/her 这是他的照片 Zhé shì tā de zhàopiàn

GLOSSARY ►

GLOSSARY

A

abalone 鲍鱼 bàoyú
ability/abilities 能力 nénglì
able (v) 能 néng
above 上面 shàngmiàn
acceleration 加速 jiāsù
accept (an idea) 认同 rèntóng
accessories 配饰 pèishì
accident (car) 事故 shìgù
accounting 会计 kuàijì
acrobatics 杂技 zájì
acrylic nails 水晶指甲 shuǐjīng zhījiǎ
activity 活动 huódòng
actor/actress 演员 yǎnyuán
acupuncture 针灸 zhēnjiū
acupuncturist 针灸师 zhēnjiūshī
add (money) 加钱 jīaqián
address 地址 dìzhǐ
adjective 形容词 xíngróngcí
adult 成年人 chéngniánrén
advertising/advertisement 广告 guǎnggào
aesthetic 美感 měigǎn
afraid 恐怕 kǒngpà
Africa 非洲 Fēizhōu
afternoon 下午 xiàwǔ
afterwards 以后 yi hòu
again 再 zài
agency fee 中介费 zhōngjiè fèi
agriculture 农业 nóngyè
ahead 前面 qiánmiàn
air bags 安全气囊 ānquán qìnáng
air conditioner 空调 kōngtiáo
air 空气 kōngqì
airline 航空公司 hángkōng gōngsī
airplane 飞机fēijī
airport 机场 jīchǎng
album 专辑 zhuānjí
alcohol 酒 jiǔ
algebra 代数 dàishù
allergic 过敏 guòmǐn
alleyway 胡同 hútòng
all-natural 全自然 quán zìrán
allow 让 ràng
almond juice 杏仁露 xìngrénlù
almond 杏仁 xìngrén
altar 祭坛 jìtán
alternative 非主流 fēi zhǔliú
alternative music 另类音乐 lìnglèi yīnyuè
altogether 一共/总共 yígòng/zǒnggòng
amazed 吃惊 chījīng
amber 琥珀 hǔpò
ambulance 救护车 jiùhùchē
amplifier (AMP) 放大器 fàngdàqì
ancient 古老 gǔlǎo
and 和/跟 hé/gēn
anesthesia 麻醉 mázuì
angry 生气 shēngqì
animal oil 荤油 hūnyóu
animals 动物 dòngwù
animation (film, TV) 动画片 dònghuà piàn
ankle 脚踝 jiǎohuái
anniversary 周年 zhōunián
annoyed 烦恼 fánnǎo
answer (n,v) 回答 huídá
antacid 抗酸剂 kàngsuānjì
antibiotics 抗生素 kàngshēngsù
antiques 古玩 gǔwán
antiseptic 防腐剂 fángfǔjì
any 任何 rènhé
apartment 楼房 lóufáng
aperture 光圈 guāngquān
apple 苹果 píngguǒ
apple sauce 苹果酱 píngguǒjiàng
application 申请表 shēnqǐngbiǎo
apply 申请 shēnqǐng
appointment 约会 yuēhuì
appreciate 欣赏 xīnshǎng
appropriate 适合 shìhé /合适 héshì
April Fool's Day 愚人节 Yúrén jié
architect 建筑师 jiànzhùshī
architecture 建筑 jiànzhù
ardent/strong/intense (a) 烈 liè
arm 胳膊 gēbo
armoire 大衣柜 dàyīguì
aromatherapy 芳香疗法 fāngxiāng liáofǎ

arrange 安排 ānpái
arrive 到达 dàodá
arrogant 自大 zìdà
art gallery 艺术画廊 yìshù huàláng
art museum 美术馆 měishùguǎn
art 艺术 yìshù
artichokes 宝塔菜 bǎotǎ cài
artist 艺术家 yìshùjiā
artist collective 艺术家群体 yìshùjiā qúntǐ
ashtray 烟灰缸 yānhuīgāng
asparagus 芦荀 lúxūn
aspirin 阿司匹林 āsīpīlín
asthma 哮喘 xiàochuǎn
astigmatism 散光 sǎnguāng
astronomy 天文学 tiānwénxué
at 在 zài
atheist 无神论者 wùshénlùnzhě
athletic shoes 运动鞋 yùndòngxié
athletics 体育 tǐyù
ATM 取款机 qǔkuǎnjī
atmosphere 气氛 qìfèn
attachment (email) (邮件)附件 (yóujiàn) fùjiàn
attack (military) 侵略 qīnlüè
attend 参加 cānjiā
auction (n) 拍卖会 pāimài huì
audio card 声卡 shēngkǎ
audio guides 语音导游 yǔyīn dǎoyóu
audit (a class) 试听 shìtīng
aunt (paternal) 姑姑 gūgu
auntie 阿姨 āyí
author 作者 zuòzhě
autobiography 自传 zìzhuàn
auxiliary road (bike lane) 辅路 fǔlù
avant-garde 先锋派 xiānfēngpài
average (n) 平均 píngjūn
avian flu 禽流感 qín liúgǎn
avocado 油梨 yóulí
award (n) 奖励 jiǎnglì
awesome ("feels so good") 爽 shuǎng
awful/horrible/annoying 讨厌 tǎoyàn
awkward 别扭 bièniu

B

baby 婴儿 yīng'ér
baby bottles 奶瓶 nǎipíng
baby formula 婴儿配方奶粉 yīng'ér pèifāng nǎifěn
baby monitor 婴儿监听器 yīng'ér jiāntīngqì
baby snow suit 婴儿雪服 yīng'ér xuěfú
baby wipes 婴儿湿巾 yīng'ér shījīn
back (body) 后背 hòubèi
back (direction) 后面 hòumiàn
backpack 背包 bēibāo
backstage 后台 hòutái
bacon 培根 péigēn
badminton 羽毛球 yǔmáoqiú
bag 包 bāo
bagel 焙果 bèiguǒ
bagpipes 风笛 fēngdí
baguette 法棒 fǎbàng
bait (for fishing) 鱼饵 yú'ěr
bake 烤 kǎo
baking powder 发酵粉 fājiàofěn
balance (v) 平衡 pínghéng
bald 光头 guāngtóu
ball 球 qiú
ballet 芭蕾舞 bāléi wǔ
bamboo 竹子 zhúzi
banana 香蕉 xiāngjiāo
band (music) 乐队 yuèduì
Band-Aid (adhesive bandage) 邦迪(创可贴) bāngdí (chuàngkětiē)
bangs 刘海儿 liúhǎir
bank account 账户 zhànghù
bank 银行 yínháng
bank book 存折 cúnzhé
bar 酒吧 jiǔbā
Barbie 芭比娃娃 Bābǐ wáwa
bargain 砍价 kǎnjià
barrettes 条形发夹 tiáoxíng fàqiā
bartender 调酒师 tiáojiǔshī
baseball 棒球 bàngqiú
baseball cap 棒球帽 bàngqiúmào
basic 基础 jīchǔ

basil 九层塔 jiǔcéngtǎ
basket (bicycle) 车筐 chēkuāng
basketball 篮球 lánqiú
basketball courts 篮球场 lánqiú chǎng
bass (electric) 贝斯 (电) bèisī (diàn)
bath house 洗浴中心 xǐyù zhōngxīn
bath toys 浴室玩具 yùshì wánjù
bath tub 浴盆 yùpén
bathe 洗澡 xǐzǎo
bathing cap 游泳帽 yóuyǒng mào
bathrobe 浴袍 yùpáo
bathroom 卫生间 wèishēngjiān
bathtub 浴缸 yùgāng
Batman 蝙蝠侠 biānfúxiá
battery 电池 diànchí
bay leaves 干月桂叶 gān yuèguì yè
BBQ sauce 烤肉酱汁 kǎoròu jiàngzhī
be (to be) 是 shì
beach 海滩 hǎitān
bean curd 豆腐 dòufu
bean sprout 豆芽 dòuyá
bean 豆子 dòuzi
bear 熊 xióng
beard 胡子 húzi
beautiful 美丽 měilì
beauty treatment 美容护理 měiróng hùlǐ
because 因为 yīnwéi
become 当 dāng
bed 床 chuáng
bed sheet 床单 chuángdān
bedroom 房间 fángjiān
bee 蜜蜂 mìfēng
bee sting 蛰 zhē
beef 牛肉 níuròu
beef broth 牛肉汤 niúròu tāng
been done (before) 老套 lǎotào
beer 啤酒 píjiǔ
beer (draught) 扎啤 zhā pí
before 以前 yǐqián
beforehand 提前 tíqián
beg 求 qiú
beginner 初级 chūjí
behind 后头 hòutóu
Beijing 北京 Běijīng
bell 钟 zhōng
bell/chime 铃 líng
bell bottoms 喇叭裤 lǎbā kù
bell tower 钟楼 zhōnglóu
belly 肚子 dùzi
bellydancing 肚皮舞 dùpí wǔ
below 下面 xiàmiàn
belt 腰带 yāodài
bench 长椅 chángyǐ
bent 变形了 biàn xíng le
beret 贝雷帽 bèiléimào
beside/next to 旁边 pángbiān
best 最好 zuì hǎo
between 中间 zhōngjiān
beware 注意 zhùyì
bib 围嘴儿 wéizuǐr
bicycle 自行车 zìxíngchē
bicycle frame 车架 chējià
biennale 双年展 shuāng nián zhǎn
big/large 大 dà
big brother 大哥 dàgē
bikini 比基尼 bǐjīní
bill (n) 账单 zhàngdān
bill (to ask for the bill) 买单 mǎidān
billiards 台球 táiqiú
billion 十亿 shíyì
bindings 固定器 gùdìngqì
biography 传记 zhuànjì
biology 生物 shēngwù
bird 鸟 niǎo
birth control pills 避孕药 bìyùnyào
birth date 出生日期 chūshēng rìqī
birthday 生日 shēngrì
bitter 苦 kǔ
bitter melon 苦瓜 kǔguā
black 黑色 hēisè
black and white 黑白 hēibái
black bread 黑面包 hēi miànbāo
black tea 红茶 hóng chá
blackboard 黑板 hēibǎn
bleach 漂白 piǎobái
blend 混合 hǔnhé

blender 搅拌机 jiǎobànjī
blessing 祝福 zhùfú
blind person 盲人 mángrén
blog 博客 bókè
blonde (hair) 金黄色头发 jīnhuángsè tóufa
blood 血 xuě
bloom 开 kāi
blouse 女式衬衫 nǚshì chènshān
blowdry 吹干 chuī gān
blue cheese 蓝奶酪 lán nǎilào
blue 蓝色 lánsè
blush 腮红 sāihóng
boat 船 chuán
body scrub 搓澡 cuōzǎo
boil 煮 zhǔ
boiled water 开水 kāishuǐ
bone 骨头 gǔtóu
bongos 手鼓 shǒugǔ
bonsai tree 盆景 pénjǐng
book 书 shū
bookcase 书柜 shūguì
booster seat 加高座椅 jiā gāo zuòyǐ
boot 靴子 xuēzi
boot (ski) 雪鞋 xuěxié
booty/bum 屁股 pìgu
boring 无聊 wúliáo
born 出生 chūshēng
borrow 借 jie
boss 老板 lǎobǎn
botox 肉毒杆菌除皱 ròudúgānjùn chúzhòu
bottle 瓶子 píngzi
bottle opener 起子 qǐzi
bounce 蹦 bèng
bowl 碗 wǎn
bowling 保龄球 bǎolíngqiú
box 盒子 hézi
box office 售票处 shòupiàochù
boxing 拳击 quánjī
boxwood 黄杨木 huángyángmù
boyfriend 男朋友 nánpéngyǒu
bra 胸罩 xiōngzhào
bracelet 手链 shǒuliàn
braids 辫子 biànzi
braise 烧 shāo
brake (a bone) (骨头)断了 (gǔtóu) duàn le
brake (v, car) 刹车 shāchē
brakes (bicycle) 车闸 chēzhá
brand name 名牌 míngpái
brandy/cognac 白兰地 báilándì
brass instruments 铜管乐器 tóngguǎn yuèqì
bread 面包 miànbāo
breakdancing 霹雳舞 pīlìwǔ
breakfast 早点/早饭 zǎodiǎn/zǎofàn
break-up 分手 fēnshǒu
breast 乳房 rǔfáng
breast enlargement 隆胸 lóngxiōng
breast meat 胸肉 xiōngròu
breast pads 乳垫 rǔdiàn
breast pump 吸乳器 xīrǔqì
breathe 呼吸 hūxī
bridge 桥 qiáo
brie 布里 bùlǐ
bring 带 dài
bring (here) 拿来 ná lái
broadband 宽带 kuāndài
broadcast 广播 guangbo
broccoli 西兰花 xīlánhuā
broken 坏了/断了 huài le / duàn le
broken (into) 撬 qiào
bronze 青铜 qīngtóng
brooch 胸针 xiōngzhēn
broom 扫帚 sàozhou
brother (older) 哥哥 gēge
brother (younger) 弟弟 dìdi
brothers 兄弟 xiōngdì
brown sugar 红糖 hóngtáng
brown 棕色 zōngsè
brunette 深褐色头发 shènhèsè tóufa
brush 毛笔 máobǐ
BTV (television station) 北京台 Běijīngtái
bubble tea (aka pearl milk tea) 珍珠奶茶 zhēnzhū nǎichá
bucket 桶 tǒng

Buddha 佛 fó
Buddhism 佛教 fójiào
Buddhist 佛教徒 Fójiàotú
budget (n) 预算 yùsuàn
buffet (self service) 自助餐 zìzhùcān
build (computer) 攒 cuán
build 建立 jiànlì
building 楼 lóu
built-in 内置 nèizhì
bullfrog 牛蛙 niúwā
bully (n) 恶霸 èbà
bully (v) 欺负 qīfù
bum/bottom 臀部 túnbù
bumper cars 碰碰车 pèngpèngchē
bungee jumping 蹦极 bèngjí
buns (steamed) 包子 bāozi
burn (CD) 刻 kè
burn incense 烧香 shāo xiāng
burner 刻录机 kèlùjī
bus 公交车 gōngjiāochē
bus station 汽车站 qìchēzhàn
bus stop 车站 chēzhàn
business trip 出差 chūchāi
business 商务 shāngwù
business/affairs 事儿 shìr
busy 忙 máng
but 但是/可是 dànshì/kěshì
butt 屁股 pìgǔ
button 扣子 kòuzi
buy 买 mǎi

C

cab (taxi) 出租车 chūzūchē
cabinet 柜子 guìzi
cable (TV or internet) 有线 yǒuxiàn
cable car 缆车 lǎnchē
cactus 仙人掌 xiānrénzhǎng
caddie 球童 qiútóng
cafe 咖啡厅 kāfēitīng
cafeteria card 饭卡 fànkǎ
cafeteria 食堂 shítáng
cake 蛋糕 dàngāo
calamine lotion 炉甘石液 lúgānshí yè
call (v) 叫 jiào
calligrapher's ink 墨 mò
calligraphy 书法 shūfǎ
calligraphy class 书法课 shūfǎ kè
calligraphy paper 宣纸 xuānzhǐ
calm down 冷静 lěngjìng
came 来了 lái le
camel 骆驼 luòtuó
camera 照相机 zhàoxiàngjī
camera lens 镜头 jìngtóu
camp (v) 野营 yěyíng
camphor 樟木 zhāngmù
campus 校园xiàoyuán
canal 运河 yùnhé
cancel 取消 qǔxiāo
candy 糖果 tángguǒ
canned (food) 罐装 guànzhuāng
canoe 皮划艇 píhuátǐng
can opener 罐头起子 guàntouqǐzi
canvas 画布 huàbù
car 车 chē
car (measure word) 辆 liàng
car accident 车祸 chēhuò
carats (jewelry) 克拉 kèlā
carbon monoxide 一氧化碳 yīyǎnghuàtàn
card 卡 kǎ
cards (poker) 扑克牌 púkèpái
career 职业 zhíyè
carefree 畅快 chàngkuài
careful 小心 xiǎoxīn
carnation 康乃馨 kāngnǎixīn
carp 鲤鱼 lǐyú
carpet 地毯 dìtǎn
carrot 胡萝卜 húluóbo
carry-on baggage 托运行李 tūoyùn xínglǐ
cash 现金 xiànjīn
cashew 腰果 yāoguǒ
cashmere 开司米 kāisīmǐ
casserole 煲 bǎo
casual/as you wish 随便 suíbiàn
casual (clothes) 休闲 xīuxián
cat 猫 māo
Catholic 天主徒 Tiānzhǔtú
cauliflower 菜花 càihuā

cave 洞穴 dòngxuè
CBD (Central Business District) 中央商务区 zhōngyāng shāngwù qū
CCTV (television station) 中央台 zhōngyāngtái
ceiling 房顶 fángdǐng'r
celery 芹菜 qíncài
cello 大提琴 dàtíqín
Celsius/centigrade 摄氏度 shèshìdù
cereal 麦片mài piàn
ceremony 庆典 qìngdiǎn
certain (firm) 确定 quèdìng
certify/certification 证明 zhèngmíng
chacha 恰恰 qiàqià
chair 椅子 yǐzi
chalk (blackboard) 粉笔 fěnbǐ
chalk (rock climbing) 滑石粉 huáshífěn
champagne 香槟酒 xiāngbīnjiǔ
champignon 香菇 xiānggū
change 换 huàn
change (small bills) 零钱 língqián
change into 换成 huàncheng
change money (v) 换钱 huànqián
changing rooms 更衣室 gēngyīshì
channel (TV) 频道 píndào
character (word) 字 zì
charcoal 炭笔 tànbǐ
charge (electricity) 充电 Chōngdiàn
charge (receive) 收 shōu
charger 充电器 chōngdiànqì
cheap (inexpensive) 便宜 piányì
check (bank) 支票 zhīpiào
check (v) 检查 jiǎnchá
checkup (physical) 体检 tǐjiǎn
cheddar 切达 qièdá
cheers 干杯 gānbēi
cheese 奶酪 nǎilào
chemical fiber 化纤 huàxiān
chemical peel 化学脱皮术 huàxué tuōpí shù
chemistry 化学 huàxué
cheongsam (long dress) 旗袍 qípáo
cherry 樱桃 yīngtáo
chest 胸 xiōng
chicken 鸡 jī
chicken broth 鸡汤 jī tāng
chicken stock 鸡精 jījīng
chicken wings 鸡翅 jī chì
child 小孩 xiǎohái
child/children 儿童 értóng
children 幼 yòu
children's book 儿童读物 értóng dúwù
chili oil 辣椒油 làjiāoyóu
chili pepper 辣椒 làjiāo
chili sauce 辣椒酱 làjiāojiàng
chimes 编钟 biānzhōng
China 中国 Zhōngguó
Chinese (language) 中文 Zhōngwén
Chinese cabbage 大白菜 dàbáicài
Chinese crepe with egg 煎饼 jiānbǐng
Chinese food 中餐 zhōngcān
Chinese wolfberries 枸杞 gǒuqí
Chips Ahoy cookies 趣多多饼干 Qùduōduō bǐnggān
chisel 凿子 záozi
Chivas 芝华士 Zhīhuáshì
choose/choice 选择 xuǎnzé
chop (mince) 剁碎 duò suì
chopping board 案板 ànbǎn
chopsticks 筷子 kuàizi
chord 和弦 héxián
Christian 基督徒 Jīdūtú
Christmas 圣诞节 Shèngdànjié
chrysanthemum 菊花 júhuā
church/cathedral 教堂 jiàotáng
cigar 雪茄 xuějiā
cigarette 烟卷 yānjuǎn
cilantro 香菜 xiāngcài
cinema 电影院 diànyǐngyuàn
cinnamon 肉桂 ròuguì
circle (v, walking or driving) 绕 rào
circular 圆形的 yuánxíng de
citizen 国民 guómín
city 城市 chéngshì
clarinet 单簧管 dānhuángguǎn
clarity 净度 jìngdù
class 班/课 bān / kè

classic 经典 jīngdiǎn
classical music 古典音乐 gǔdiǎn yīnyuè
classmate 同学 tóngxué
classroom 教室 jiàoshì
clay 陶土 táotǔ
clay packs 黏土护理 niántǔ hùlǐ
clean (adj) 干净 gānjìng
clean (v) 打扫 dǎsǎo
clean up (tidy) 清理 qīnglǐ
clear (see-through) 透明 tòumíng
clear day 晴天 qíngtiān
client 客户 kèhù
climate 气候 qìhòu
climbing 攀爬 pānpá
clinic 诊所 zhěnsuǒ
clips 夹子 jiāzi
clock 钟 zhōng
close (turn off) 关上 guānshàng
closed 关门 guān mén
closest 最近 zuìjìn
closet 壁橱 bìchú
clothing 服装 fúzhuāng
cloud 云 yún
clown 丑角 chǒujué
club (golf) 球杆 qiúgān
clubhouse 俱乐部会所 jūlèbù huìsuǒ
coach 教练 jiàoliàn
coconut 椰子 yēzi
codeine 可待因 kědàiyīn
coffee 咖啡 kāfēi
coffee liquor 咖啡酒 kāfēijiǔ
coffee machine 咖啡机 kāfēi jī
Cointreau 君度酒 jūndùjiǔ
cola 可乐 kělè
cold 冷 lěng
cold (frozen) 冰 bīng
cold dish 凉菜 liángcài
collage 拼贴 pīntiē
collagen (fat injections) lips 嘴唇增厚术 zuǐchǔn zēnghòu zhù
collar 领子 lǐngzi
colleague 同事 tóngshì
collection (of art) 收藏品 shōucáng pǐn
collector (of art) 收藏家 shōucáng jiā
color 颜色 yánsè
colorful 色彩 sècǎi
coloring books 彩色图书 cǎisè túshū
comb 梳 shū
come 来 lái
come down 下来 xiàlái
comedy 喜剧 xǐjù
comfortable 舒服 shūfu
comic books 连环画 liánhuán huà
common (ordinary) 普通 pǔtōng
Communist Party 共产党 Gòngchǎndǎng
company 公司 gōngsī
compass 指南针 zhǐnánzhēn
competition (game) 比赛 bǐsài
compilation 合辑 héjí
completely 完全 wánquán
composition 构图 gòutú
compound (residential) 小区 xiǎoqū
computer 电脑 diànnǎo
concern (v) 关心 guānxīn
concert 演唱会 yǎnchànghuì
conch 海螺 hǎiluó
concubine 妃嫔 fēipín
conditioner (hair) 护发素 hùfàsù
condolences 悼词 dàocí
condom 安全套 ānquántào
conductor (music) 指挥 zhǐhuī
conference 大会 dàhuì
congratulations 祝贺 zhùhè
connect 连接 liánjiē
connections (personal/professional network) 关系 guānxi
consider 考虑 kǎolǜ
constipation 便秘 biànmì
construction 建设 jiànshè
consultant 顾问 gùwèn
contact lenses 隐形眼镜 yǐnxíng yǎnjìng
contemporary art 当代艺术 dāngdài yìshù
context 上下文 shàngxiàwén
continue 继续 jìxù
contrast (compare) 对比 duìbǐ

control 控制 kòngzhì
convenience store 便利店 biànlìdiàn
convenient 方便 fāngbiàn
conveniently 顺便 shùnbiàn
conversation class 会话课 huìhuà kè
convey (express) 表达 biǎodá
cook 做饭 zuò fàn
cookbook 菜谱 càipǔ
cookie 饼干 bǐnggān
cool (cold) 凉 liáng
cool (hip) 酷 kù
coral 珊瑚 shānhú
corduroy 灯芯绒 dēngxīnróng
corkscrew 开瓶器 kāipíngqì
cornflakes 玉米片 yùmǐ piàn
corn 玉米 yùmǐ
cornichons 淹瓜 yān guā
cornrows 玉米辫子头 yùmǐ biànzi tóu
cornstarch 淀粉 diànfěn
corpse 遗体 yítǐ
correct 对 duì
correct (proper) 正确 zhèngquè
cosmetics 化妆品 huàzhuāngpǐn
costume (for a performance) 演出服 yǎnchūfú
cotton 棉 mián
couch 沙发 shāfā
cough 咳嗽 késou
cough medicine 止咳药 zhǐkéyào
cough syrup 止咳糖浆 zhǐké tángjiāng
counter 柜台 guìtái
counterfeit 赝品 yànpǐn
countryside 乡村 xiāngcūn
couple (romantic) 一对 yí duì
courier 快递 kuàidì
courthouse 法庭 fǎtíng
courtyard 院子 yuànzi
courtyard house 四合院 sìhéyuàn
cover (n) 封面 fēngmiàn
cowboy hat 牛仔帽 níuzǎimào
CPU 中央处理器 zhōngyāng chùlǐ qì
crab 螃蟹 pángxiè
cradle (n) 摇篮 yáolán
cranberry 蔓越莓 mànyuèméi
crayfish 小龙虾 xiǎo lóngxiā
crayon 蜡笔 làbǐ
cream cheese 奶油芝士 nǎiyóu zhīshì
credit card 信用卡 xìnyòngkǎ
creel 鱼篓 yúlǒu
criminal 罪犯 zuìfàn
critic 评论家 pínglùnjiā
critique 批判 pīpàn
croissant 牛角面包 niújiǎo miànbāo
crucian carp 鲫鱼 jìyú
cry 哭 kū
crystal 水晶 shuǐjīng
cube 立方体 lìfāngtǐ
cubic meter 立方 lìfāng
cubic zirconium 锆石 gàoshí
cucumber 黄瓜 huángguā
cudgel 棍 gùn
cue ball 白球 báiqiú
cue stick 球杆 qiúgān
cup 杯子 bēizi
cupping (moxibustation) 拔火罐儿 bá huǒguàn'r
curator 策展人 cèzhǎn rén
cured tobacco 烤烟 kǎoyān
curious 好奇 hàoqí
curlers 卷发夹子 juǎnfà jiāzi
curls (hair) 卷发 juǎnfà
curriculum 课程 kèchéng
curry 咖喱 gāli
curtain 窗帘 chuānglián
cushion 垫子 diànzǐ
custom (convention) 习俗 xísú
customs 海关 hǎiguān
cut 切 qiè
cut tobacco 烟丝 yānsī
cute 可爱 kě'ài
cuticles 死皮 sǐpí
cutting (in line) 插队 chāduì
cutting edge (style) 前卫 qiánwèi
cylinder 圆柱体 yuánzhùtǐ
cymbal 镲 chǎ

D

dagger 匕首 bǐshǒu
dairy products 奶制品 nǎi zhìpǐn
dance partner 舞伴 wǔbàn
dance 跳舞 tiàowǔ
dancing 跳舞 tiàowǔ
dandruff 头皮屑 tóupíxiè
dangerous 危险 wēixiǎn
dare (v) 敢 gǎn
dark blue 深蓝色 shēnlánsè
date (time)日期 rìqī
daughter 女儿 nǚ'ér
day 天 tiān
day after tomorrow 后天 hòutiān
day before yesterday 前天 qiántiān
daytrip 一日游 yí rì yóu
deadline 截止日期 jíezhǐ rìqī
dear (letter greeting) 尊敬 zūnjìng
decide 决定 juédìng
deconstruct 解构拆析 jiěgòu chāixī
decorate 装饰 zhuāngshì
deductible 免赔 miǎn péi
deep 深 shēn
deep fry 炸 zhá
deep tissue massage 深层肌肉放松按摩 shēncén jīròu fàngsōng ànmó
degree 学位 xúewèi
delay (v) 延误 yánwù
deliver 送货/发货sònghuò / fāhuò
Deng Xiaoping 邓小平 Dèng Xiǎopíng
dental floss 牙线yáxiàn
dentist 牙医 yáyī
deodorant 除臭剂 chúchòujì
departure 出发 chūfā
deposit (n) 押金 yājīn
deposit (v) 存钱 cúnqián
depressed 沮丧 jǔsàng
dermatology 皮肤科 pífūkē
design (v) 设计 shèjì
desk 书桌 shūzhuō
desktop computer 台式电脑 táishì diànnǎo
desserts 甜点 tiándiǎn
detail (n) 细节 xìjié
detergent 洗衣粉 xǐyīfěn
develop 冲印/冲洗 chōngyìn/chōngxǐ
devil 魔鬼 móguǐ
diabetes 糖尿病 tángniàobìng
dialogue 对话 duìhuà
diamond 钻石 zuànshí
diapers 尿布 niàobù
diarrhea 拉肚子 lādùzi
dictionary 字典 zìdiǎn
diet tea 减肥茶 jiǎnféi chá
dietary preference 忌口 jìkǒu
different 不同 bù tóng
difficult 困难 kùnnàn
digital 数码 shùmǎ
dill 茴香 huíxiāng
dining table 餐桌 cānzhuō
dinner 晚饭 wǎnfàn
diplomat 外交官 wàijiāoguān
direct (adj) 直接 zhíjiē
direction 方向 fāngxiàng
director 导演 dǎoyǎn
dirty 脏 zāng
photography 摄影 Shèyǐng
disabled 残 cán
disagree 分歧 fēnqí
disappointed 失望 shīwàng
disco 迪厅 dītīng
discount (n) 打折/优惠 dǎzhé/yōuhuì
discuss 商量 shāngliàng
disembowel 内脏取出来 nèizàng qǔ chūlái
disgusting 恶心 ěxīn
dish 盘子 pánzi
dish soap 洗涤灵 xǐdílíng
dishwasher 洗碗机 xǐwǎnjī
disk 盘 pán
display piece 展品 zhǎnpǐn
disposable 抛弃型 pāoqì xíng
distinguish/discern 识别 shíbié
district 区 qū
diving pool 跳水池 tiàoshuǐ chí
dizziness 头晕 tóuyūn

dizzy (out of it) 头晕 tóuyūn
do (make) 做 zuò
do illegal drugs 吸毒 xī dú
doctor 大夫/医生 dàifu/yīshēng
document (n) 资料 zīliào
documentary 纪录片 jìlù piàn
dog 狗 gǒu
doll 洋娃娃 yángwáwa
domestic 国内 guónèi
don't have 没有 méiyǒu
donkey 驴 lǘ
door 门 mén
double room 双人房间 shuāngrén fángjiān
down (below) 下 xià
down (feathers) 羽绒 yǔróng
download下载 xiàzǎi
doze 打盹 dǎdǔn
dragon 龙 lóng
dragon boat 龙舟 lóngzhōu
drama 戏剧 xìjù
Dramamine 晕海宁 yūnhǎiníng
draw 画 huà
dreadlocks 骇人发髻 hàirén fàjiū
dream (n) 梦 mèng
dress (n) 连衣裙 liányī qún
drink (n) 饮料 yǐnliào
drink (v) 喝 hē
drive (v) 开车 kāi chē
driver 司机 sījī
driver's license 驾照 jiàzhào
drum 鼓 gǔ
drumstick 鼓槌 gǔchuí
Drum Tower 鼓楼 Gǔlóu
drunk 醉 zuì
drunken-style boxing 醉拳 zuìquán
dry (v) 干燥 gānzào
dry clean 干洗 gān xǐ
dryer (clothes) 烘干机 hōnggānjī
dub (v, n) 配音 pèiyīn
duck 鸭子 yāzi
duck foot (food) 鸭掌 yāzhǎng
dude 哥们儿 gēmenr
dulcimer 扬琴 yángqín
dumbbells 哑铃 yǎlíng
dumpling flour 饺子粉 jiǎozi fěn
dumplings (boiled) 水饺 shuǐjiǎo
dumplings (fried) 锅贴 guōtiē
duplicate 复印 fùyìn
dusk 黄昏 huánghūn
dust storm 沙尘暴 shāchénbào
dustpan 簸箕 bòji
DVD player DVD机 DVD jī
dye 染 rǎn

E

ear 耳朵 ěrduo
ear plugs 耳塞 ěrsāi
early 早 zǎo
earmuffs 耳罩 ěrzhào
earn money 赚钱 zhuànqián
earring 耳环 ěrhuán
easel 画架 huàjià
east 东 dōng
Easter 复活节 Fùhuójié
easy 容易 róngyì
eat 吃饭 chīfàn
eat in 在家吃饭 zài jiā chīfàn
ebony 乌木 wūmù
echo 回声 huí shēng
economy ticket 经济仓票 jīngjìcāng piào
edam cheese 红球奶酪 hóngqiú nǎilào
education 教育 jiàoyù
effect (result) 效果 xiàoguǒ
effects pedals 效果器 xiàoguǒqì
egg (chicken) 鸡蛋 jīdàn
eggplant (aubergine) 茄子 qiézi
eight 八 bā
elbow 肘 zhǒu
elderly 老人 lǎorén
electrolysis 电子除痣 diànzǐ chú zhì
electronica (music) 电子乐 diànzǐyuè
electronics 电子产品 diànzǐ chǎnpǐn
elegant (graceful) 秀美 xiùměi
elementary school 小学 xiǎoxué
elphant 大象 dàxiàng
elevation 海拔 hǎibá

elevator 电梯 diàntī
elope 私奔 sībēn
email address 电子邮箱 diànzǐ yóuxiāng
email 电子邮件 diànzǐ yóujiàn
embalming 防腐处理 fángfǔ chùlǐ
embarrassed 丢脸 diūliǎn
embassy 大使馆 dàshǐguǎn
embroidery 刺绣 cìxiù
emerald 玛瑙/绿宝石 mǎnǎo/lǜbǎoshí
emergency room 急救室 jíjiùshì
emergency 急事儿/急救jíshìr/jíjiù
emmental (Swiss cheese) 瑞士多孔干酪 Ruìshì duōkǒng gānlào
emperor 皇帝 huángdì
employ (v) 雇佣gùyōng
empress 皇后 huánghòu
empty 空 kōng
enemy 敌人 dírén
energetic 精力旺盛 jīnglì wàngshèng
engagement ring 订婚戒指 dìnghūn jièzhǐ
engine 发动机 fādòngjī
engineer 工程师 gōngchéngshī
English (language) 英语 yīngyǔ
English language menu 英文菜单 yīngwén càidān
English tea 英国茶 yīngguó chá
enlarge 放大 fàngdà
enough 够 gòu
enroll 报名 bàomíng
enter 进入 jìnrù
enter (input) 输入 shūrù
entertainment 娱乐 yúlè
entrance 入口 rùkǒu
entrance ticket 门票 ménpiào
envelope 信封 xìnfēng
environment 环竟 huánjìng
environmentally safe 环保 huánbǎo
equal 平等 píngděng
equipment 设备 shèbèi
erhu 二胡 èrhú
especially 特别 tèbié
essential (fundamental) 基础 jīchǔ
estimate 估价 gūjià

etcetera 等等 děngděng
eunuch 太监 tàijiān
evening 晚上 wǎnshàng
everybody 大家 dàjiā
everyday 每天 měitiān
examine 检查 jiǎnchá
example 例子 lìzi
exceed 超过 chāoguò
excellent (colloquial) 棒 bàng
excellent 非常好 fēicháng hǎo
excessive/too far (behavior) 过分 guòfèn
exchange rate 汇率 huìlǜ
excited (hyperactive) 兴奋 xīngfèn
excursion 郊游 jiāoyóu
exercise (movement) 运动 yùndòng
exhibit (n, v) 展览 zhǎnlǎn
exit (n) 出口 chūkǒu
exit (v) 出去 chūqù
expensive 贵 guì
experience (n, v) 经验 jīngyàn
experiment/experimental 实验 shíyàn
expired 过期了 guòqī le
export 出口 chūkǒu
express mail 快递 kuàidì
extend (v) 延长 yáncháng
extend (visa) 续(签证) xù (qiānzhèng)
extension number 分机号 fēnjī hào
extensions (hair) 接发 jiē fà
external medicine 外用药 wàiyòng yào
extravagance 奢华 shēhuá
eye 眼睛 yǎnjīng
eye drops 眼药水 yǎnyàoshuǐ
eyebrow 眉毛 méimáo
eyelid surgery 眼睑手术 yǎnjiǎn shǒushù
eyeliner 眼线笔 yǎnxiànbǐ
eyeshadow 眼影 yǎnyǐng
eyesight 视力 shìlì

fabric 布料 bùliào
facelift 面部整容 miànbù zhěngróng

facial 面部护理 miànbù hùlǐ
fail/failure 失败 shībài
fail (exam) 不及格 bùjígé
faint (v) 晕倒 yūn dǎo
fall (season) 秋天 qiūtiān
fall in love 谈恋爱 tán liàn'ài
familiar 熟悉 shúxi
famous 知名 zhīmíng
fan (electric) 电扇 diànshàn
fantastic (formidable) 厉害 lìhài
far 远 yuǎn
farsighted 远视 yuǎnshì
fascinating (full of mystery) 充满神密感 chōngmǎn shénmìgǎn
fashionable 时尚 shíshàng
fast 快 kuài
faster 快点儿 kuài diǎn'r
fastest 最快的 zuì kuài de
fasting 斋戒 zhāijiè
fat 胖 pàng
fate 缘分 yuánfen
father父亲 fùqīn
faucet 水龙头 shuǐlóngtóu
fault (responsibility) 全责 quánzé
favorite 最喜欢 zuì xǐhuān
fax 传真 chuánzhēn
fax machine 传真机 chuánzhēnjī
fee (application) 报名费 bàomíngfèi
feed (pet) 喂 wèi
feedback 反馈 fǎnkuì
feel (perceive) 感觉 gǎnjué
feel (think) 觉得 juéde
feelings 感觉 gǎnjué
female 女性 nǚxìng
fencing 击剑 jījiàn
ferris wheel 大观览车 dà guānlǎnchē
fetch 取来 qǔ lái
fever 发烧 fāshāo
fight (n, v) 打架 dǎjià
file (n) 文件 wénjiàn
file/document 档案 dàng'àn
fill out (form) 填 tián
filling (teeth) 补(牙) bǔ (yá)
film (roll) 胶卷 jiāojuǎn
filter 过滤嘴 guòlǜzuǐ
find (look for) 找 zhǎo
fire 火 huǒ
fire detector 烟感器 yāngǎnqì
fire escape 消防通道 xiāofáng tōngdào
fire extinguisher 灭火器 mièhuǒqì
fired 被炒 bèi chǎo
first 第一 dìyī
first aid kit 急救包 jíjiù bāo
first class ticket 头等舱票 tóuděngcāng piào
firstly 首先 shǒuxiān
fish 鱼 yú
fish sauce 海鲜调料 hǎixiān tiáoliào
fishing line 渔线 yúxiàn
fishing pole 鱼竿 yúgān
fishing 钓鱼 diàoyú
fitness centers 健身中心 jiànshēn zhōngxīn
fitting room 试衣间 shìyījiān
five 五 wǔ
five color enamel 五彩珐琅 wǔcǎi fǎláng
five spice flavoring 五香 wǔxiāng
fix 修 xiū
flag lowering 降旗 jiàngqí
flag raising 升旗 shēngqí
flamboyant 妖艳 yāoyàn
flanger 弗兰格效果器 fúlángé xiàoguǒqì
flash (camera) 闪光灯 shǎnguāngdēng
flashlight 手电 shǒudiàn
flat tire 爆胎了 bàotāi le
flats (shoes) 平底鞋 píngdǐ xié
flipper 脚蹼 jiǎopǔ
float 鱼漂 yúpiāo
floor (building) 楼 lóu
flooring/floor 地板 dìbǎn
floppy disk 软盘 ruǎnpán
floppy drive 软驱 ruǎnqū
floss (n) 牙线 yáxiàn
flour 面粉 miànfěn
flower 花 huā
flowerpot 花盆 huāpén

flu 感冒 gǎnmào
flute 长笛 chángdí
fly a kite 放风筝 fàng fēngzhēng
focus (n) 焦点 jiāodiǎn
focus (v) 对焦 duìjiāo
fog 雾 wù
forder文件夹wénjiànjiá
folk (music) 民谣 mínyáo
folk art 民间艺术 mínjiān yìshù
folk dance 民族舞 mínzúwǔ
follow 跟着 gēnzhe
food 食品 shípǐn
foot 脚 jiǎo
foot massage 足疗 zúliáo
football (soccer) 足球 zúqiú
football (USA) 美式足球 měishì zúqiú
footrest 脚凳 jiǎodèng
Forbidden City 故宫 Gùgōng
forehead 额头 étóu
foreign country 外国 wàiguó
foreign currency 外币 wàibì
foreign language 外语 wàiyǔ
foreign students' office 留学生办公室 liúxuéshēng bàngōngshì
foreign students' dorms 留学生宿舍 liúxuéshēng sùshè
foreigner 老外 lǎowài
forest 森林 sēnlín
forget it 算了 suàn le
forgive me 抱歉 bàoqiàn
fork 叉子 chā zi
form (document) 表 biǎo
formal 正式 zhèngshì
formaldehyde 甲醛 jiǎquán
formula (baby) 奶粉 nǎifěn
for sale 出售 chūshòu
foul 犯规 fànguī
found 找到 zhǎodào
foundation (makeup) 粉底 fěndǐ
four 四 sì
fragrant 香 xiāng
frame (picture 画框 huàkuàng
free (adj, no cost) 免费 miǎnfèi
free/freedom 自由 zìyóu
freelance photographer 自由摄影师 zìyóu shèyǐngshī
freeze 冻 dòng
French (language) 法文 fǎwén
fresh 新鲜 xīnxīan
fried rice 炒饭 chǎofàn
friend 朋友 péngyǒu
friendly 友好 yǒuhǎo
friendship 友谊 yǒuyí
frisbee 飞盘 fēipán
frog 田鸡 tiánjī
from 从 cóng
front 前面 qiánmiàn
fruit juice 果汁 guǒzhī
fruit 水果 shuǐguǒ
fry 炒 chǎo
frying pan 平底锅 píngdǐguō
fuel refilling station加油站 jiāyóuzhàn
full (container) 满 mǎn
full (hope) 充满 chōngmǎn
full-time (work) 全职 quánzhí
fun 好玩儿 hǎowánr
funny (humorous) 幽默 yōumò
funny (silly) 逗 dòu
furious 气死了 qì sǐ le
furniture 家具 jiājù
furthest 最远的 zuì yuǎn de
fur 毛/皮草 máo/pícǎo
fusili 意大利螺丝粉 yìdàlì luósīfěn
future rock (music) 未来摇滚 wèilái yáogǔn

G

Gaelic rules football 爱尔兰式足球 ài'erlán shì zúqiú
game 游戏 yóuxì
game show 娱乐节目 yúlè jiémù
garbage 垃圾 lājī
garlic 蒜 suàn
garlic salt 蒜盐 suànyán
gas 煤气 méiqì
gasolene 石油 shíyóu
Gate of Heavenly Peace 天安门 Tiān'ānmén
Gaudy Art 艳俗艺术 Yànsú Yìshù
gear 装备 zhuāngbèi

gender 性别 xìngbié
general 一般 yībān
genius 天才 tiāncái
gentle (light) 轻 qīng
geomancy (Fengshui) 风水 fēngshuǐ
Germany 德国 Déguó
German (language) 德文 Déwén
get (earn/achieve) 得到 dédào
get online 上网 shàngwǎng
get sick (v) 生病 shēngbìng
gherkins 酸瓜 suān guā
ghost 鬼 guǐ
gin 金酒 jīn jiǔ
ginger 姜 jiāng
girlfriend 女朋友 nǚpéngyǒu
give 给 gěi
glass (cup) 杯子 bēizi
glass 玻璃 bōli
glass noodle 粉丝 fěnsī
glasses 眼镜 yǎnjìng
gloves 手套 shǒutào
glue 胶水 jiāoshuǐ
glutinous rice 糯米 nuòmǐ
go (towards somewhere) 往...走 wǎng ... zǒu
go 去 qù
go! (cheer) 加油 jiāyóu
goal (football) 进球 jìnqiú
goal (for life) 目标 mùbiāo
goat cheese 羊奶酪 yáng nǎilào
goatee 山羊胡 shānyánghú
goggles (swim) 泳镜 yǒngjìng
going out 出去 chūqù
gold (color) 金色 jīnsè
gold (n) 黄金 huángjīn
gold plated 镀金 dùjīn
golf 高尔夫 gāo'erfū
gong 锣 luó
good enough/ok 还可以 hái kěyǐ
good luck 好运气 hǎo yùnqì
good morning 早上好 zǎoshàng hǎo
good night 晚安 wǎn ān
goodbye 再见 zàijiàn
goodbyes 分别 fēnbié
gorge 峡谷 xiágǔ
gouda 豪达 háodá
government 政府 zhèngfǔ
grade (in school) 年级 niánjí
grade (mark) 成绩 chéngjì
graduate (v) 毕业 bìyè
graffiti 亲笔 qīnbǐ
graffiti art 涂鸦 túyā
grain alcohol 白酒 báijiǔ
gram 克 kè
grandfather (maternal) 姥爷 lǎoyé
grandfather (paternal) 爷爷 yéye
grandmother (maternal) 姥姥 lǎolao
grandmother (paternal) 奶奶 nǎinai
grape 葡萄 pútáo
grass carp 草鱼 cǎoyú
grass script (calligraphy) 草书 cǎo shū
grass 草 cǎo
grassland 草地 cǎodì
gray 灰色 huīsè
Great Wall 长城 Chángchéng
greedy 贪心 tānxīn
green 绿色 lǜsè
green beans 四季豆 sìjìdòu
green soybean 毛豆 máodòu
green tea 绿茶 lǜchá
greenhouse 温室 wēnshì
greet (v) 打招呼 dǎ zhāohu
grill (n) 烧烤 shāokǎo
grocery store 超市 chāoshì
grouper 石斑 shíbān
grow up 成长 chéngzhǎng
guest (client) 客人 kèrén
guest (formal) 来宾 láibīn
guide/guidebook 指南 zhǐnán
guitar (acoustic) 箱琴 xiāngqín
guitar (electric) (电) 吉他 (diàn) jítā
guitar pick 吉他拨片 jítā bōpiàn
gum 口香糖 kǒuxiāngtáng
gun 枪 qiāng
gym 健身 jiànshēn
gymnasium 体育馆 tǐyùguǎn
gynecology 妇科 fùkē

H

habit/custom 习惯 xíguàn
haggle 讲价 jiǎngjià
hair 头发 tóufà
hair cut 剪发 jiǎnfà
hair gel 啫喱 zhěli
hair salon 美发厅 měifàtīng
hair spray 发胶 fàjiāo
hair stylist 理发师 lǐfàshī
hair wash 洗头 xǐtóu
hairstyle 发型 fàxíng
halal 清真 qīngzhēn
half 一半 yī bàn
half kilogram 一斤 yì jīn
ham 火腿 huǒtuǐ
Han dynasty 汉(代/朝) Hàn (dài/cháo)
hand 手 shǒu
hand moisturizer 护肤霜 hùfūshuāng
hand soap 香皂 xiāngzào
handbag 手提包 shǒutíbāo
handbook 手册 shǒucè
handlebar 车把 chēbǎ
handmade 手工 shǒugōng
handsome 帅 shuài
Hanukkah 光明节 Guāngmíngjié
happy 快乐 kuàilè
happy hour (discount time) 打折时光 dǎzhé shíguāng
happy in poverty 穷欢乐 qióng huānlè
happy 快乐/高兴 kuàilè/gāoxìng
hard 硬 yìng
hard drive 硬盘 yìngpán
hard seat 硬座 yìngzuò
hard sleeper 硬卧 yìngwò
hardcover 精装 jīngzhuāng
harder 重一点儿 zhòng yīdiǎnr
have 有 yǒu
have to (must) 得 děi
hawthorn 山楂 shānzhā
hazelnut 栗子 lìzi
he/him 他 tā
head 头 tóu
headache 头疼 tóu téng
headgear 帽子 màozi
headphones 耳机 ěrjī
health care 保健 bǎojiàn
health insurance 健康保险 jiànkāng bǎoxiǎn
health/healthy 健康 jiànkāng
heart 心脏 xīnzàng
heater/heating 暖气 nuǎnqì
heavy 重 zhòng
heaven 天堂 tiāntáng
hegemony 霸权 bàquán
height (of a person) 身高 shēn gāo
hell 地狱 dìyù
hello 你好 nǐ hǎo
hello (telephone) 喂 wèi
helmet 头盔 tóukuī
help (v) 帮助/帮忙 bāngzhù/bāng máng
help! 救命! jiù mìng!
hepatitis 肝炎 gānyán
herbal medicine 草药 cǎoyào
here 这儿 zhèr
hero 英雄 yīngxióng
high 高 gāo
high chair 高脚婴儿椅 gāojiǎo yīng'ér yǐ
high heels 高跟鞋 gāogēnxié
high school 高中 gāozhōng
highlights 挑染 tiǎo rǎn
hike (n, v) 徒步旅行 túbù lǚxíng
hiking boots 登山鞋 dēngshān xié
hinges 合页 héyè
hip (fashionable) 时尚 shíshàng
history 历史 lìshǐ
hit/play 打 dǎ
hoisin sauce 海鲜沙司 hǎixiān shāsī
holiday excursion 度假 dù jià
holidays (festivals) 节日 jiérì
home 家 jiā
home altar 家用小祭台 jiāyòng xiǎo jìtái
homemaker 家庭主妇 jiātíng zhǔfù
homework 作业 zuòyè
honey 蜂蜜 fēngmì
Hong Kong 香港 Xiānggǎng

honor (n) 荣誉 róngyù
honored guest 嘉宾 jiābīn
hook (fish) 鱼钩 yúgōu
hope 希望 xīwàng
horn 喇叭 lǎba
horror 恐怖 kǒngbù
horse 马 mǎ
horseback riding 骑马 qímǎ
hospital 医院 yīyuàn
host (of a TV show) 主持人 zhǔchírén
hot 热 rè
hot (spicy, sexy) 辣 là
hot mud spa 火山泥温泉浴 huǒshānní wēnquán yù
hot pot 火锅 huǒguō
hot springs 温泉 wēnquán
hot tub 热浴盆 rè yùpén
hot water heater 热水器 rèshuǐqì
hot water thermos 暖壶 nuǎnhú
hotel 旅馆 lǚguǎn
hour 小时 xiǎoshí
house 房子 fángzi
housing permit 住宿登记证 zhùsù dēngjìzhèng
how 怎么 zěnme
how many 多少 duōshǎo
hub (computer) 集线器 jíxiànqì
hug (v) 抱 bào
humid 潮湿 cháoshī
humidor 雪茄盒 xuějiā hé
hundred 一百 yìbǎi
hungry 饿 è
hurry up (food) 催一下 cuī yī xià
hurt 疼 téng
hurt (injured) 受伤 shòu shāng
husband 丈夫/老公 zhàngfu/lǎogōng
hustle and bustle 喧嚣 xuānxiāo
hutong (lane, alley) 胡同 hútòng
hypermetropia 远视 yuǎnshì

I

I 我 wǒ
ibuprofen 布洛芬 bùluòfēn
ice chair 冰车 bīng chē
ice hockey 冰球 bīngqiú
ice skating 滑冰 huábīng
iced tea 冰茶 bīng chá
ID card 身份证 shēnfènzhèng
if 要是/如果 yàoshì/rúguǒ
imagine 想象 xiǎngxiàng
imam 阿訇 ā hòng
immediately 马上 mǎshàng
Immodium 缓泻剂 huǎnxièjì
import 进口 jìnkǒu
important 重要 zhòngyào
in/at/on 在 zài
incense 香 xiāng
inch 寸 cùn
include 包括 bāokuò
incorrect 错 cuò
India 印度 Yìndù
individual 个人 gèrén
indoor 室内 shìnèi
industrial 工业 gōngyè
influence 印象 yìnxiàng
information booth 问讯处 wènxúnchù
information technology (IT) 资讯科技 zīxùn kējì
infrared 红外 hóngwài
infrared device 红外设备 hóngwài shèbèi
ingredients 配料 pèiliào
inhaler 吸入剂 xīrùjì
injector 注射器 zhùshèqì
injured/injury 受伤 shòushāng
ink stone 砚台 yàntái
insensitive 冷漠 lěngmòu
inside 里面 lǐmiàn
install 装 zhuāng
installation art 装制艺术 zhuāngzhì yìshù
instructions 指示 zhǐshì
insurance 保险 bǎoxiǎn
intentional/on purpose 故意 gùyì
interesting 有趣 yǒuqù
intermediate 中级 zhōngjí
intermission 中场休息 zhōngchǎng xiūxi

internal medicine 内服药 nèifú yào
international 国际 guójì
Internet 网络 wǎngluò
Internet café 网吧 wǎngbā
Internet connection 网络连接 wǎngluò liánjiē
interplay (mutual influence) 相互影响 xiānghù yǐngxiǎng
intersection 十字路口 shízì lùkǒu
interview 面试 miànshì
introduce (v) 介绍 jièshào
introduce/introduction 介绍 jièshào
invest 投资 tóuzī
invitation letter 邀请书 yāoqǐng shū
invite 邀请 yāoqǐng
iodine 碘酒 diǎnjiǔ
iron (v) 熨烫 yùntàng
is (to be) 是 shì
Islam 伊斯兰教 Yīsīlánjiào
island 岛 dǎo
Italy 意大利 Yìdàlì
Italian (language) 意大利文 Yìdàlìwén

J

jacket 夹克 jiákè
jade 玉 yù
jade carving 玉雕 yù diāo
jam (jelly) 果酱 guǒjiàng
Japan 日本 Rìběn
Japanese (language) 日文 Rìwén
Japanese encephalitis 乙型脑炎 yǐxíng nǎoyán
jasmine tea 茉莉花茶 mòlìhuā chá
jazz 爵士 juéshì
jeans 牛仔裤 niúzǎikù
jelly snacks 果冻 guǒdòng
jellyfish 蛰头 zhétóu
jerky (cured meat) 牛肉干 niúròugān
jewelry 珠宝 zhūbǎo
Jewish 犹太人 Yóutàirén
job (n) 工作 gōngzuò
joint venture 合资 hézī
joke (v) 开玩笑 kāi wánxiào
joss sticks and candles 香烛 xiāngzhú
journalist 记者 jìzhě
Judaism 犹太教 Yóutàijiào
judgments 判断 pànduàn

K

karaoke 卡拉OK / KTV kǎlā ok
kayak 皮艇 pítǐng
kebab 串儿 chuànr
kelp 海带 hǎidài
kennel 寄养 jìyǎng
key 钥匙 yàoshì
keyboard 键盘 jiànpán
kick (v) 踢 tī
kilogram 公斤 gōngjīn
kilometer 公里 gōnglǐ
kindergarten 幼儿园 yòu'éryuán
kitchen 厨房 chúfáng
kite 风筝 fēngzhēng
kiwi 猕猴桃 míhóutáo
knee 膝盖 xīgài
knee pad 护膝 hùxī
knife 刀子 dāozi
knock (v) 敲门 qiāomén
knot 绳结 shéngjié
know 知道 zhīdào
Korea 韩国 Hánguó
Korean (language) 韩文 Hánwén
kosher 清真 qīngzhēn
kowtow (genuflect) 磕头 kē tóu
kung fu tea 功夫茶 gōngfu chá
kungfu shoes 功夫鞋 gōngfu xié

L

label 标签 biāoqiān
lace 蕾丝 léisī
lacquer 漆器 qīqì
lacrosse 长曲棍球 cháng qūgùnqiú
lake 湖 hú
lamp 灯 dēng
landlord 房东 fángdōng
landscape painting 风景画 fēngjǐng huà
Lantern Festival 元宵节 Yuánxiāojié
laptop computer 笔记本 bǐjìběn
large corporation 大集团 dà jítuán

lasagna 意大利宽面 Yìdàlì kuān miàn
last year 去年 qùnián
last 上个 shànggè
late (person) 迟到 chídào
late (time) 晚 wǎn
late-night meal 宵夜 xiāoyè
latin dance 拉丁舞 lādīng wǔ
laugh 笑 xiào
lavender 薰衣草 xūnyīcǎo
lawyer 律师 lǜshī
laxative 泻药 xièyào
LCD monitor 液晶屏 yèjīng píng
leaf 叶子 yèzi
learn 学 xué
lease （n） 合同 hétong
leather handbag/briefcase 皮包 píbāo
leather 皮革 pígé
leave (exit / go out) 出去 chūqù
leave 离开 líkāi
leeks 韭菜 jiǔcài
left 左 zuǒ
leg 腿部 tuǐ
Lego 乐高 Lègāo
lemon 柠檬 níngméng
length 长度 chángdù
lens (for spectacles) 眼镜片 yǎnjìng piàn
less 少 shǎo
letter (n, postal) 信 xìn
lettuce 生菜 shēngcài
level 水平 shuǐpíng
liberate/liberation 解放 jiěfàng
library 图书馆 túshūguǎn
librette 唇下 chúnxià
lice 虱子 shīzi
license plate 牌照 páizhào
life partner 爱人 àirén
life 生活 shēnghuó
light fixtures 灯座 dēngzuò
light meter 测光表 céguāngbiǎo
light 灯 dēng
lighter 打火机 dǎhuǒjī
lightning 闪电 shǎndiàn

like 喜欢 xǐhuān
lily 百合 bǎihé
lime 酸橙/莱姆 suānchéng/láimǔ
limit 限额 xiàn'é
line up 排队 páiduì
line 线条 xiàntiáo
linen 亚麻 yàmá
lip/s 嘴唇 zuǐchún
lip balm 润唇膏 rùnchúngāo
lipgloss 唇彩 chúncǎi
liposuction 抽脂手术 chōuzhǐ shǒushù
lipstick 唇膏 chúngāo
list 列表 lièbiǎo
listen 听 tīng
listening comprehension class 听力课 tīnglì kè
little while 一会儿 yíhuìr
live (eg. music, entertainment) 现场 xiànchǎng
live (place) 住 zhù
living room 客厅 tīng
liver 肝 gān
loafers 无带皮鞋 wúdài píxié
lobster 龙虾 lóngxiā
lock (n,v) 锁 suǒ
login 登录 dēnglù
lomotil 止泻宁 zhǐxièníng
lonely 孤单 gūdān
long 长 cháng
long distance 长途 chángtú
long time 久 jiǔ
long underwear 保暖内衣 bǎonuǎn nèiyī
look for 找 zhǎo
looking forward to 期待 qīdài
loose 松 sōng
lose (a game) 输 shū
lose (v, something) 丢 diū
lose money 赔钱 péiqián
lost (oneself) 迷路 mílù le
lotus flowers 莲花 liánhuā
lotus root 莲藕 lián'ǒu
love 爱 ài
love/romance 爱情 àiqíng

love at first sight 一见钟情 yí jiàn zhōngqíng
low 低 dī
lucky 幸运 xìngyùn
luggage 行李 xíngli
lunch 午饭 wǔfàn
luxury apartment 公寓 gōngyù
luxury hotel 饭店/酒店 fàndiàn/jiǔdiàn
lychee 荔枝 lìzhī

M

machine 机器 jīqì
machine wash 机洗 jīxǐ
madam 女士 nǚshì
magazine 杂志 zázhì
magnesium powder 镁粉 měifěn
magnificent 伟大 wěidà
mahogany 红木 hóngmù
mail (n) 邮件 yóujiàn
mail (v) 寄 jì
mailbox 信箱 xìnxiāng
mainstream 主流 zhǔliú
make 做 zuò
make a phone call 打电话 dǎ diànhuà
malaria 疟疾 nüèji
male 男生 nánxing
mambo 曼波 mànbō
mammal 哺乳动物 bǔrǔ dongwu
man 男人 nánrén
management 物业 wùyè
manager 经理 jīnglǐ
mandarin fish 桂鱼 guìyú
mango 芒果 mángguǒ
manicure 修指甲 xiū zhǐjiǎ
manufacture 制造 zhìzào
many 多 duō
Mao Zedong 毛泽东 Máo Zédōng
map 地图 dìtú
maple syrup 枫糖 fēngtáng
market 市场 shìchǎng
marriage 婚姻 hūnyīn
marry (v) 结婚 jiéhūn
martial arts 武术 wǔshù
mascara 睫毛膏 jiémáogāo
massage 按摩 ànmó
masses 大众 dàzhòng
master (n) 师傅 shīfu
match (n) 火柴 huǒchái
materials 材料 cáiliào
math 数学 shùxué
matting 卡纸 kǎzhǐ
May Fourth Movement 五四运动 Wǔsì Yùndòng
maybe 也许 yěxǔ
mayonnaise 蛋黄酱 dànhuángjiàng
maze 迷宫 mígōng
meaning 意思 yìsi
measurements 量尺寸 liáng chǐcùn
measuring cup 量杯 liángbēi
measuring spoons 量勺 liángsháo
meat dish 荤菜 hūncài
meat 肉 ròu
media 媒体 méitǐ
medical records 病历档案 bìnglì dàngàn
medicine 药 yào
meet up 见面 jiànmiàn
meeting (formal) 开会 kāihuì
meeting room 会议室 hùiyìshì
mega pixels 像素 xiàngsù
member 会员 huìyuán
memorial hall 纪念馆 jìniànguǎn
memory (computer) 内存 nèicún
menstrual period 例假 lìjià
menu (food) 菜单 càidān
merry-go-round 旋转木马 xuánzhuàn mùmǎ
message (phone) 留言 liúyán
messy 杂乱 záluàn
metal 金属 jīnshǔ
meter (length) 米 mǐ
meter (taxi) 表 biǎo
method 方式 fāngshì
microlight 动力伞 dònglì sǎn
microphone 麦克风 màikèfēng
microwave 微波炉 wēibōlú
Mid-Autumn Festival 中秋节 Zhōngqiūjié
middle/medium 中 zhōng

middle school 中学 zhōngxué
midnight 午夜 wǔyè
migrant 外地人 wàidìrén
military 军事 jūnshì
milk 牛奶 niúnǎi
milk baths 牛奶浴 niúnǎiyù
milk chocolate 巧克力牛奶 qiǎokèlì niúnǎi
milk powder 奶粉 nǎifěn
million 一百万 yībǎiwàn
mineral water 矿泉水 kuàngquánshuǐ
Ming dynasty 明(代/朝) Míng (dài/cháo)
Minimalism 极简主义 Jíjiǎn Zhǔyì
mint 薄荷 bòhé
mirror 镜子 jìngzi
miss (Ms.) 小姐/姑娘 xiǎojiě/gūniáng
miss (v) 想念 xiǎngniàn
missing home 想家 xiǎngjiā
mister (Mr.) 先生 xiānshēng
mobile phone 手机 shǒujī
modem 调制解调器 tiáozhìjiětiáoqì
modern 现代 xiàndài
modern dance 现代舞 xiàndàiwǔ
modern theater 现代剧院 xiàndài jùyuàn
modernize/modernization 现代化 xiàndàihuà
monitor 显示器(液晶) xiǎnshìqì
monk 和尚/僧人 héshàng/sēngrén
monkey 猴子 hóuzi
Monkey King 美猴王/孙悟空 Měihóuwáng/Sūn Wùkōng
monosodium glutamate (MSG) 味精 wèijīng
Monterey Jack 蒙特里杰克干酪 méngtèlǐ jiékè gānlào
month 月 yuè
moon 月亮 yuèliàng
mop (v) 拖 tuō
mop 拖把 tuōbǎ
more 多 duō
morning 早上 zǎoshàng
morning exercises 早操 zǎocāo
mosque 清真寺 qīngzhēnsì
mother 母亲 mǔqīn
motherboard 主板 zhǔbǎn
motor scooters 迷你摩托车 mínǐ mótuóchē
motorcycles 摩托车 mótuóchē
mount (v, art) 裱 biǎo
mountain 山 shān
mountain climbing 爬山 páshān
mourning 悼念 dàoniàn
mouse 鼠标 shǔbiāo
mousse 摩丝 mósī
mouth 嘴巴 zuǐba
mouth-numbing pepper oil 花椒油 huājiāoyóu
move down (level) 降级 jiàngjí
move up (level) 跳级 tiàojí
movie theater 电影院 dianyìngyuan
movie/film 电影 diànyǐng
moving (house) 搬家 bānjiā
moxibustion 针灸 zhēnjiū
mozzarella 马苏里拉/意大利干酪 mǎsūlǐlā / yìdàlì gānlào
muesli 瑞士风味早餐食品 ruìshì fēngwèi zǎocān shípǐn
muffin 松饼 sōngbǐng
mullet 魔雷 móléi
multiculturalism 多元文化主义 duōyuán wénhuà zhǔyì
multimedia 多媒体 duōméitǐ
muscle 肌肉 jīròu
museum 博物馆 bówùguǎn
mushrooms 蘑菇 mógū
music 音乐 yīnyuè
musical instruments 乐器 yuèqì
musical performance 音乐会 yīnyuèhuì
musical score 曲谱 qǔpǔ
Muslim (believer) 伊斯兰教徒 Yīsīlán jiàotú
mussel 蚌 bàng
mustard 芥末 jièmò
mutton 羊肉 yángròu
myopia 近视 jìnshì
myself 我自己 wǒ zìji
mystery/mysterious 神密 shénmì

N

nail polish 指甲油 zhǐjiǎyóu
nail polish remover 洗甲水 xǐjiǎshuǐ
name 名字 míngzi
name card 名片 míngpiàn
nanny/maid 阿姨 āyí
napkins 餐巾 cānjīn
narrow 窄 zhǎi
nasal aspirator 鼻腔吸管 bíqiāng xīguǎn
nation/country 国家 guójiā
National Day 国庆节 Guóqìngjié
national humiliation 国耻 guóchǐ
National People's Congress 人民代表大会 Rénmín Dàibiǎo Dàhuì
navel 肚脐 dùqí
near 近 jìn
neck 颈 jìng
necklace 项链 xiàngliàn
need (require) 需要 xūyào
negative space 实体周围的空间 shítǐ zhōuwéi de kōngjiān
negatives 底片 dǐpiàn
negotiate 谈判 tánpàn
neighbor 邻居 línjū
neighborhood 小区 xiǎoqū
nephew (father's side) 侄子 zhízi
new 新 xīn
new jazz 新爵士 xīn juéshì
new media 新媒体 xīn méitǐ
new rock (music) 新摇滚 xīn yáogǔn
New Year's 新年 Xīnnián
news 新闻 xīnwén
newspaper 报纸 bàozhǐ
newspaper reading class 报刊课 bàokān kè
newsstand 报刊亭 bàokāntíng
next (one) 下个 xiàgè
next week 下星期 xià xīngqī
next year 明年 míngnián
nicotine 烟碱 yānjiǎn
niece (father's side) 侄女 zhínǚ
night 晚上 wǎnshàng
nightclub 夜总会 yèzǒnghuì
nine 九 jiǔ
nitrous (oxide) 笑气(一氧化二氮) xiàoqì (yīyǎnghuà'èrdàn)
no 不 bù
no problem 没有关系 méiyǒu guānxi
no way 没门儿 méi ménr
noisy 吵(闹) chǎo(nào)
non-profit organization 非盈利组织 fēi yínglì zǔzhi
nonsense/bullshit 胡说 húshuō
non-smoking area 禁烟区 jìnyān qū
non-stop (flight) 直飞 zhífēi
noodles 面 miàn
noon 中午 zhōngwǔ
north 北 běi
north gate 北门 běimén
nose 鼻子 bízi
nose job 隆鼻 lóngbí
nose ring 鼻环 bíhuán
not a lot 不太多 bú tài duō
not bad / ok 不错 búcuò
not have / there is not 没有 méiyǒu
novel 小说 xiǎoshuō
novocaine 局部麻醉 júbù mázuì
now 现在 xiànzài
nudity 裸露 luǒlù
number (phone) 号码 hàomà
numeral 数字 shùzì
numerology 生辰八字占卜 shēngchénbāzì zhānbǔ
nun 修女/尼姑 xiūnǚ/nígū
nutrition 营养 yíngyǎng
nuts 坚果 jiānguǒ
nylon 尼龙 nílóng

O

oar 桨 jiǎng
oatmeal (燕)麦片/(燕)麦粥 (yàn) màipiàn/(yàn) màizhōu
obey 听话 tīng huà
object 实体 shítǐ
obstetry 产科 chǎnkē
octopus 章鱼 zhāngyú
of course 当然 dāngrán
office 办公室 bàngōngshì

offside 越位 yuèwèi
oil 油 yóu
oil painting 油画 yóuhuà
oily 油腻 yóunì
ok 行 xíng
old (person) 老 lǎo
old (thing) 旧 jiù
olive/s 橄榄 gǎnlǎn
olive oil 橄榄油 gǎnlǎnyóu
Olympics 奥林匹克 àolínpǐkè
Olympic Games 奥运会 àoyùnhuì
on/above 上/上面 shàng/shàngmiàn
once 一次 yí cì
one 一 yī
one/each 一个 yí gè
one minute 一分钟 yì fēnzhōng
one size fits all 均码 jūnmǎ
one-on-one class 一对一授课 yīduìyī shòukè
one-way ticket 单程票 dānchéng piào
onion, red 洋葱 yángcōng
online (go) 上网 shàngwǎng
only 只 zhǐ
oolong tea 乌龙茶 wūlóngchá
opal 猫眼石 māoyǎnshí
open (adj) 开放 kāifàng
open (v, turn on) 打开 dǎkāi
opening (of an event) 开幕式 kāimùshì
opening (secuence of a play or film) 开场 kāichǎng
operating system 操作系统 cāozuò xìtǒng
opiates 安眠药 ānmiányào
opinion 想法 xiǎngfǎ
opium 鸦片 yāpiàn
opposite (location) 对面 duìmiàn
opposite (inverted, e.g. opposite day) 相反 xiāngfǎn
oppress 压迫 yāpò
oppressed 压抑 yāyì
optometrist (office) 眼镜店 yǎnjìng diàn
oral (medication) 口服 kǒufú
oral language 口语 kǒuyǔ
orange (color) 桔红色 júhóngsè
orange (fruit) 橙子 chéngzi
orchestra 管弦乐队 guǎnxián yuèduì
orchid 兰花 lánhuā
order (food) 点菜 diǎncài
oregano 牛至 niúzhì
Oreo cookies 奥力奥饼干 àolì'ào bǐnggān
organ 风琴 fēngqín
organization (government) 机关 jīguān
orientation 方位 fāngwèi
original sound/language (movie) 原声 yuánshēng
orthodontics 畸齿矫正 jīchǐ jiàozhèng
other 其他 qítā
outdoor 室外 shìwài
outgoing 开朗 kāilǎng
outside 外面 waimiàn
oven (or toaster oven) 烤箱 kǎoxiāng
overalls 背带裤 bēidàikù
overcoat 大衣 dàyī
overhead projector 投影仪 tóuyǐngyí
overnight success 一夜成名 yí yè chéngmíng
oyster mushrooms 平菇 píngū
oyster sauce 蚝油 háoyóu

P

pacifier 橡皮奶嘴儿 xiàngpí nǎizuǐr
page 页 yè
pain killers 止疼药 zhǐténgyào
paint (n, color) 颜料/漆 yánliào/qī
paint (v) 绘画 huìhuà
painting (n) 画 huà
pair 双 shuāng
pajamas/nightie 睡衣 shuìyī
pancake 煎饼 jiānbǐng
pandean pipe 笙 shēng
pants 裤子 kùzi
papaya 木瓜 mùguā
paper cuttings 剪纸 jiǎn zhǐ

paper shredder 碎纸机 sùizhǐjī
paper towel 纸巾 zhǐjīn
paper towels 纸巾 zhǐjīn
paperback (book) 平装 píngzhuāng
paperclips 别针 biézhēn
parachute 跳伞 tiàosǎn
paragliding 滑翔伞 huáxiángsǎn
parametric EQ 参数均衡器 cānshù jūnhéngqì
parcel 包裹 bāoguǒ
pardon me 不好意思 bùhǎo yìsi
park (v, car) 停车 tíngchē
park 公园 gōngyuán
parmesan 帕尔马干酪 pà'ěrmǎ gānlào
parsley 香菜 xiāngcài
part (n) 零件 língjiàn
part-time (work) 兼职 jiānzhí
pass (exam) 及格 jígé
pass away (die) 去世 qùshì
pass by 通过 tōngguò
Passover 逾越节 Yúyuèjié
passport 护照 hùzhào
password 密码 mìmǎ
pasta 意大利面食 Yìdàlì miànshí
pasta sauce 意大利面酱 Yìdàlìmiàn jiàng
pate 冻肉 dòngròu
patience 耐心 nàixīn
pay (money) 付 fù
pay salary 发工资 fā gōngzī
payment 交款 jiāo kuǎn
payment method 付款方式 fùkuǎnfāngshì
peace 和平 hépíng
peach 桃子 táozi
peak (of a mountain) 山峰 shānfēng
peanut butter 花生酱 huāshēngjiàng
peanut oil 花生油 huāshēngyóu
peanuts 花生 huāshēng
pear 梨 lí
pearl 珍珠 zhēnzhū
peas 豌豆 wāndòu
pecans 长寿果 chángshòu guǒ
pedestrian bridge 天桥 tiānqiáo
pediatrician 儿科医生 érkē yīshēng
pediatry 儿科 érkē
pedicab / three-wheeled vehicles 三轮车 sānlúnchē
pedicure 修脚 xiū jiǎo
piercings 穿孔 chuānkǒng
Peking Opera 京剧 jīngjù
pen 笔 bǐ
penalty 判罚 pànfá
pencils 铅笔 qiānbǐ
penguin 企鹅 qǐ'é
penicillin 青霉素 qīngméisù
penis 阴茎 yīnjīng
penis enlargement 阴茎增长术 yīnjīng zēngchǎng shù
penne 通心粉 tōngxīnfěn
peony 牡丹/芍药 mǔdān/sháoyào
people 人 rén
people, the 人民 rénmín
People's Republic of China 中华人民共和国 Zhōnghuá Rénmín Gònghéguó
pepper (black) 黑胡椒 hēi hújiāo
pepper (spicy) 辣椒 làjiāo
pepper, green 青椒 qīngjiāo
percussion (instruments) 打击乐器 dǎjī yuèqì
performance 表演 biǎoyǎn
performance art 行为艺术 xíngwéi yìshù
period (of time) 时期 shíqī
perm (v) 烫发 tàngfà
permit (v, allow) 让 ràng
person 人 rén
personal information 个人信息 gèrén xìnxī
personal style 个人风格 gèrén fēnggé
personality 个性 gèxìng
perspective (visual) 透视法 tòushìfǎ
perspective/opinion 看法 kànfǎ
pesto sauce 九层塔酱 jiǔcéngtǎ jiàng
pet (n) 宠物 chǒngwù
pharmaceutical 制药 zhìyào

pharmacy 药房 yàofáng
pheasant or peacock feathers on top of a warrior's helmet (in Peking opera) 翎子 língzi
phlegm 痰 tán
phone 电话 diànhuà
phonecall 打电话 dǎ diànhuà
photocopier 复印机 fùyìnjī
photography 摄影 shèyǐng
phrase/word 词 cí
physical examination 体检 tǐjiǎn
physique 身材 shēncái
piano 钢琴 gāngqín
pick up (clean, collect) 捡起 jiǎn qǐ
pick up / meet (someone) 接 jiē
pick up / take away 取 qǔ
pick/choose 挑 tiāo
pick/pluck (e.g. fruit) 采摘 cǎizhāi
pickle/kimchee 泡菜 pàocài
picture books 画册 huàcè
pierce (body) 打孔 dǎkǒng
pig 猪 zhū
pig's trotters 猪蹄 zhūtí
pillow 枕头 zhěntóu
pine nuts 松仁 sōngrén
pineapple 菠萝 bōluó
ping pong 乒乓球 pīngpāngqiú
pink 粉色 fěnsè
pinky toe 小拇指 xiǎomǔzhǐ
pipa (Chinese lute) 琵琶 pípā
pipe (for smoking) 烟斗 yāndǒu
pipe (plumbing) 管道 guǎndào
pirated 盗版 dàobǎn
pistachio 开心果 kāixīnguǒ
pita 皮塔饼 pítǎ bǐng
pity / a shame 可惜 kěxī
place (n) 地方 dìfāng
placement exam 入学考试 rùxué kǎoshì
plan 计划 jìhuà
plank of wood 木板 Mùbǎn
plants 植物 zhíwù
plaster 石膏 shígāo
plastic 塑料 sùliào
plastic surgeon 整形外科医生 zhěngxíng wàikē yīshēng
plastic surgery 整形外科手术 zhěngxíng wàikē shǒushù
plate盘子pánzi
platform (train) 站台 zhàntái
platinum 铂金 bójīn
play (theatre) 剧本 jùběn
play (v) 玩儿 wánr
play (video) games 打游戏 dǎ yóuxì
play area 游乐区 yóulè qū
Playdoh 培乐多 Péilèduō
player 运动员 yùndòngyuán
playpen 婴儿围栏 yīng'ér wéilán
playwright 剧作家 jùzuòjiā
please 请 qǐng
please! 拜托! bàituō!
pleather PU皮 PU pí
pleats 褶子 zhězi
plot 情节 qíngjié
pluck eyebrows 修眉毛 xiū méimáo
plug in 插入 chārù
plum sauce 梅子酱 méizijiàng
plywood 大芯板 dàxīnbǎn
pneumonia 肺炎 fèiyán
pocket 口袋 kǒudài
poetry 诗歌 shīgē
point out 指出 zhǐchū
pointless/empty 虚空 xūkōng
police 警察 jǐngchá
Political Pop (art) 政治波普 Zhèngzhì Bōpǔ
politics 政治 zhèngzhì
pollution 污染 wūrǎn
polyester 涤纶 dílún
pomelo 柚子 yòuzi
pool hall 台球厅 táiqiú tīng
poor 穷 qióng
poor/pitiable (adj) 可怜 kělián
popcorn 爆米花 bàomǐhuā
popular/pop 流行 liúxíng
porcelain 瓷器 cíqì
pork 猪肉 zhūròu
porkchop 排骨 páigǔ
porter 挑夫 tiāofū
possibly 可能 kěnéng
post (mail) 寄信 jì xìn
post office 邮局 yóujú

postcards 名信片 míngxìnpiàn
postcode 邮编 yóubiān
post-modern 后现代 hòu xiàndài
post-structuralism 后结构主义 hòu jiégòu zhǔyì
pot/wok 锅 guō
potato 土豆 tǔdòu
pottery 陶瓷 táocí
pottery wheel 制陶转台 zhìtáo zhuàntái
poultry 禽类 qínlèi
power outlets 电源出口 diànyuán chūkǒu
power supply 电源 diànyuán
practice (v) 练(习) liàn(xí)
pray (v) 祈福/拜 qǐ fú/bài
prayer 祈祷 qǐdǎo
prayer beads (Bhuddist) 佛珠 fó zhū
prayer wheel 法轮 fǎlún
pregnancy test 妊娠测试 rènshēn cèshì
pregnant 怀孕 huáiyùn
prepaid cards 预付卡 yùfùkǎ
prepare 准备 zhǔnbèi
prescription 处方 chǔfāng
press (v, button, etc.) 按 àn
pretty 漂亮 piàoliàng
price 价格 jiàgé
priest 牧师 mùshī
primary school 小学 xiǎoxué
print (e.g. T-shirt) 喷绘 pēnhuì
print (v) 打印 dǎyìn
printer paper 打印纸 dǎyìn zhǐ
printer 打印机 dǎyìnjī
private learning center 私立学校 sīlì xúexiào
private room 包间 bāojiān
probation period 试用期 shìyòngqī
problem 毛病 máobìng
program (TV show) 节目 jiémù
pronounce/pronounciation 发音 fāyīn
propaganda posters 宣传画 xuānchuán huà
property agent 中介 zhōngjiè
property deed 房产证 fángchǎnzhèng
protect 保护 bǎohù
proud 自豪 zìháo
provide 提供 tígōng
prunes 李子干 lǐzi gān
psychiatry 精神病科 jīngshénbìngkē
psychologist 心理医生 xīnlǐ yīshēng
publish 出版 chūbǎn
publisher 出版商 chūbǎnshāng
pudding 布丁 bùdīng
pull 拉 lā
pumpkin 南瓜 nánguā
punch/beat 打 dǎ
punk (music) 朋克 péngkè
puppet (wooden) 木偶 mù'ǒu
purity 纯度 chúndù
purple 紫色 zǐsè
push 推 tuī
puzzles 拼图 pīntú
pyramid 金字塔 jīnzìtǎ

Q

Qing dynasty 清(代/朝) Qīng (dài/cháo)
quail 鹌鹑 ānchún
quality 质量 zhìliàng
quarterly (payment) 季付 jìfù
question/problem 问题 wèntí
quiet 安静 ānjìng
quilt (cover) 被子(罩) bèizi(zhào)
quit (job) 离职 lízhí

R

rabbit 兔 tù
rabies 狂犬病 kuángquǎnbìng
racing cars (n,v) 赛车 sàichē
radio (n) 收音机 shōuyīnjī
rag 抹布 mǒbù
rain (n) 雨 yǔ
rain (v) 下雨 xiàyǔ
raincoat 雨衣 yǔyī
raise (v) 调高 tiáo gāo
raisin 葡萄干 pútáo gān
Raisin Bran 葡萄干麦片 pútáogān màipiàn

rap (v) 说唱 shuōchàng
rattan matting 藤席 téng xí
rattle (baby) 儿童沙锤 értóng shāchuí
ravioli 意大利饺 yìdàlì jiǎo
razorblade 剃刀 tìdāo
read (pronounce) 念 niàn
reading comprehension class 阅读课 yuèdú kè
real/true 真的 zhēnde
really/extremely 实在 shízài
rear-end (accident) 追尾 zhuīwěi
receipt 发票 fāpiào
receive 收到 shōudào
recipient 收货人 shōuhuòrén
recognize/know 认识 rènshi
recommend 推荐 tuījiàn
record (movies) 拍(视频) pāi shìpín
rectangular 长方形 chángfāngxíng
red 红色 hóngsè
red bean cream 红豆沙 hōngdòushā
red cherry 樱桃 yīngtáo
red wine 红酒 hóngjiǔ
redhead 红褐色头发 hónghèsè tóufa
reduce 减少 jiǎnshǎo
reduce taxes 减免税 jiǎnmiǎn shuì
reel (fishing) 渔线轮 yúxiànlún
refill card (mobile phone) 手机充值卡 shǒujī chōngzhíkǎ
refrigerate 晾凉 liàngliáng
refrigerator 冰箱 bīngxiāng
reggae 雷鬼 léiguǐ
register/registration 挂号 guàhào
regular script (calligraphy) 楷书 kǎishū
reheat 再热一下 zài rè yí xià
re-hydration salts 盐水 yánshuǐ
reimburse (expenses) 报销 bàoxiāo
rejuvenation 复兴 fùxīng
release/let go 放开 fàngkāi
religioun 宗教 zōngjiào
renovation 翻修 fānxiū
rent (n) 房租 fángzū
rent (v) 租 zū
rent out 出租 chūzū
repair 修 xiū
repairs 修理 xiūlǐ
repeat 重复 chóngfù
replace 换 huàn
report card 成绩单 chéngjìdān
republic 民国 mínguó
research 研究 yanjiu
reserve (in advance) 预定 yùdìng
reserve 订 dìng
residence permit (Chinese) 户口本儿 hùkǒuběn'r
resident permit (foreigner) 居留证 jūliúzhèng
responsibilities (professional) 职责 zhízé
responsible 负责 fùzé
rest 休息 xiūxi
restaurant 餐厅/餐馆/饭馆 cāntīng/cānguǎn/fànguǎn
resting room 休息厅 xiūxītīng
restriction 限制 xiànzhì
restroom 洗手间 xǐshǒujiān
resume/cv 简历 jiǎnlì
return (something) 退 tuì
return (turn back/around) 返回 fǎnhuí
return/come back 回来 huílái
revolution 革命 gémìng
reward 报酬 bàochóu
rhumba 伦巴 lúnbā
rhythm 节奏 jiézòu
rice 米饭 mǐfàn
rice paper 宣纸 xuānzhǐ
rice vinegar 米醋 mǐcù
rice cooker 电饭锅 diànfànguō
rich (person) 富 fù
riches 财产 cáichǎn
ride (bike, horse) 骑 qí
ride in a cab 打车 dǎ chē
rigatoni 意大利大弯管通心粉 Yìdàlì dà wānguǎn tōngxīnfěn
right 右 yòu
ring (n) 戒指 jièzhǐ
ring tone 铃声 língshēng
rinse mouth 漱口 shùkǒu

ripe/cooked 熟 shóu
Ritz cracker 乐之饼干 lèzhī bǐnggān
river 河 hé
road 路 lù
road entrance 路口 lùkǒu
road tolls 过路费 guòlùfèi
robb 抢 qiǎng
rock climbing 攀岩 pānyán
rock 石头 shítou
rock & roll 摇滚 yáogǔn
roller coaster 过山车 guòshānchē
rolling paper 卷烟纸 juǎnyān zhǐ
Romanian (language) 罗马尼亚语 Luòmǎníyà yǔ
romantic 浪漫 làngmàn
roof creatures 檐兽 yánshòu
roof tiles 房瓦 fángwǎ
rope/line 绳 shéng
roquefort 羊乳干酪 yángrǔ gānlào
rose 玫瑰 méiguī
rosemary 迷迭香 mídiéxiāng
rosewood 红木 hóngmù
Rosh Hashanah 岁首节 Suìshǒujié
round 圆 yuán
roundtrip ticket 往返票 wǎngfǎn piào
router 路由器 lùyóuqì
row (a boat) 划 huá
rubber 橡胶 xiàngjiāo
rubbing alcohol 外用酒精 wàiyòng jiǔjīng
ruby 红宝石 hóngbǎoshí
rugby 橄榄球 gǎnlǎnqiú
ruins/relics 遗址 yízhǐ
ruler 尺子 chǐzi
rum 朗姆酒 lǎngmǔ jiǔ
run/running 跑步 pǎobù
running (semi-cursive) script (calligraphy) 行书 xíngshū
rush hour 高峰期 gāofēngqī
Russian (language) 俄文 éwén

S

sacrifices 祭品 jìpǐn
sad/depressed 难过 nánguò
safe 安全 ānquán
safety 治安 zhì'ān
sage (salvia, dried) 撒尔维亚干叶 sā'ěrwéiyà gānyè
sailing 帆船 fānchuán
salad dressing 沙拉酱 shālājiàng
salami 萨拉米 sālāmǐ
salary 工资/薪水 gōngzī/xīnshǔi
salmon 鲑鱼 guìyú
salt 盐 yán
salty 咸 xián
samba 桑巴 sāngbā
same 一样 yíyàng
sand 沙子 shāzi
sandals 便鞋 biànxié
sandalwood 檀木 tánmù
sandwich 三明治 sānmíngzhì
sanitary pads 卫生巾 wèishēngjīn
sapphire 蓝宝石 lánbǎoshí
satellite 卫星 wèixīng
sauce 酱 jiàng
sauna 桑拿 sāngná
sausage 香肠 xiāngcháng
savvy 懂事 dǒngshì
saxophone 萨克斯 sàkèsī
scallop 扇贝 shànbèi
scalping (reselling tickets) 倒票 dǎopiào
scanner 扫描仪 sǎomiáoyí
scare 吓 xià
scarf 围巾 wéijīn
scenery 风景 fēngjǐng
scented tea 花茶 huāchá
schedule (of classes) 课程表 kèchéngbiǎo
schema (composition) 构图 gòutú
school 学校 xuéxiào
science 科学 kèxué
science and technology building 科技楼 kējìlóu
science fiction 科幻 kēhuàn
scissors 剪子 jiǎnzi
scones 司康 sīkāng
score (music) 乐谱 yuèpǔ
score (n, sports) 分数 fēnshù
score (v, point) 得分 défēn

scotch (Chivas) 苏格兰威士忌（芝华士）sūgélán wēishìjì (zhīhuáshì)
screen 屏幕 píngmù/屏风 píngfēng
screens 影壁 yǐngbì
screw (n) 螺丝 luósī
scripture 圣经 shèngjīng
scroll mounting 装裱 zhuāng biǎo
scrub 刷 shuā
scrubber 刷子 shuāzi
scuba diving 潜水 qiánshuǐ
scuba mask 潜水面具 qiánshuǐ miànjù
sculpture 雕塑 diāosù
sea bass 鲈鱼 lúyú
sea cucumber 海参 hǎishēn
seafood 海鲜 hǎixiān
seal (mammal) 海豹 hǎibào
seal script (calligraphy) 隶书 lìshū
search (internet) 搜索 sōusuǒ
search / look for 寻找 xúnzhǎo
seaside 海边 hǎibiān
seasoning 调料 tiáoliào
seatbelt 安全带 ānquándài
seats 座位 zuòwèi
second 第二 dì-èr
second hand / used 二手 èrshǒu
secret 秘密 mìmì
secretary 秘书 mìshū
security guard 保安 bǎo'ān
sedan chairs 轿子 jiàozi
see (v) 看 kan
selfish 自私 zìsī
self-rising flour 自发粉 zìfā fěn
self-tanning spray 美黑喷雾 měihēi pēnwù
sell 卖 mài
send (mail) 寄 jì
send (transmit) 发送 fāsòng
sensitive 敏感 mǐn'gǎn
sentence 句型 jùxíng
separate(ly) 分开 fēnkāi
server (waiter) 服务员 fúwùyuán
server (computer) 服务器 fúwùqì
service charge 服务费 fúwùfèi
sesame 芝麻 zhīmá
sesame oil 芝麻油 zhīmáyóu
set (for a play) 布景 bùjǐng
set out / leave 出发 chūfā
set table 摆桌子 bǎi zhuōzi
seven 七 qī
sex 性交 xìngjiao
sexually transmitted disease 性病 xìngbìng
sexy 性感 xìnggǎn
shag head 蓬乱一团的头发 péngluànyītuán de tóufà
shake hands 握手 wò shǒu
shallow 浅 qiǎn
shampoo 洗发水 xǐfàshuǐ
Shanxi vinegar 山西陈醋 Shānxī chéncù
shape 形状 xíngzhuàng
shave (bald) 剃 tì
shave (beard) 刮 guā
she/her 他 tā
sheep/goat 羊 yáng
shellfish 贝类 bèilèi
shield 盾 dùn
shinier 亮点儿 liàng diǎnr
shirt 衬衫 chènshān
Shock Art 冲击艺术，修克艺术 Chōngjī Yìshù, Xiūkè Yìshù
shoe/s 鞋 xié
shoe laces 鞋带 xiédài
shoe shine 鞋油 xiéyóu
shoe sole 鞋底 xiédǐ
shoot 射击 shèjī
shopping 购物 gòuwù
short (not tall) 矮 ǎi
short 短 duǎn
shorts 短裤 duǎnkù
shoulder 肩膀 jiānbǎng
shower (n) 淋浴 línyù
shrimp 虾 xiā
shrine 神殿 shéndiàn
shrink 缩 suō
shutter (photo) 快门 kuàimén
shuttlecock 毽子 jiànzi
shy 害羞 hàixiū
siblings 兄弟姐妹 xiōngdì jiěmèi
sick (v) 病 bìng

sideburns 鬓角 bìnjiǎo
sight 验光 yànguāng
sign (v) 签 qiān
sign up 注册 zhùcè
signature 签名 qiānmíng
silk 丝绸 sīchóu
silver (color) 银色 yínsè
silver (metal) 白银 báiyín
simple 简单 jiǎndān
sing 唱歌 chànggē
singer 歌手 gēshǒu
single room 单人房间 dānrén fángjiān
sink 水盆 shuǐpén
sipping cups 婴儿吮杯 yīng'ér shǔnbēi
sister (older) 姐姐 jiějie
sister (younger) 妹妹 mèimei
sisters 姐妹 jiěmèi
sit 坐 zuò
situation 情况 qíngkuàng
six 六 liù
size 尺寸 chǐcùn
sketchbook 写生簿 xiěshēng bù
ski mask 护脸 hùliǎn
ski poles 雪杖 xuězhàng
ski suit 滑雪服 huáxuě fú
skiing 滑雪 huáxuě
skillful 熟练 shúliàn
skin 皮肤 pífū
skin (v) 剥皮 bāo pí
skinny 瘦 shòu
skirt 短裙 duǎnqún
skis 双板 shuāngbǎn
sleep 睡觉 shuìjiào
sleeping bag 睡袋 shuìdài
sleeping pill 安眠药 ānmiányào
sleepy 困 kùn
sleeve 袖子 xiùzi
slice (v) 切片 qiē piàn
slides 滑梯 huátī
slimming treatments 减肥疗程 jiǎnféi liáochéng
slippers 拖鞋 tuōxié
slogans 口号 kǒuhào
slow 慢 màn
slowest 最慢的 zuìmàn
small 小 xiǎo
small change (n) 零钱 língqián
smart/clever 聪明 cōngmíng
smash/shatter 碎 suì
smelly 臭 chòu
smile 微笑 wēixiào
smile 笑容 xiàoróng
smoke (n) 烟 yān
smoke (v) 抽烟/吸烟 chōu yān / xī yān
snack (n) 零食 língshí
snack shop 小吃店 xiǎochīdiàn
snake 蛇 shé
sneakers 帆布鞋 fānbù xié
snooker 斯诺克 sīnuòkè
snow (n) 雪 xuě
snow (v) 下雪 xiàxuě
snow boots 雪靴 xuěxuē
snow peas 荷兰豆 hélándòu
snowboard 单板 dānbǎn
snowboarding 滑单板 huá dānbǎn
so so 一般般/马马虎虎的 yì bānbān / mǎmǎ hūhū de
socialism 社会主义 shèhuì zhǔyì
socks 袜子 wàzi
soda water 苏打水 sūdǎshuǐ
soft 软 ruǎn
soft seat (train) 软座 ruǎnzuò
soft sleeper (train) 软卧 ruǎnwò
softball 垒球 lěiqiú
softener 软化剂 ruǎnhuà jì
software 软件 ruǎnjiàn
sold out 卖完了 mài wán le
soldiers 军人 jūnrén
some 一些 yìxiē
someone else / another person 别人 biérén
son 儿子 érzi
song 歌 gē
sorry 对不起 duìbùqǐ
sound 声音 shēngyīn
soup 汤 tāng
sour 酸 suān
sour cream 酸奶 suānnǎi
south 南 nán

south gate 南门 nánmén
soy milk 豆浆 dòujiāng
soy sauce 酱油 jiàngyóu
soybean milk 豆浆 dòujiāng
spaghetti 意大利面 yìdàlì miàn
Spain 西班牙 Xībānyá
Spanish (language) 西班牙文 xībānyáwén
spank/hit 打 dǎ
spayed 绝育 juéyù
speak (language) 讲 jǐang
speak/say (v) 说 shuō
speakers 音箱 yīnxiāng
special 特别 tèbié
special/particularly 特别 tèbié
specialist 专家 zhuānjiā
specialty 特色菜 tèsè
spectacular/wicked 倍儿棒 bèir bàng
speed 速度 sùdù
spend (money) 花 huā
sphere 球体 qiútǐ
spicy 辣 là
spinach 菠菜 bōcài
spit (mucous) 吐痰 tùtán
split ends 发尾分岔 fàwěi fēnchà
spokes 车条 chētiáo
sponge 海绵 hǎimián
spoon 汤匙 tāngchí
sports arena / gym 体育馆 tǐyùguǎn
sportswear 运动衣 yùndòngyī
spouse 爱人 àiren
spring 春天 chūntiān
Spring and Autumn period 春秋时代 chūnqiū shídài
Spring Festival (Chinese New Year) 春节 Chūnjié
spring onions / shallots 葱 cōng
spring rolls 春卷 chūnjuǎn
sprite 雪碧 xuěbì
square 方型 fāngxìng
square meter(s) 平米 píngmǐ
squid 鱿鱼 yóuyú
squirrel 松鼠 sōngshǔ
stable 安定 āndìng
stadium 体育场 tǐyùchǎng
stain 污渍 wūzì
stairs 楼梯 lóutī
stamp 邮票 yóupiào
stand 站 zhàn
staple foods 主食 zhǔshí
starch 上浆 shàngjiāng
stare (v) 盯 dīng
stars (movie) 明星 míngxīng
starving 饿死了 è sǐ le
statue 雕像 diàoxiàng
stay behind 留 liú
steak (beef) 牛排 niúpái
steal 偷 tōu
steam (v) 蒸 zhēng
steam room 蒸汽浴房 zhēngqì yùfáng
steamed buns 馒头 mántou
steep climb 陡坡 dǒu pō
steles 石碑 shí bēi
steralize 杀菌 shā jūn
stereo 立体声 lìtǐshēng
stickers 贴纸 tiēzhǐ
sticky notes 便条 biàntiáo
stir fry 炒 chǎo
stomach 胃 wèi
stomach ache 胃疼 wèi téng
stone statues 石像 shíxiàng
stone lion sentries 石狮子 shí shìzi
stool (seat) 凳子 dèngzi
stool sample 大便样本 dàbiàn yàngběn
stop (v) 停 tíng
stoplight 红灯 hóngdēng
storage capacity 存储容量 cúnchǔ róngliàng
storage card 存储卡 cúnchǔkǎ
stove 炉灶 lúzào
straight (direction) 直走 zhí zǒu
straighten up / clean 清理 qīnglǐ
strange 奇怪 qíguài
strangers 陌生人 mòshēngrén
straw mushroom 草菇 cǎogū
strawberry 草莓 cǎoméi
stream 溪 xī
street 大街 dàjiē
street dancing 街舞 jiēwǔ

street food 街边食品 jiēbiān shípǐn
street vendor 路边摊儿 lùbiān tānr
string 琴弦 qínxián
strings (music) 弦乐器 xiányuèqì
stroller 幼儿车 yòu'ér chē
strong 强 qiáng
structuralism 结构主义 jiégòu zhǔyì
structure 结构 jiégòu
struggle 奋斗 fèngdòu
student discount ticket 学生票 xúeshēngpiào
student dorms 宿舍 sùshè
student ID card 学生证 xuéshēngzhèng
students 学生 xuéshēng
studio 工作室 gōngzuò shì
study 学习 xuéxí
stuffed animals 毛绒动物玩具 máoróng dòngwù wánjù
stupid 笨 bèn
style 风格 fēnggé
sublet 转租 zhuǎnzū
substitution 替换 tìhuàn
subtitle 字幕 zìmù
subway 地铁 dìtiě
suckup (swot) 马屁精 mǎpì jīng
sue (v) 起诉 qǐsù
suede 羊皮 yángpí
sugar 糖 táng
suit 套装 tàozhuāng
suit (business) 西服 xīfú
suitcase 手提箱 shǒutíxiāng
sulfa drugs 磺胺药 huáng'ānyào
summer 夏天 xiàtiān
summer school 暑期班 shǔqībān
sun 太阳 tàiyáng
sunflower 向日葵 xiàngrìkuí
sunflower oil 葵花籽油 kuíhuāzǐyóu
sunflower seeds 瓜子 guāzǐ
sunglasses 太阳眼镜 tàiyáng yǎnjìng
sunlight 阳光 yángguāng
sunrise 日出 rìchū
sunscreen 防晒霜 fángshàishuāng
sunset 日落 rìluò
suona (trumpet like Chinese instrument) 唢呐 suǒnà
supermarket 超市 chāoshì
surge protector 插座 chāzuò
surgery 外科 wàikē
surgical operation 手术 shǒushù
surprised 惊讶 jīngyà
surrounding 周围 zhōuwéi
suspension 减震 jiǎnzhèn
sweater 毛衣 máoyī
sweatshirt 卫衣 wèiyī
Sweden 瑞典 Ruìdiǎn
sweet potato 红薯/地瓜 hóngshǔ/dìguā
sweet 甜 tián
swimming 游泳 yóuyǒng
swimming cap 泳帽 yǒngmào
swimming pool 游泳池 yóuyǒng chí
swimsuit 泳衣 yǒngyī
swing 秋千 qiūqiān
Swiss cheese 瑞士多孔干酪 Ruìshì duōkǒng gānlào
Switzerland 瑞士 Ruìshì
sword 剑 jiàn
sympathy 同情 tóngqíng
symphony 交响乐 jiāoxiǎngyuè
symptoms 症状 zhèngzhuàng
syringe 注射器 zhùshèqì
system 系统 xìtǒng
step 踏板 tàbǎn

T

table 桌子 zhuōzi
tacit understanding 默契 mòqì
tackle (fishing) 渔具 yújù
taichi 太极拳 tàijíquán
tailor/tailoring 裁缝 cáifeng
take a bus 坐公车 zuò gōngchē
take away (food) 带走 dài zǒu
take care of 照顾 zhàogù
take off (clothing) 拖 tuō
take pictures 拍照 pāizhào
takeaway (doggy bag) 打包 dǎbāo
tall 高 gāo
tampons 棉球 miánqiú
Tang dynasty 唐(代/朝) Táng (dài/cháo)

tangerines 柑橘 gānjú
tango 探戈舞 tāngē wǔ
tank top 吊带背心 diàodài bèixīn
tank 坦克 tǎnkè
tanning bed 日光浴床 rìguāngyù chuáng
Taoism 道教 Dàojiào
tap dancing 踢踏舞 tītā wǔ
tape 胶条 jiāotiáo
tape recorder 录音机 lùyīnjī
tapestry 挂毯 guàtǎn
tar 焦油 jiāoyóu
tarp 防雨布 fángyǔ bù
taste/try (v) 尝 cháng
tasteful (n) 品味 pǐnwèi
tattoos 纹身 wénshēn
tax (v) 扣税 kòushuì
tax rate 税率 shuìlǜ
taxi driver 司机 sījī
tea 茶 chá
tea ceremony 茶道 chádào
tea leaves (loose) 茶叶 cháyè
tea set 茶具 chájù
teabag 袋泡茶 dài pào chá
teach 教 jiāo
teacher 老师 lǎoshī
teahouse 茶馆 cháguǎn
team (sport) 队 duì
teapot 茶壶 cháhú
tear down/apart 拆 chāi
tease (v) 逗 dòu
technique 技术 jìshù
telecommunications 电讯 diànxùn
telephone 电话 diànhuà
telephone number 电话号码 diànhuà hàomà
television 电视 diànshì
television series 电视剧 diànshìjù
tell (difference) 分得出来 fēn de chūlái
tell 告诉 gàosù
temperature 温度 wēndù
temple 寺庙 sìmiào
temporary 临时 línshí
temporary housing permit 住宿许可证 zhùsù xǔkě zhèng
ten 十 shí
tennis 网球 wǎngqiú
tent 帐篷 zhàngpéng
tequila 龙舌兰酒 lóngshélánjiǔ
terrible 差劲 chàjìn
terminus 终点站 zhōngdiǎnzhàn
terrorism 恐怖主义 kǒngbùzhǔyì
terrorist 恐怖分子 kǒngbùfènzǐ
test (exam) 考试 kǎoshì
tetanus 破伤风 pòshāngfēng
textbook 课本 kèběn
text message 短信 duǎnxìn
Thailand 泰国 Tàiguó
thank you 谢谢 xièxie
Thanksgiving 感恩节 Gǎn'ēnjié
that 那 nà
that one 那个 nà gè
theater 剧场 jùchǎng
therefore 结果/所以 jiéguǒ/suǒyǐ
thermometer 体温计 tǐwēnjì
these 这些 zhèxiē
they/them 他们 tāmen
thick 粗/厚 hòu/cū
thief 小偷 xiǎotōu
thin 薄 báo
thing/s 东西 dōngxi
think 想 xiǎng
third 第三 dì-sān
thirsty 渴 kě
this 这 zhè
this one 这个zhègè
this year 今年 jīnnián
thong 丁字裤 dīngzìkù
those 那些 nàxiē
thousand island dressing 千岛酱 qiāndǎojiàng
thousand 一千 yìqiān
Three Kingdoms 三国 Sānguó
three 三 sān
throat 嗓子 sǎngzi
throw away 扔掉 rēngdiào
thumb 大拇指 dàmǔzhǐ
thunder 雷 léi
Tibet 西藏 Xīzàng
ticket 票 piào

ticket booth 售票口 shòupiàokǒu
tidy 整洁 zhěngjié
tidy up (verb) 收拾 shōushi
tie (game) 平局 píngjú
tie (n) 领带 lǐngdài
tight 紧 jǐn
tights 裤袜 kùwà
tiles 瓷砖 cízhuān
time 时间 shíjiān
tire pump 打气筒 dǎqìtǒng
tired 累 lèi
title (name) 称呼 chēnghū
to the end 到底 dàodǐ
toast bread 吐司面包 tǔsī miànbāo
tobacco leaf 烟叶 yānyè
tobacco products 烟草 yāncǎo
toboggan ride 滑道 huádào
today 今天 jīntiān
toe ring 趾戒 zhǐjiè
together 一起 yìqǐ
toilet 厕所 cèsuǒ
toilet bowl cleaner 洁厕剂 jiécèjì
tomato 西红柿 xīhóngshì
tomato sauce 番茄酱 fānqié jiàng
tombs 陵墓 língmù
tomorrow 明天 míngtiān
tone (Chinese) 声调 shēngdiào
tongue 舌头 shétóu
tonsil 扁桃腺 biǎntáoxiàn
too clever for his/her britches 爱耍小聪明 ài shuǎ xiǎo cōngmíng
tooth 牙齿 yáchǐ
topographical map 地形图 dìxíng tú
tortilla chips 墨西哥玉米脆片 mòxīgē yùmǐ cuìpiàn
total 一共 yígòng
touch (v) 碰 pèng
tour 旅游 lǚyǒu
tour guides 导游 dǎoyóu
tourist 游客 yóukè
tow truck 拖车 tuōchē
towel 毛巾 máojīn
tower 塔 tǎ
toy 玩具 wánjù
track (sports) 田径场 tiánjìng chǎng
trade 贸易 maoyì
tradition 传统 chuántǒng
traditional Chinese Medicine 中医 zhōngyī
traffic jam 堵车 dǔ chē
traffic light / stoplight 红绿灯 hóng lǜ dēng
tragedy 悲剧 bēijù
trail/road 路 lù
train (n) 火车 huǒchē
train station 火车站 huǒchēzhàn
training 培训 péixùn
trampoline 蹦蹦床 bèngbèng chuáng
transfer (call) 转 zhuǎn
translate/translation/translator/interpreter 翻译 fānyì
transportation 交通 jiāotōng
transsexual/s 人妖 rényāo
travel 旅游 lǚyóu
traveler's check 旅游支票 lǚyóu zhīpiào
treadmill 跑步机 pǎobùjī
treatment (medical) 治疗 zhìliáo
treaty 条约 tiáoyuē
treble 高音 gāoyīn
tree 树 shù
trendy/popular 流行 liúxíng
triangle 三角形 sānjiǎoxíng
triennale 三年展 sān nián zhǎn
trigonometry 几何 Jǐhé
tripod 三脚架 sānjiǎojià/鼎 dǐng
trout 鲑鱼 guìyú
trumpet 小号 xiǎohào
trunk (car) 后备箱 hòubèixiāng
try (v) 试试 shìshi
T-shirt T恤衫 tìxùshān
tuition 学费 xuéfèi
tulip 郁金香 yùjīnxiāng
tumble dry 滚筒烘干 gǔntǒng hōnggān
tummy tuck 腹部整形术 fùbù zhěngxíng shù
tuna 金枪鱼 jīnqiāngyú
tuner 调音器 tiáoyīnqì
turkey 火鸡 huǒjī

turn (n, v) 转弯 zhuǎnwān
turn 转 zhuǎn
turn off 关 guān
turn on 开 kāi
turquoise 绿松石 lǜsōngshí
turtle 甲鱼 jiǎyú
turtleneck 圆翻领毛衣
yuán fānlǐng máoyī
tutor (n) 辅导老师 fúdǎo lǎoshī
tutor (v) 辅导 fǔdǎo
tuxedo 燕尾服 yànwěifú
twenty 二十 èrshí
twice 两次 liǎng cì
twist/shake 扭 niǔ
twisted ankle 脚崴了 jiǎo wǎi le
two 二 èr
typhoid 伤寒 shānghán

U

UFO 飞碟 fēidié
ugly 丑陋 chǒulòu
umbrella 雨伞 yǔsǎn
unbearable 受不了 shòubùliǎo
uncle (paternal) 叔叔 shūshu
uncomfortable 不舒服 bu shūfú
under 下 xià
underground 地下 dìxià
underground metal (music)
地下金属 dìxià jīnshǔ
understand (at all) 理解 lǐjiě
understand (clearly) 明白 míngbái
underwear 内衣 nèiyī
unemployed 下岗 xiàgǎng
unequal 不平等 bù píngděng
uniform (school) 校服 xiàofú
university 大学 dàxúe
unlucky 不幸 búxìng
up 上 shàng
upload 上传 shàngchuán
urban 都市 dūshì
urine 尿 niào
USA 美国 Měiguó
USB drive 优盘 yōupán
use 用 yòng
useful 实用 shíyòng
utopia 乌托邦 wūtuōbāng
U-turn 调头 diàotóu

V

vacation (period) 假期 jiàqī
vaccinate 预防针 yùfángzhēn
vaccine 疫苗 yìmiáo
vacuum (n) 吸尘器 xīchénqì
vacuum (v) 吸尘 xīchén
vacuum cleaner 吸尘器 xīchénqì
Valentine's Day 情人节 Qíngrénjié
valley 谷 gǔ
valuable 贵重 guìzhòng
variety show 综艺节目 zōngyì jiémù
vase 花瓶 huāpíng
vegetable dish 素菜 sùcài
vegetables 蔬菜 shūcài
vegetarian (n) 吃素的 chī sù de
vagina 阴道 yīndào
venison 鹿肉 lùròu
verbs 动词 dòngcí
vermicelli 米粉 mǐfěn
vest 背心 bèixīn
veterinarian 兽医 shòuyī
video art 媒介艺术 méijiè yìshù
video card 显卡 xiǎnkǎ
videotape (v) 录 lù
villa 别墅 biéshù
village 乡村 xiāngcūn
villain 奸臣 jiānchén
vinegar 醋 cù
violin 小提琴 xiǎotíqín
VIP 贵宾 guìbīn
virtual reality 虚拟世界 xūnǐ shìjiè
visa 签证 qiānzhèng
visit (person) 看 kàn
visit 参观 cānguān
vitamin 维他命 wéitāmìng
vocabulary 词汇 cíhuì
vodka 伏特加 fútèjiā
voice recorder 录音器 lùyīnqì
volume 体积 tǐjī
volume 音量 yīnliàng
vomit 吐了 tù le

W

waist 腰 yāo
waistcoat 马甲 mǎjiǎ
wait 等 děng
waiter/waitress服务员fúwùyuán
wake up 醒 xǐng
walk 走路 zǒulù
walk/leave/go 走 zǒu
walking stick 手杖 shǒuzhàng
walkman 随身听 suíshēntīng
wall 墙 qiáng
wallet 钱包 qiánbāo
walnuts 桃仁 táorén
wander (around and around) 转转 zhuànzhuan
want/will 要 yào
want/think 想 xiǎng
war 战争 zhànzhēng
warm 暖和 nuǎnhé
warm up (food) 热一下 rè yíxià
warmth/temperature 温度 wendu
warranty 保修 bǎoxiū
Warring States period 战国时代 Zhànguó shídài
washing machine 洗衣机 xǐyījī
watch out 当心 dāngxīn
watch 看 kàn
watchtower 烽火台 fēnghuǒtái
water 水 shuǐ
water bottle 水壶 shuǐhú
water chestnut 荸荠 bíqì
water filter 净水器 jìngshuǐqì
water pressure 水压 huǐyā
water skiing / water slide 滑水 huáshuǐ
watercolors 水彩画 shuǐcǎi huà
waterfall 瀑布 pùbù
watermelon 西瓜 xīguā
waterproof 防水 fángshuǐ
wax 脱毛腊 tuōmáolà
we/us 我们 wǒmen
weak 弱 ruò
wear (v) 穿 chuān
wear and tear 磨损 mósǔn
weather 天气 tiānqì
website 网站 wǎngzhàn
wedding 婚礼 hūnlǐ
weeds 杂草 zácǎo
week (n) 星期 xīngqī
weekend 周末 zhōumo
weever 鲈鱼 lúyú
weight 重量 zhòngliàng
well done 干得好 gàn de hǎo
west gate 西门 ximén
west 西 xī
western food 西餐 xīcān
western medicine 西药 xīyào
wet 湿润 shīrùn
WFOE (wholly foreign-owned enterprise) 外资企业 wàizī qǐyè
what 什么 shénme
what's up? 什么事? shénme shì?
whatever 无所谓 wúsuǒwèi
wheat bread 全麦面包 quánmài miànbāo
wheel 轮胎 lúntāi
when 什么时候 Shénme shíhòu
where 哪儿 nǎr
whipping cream 淡奶油 dàn nǎiyóu
whisky 威士忌 wēishìjì
white eel 白鳝 báishàn
white fungus 银耳 yín'ěr
white mushrooms 草菇 cǎogū
white 白色 báisè
who 谁 shéi
whole 整 zhěng
wholesale price 批发价 pīfā jià
wide angle 广角 guǎngjiǎo
wide/width 宽 kuān
wife 妻子/老婆 qīzǐ/lǎopo
Wi-Fi 高保真 gāobǎozhēn
wild 野 yě
win 赢 yíng
wind (blowing) 刮风 guāfēng
wind (instruments) 吹奏乐器 chuīzòu yuèqì
wind (n) 风 fēng
window 窗户 chuānghù
windshield 前挡风 qiándǎngfēng
wind-surfing 帆板 fānbǎn
winning 领先 lǐngxiān

winter 冬天 dōngtiān
winter swimming 冬泳 dōngyǒng
wipe (v) 擦 cā
wireless (card) 无线(卡) wúxiàn (kǎ)
wiring 走线 zǒu xiàn
wisdom 知识 zhīshí
wish (well) 祝 zhù
withdraw money 提钱 tíqián
withdrawal (fee) 扣钱 kòuqián
witness 目击证人 mùjī zhèngrén
wok 锅 guō
woman 女人 nǚrén
wonderful/brilliant 精彩 jīngcǎi
wood 木材 mùcaí
woodblock print 套色板画 tàosè bǎnhuà
woodcut 木刻 mù kè
wool 羊毛 yángmáo
work (n, v) 工作 gōngzuò
work (v) 上班 shàng bān
work unit (company) 单位 dānwèi
worried 担心 dānxīn
wristguard 护腕 hùwàn
wrist 手腕 shǒuwàn
write down 写下来 xiěxiàlái
write 写 xiě
writer 作家 zuòjiā
wrong number 打错了 dǎ cuò le

X

x-ray (v) 照X光 zhào x guāng

Y

yeah/alright 好啊 hǎo a
yell 大吼大叫 dàhǒudàjiào
yellow 黄色 huángsè
yes 是 shì
yesterday 昨天 zuótiān
yoga 瑜珈 yújiā
yoghurt 酸奶酪 suān nǎilào
Yom Kippur 赎罪日 Shúzuìrì
you 你 nǐ
you all 你们 nǐmen
young person / people 年轻人 niánqīngrén
you're welcome 不客气 bú kèqì
youth hostel 青年旅馆 qīngnián lǚguǎn

Z

zero 零 líng
zheng (Chinese zither with 25 strings) 古筝 gǔzhēng
zipper 拉链 lāsuǒ
zoom (photo) 变焦 biànjiāo
zucchini 西葫芦 xīhúlu

GLOSSARY

A

āsīpīlín 阿司匹林 aspirin
āyí 阿姨 auntie/ nanny/maid
ǎi 矮 short (not tall)
ài 爱 love
àiqíng 爱情 love/romance
àirén 爱人 spouse
āndìng 安定 stable (a)
ānjìng 安静 quiet
ānmiányào 安眠药 sleeping pil
ānpái 安排 arrange
ānquán 安全 safe
ānquándài 安全带 seatbelt
ānquánmào 安全帽 helmet
ānquántào 安全套 condom
àn 按 press (v, button, etc.)
ànmō 按摩 massage
àolínpǐkè 奥林匹克 Olympics
àoyùn 奥运 Olympic Games

B

bàba 爸爸 father
báijiǔ 白酒 grain alcohol
báilándì 白兰地 brandy
báisè 白色 white
báiyín 白银 silver (metal)
bān 班 class
bānjiā 搬家 moving (house)
bàngōngshì 办公室 office
bāngmáng 帮忙 help (v)
bāngzhù 帮助 help (v)
bàng 棒 excellent (colloquial)
bàngqiú 棒球 baseball
bāo 包 bag
bāoguǒ 包裹 parcel
bāojiān 包间 private room
bāokuò 包括 include
bāopí 剥皮 skin (v)
bāozi 包子 steamed buns
báo 薄 thin
bǎo'ān 保安 security guard
bǎohù 保护 protect
bǎolíngqiú 保龄球 bowling
bǎoxiǎn 保险 insurance
bǎoxiū 保修 warranty
bào 抱 hug (v)
bàochou 报酬 reward
bàomíng 报名 enroll
bàoqiàn 抱歉 forgive me
bàoxiāo 报销 reimburse (expenses)
bàoyú 鲍鱼 abalone
bàozhǐ 报纸 newspaper
bēi 杯 cup
bēibāo 背包 backpack
bēizi 杯子 glass (cup)
běi 北 north
Běijīng 北京 Beijing
bèir bàng 倍儿棒 spectacular/wicked
bèn 笨 stupid
bèng 蹦 bounce
bèngbèng chuáng 蹦蹦床 trampoline
bízi 鼻子 nose
bǐ 笔 pen
bǐ sài 比赛 competition (game)
bìyùnyào 避孕药 birth control pills
biànlìdiàn 便利店 convenience store
biànzi 辫子 braid/s
biǎo 表 form (document)/taxi meter
biǎodá 表达 convey (express)
biǎoyǎn 表演 performance
bié 别 don't
biérén 别人 someone else/another
bièniu 别扭 awkward person
bīng 冰 cold (frozen)
bīngxiāng 冰箱 refrigerator
bǐnggān 饼干 cookie
bìng 病 sick (v)
bōcài 菠菜 spinach
bōli 玻璃 glass
bōluó 菠萝 pineapple
bówùguǎn 博物馆 museum
bózi 脖子 neck
bòhé 薄荷 mint
búcuò 不错 not bad/ok
bú kèqi 不客气 you're welcome
bù 不 no
bùhǎo yìsi 不好意思 pardon me
bù kěnéng 不可能 impossible
bùliào 布料 fabric
bù píngděng 不平等 unequal

bù shūfú 不舒服 uncomfortable
bù tóng 不同 different

C

cā 擦 wipe (v)
cáichǎn 财产 riches
cáifeng 裁缝 tailor/tailoring
cáiliào 材料 materials
càidān 菜单 menu (food)
càipǔ 菜谱 recipe
cānguān 参观 visit
cānguǎn 餐馆 restaurant
cānjiā 参加 attend
cānjīn 餐巾 napkins
cāntīng 餐厅 restaurant
cǎo 草 grass
cǎoméi 草莓 strawberry
cèsuǒ 厕所 toilet
chāduì 插队 budge/cutt (in line)
chá 茶 tea
chà 差 subtract/missing
chàbùduō 差不多 more or less
chàjìn 差劲 terrible
chāzi 叉子 fork
chāi 拆 tear down/apart
cháng 尝 taste/try (v)
cháng 长 long
chángchéng 长城 Great Wall
chángdí 长笛 flute
chángdù 长度 length
chángtú 长途 long distance
chànggē 唱歌 sing
chàngkuài 畅快 carefree
chāoshì 超市
grocery store/supermarket
cháoshī 潮湿 humid
chǎo 炒 stir fry
chǎo(nào) 吵(闹) noisy
chǎo fàn 炒饭 fried rice
chē 车 car
chēhuò 车祸 car accident
chēzhá 车闸 bicycle brakes
chēzhàn车站bus stops
chènshān 衬衫 shirt
chēnghū 称呼 title (name)
chéng 橙 orange (fruit)
chéngniánrén 成年人 adult
chéngshì 城市 city
chī(fàn) 吃(饭) eat (rice)
chījīng 吃惊 amazed
chī sù de 吃素的 vegetarian (n)
chídào 迟到 late (person)
chōngxǐ 冲洗 develop pictures
chōngdiàn 充电 charge (electricity)
chōngdiànqì 充电器 charger
chōngmǎn 充满 full
chōngzhíkǎ 手机充值卡 refill card (mobile phone)
chóngfù 重复 repeat
chǒngwù 宠物 pet (n)
chóu yān 抽烟 smoke (v)
chǒulòu 丑陋 ugly
chòu 臭 stinky
chūbǎn 出版 publish
chūchāi 出差 business trip
chūfā 出发 set out/leave
chūjí 初级 beginner
chūkǒu 出口 exit (n)
chūkǒu 出口 export
chūqù 出去 exit (v)
chūqù 出去 going out
chūshēng 出生 born
chūshòu 出售for sale
chūzū 出租 rent out
chūzūchē 出租车 cab (taxi)
chúfáng 厨房 kitchen
chuān 穿 wear (v)
chuán 船 boat
chuántǒng 传统 tradition
chuánzhēn 传真 fax
chuànr 串儿 kebab
chuáng 床 bed
chuānghù 窗户 window
Chūnjié 春节 Spring Festival
(Chinese New Year)
chūnqiū shídài 春秋时代 Spring and Autumn period
chūntiān 春天 spring
cí 词 phrase/word
cíhuì 词汇 vocabulary
cíqì 瓷器 porcelain
cōng 葱 onion

cōngmíng 聪明 smart/clever
cóng 从 from
cū 粗 thick
cuī yí xià 催一下 hurry up (food)
cúnqián 存钱 deposit (v)
cuò 错 incorrect

D

dǎ 打 hit/play/punch/beat
dǎsǎo 打扫 clean (v)
dǎbāo 打包 takeaway (doggy bag)
dǎ dī 打的 take a taxi cab
dǎ diànhuà 打电话 make a phone call/phonecall
dǎjià 打架 fight (n, v)
dǎkāi 打开 open (v, turn on)
dǎyìn 打印 print (v)
dǎ zhāohu 打招呼 greet (v)
dǎzhé 打折 discount (n)
dà 大 big/large
dàbáicài 大白菜 Chinese cabbage
dàgē 大哥 big brother
dàhǒudàjiào 大吼大叫 yell
dàhuì 大会 conference
dàjiā 大家 everybody
dàmǔzhǐ 大拇指 thumb
dàshǐguǎn 大使馆 embassy
dàxiàng 大象 elephant
dàxúe 大学 university
dàyī 大衣 overcoat
dài 带 bring
dàifu 大夫 doctor
dài zǒu 带走 take away (food)
dānrén fángjiān 单人房间 single room
dānwèi 单位 work unit (company)
dānxīn 担心 worried
dàngāo 蛋糕 cake
dànshì 但是 but
dāng 当 become
dāngrán 当然 of course
dāngxīn 当心 be careful/watch out
dǎo 岛 island
dǎoyǎn 导演 director
dǎoyóu 导游 tour guide
dào 到 arrive
dàobǎn 盗版 pirated
dàocí 悼词 condolences
dàodǐ 到底 to the end
dàojiào 道教 Taoism
dédào 得到 get (achieve)
déwén 德文 German language
dēng 灯 light/lamp
děng 等 wait
děngděng 等等 etcetera
dī 低 low
dǐpiàn 底片negatives
dìfāng 地方 place (n)
dìguā 地瓜 sweet potato
dírén 敌人 enemy
dìtǎn 地毯 carpet
dìtiě 地铁 subway
dìtú 地图 map
dìxià 地下 underground
dìyù 地狱 hell
dìzhǐ 地址 address
diǎncài 点菜 order food
diànchí 电池 battery
diànhuà 电话 telephone
diànhuà hàomà 电话号码 telephone number
diànnǎo 电脑 computer
diànshì 电视 television
diàntí 电梯 elevator
diànyǐng 电影 movie/film
diànyǐngyuàn 电影院 movie theater
diànzǐ yóuxiāng 电子邮箱 email address
diāosù 雕塑 sculpture
diàotóu 调头 U-turn
diàoyú 钓鱼 fishing
dīng 盯 stare (v)
dīngzìkù 丁字裤 thong
dǐng 鼎 tripod
dìng 订 reserve
diū 丢 lose (v, something)
diūliǎn 丢脸 lose face
dōng 东 east
dōngtiān 冬天 winter
dōngxi 东西 thing/s
dǒngshì 懂事 savvy
dòng 冻 freeze

dòngwù 动物 animals
dòngxuè 洞穴 cave
dǒu pō 陡坡 steep climb
dòu 逗 funny
dòufu 豆腐 bean curd
dòujiāng 豆浆 soy milk
dòuyá 豆芽 bean sprout
dòuzi 豆子 bean
dǔ chē 堵车 traffic jam
dǔ shū 读书 read books (study)
dùpí wǔ 肚皮舞 bellydancing
dùqí 肚脐 navel
dùzi 肚子 belly
duǎn 短 short length
duǎnkù 短裤 shorts
duǎnqún 短裙 skirt
duǎnxìn 短信 text message
duàn le 断了 cut off/broken off
duì 对 correct
duì 队 team (sport)
duìbǐ 对比 contrast (compare)
duìbùqǐ 对不起 sorry
duìhuà 对话 dialogue
duìmiàn 对面 opposite (lit)
duō 多 many/more
duōshǎo 多少 how many

E

é'tóu 额头 forehead
ěxīn 恶心 disgusting
è 饿 hungry
èbà 恶霸 bully (n)
è sǐ le 饿死了 starving
értóng 儿童 child/children
érzi 儿子 son
ěrduo 耳朵 ear
ěrjī 耳机 headphones
èrshǒu 二手 second hand/used

F

fādòngjī 发动机 engine
fājiàofěn 发酵粉 baking powder
fāpiào 发票 receipt
fāshāo 发烧 fever
fāsòng 发送 send
fāyīn 发音 pronounce/pronounciation
fǎwén 法文 French language
fàxíng 发型 hairstyle
fānyì 翻译 translate/translation/translator/interpreter
fánnǎo 烦恼 annoyed
fàndiàn 饭店 luxury hotel
fànguǎn 饭馆 restaurant
fāngbiàn 方便 convenient
fāngxing 方型 square
fāngshi 方式 method
fāngxiàng 方向 direction
fángdōng 房东 landlord
fángshàishuāng 防晒霜 sunscreen
fángjiān 房间 room
fángzi 房子 house
fángzū 房租 rent (n)
fàngdà 放大 enlarge
fàng fēngzhēng 放风筝 fly a kite
fàngkāi 放开 release/let go
fēidié 飞碟 UFO
fēijī 飞机airplane
fēnjī hào 分机号 extension number
fēnkāi 分开 separate(ly)
fēnqí 分歧 disagreement
fēnshǒu 分手 break-up
fēng 风 wind (n)
fēnggé 风格 style
fēngjǐng 风景 scenery
fēngmì 蜂蜜 honey
fēngshuǐ 风水 geomancy (Fengshui)
fēngzhēng 风筝 kite
fèngdòu 奋斗 struggle
fó 佛 Buddha
fójiào 佛教 Buddhism
fúwù 服务 serve/service
fúwùyuán 服务员 server/waiter/waitress
fúzhuāng 服装 clothing
fǔdǎo 辅导 tutor (v)
fǔlù 辅路 auxiliary road (bike lane)
fǔdǎo lǎoshī 辅导老师 tutor (n)
fù 付 pay
fùchū dàijià 付出代价 pay the price (for your actions)

fùxīng 复兴 rejuvenation
fùyìn 复印 photocopy (n/v)
fùyǒu 富有 rich
fùzé 负责 responsible

G

gān 肝 liver
gānbēi 干杯 cheers
gāngà 尴尬 embarrassed
gānjìng 干净 clean (a)
gānzào 干燥 dry (v/a)
gǎn 敢 dare (v)
gǎnjué 感觉 feel/feelings (n, v)
gǎnmào 感冒 flu
gàn de hǎo 干得好 well done
gāngqín 钢琴 piano
gāo 高 high/tall
gāoxìng 高兴 happy
gāozhōng 高中 high school
gàosù 告诉 tell
gē 歌 song
gēbei 胳臂 arm
gēge 哥哥 brother (older)
gēmenr 哥们儿 dude
gēshǒu 歌手 singer
gémìng 革命 revolution
gèrén 个人 individual
gèxìng 个性 personality
gèzhǒnggèyàng 各种各样 all sorts
gěi 给 give
gēn 跟 and
gōngchéngshī 工程师 engineer
gōngjiāochē 公交车 bus
gōngjīn 公斤 kilogram
gōnglǐ 公里 kilometer
gōngsī 公司 company
gōngyè 工业 industrial
gōngyuán 公园 public park
gōngzī 工资 salary
gōngzuò 工作 work (n, v)
gōngzuò shì 工作室 studio
gòngchǎndǎng 共产党 Communist Party
gǒu 狗 dog
gòu 够 enough
gòuwù 购物 shopping
gūdān 孤单 lonely
gūniáng 姑娘 miss (ms.)
gǔ 谷 valley
gǔ 鼓 drum
gǔdiǎn yīnyuè 古典音乐 classical music
gǔlǎo 古老 ancient
gǔlóu 鼓楼Drum Tower
gǔtóu 骨头 bone
gǔwán 古玩 antiques
gùwèn 顾问 consultant
Gùgōng 故宫 Forbidden City
gùyì 故意 intentional/on purpose
gùyōng 雇佣 employ (v)
guā 刮 shave (beard)
guāfēng 刮风 wind (blowing)
guāzǐ 瓜子 sunflower seeds
guàhào 挂号 register/registration
guān 关 turn off
guān mén 关门 closed
guānshàng 关上 close (turn off)
guānxì 关系 connections (personal/professional network)
guānxīn 关心 concern (v)
guànzi 罐子 can (n)
guǎngbō 广播 broadcast
guāngtóu 光头 bald
guǎnggào 广告 advertising/advertisement
guǐ 鬼 ghost
guì 贵 expensive
guìbīn 贵宾 VIP
guìtái 柜台 counter (n)
guìzhòng 贵重 valuable
guìzi 柜子 cabinet
gùnzi 棍子 cudgel
guō 锅 pot/wok
guójì 国际 international
guojia 国家 nation/country
Guóqìngjié 国庆节 National Day
guǒzhī 果汁 fruit juice
guòfèn 过分 excessive/too far (behavior)
guòmǐn 过敏 allergic

H

hái kěyǐ 还可以 good enough/ok
hǎibiān 海边 seaside
hǎiguān 海关customs
hǎitān 海滩 beach
hǎixiān 海鲜 seafood
hàixiū 害羞 shy
hǎowánr 好玩儿 fun
hǎo yùnqì 好运气 good luck
hàomà 号码 number (phone)
hàoqí 好奇 curious
hē 喝 drink (v)
hé 河 river
hélándòu 荷兰豆 snow peas
hépíng 和平 peace
héshì合适 appropriate
hétong 合同 contract (n)
hézì 盒子 box
hēibái 黑白 black and white
hēisè 黑色 black
hōngdòushā 红豆沙 red bean cream/paste
hóngjiǔ 红酒 red wine
hóng lǜ dēng 红绿灯 traffic light/ stoplight
hóngsè 红色 red
hóngshǔ 红薯 sweet potato
hòu 厚 thick
hòubèi 后背 back (body)
hòubēixiāng 后备箱 trunk (car)
hòumiàn 后面 back, behind (direction)
hòutiān 后天 day after tomorrow
hòutóu 后头 behind
hūxī 呼吸 breathe
hú 湖 lake
hǎiyáng 海洋 ocean
hé 和 and
húluóbo 胡萝卜 carrot
húshuō 胡说 nonsense/bullshit
hútòng 胡同 alleyway
húzi 胡子 beard
hùkǒu 户口 registered residence status for Chinese
hùzhào 护照 passport
huā 花 flower
huā 花 spend (money)
huāchá 花茶 scented tea
huāpíng 花瓶 vase
huāshēng 花生 peanuts
huá 划 row (a boat)
huábīng 滑冰 ice skating
huáxuě 滑雪 skiing
huà 画 draw/painting (n)
huàxué 化学 chemistry
huàzhuāngpǐn 化妆品 cosmetics
huáiyùn 怀孕 pregnant
huài 坏 broken
huánbǎo 环保 environmental protection
huánjìng 环镜 environment
huángdì 皇帝 emperor
huángguā 黄瓜 cucumber
huánghòu 皇后 empress
huángjīn黄金 gold
huángsè 黄色 yellow
huàn 换 change
huàn 换 replace
huàncheng 换成 change into
huànqián 换钱 change money (v)
huīsè 灰色 gray
huí 回 return/come back
huídá 回答 answer (n,v)
huí shēng 回声 echo
huìhua 绘画 paint (v)
huìlǜ 汇率 exchange rate
huí 回 return/come back
huídá 回答 answer (n,v)
hǔnhé 混合 blend
hǔnluàn 混乱 chaos
huódòng 活动 activity
huǒ 火 fire
huǒchē 火车 train (n)
huǒchēzhàn 火车站 train station
huǒguō 火锅 hot pot

J

jī 鸡 chicken
jīchǎng 机场 airport
jīchǔ 基础 basic
jīdàn 鸡蛋 egg (chicken)
Jīdūtú 基督徒 Christian

jīguān 机关
governmental organization
jīqì 机器 machine
jīròu 肌肉 muscle
jídù 嫉妒 jealous
jítā 吉他 guitar
jì 寄 mail (v)/send
jìhuà 计划 plan
jìkǒu 忌口 dietary preference
jìshù 技术 technique/skill
jìxìn 寄信 post mail
jìxù 继续 continue
jìzhě 记者 journalist
jiā加 add
jiā 家 home
jiājù 家具 furniture
jiāsù 加速 acceleration
jiāyóu 加油 go! (cheer)
jiǎ 假 false
jiàgé 价格 price
jiàqī 假期 vacation (period)
jiàzhào 驾照 driver's license
jiānbǎng 肩膀 shoulder
jiānbǐng 煎饼 Chinese crepe
with egg
jiānzhí 兼职 part-time (work)
jiǎnchá 检查 check (v)
jiǎndān 简单 simple
jiǎnlì 简历 resume/cv
jiǎn qǐ 捡起 pick up (clean, collect)
jiǎnshǎo 减少 reduce
jiàn 剑 sword
jiànkāng 健康 healthy
jiànkāng bǎoxiǎn 健康保险
health insurance
jiànlì 建立 build
jiànmiàn 见面 meet up
jiànshè 建设 construction
jiànshēn zhōngxīn 健身中心
fitness center
jiāng 姜 ginger
jiǎng 讲 speak (language)
jiǎngpin 奖品 prize/award (n)
jiàng 酱 sauce
jiàngyóu 酱油 soy sauce
jiāojuǎn 胶卷 film (roll)
jiāotiáo 胶条 tape
jiāotōng 交通 transportation
jiàoliàn 教练 coach
jiàoshì 教室 classroom
jiàotáng 教堂 church/cathedral
jiàoyù 教育 education
jiē 接 pick up/meet (someone)
jiē 街 street
jiégòu 结构 structure
jiéguǒ 结果 therefore/as a result
jiéhūn 结婚 marry (v)
jiémù 节目 program (TV show)
jiézòu 节奏 rhythm
jiěfàng 解放 liberate/liberation
jiè 借 lend/borrow
jièshào 介绍 introduce/introduction
jièzhǐ 戒指 ring (n)
jīnnián 今年 this year
jīnsè 金色 gold (color)
jīnshǔ 金属 metal
jīntiān 今天 today
jǐn 紧 tight
jìn 近 near
jìnkǒu 进口 import
jìnrù 进入 enter
jīngcǎi 精彩 wonderful/brilliant
jīngdiǎn 经典 classic
jīngjù 京剧 Peking Opera
jīnglǐ 经理 manager
jīnglì wàngshèng 精力旺盛
energetic
jǐngchá 警察 police
jìngdù 净度 clarity
jìngtóu 镜头 camera lens
jìngzi 镜子 mirror
jiǔ 久 long time
jiǔ 酒 alcohol
jiǔbā 酒吧 bar
jiǔdiàn 酒店 luxury hotel
jiù 旧 old (thing)
jiùhùchē 救护车 ambulance
jiù mìng! 救命！ help!
júhóngsè 桔红色 orange (color)
jǔsàng 沮丧 depressed
jùchǎng 剧场 theater

jùzi 句子 sentence
juéde 觉得 feel (think)
juédìng 决定 decide
juéshì 爵士 jazz
jūnrén 军人 soldiers
jiànzhù 建筑 architecture
jiǎnzi 剪子 scissors
jiànzi 毽子 shuttlecock
jiào 叫 call (v)
jiào 教 teach
jiǎo 脚 foot
jiǎohuái 脚踝 ankle
jīngyà 惊讶 surprised
jīngyàn 经验 experience (n, v)
juéduì 绝对 absolute/absolutly

K

kāfēi 咖啡 coffee
kāfēitīng 咖啡厅 café
kǎ 卡 card
kǎlā ok 卡拉OK / KTV kareoke
kāi 开 turn on/bloom
kāi chē 开车 drive car (v)
kāifàng 开放 open (a)
kāihuì 开会 meeting (formal)
kāilǎng 开朗 outgoing
kāishuǐ 开水 boiled water
kāi wánxiào 开玩笑 joke (v)
kǎnjià 砍价 bargain (v)
kàn 看 visit (person)
kàn 看 watch
kànfǎ 看法 perspective/opinion
kǎo 烤 bake
kǎolǜ 考虑 consider
kǎoshì 考试 test (exam)
kǎoxiāng 烤箱 oven (or toaster oven)
kētóu 磕头 kowtow (genuflect)
kēxué 科学 science
késòu 咳嗽 cough
kě 渴 thirsty
kě'ài 可爱 cute
kělè 可乐 cola
kělián 可怜 unfortunate, pitiable
kěnéng 可能 possibly
kěshì 可是 but
kěxī 可惜 what a pity/a shame
kè 刻 burn (cd)/cut/carve
kè 课 class
kèchéng 课程 curriculum
kèhù 客户 client
kèlùjī 刻录机 cd burner
kèrén 客人 guest (client)
kōng 空 empty
kōngqì 空气 air
kōngtiáo 空调 air conditioner
kǒngbù 恐怖 horror
kǒngpà 恐怕 afraid
kòngzhì 控制 control
kǒudài 口袋 pocket
kǒuhào 口号 slogan
kǒuyǔ 口语 oral language
kòuqián 扣钱 charge a fee
kòushuì 扣税 tax (v)
kòuzi 扣子 button
kū 哭 cry
kǔ 苦 bitter
kǔguā 苦瓜 bitter melon
kù 酷 cool (hip)
kùzi 裤子 pants
kuài 快 fast
kuàidì 快递 courier
kuàijì 会计 accounting
kuàilè 快乐 happy
kuàizi 筷子 chopsticks
kuān 宽 wide/width
kuāndài 宽带 broadband
kùn 困 sleepy
kùnnàn 困难 difficult

lā 拉 pull
lādùzi 拉肚子 diarrhea
lājī 垃圾 garbage
lāsuǒ 拉链 zipper
là 辣 spicy
làjiāo 辣椒 chili pepper
lái 来 come
lánqiú 篮球 basketball
lánsè 蓝色 blue

lǎnchē 缆车 cable car
làngmàn 浪漫 romantic
lǎo 老 old (person)
lǎobǎn 老板 boss
lǎogōng 老公 husband
lǎopo 老婆 wife
lǎorén 老人 elderly
lǎoshī 老师 teacher
lǎotào 老套 been done (before)
lǎowài 老外 foreigner
léi 雷 thunder
lèi 累 tired
lěng 冷 cold
lěngjìng 冷静 calm down/calm
lěngmòu 冷漠 insensitive
lí 梨 pear
líkāi 离开 leave
lǐjiě 理解 understand (at all)
lǐmiàn 里面 inside
lìhài 厉害 fantastic (formidable)
lìjià 例假 menstrual period
lìshǐ 历史 history
lìzi 栗子 hazlenut
lìzi 例子 example
liánjiē 连接 connect
liànxí 练习 practice (v)
liáng 凉 cool (cold)
liángcài 凉菜 cold dish
liàng 晾 cool
liè 烈 ardent/strong/intense (a)
línjū 邻居 neighbor
línshí 临时 temporary
líng 铃 bell/chime
língjiàn 零件 part (of a machine)
língmù 陵墓 tombs
língqián 零钱 small change (n)
língshí 零食 snack (n)
lǐngdài 领带 tie (n)
liú 留 stay behind
liúxíng 流行 popular/trendy
liúyán 留言 message (phone)
lóng 龙 dragon
lóngxiā 龙虾 lobster
lóu 楼 building
lóutī 楼梯 stairs
lúzào 炉灶 stove
lù 路 road
lùkǒu 路口 road entrance
lùyin 录音 videotape (v)
lùyīnqì 录音器 voice recorder
lǘ 驴 donkey
lǚguǎn 旅馆 hotel
lǜsè 绿色 green
lǜshī 律师 lawyer
lǚyóu 旅游 travel
lǚyóu zhīpiào 旅游支票 traveler's check
lúntāi 轮胎 wheel
luǒlù 裸露 nudity
luòtuó 骆驼 camel

M

māma 妈妈 mother
mǎ 马 horse
mǎshàng 马上 immediately
mǎmǎ hūhū de 马马虎虎的 so so/not so great
mǎpì jīng 马屁精 suckup (swot)
mǎi 买 buy
mǎidān 买单 bill, please!
mài 卖 sell
mántou 馒头 steamed buns
mǎn 满 full (container)
màn 慢 slow
máng 忙 busy
mángrén 盲人 blind person
māo 猫 cat
máobǐ 毛笔 painting/calligraphy brush
máobìng 毛病 problem
máojīn 毛巾 towel
máoyī 毛衣 sweater
máoyì 贸易 trade
Máo Zédōng 毛泽东 Mao Zedong
màozi 帽子 hat
méiguī 玫瑰 rose
méi ménr 没门儿 no way
méiyǒu 没有 don't have/there is not
méiyǒu guānxi 没有关系 no problem

méitǐ 媒体 media
měilì 美丽 beautiful
měiróng hùlǐ 美容护理 beauty treatment
měitiān 每天 everyday
mèimei 妹妹 sister (younger)
mén 门 door
ménpiào 门票 entrance ticket
mèng 梦 dream (n)
mílù 迷路 to get lost
mígōng 迷宫 maze
mǐn'gǎn 敏感 sensitive
mǐ 米 meter (length)
mǐfàn 米饭 rice
mǐfěn 米粉 rice noodles/vermicelli
mìfēng 蜜蜂 bee
mìmǎ 密码 password
mìmì 秘密 secret
mìshū 秘书 secretary
mián 棉 cotton
miánqiú 棉球 tampons
miǎnfèi 免费 free
miàn 面 noodles
miànbāo 面包 bread
miànfěn 面粉 flour
miànshì 面试 interview
míngbai 明白 understand (clearly)
míngnián 明年 next year
míngpái 名牌 brand name
míngpiàn 名片 name card
míngtiān 明天 tomorrow
míngxīng 明星 stars (movie)
míngxìnpiàn 名信片 postcards
míngzi 名字 name
mógū 蘑菇 mushrooms
móguǐ 魔鬼 devil
móléi 魔雷 mullet
mótuóchē 摩托车 motorcycles
mòqì 默契 tacit understanding
mòshēngrén 陌生人 strangers
mò 墨 calligrapher's ink
mòbānchē 末班车 last bus
mùbiāo 目标 goal (for life)
mùjī zhèngrén 目击证人 witness
mùtou 木头 wood

N

ná lái 拿来 bring (here)
nǎr? 哪儿? where?
nà 那 that
nàgè 那个 that one
nàxiē 那些 those
nǎilào 奶酪 cheese
nǎinai 奶奶 grandma
nǎipíng 奶瓶 baby bottles
nàixīn 耐心 patience
nán 南 south
nánguò 难过 sad/depressed
nánpéngyǒu 男朋友 boyfriend
nánrén 男人 man
nèiyī 内衣 underwear
nèizhì 内置 built-in
néng 能 able (v)
nénglì 能力 ability/abilities
nǐ 你 you
nǐ hǎo 你好 hello
nǐmen 你们 you all
niánqīngrén 年轻人 young person/people
niàn 念 read (pronounce)
niǎo 鸟 bird
niào 尿 urine
níngméng 柠檬 lemon
niúbī 牛B awesome
niúnǎi 牛奶 milk
niúpái 牛排 steak (beef)
niúròu 牛肉 beef
niúzǎikù 牛仔裤 jeans
niǔ 扭 twist/shake
nóngyè 农业 agriculture
nǚ'er 女儿 daughter
nǚpéngyǒu 女朋友 girlfriend
nǚren 女人 woman
nuǎnhé 暖和 warm
nuǎnqì 暖气 heating

P

páshān 爬山 mountain climbing
pà 怕 fear/afraid
pāimǎpì 拍马屁 kiss ass

pāi shìpín 拍(视频) record (movies)
pāizhào 拍照 take pictures
páiduì 排队 line up
pānpá 攀爬 climbing
pānyán 攀岩 rock climbing
pánzi 盘子 dish/plate/disk
pànduàn 判断 judgments
pángbiān 旁边 beside/next to
pángxiè 螃蟹 crab
pàng 胖 fat
pǎobù 跑步 run/running
pàocài 泡菜 pickle/kimchee
péigēn 培根 bacon
péiqián 赔钱 lose money
péixùn 培训 training
pèishì 配饰 accessories
péngyǒu 朋友 friend
pèng 碰 touch (v)
pīfā jià 批发价 wholesale price
pīlìwǔ 霹雳舞 breakdancing
pīpàn 批判 critique/criticize
pífū 皮肤 skin
pígé皮革leather
píjiǔ 啤酒 beer
pìgu 屁股 booty/bum/butt
piányì 便宜 cheap (inexpensive)
piào 票 ticket
piàoliàng 漂亮 pretty
píndào 频道 channel (TV)
pǐnwèi 品味 tasteful (n)
pīngpāngqiú 乒乓球 ping pong
píngdeng 平等 equality/equal
píngguǒ 苹果 apple
pínghéng 平衡 balance (n, v)
píngjūn 平均 average (n)
píngmǐ 平米 square meter(s)
píngzi 瓶子 bottle
púkèpái 扑克牌 poker cards
pútáo 葡萄 grape
pútáo gān 葡萄干 raisin
pǔtōng 普通 common (ordinary)
pùbù 瀑布 waterfall

Q

qīdài 期待 looking forward to
qīfù 欺负 tease (v)
qīzǐ 妻子 wife
qí 骑 ride (bike, horse)
qíguài 奇怪 strange
qítā 其他 other
qǐsù 起诉 sue (v)
qìfèn 气氛 atmosphere
qìhòu 气候 climate
qì sǐ le 气死了 furious
qiān 签 sign (v)
qiānmíng 签名 signature
qiānzhèng 签证 visa
qiánbāo 钱包 wallet
qiánmiàn 前面 front/ahead
qiántiān 前天 day before yesterday
qiāng 枪 gun
qiáng 强 strong
qiǎng 抢 robb
qiāomén 敲门 knock (v)
qiáo 桥 bridge
qiē 切 cut
qiézi 茄子 eggplant (aubregine)
qīnlüè 侵略 attack (millitary)
qín liúgǎn 禽流感 avian flu
qīng 轻 gentle (light)
qīnglǐ 清理 straighten up/clean
qíngkuàng 情况 situation
Qíngrén jié 情人节 Valentine's Day
qíngtiān 晴天 clear day
qǐng 请 please
qióng 穷 poor
qiūtiān 秋天 fall (season)
qiú 球 ball
qiú 求 beg
qū 区 district
qǔ 取 pick up/take away/fetch
qǔkuǎnjī 取款机 ATM
qǔxiāo 取消 cancel
qù 去 go
qùnián 去年 last year
qùshì 去世 pass away (die)
quánjī 拳击 boxing
quánzhí 全职 full-time (work)
quèdìng 确定 certain/confirm (n, v)

R

ràng 让 permit/allow

 rào 绕 circle (walking or driving v)
rè 热 hot
rén 人 person
rénmín 人民 the people
rényāo 人妖 transsexual
rènhé 任何 any
rènshi 认识 recognize/know
rèntóng 认同 accept (an idea)
rēngdiào 扔掉 throw away
rìchū 日出 sunrise
rìluò 日落 sunset
rìqī 日期 date (time)
róngyì 容易 easy
róngyù 荣誉 honor (n)
ròu 肉 meat
ròuguì 肉桂 cinnamon
rúguǒ 如果 if
rǔfáng 乳房 breast
rùkǒu 入口 entrance
ruǎn 软 soft
ruǎnjiàn 软件 software
ruǎnwò 软卧 soft sleeper (train)
ruò 弱 weak

S

sānjiǎoxíng 三角形 triangle
sānlúnche 三轮车 pedicab/ three wheeled vehicle
sānmíngzhì 三明治 sandwich
sāngná 桑拿 sauna
sǎngzi 嗓子 throat
sàozhou 扫帚 broom
sècǎi 色彩 colorful
sēnlín 森林 forest
shāchē 刹车 brakes/brake
shāchénbào 沙尘暴 dust storm
shāfā 沙发 couch
shā jūn 杀菌 steralize / kill germs
shāzi 沙子 sand
shān 山 mountain
shānfēng 山峰 mountain peak
shānzhā 山楂 hawthorn
shāngwù 商务 business
shàng bān 上班 work (v)
shàng 上 on/above
shāngliàng 商量 discuss
shàngmiàn 上面 on/above
shàngwǎng 上网 get online
shàngxiàwén 上下文 context
shāo 烧 braise
shāo xiāng 烧香 burn incense
shǎo 少 less
shé 蛇 snake
shétóu 舌头 tongue
shèbèi 设备 equipment
shèhuì zhǔyì 社会主义 socialism
shèjī 射击 shoot
shèjì 设计 design (v)
shèyǐng 摄影 photography
Shéi? 谁? Who?
shēncái 身材 physique
shēnfènzhèng 身份证 ID card
shēnqǐng 申请 apply
shēntǐ 身体 body
Shénme? 什么? What?
Shénme shíhòu? 什么时候? When?
shénmì 神密 mystery/mysterious
shēngbìng 生病 get sick (v)
shēngdiào 声调 tone (Chinese language)
shēnghuó 生活 life
shēngqì 生气 angry
shēngrì 生日 birthday
shēngwù 生物 biology
shēngyīn 声音 sound
shéng 绳 rope/line
Shèngdànjié 圣诞节 Christmas
shèngjīng 圣经 scripture
shīfu 师傅 master (n)
shīgē 诗歌 poetry
shīrùn 湿润 wet
shīwàng 失望 disappointed
shíjiān 时间 time
shípǐn 食品 food
shíshàng 时尚fashionable
shítáng 食堂 cafeteria
shíyàn 实验 experiment/experimental
shíyòng 实用 useful
shíyóu 石油 gasoline/petrol
shízài 实在 indeed/true/really/honest

shì 是 is (to be)/yes
shìchǎng 市场 market
shìgù 事故 accident (car)
shìhé 适合 appropriate
shìmín 市民 citizen
shìr 事儿 business/affairs
shìshi 试试 try (v)
shìwài 室外 outdoor
shìyī jiān 试衣间 fitting room
shōu(dào) 收到 charge (receive)
shōushi 收拾 tidy up (verb)
shóu 熟 ripe/cooked
shǒu手hand
shǒubānchē 首班车 first bus
shǒujī 手机 mobile phone
shǒuliàn 手链 bracelet
shǒushù 手术 surgical operation
shǒutào 手套 gloves
shǒuwàn手腕wrist
shòu 瘦 skinny
shòubùliǎo 受不了 unbearable
shòupiàochù 售票处 box office
shòu shāng 受伤 hurt (injured)
shòuyī 兽医 veterinarian
shū 梳 comb
shū 输 lose (a game)
shū 书 book
shūcài 蔬菜 vegetables
shūfǎ 书法 calligraphy
shūfu 舒服 comfortable
shūguì 书柜 bookcase
shúliàn 熟练 skillful
shúxī 熟悉 familiar
shǔtiáo 薯条 french fries
shù 树 tree
shùmǎ 数码 digital
shùxué 数学 math
shùzì 数字 numeral
shuā 刷 scrub
shuài 帅 handsome
shuāng 双 pair
shuāngrén fángjiān 双人房 double room
shuǎng 爽 awesome ("feels so good")
shuǐ 水 water
shuǐguǒ 水果 fruit
shuǐjīng zhījiǎ 水晶指甲 acrylic nails
shuǐpíng 水平 level
shuì 税 taxes
shuìjiào 睡觉 sleep
shuìlǜ 税率 tax rate
shuìyī 睡衣 pajamas/nightie
shùnbiàn 顺便 conveniently
shuō 说 speak/say (v)
sī(chóu) 丝(绸) silk
sījī 司机 driver
sìmiào 寺庙 temple
sōng 松 loose
sōngshǔ 松鼠 squirrel
sōusuǒ 搜索 search (internet)
sùdù 速度 speed
sùliào 塑料 plastic
sùshè 宿舍 student dorms
suān 酸 sour
suàn 蒜 garlic
suàn le 算了 forget it
suíbiàn 随便 casual/as one pleases
suíshēntīng 随身听 walkman
suì 碎 smash/shatter
Sūn Wùkōng 孙悟空 Monkey King
suō 缩 shrink
suǒ 锁 lock (n,v)
suǒyǐ 所以 therefore

T

tā 他 he/she/him/her
tāmen 他们 they/them
tǎ 塔 tower
táiqiú 台球 billiards
tàijíquán 太极拳 taichi
tàiyáng 太阳 sun
tàiyáng yǎnjìng 太阳眼镜 sunglasses
tānxīn 贪心 greedy
tán 痰 phlegm
tán liàn'ài 谈恋爱 fall in love
tánpàn 谈判 negotiate
tāng 汤 soup
tāngchí 汤匙 spoon
tángguǒ 糖果 candy

táng 糖 sugar
táocí 陶瓷 pottery
táozi 桃子 peach
tǎoyàn 讨厌 awful/horrible/annoying
tàozhuāng 套装 suit
tèbié 特别 special/particularly
tèsècài 特色菜 specialty dish
téng 疼 pain
tī 踢 kick (v)
tígòng 提供 provide
tíqián 提钱 withdraw money
tíqián 提前 beforehand
tǐyù 体育 athletics
tǐyùchǎng 体育场 stadium
tǐyùguǎn 体育馆 sports arena/gym
tì 剃 shave (bald)
tìdāo 剃刀 razorblade
tìhuàn 替换substitute
tìxùshān T恤衫 T-shirt
tiān 天 heaven/day
Tiān'ānmén 天安门 Gate of Heavenly Peace
tiāncái 天才 genius
tiānqì 天气 weather
Tiānzhǔtú 天主徒 Catholic
tiándiǎn 甜点 desserts
tián 甜 sweet
tián 填 fill out (form)
tiāo 挑 pick/choose
tiáoliào 调料 seasoning
tiàowǔ 跳舞 dance
tiēzhǐ 贴纸 stickers
tīng 听 listen
tīng huà 听话 obey/obedient
tíng 停 stop (v)
tíngchē 停车 park (v, car)
tōngguò 通过 pass by
tóngqíng 同情 sympathy
tóngshì 同事 colleague
tóngxué 同学 classmate
tǒng 桶 bucket
tōu 偷 steal
tóu 头 head
tóufa 头发 hair
tóukuī 头盔 helmet
tóu téng 头疼 headache
tóuyūn 头晕 dizzy
tóuzī 投资 invest
tòumíng 透明 clear/translucent/see-through
tǔdòu 土豆 potato
túshūguǎn 图书馆 library
tù 吐 vomit/spit
tùtán 吐痰 spit
tùzi 兔子 rabbit
tuī 推 push
tuījiàn 推荐 recommend
tuǐ 腿部 leg
tuì 退 return (something)
tuō 拖 take off (clothing)
tuōxié 拖鞋 slippers

wàzi 袜子 socks
wàibì 外币 foreign currency
wàidìrén 外地人 migrant
wàiguó 外国 foreign country
wàimiàn 外面 outside
wāndòu 豌豆 peas
wánquán 完全 completely
wánr 玩儿 play (v)
wǎn ān 晚安 good night
wǎnfàn 晚饭 dinner
wǎn 晚 late (time)
wǎnshàng 晚上 evening/night
wǎngbā 网吧 Internet café
wǎngluò 网络 Internet
wǎngqiú 网球 tennis
wǎngzhàn 网站 website
wēibōlú 微波炉 microwave
wéijīn 围巾 scarf
wéitāmìng 维他命 vitamin
wěidà 伟大 magnificent
wèi 胃 stomach
wèi 喂 hello (telephone)
wèijīng 味精 MSG (monosodium glutamate)
wèixīng 卫星 satellite
wēndù 温度 temperature
wēnquán 温泉 hot springs
wénshēn 纹身 tattoos
wèntí 问题 question/problem

wǒ 我 I
wǒmen 我们 we/us
wòshǒu 握手 shake hands
wūrǎn 污染 pollution
wūtuōbāng 乌托邦 utopia
wúliáo 无聊 boring
wúsuǒwèi 无所谓 whatever
wǔfàn 午饭 lunch
wǔshù 武术 martial arts
wù 雾 fog

X

x guāng X光 x-ray
xī 西 west
xīcān 西餐 western food
xīdú 吸毒 do illegal drugs
xīfú 西服 suit
xīgài 膝盖 knee
xīguā 西瓜 watermelon
xīhóngshì 西红柿 tomato
xīlánhuā 西兰花 broccoli
xīwàng 希望 hope
xīyān 吸烟 smoke (v)
xīyào 西药 western medicine
xīzàng 西藏 Tibet
xíguān 习惯 habits/customs
xísú 习俗 custom (convention)
xǐfàshuǐ 洗发水 shampoo
xǐhuān 喜欢 like
xǐshǒujiān 洗手间 restroom
xǐyījī 洗衣机 washing machine
xǐyù zhōngxīn 洗浴中心 bath house
xǐzǎo 洗澡 bathe
xìjié 细节 detail (n)
xìjù 戏剧 drama
xìtǒng 系统 system
xiā 虾 shrimp
xiágǔ 峡谷 gorge
xià 下 down (below)/under
xià 吓 scare
xiàgǎng le 下岗了 unemployed
xiàgè 下个 next (one)
xiàmiàn 下面 below
xiàtiān 夏天 summer
xiàwǔ 下午 afternoon
xiàxuě 下雪 snow (v)
xiàyǔ 下雨 rain (v)
xiàzài 下载 download
xiān 先 first
xiānshēng 先生 mister (mr.)
xián 咸 salty
xiànchǎng 现场 live (eg. music, entertainment)
xiàndài 现代 modern
xiàndàihuà 现代化 modernize/modernization
xiàn'é 限额 limit
xiànjīn 现金 cash
xiànzài 现在 now
xiànzhì 限制 restriction
xiāng 香 fragrant
xiāngcháng 香肠 sausage
xiāngcūn 乡村 countryside
xiānggǎng 香港 Hong Kong
xiānggū 香菇 shitake mushroom
xiāngjiāo 香蕉 banana
xiǎng 想 want/think
xiǎngfǎ 想法 opinion
xiǎngniàn 想念 miss (v)
xiǎngxiàng 想象 imagine
xiàngjiāo 橡胶 rubber
xiàngrìkuí 向日葵 sunflower
xiāoyè 宵夜 late-night meal
xiǎo 小 small
xiǎochǒu 小丑 clown
xiǎohái 小孩 child
xiǎojiě 小姐 miss (ms.)
xiǎoqū 小区 neighborhood
xiǎoshí 小时 hour
xiǎotíqín 小提琴 violin
xiǎotōu 小偷 thief
xiǎoxīn 小心 careful
xiǎoxué 小学 elementary school
xiào 笑 laugh
xiàochuǎn 哮喘 asthma
xiàoguǒ 效果 effect (result)
xiàoróng 笑容 smile
xiàoyuán 校园 campus
xié 鞋 shoes
xiě 写 write
xièxie 谢谢 thank you
xīn 新 new

xīn 心 heart
Xīnnián 新年 New Year's
xīnshǎng 欣赏 appreciate
xīnshǔi 薪水 salary
xīnwén 新闻 news
xīnxiān 新鲜 fresh
xìn 信 letter
xìnhào 信号 signal reception
xìnyòngkǎ 信用卡 credit card
xīngfèn 兴奋 excited (hyperactive)
xīngqī 星期 week (n)
xíng 行 ok
xínglǐ 行李 luggage
xíngróngcí 形容词 adjective
xíngzhuàng 形状 shape
xǐng 醒 wake up
xìngbié 性别 gender
xìngbìng 性病 sexually transmitted disease
xìngfú 幸福 lucky/happy
xìnggǎn 性感 sexy
xìngjiāo 性交 sexual intercourse
xìngrén 杏仁 almond
xìngyùn 幸运 lucky
xiōngbù 胸部 breast/chest
xiōngdì jiěmèi 兄弟姐妹 siblings
xiōngzhào 胸罩 bra
xióng 熊 bear
xiū 修 repair/fix
xiūxi 休息 rest
xiùměi 秀美 elegant (graceful)
xiùzi 袖子 sleeve
xūkōng 虚空 pointless/empty
xūyào 需要 need (require)
xuānchuán 宣传 propaganda
xuǎnzé 选择 choose/choice
xuēzi 靴子 boot
xué 学 learn
xuéfèi 学费 tuition
xuéshēng 学生 student
xuéshēngpiào 学生票 student discount ticket
xuéshēngzhèng 学生证 student ID card
xuéwèi 学位 academic degree
xuéxí 学习 study
xuéxiào 学校 school
xuě 雪 snow (n)
xuě 血 blood
xuěbì 雪碧 sprite
xúnzhǎo 寻找 search/look for

Y

yājīn 押金 deposit (n)
yāpiàn 鸦片 opium
yāpò 压迫 oppress
yāzi 鸭子 duck
yáchǐ 牙齿 tooth
yáyī牙医 dentist
yān 烟 smoke (noun)
yānhuīgāng 烟灰缸 ashtray
yán 盐 salt
yáncháng 延长 extend (v)
yánjiū 研究 Research
yánsè 颜色 color
yánshòu檐兽roof creatures
yǎnchànghuì 演唱会concert
yǎnjīng 眼睛 eye
yǎnjìng 眼镜 glasses
yǎnyuán 演员 actor/actress
yànpǐn 赝品 counterfeit
yáng 羊 sheep/goat
yángguāng 阳光 sunlight
yángmáo 羊毛 wool
yángròu 羊肉 mutton
yāo 腰 waist
yāodài 腰带 belt
yāoguǒ 腰果 cashew
yāoqǐng 邀请 invite
yāoyàn 妖艳 flamboyant
yáogǔn 摇滚 rock n' roll
yào 药 medicine
yào 要 want / will
yàofáng 药房 pharmacy
yàoshi 钥匙 key
yàoshì 要是 if
yēzi 椰子 coconut
yéye 爷爷 grandpa
yě 野 wild
yěxǔ 也许 maybe
yè 页 page
yèzi 叶子 leaf

yī fēnzhōng 一分钟 one minute
yīhuìr 一会儿 a little while
yīshēng 医生 doctor
yīyuàn 医院 hospital
yí cì 一次 once
yígè 一个 one/each
yígòng 一共 altogether/total
yí jiàn zhōngqíng 一见钟情 love at first sight
yítǐ 遗体 corpse
yíyàng 一样 same
yízhǐ 遗址 ruins/relics
yǐhòu 以后 afterwards
yǐqián 以前 before
yǐzi 椅子 chair
yìdàlì miàn 意大利面 spaghetti
yìmiáo 疫苗 vaccine
yìqǐ 一起 together
yìshù 艺术 art
yìshùjiā 艺术家 artist
yìsi 意思 meaning
yìxiē 一些 some
yīndào 阴道 vagina
yīnjīng 阴茎 penis
yīnliàng 音量 volume (of sound)
yīnwéi 因为 because
yīnxiāng 音箱 speakers
yīnyùe 音乐 music
yínháng 银行 bank
yínsè 银色 silver (color)
yǐnliào 饮料 drink (n)
yìnxiàng 印象 influence
yīng'ér 婴儿 baby
yīngtáo 樱桃 cherry
yīngxióng 英雄 hero
yīngyǔ 英语 English (language)
yíng 赢 win
yíngyǎng 营养 nutrition
yǐngbì 影壁 screen
yìng 硬 hard
yòng 用 use
yōuhuì 优惠 discount (n)
yōumò 幽默 funny (humorous)
yōupán 优盘 USB drive
yóu 油 oil
yóujiàn 邮件 mail (n)
yóujú 邮局 post office
yóunì 油腻 oily
yóupiào 邮票 postal stamp
yóuxì 游戏 game
yóuyǒng 游泳 swim
yóuyú 鱿鱼 squid
yǒu 有 have
yǒuqù 有趣 interesting
yǒuxiàn 有线 cable (TV or internet)
yòu 右 right
yòuzi 柚子 pomelo
yú 鱼 fish
yújiā 瑜珈 yoga
yúlè 娱乐 entertainment
yú 预订 make a reservation
yǔ 雨 rain (n)
yǔsǎn 雨伞 umbrella
yǔmáoqiú 羽毛球 badminton
yù 玉 jade
yùdìng 预定 reserve (in advance)
yùgāng 浴缸 bathtub
yùmǐ 玉米 corn
yùsuàn 预算 budget (n, v)
yuán 圆 round
yuánfen 缘分 fate
Yuánxiāojié 元宵节 Lantern Festival
yuánxíng 圆形 circular
yuánzi 园子 courtyard
yuǎn 远 far
yuēhuì 约会 appointment
yuè 月 month
yuèduì 乐队 band (music)
yuèqiú 月球 moon
yūn dǎo 晕倒 faint (v)
yún 云 cloud
yùndòng 运动 exercise (movement)
yùnhé 运河 canal

zájì 杂技 acrobatics
záluàn 杂乱 messy
zázhì 杂志 magazine
zài 再 again
zài 在 in/at/on
zàijiàn 再见 goodbye
zāng 脏 dirty

zǎo 早 early
zǎodiǎn 早点 breakfast
zǎoshàng 早上 morning
zǎoshàng hǎo 早上好 good morning
zěnme 怎么 how
zhá 炸 deep fry
zhǎi 窄 narrow
zhǎnlǎn 展览 exhibit (n, v)
zhàn 站 stand (v)
zhàntái 站台 platform (train)
zhànzhēng 战争 war
zhàngdān 账单 bill (n)
zhàngfu 丈夫 husband
zhànghù 账户 bank account
zhǎo 找 look for
zhàogù 照顾 take care of
zhàoxiàngjī 照相机 camera
zhè 这 this
zhègè 这个 this one
zhèr 这儿 here
zhèxiē 这些 these
zhēn 真 real/true
zhēnjiǔ 针灸 acupuncture
zhēnzhū 珍珠 pearl
zhēnzhū nǎichá 珍珠奶茶
bubble tea (aka pearl milk tea)
zhěnsuǒ 诊所 clinic
zhēng 蒸 steam (v)
zhěng 整 whole
zhěngjié 整洁 tidy
zhèngfǔ 政府 government
zhèngmíng 证明
certify/cerrtification
zhèngquè 正确 correct (proper)
zhèngshì 正式 formal
zhèngzhi 政治 politics
zhèngzhuàng 症状 symptoms
zhīdào 知道 know
zhīmá 芝麻 sesame
zhīmíng 知名 famous
zhīpiào 支票 check (bank)
zhīshí 知识 wisdom
zhíjiē 直接 direct (a)
zhíwù 植物 plants
zhíyè 职业 career
zhí zǒu 直走 go straight
zhǐjīn 纸巾 paper towel
zhǐ 只 only
zhǐténgyào 止疼药 pain killers
zhì'ān 治安 safety
zhìliàng 质量 quality
zhìliáo 治疗 treatment (medical)
zhìzào 制造 manufacture
zhōng 中 middle/medium
zhōng 钟 bell
zhōng 钟 clock
zhōngcān 中餐 Chinese food
zhōngguó 中国 China
Zhōnghuá Rénmín Gònghéguó
中华人民共和国
Peoples Republic of China
zhōngjí 中级 intermediate
zhōngjiān 中间 between
zhōnglóu 钟楼 Bell Tower
Zhōngqīujié 中秋节
Mid-Autumn Festival
zhōngwén 中文 Chinese
zhōngwǔ 中午 noon
zhōngxué 中学 middle school
zhōngyī 中医
traditional Chinese Medicine
zhòng 重 heavy
zhòngliàng 重量 weight
zhòngyào 重要 important
zhōumo 周末 weekend
zhǒu 肘 elbow
zhū 猪 pig
zhūbǎo 珠宝 jewelry
zhūròu 猪肉 pork
zhúzi 竹子 bamboo
zhǔ 煮 boil
zhǔliú 主流 mainstream
zhǔshí 主食 staple food
zhù 住 live (place)
zhù 祝 wish (well)
zhùcè 注册 sign up/register
zhùfú 祝福 blessing
zhùhè 祝贺 congratulations
zhùyì 注意 beware
zhuānjiā 专家 specialist
zhuǎn 转 turn (v)/ transfer (call)
zhuǎnwān 转弯 turn (n, v)

zhuànjì 传记 biography
zhuànqián 赚钱 earn money
zhuànzhuan 转转 wander (around and around)
zhuāng 装 install
zhuāngshì 装饰 decorate
zhǔnbèi 准备 prepare
zhuōzi 桌子 table
zīliào 资料 document/s (n)
zǐsè 紫色 purple
zì 字 character (word)
zìdà 自大 arrogant
zìdiǎn 字典 dictionary
zìháo 自豪 proud
zìjǐ 自己 myself
zìmù 字幕 subtitle
zìsī 自私 selfish
zìxíngchē 自行车 bicycle
zìyóu 自由 free/freedom
zìzhùcān 自助餐 buffet (self service)
zōngjiào 宗教 religioun
zōngsè 棕色 brown
zǒu 走 walk/leave/go
zū 租 rent (v)
zúliáo 足疗 foot massage
zúqiú 足球 football (soccer)
zuǐchún 嘴唇 lips
zuì 醉 drunk
zuì hǎo 最好 best
zuìjìn 最近 closest, recently
zuótiān 昨天 yesterday
zuǒ 左 left
zuò 做 do (make)
zuò 做 make
zuò 坐 sit
zuò fàn 做饭 cook
zuò gōngchē 坐公车 take a bus
zuòjiā 作家 writer
zuòwèi 座位 seats
zuòyè 作业 homework
zuòzhě 作者 author